The Drug User

Documents: 1840–1960

Edited by John Strausbaugh
and Donald Blaise

Foreword by
William S. Burroughs

Blast Books New York • *Dolphin-Moon Press Baltimore*

Foreword © 1990 William S. Burroughs, reprinted by permission of New American Library and published in a slightly different version in *High Risk: An Anthology of Forbidden Writings* edited by Amy Scholder and Ira Silverberg

Permissions appear on pages 239–40.

The publishers gratefully acknowledge the generous contributions made by William S. Burroughs, T. K. Christopher, Beth Escott, José Férez, Raymond Foye, Daniel Gerould, James Grauerholz, Herbert Huncke, Paola Igliori, John Jessen, Dan Levy, Ann Nocenti, Chris O'Connell, Paul Rickert, Charles Schneider, Roger Shattuck, Ira Silverberg, Kim Spurlock, Rain Spurlock, and Washoe's Native American Church.

Published by
BLAST BOOKS, INC.
P.O. Box 51
Cooper Station
New York, NY 10276-0051

Designed by Beth Escott

Manufactured in the United States of America

FIRST EDITION 1991

10 9 8 7 6 5 4 3 2 1

The Drug User

Opium Eater's Soliloquy

Sir Patrick Hehir, M.D.

I'd been cheered up, at my *chandoo*-shop, for years
    at least two-score,
To perform my daily labour, and was never sick or sore,
      But they said this must not be;
      So they've passed a stern decree,
And they've made my chandoo-seller shut his
    hospitable door.

If I'd only cultivated, now, a taste for beer and gin,
Or had learnt at pool or baccarat my neighbour's
    coin to win,
      I could roam abroad o' nights,
      And indulge in these delights,
And my soul would not be stigmatized, as being
    steeped in sin.

But as mine's a heathen weakness for a
    creature-comfort far
Less pernicious than their alcohol, more clean
    than their cigar,
      They have sent their howlings forth
      From their platform in the North,
And 'twixt me and my poor pleasure have opposed a
    righteous bar.

London, 1894

Contents

The Drug User

Foreword

William S. Burroughs

"My advice to the
young is: Just Say No
to Drug Hysteria!"

AN INTERESTING CASE OF MASS HYSTERIA is described in a book called *The Medical Detectives,* by Berton Roueché. The outbreak occurred at the Bay Harbor Elementary School in Dade County, Florida. A girl named Sandy, who was slightly ill with the flu, collapsed in the school cafeteria and was carried out on a stretcher as the next shift of students was coming in.

Sandy, it seems, was a sort of leader. In any case, the students started keeling over in droves. An officer from the Department of Public Health was dispatched to the scene. Fortunately, he recalled a similar case some years back from another high school, and quickly made a diagnosis of mass hysteria.

The remedy is very simple—get back to a calm, normal routine as expeditiously as possible. Get the children back to their classes. And that was the end of the outbreak. However, if the hysteria is not recognized and acted upon, it will go on and get worse and worse, as happened in the previous outbreak.

When hysteria is deliberately and systematically cultivated and fomented by a governing party, it can be relied upon to get worse and worse, to spread and deepen. Recent examples are Hitler's anti-semitic hysteria and present-day drug hysteria. The remedy is simple—a calm, objective, commonsense approach.

Remember that during the 19th and early 20th centuries—the "good old days," which conservatives so fondly evoke—opiates, cannabis tinctures and cocaine were sold across the counter from sea to shining sea, and the United States did not founder as a result. There's no way to know exactly how many addicts there were, but my guess would be—surprisingly few. Many people simply *don't like these drugs.*

In England, before America persuaded the English government to adopt our own tried-and-failed, police-and-sanction approach, any addict could get heroin on prescription and fill his script on the National Health. As a result there was no black market, since there was no profit involved. In 1957 there were about 500 addicts in the UK, and two narcotics officers for metropolitan London. Now England presents the same dreary spectrum as the USA—thousands of addicts, hundreds of drug agents, some of them on the take, a flourishing black market, addicts dying from OD's and contaminated heroin.

Obviously the sane, commonsense solution is maintenance for those who cannot or will not quit, and effective treatment for those who want to quit. The only treatment currently available is abrupt withdrawal, or withdrawal with substitute drugs. Withdrawal treatment dates back to early 19th-century British drug essayist Thomas De Quincey. Surely they could do better than that. Indeed, they *could,* but they show no signs of doing so.

Consider alternative therapy that is available: acupuncture, apomorphine. Both therapies work because they stimulate the production of endorphins, the body's natural regulators and pain killers. The discovery and isolation of endorphins has been called the most crucial breakthrough towards understanding and treatment of addiction since addiction was first recognized as a syndrome.

If you don't use it, you lose it. The addict is ingesting an artificial painkiller, so his body ceases to produce endorphins. If opiates are then withdrawn, he is left without the body's natural painkiller, and what would be normally minor discomfort becomes excruciatingly painful, until the body readjusts and produces endorphins. This is the basic mechanism of addiction, and explains why any agent that stimulates the production of endorphins will afford some relief from withdrawal symptoms.

De Quincey suggested that there may be a *constitutional* predisposition to the use of opium, and modern researchers speculate that addicts may be genetically deficient in insulin. I have heard from one addict who received an experimental injection of endorphins during heroin withdrawal. He reported that there was none of the usual euphoria experienced from an opiate injection, but rather "a shift of gears," and he was suddenly free from withdrawal symptoms. Researchers believe that endorphins, since it is a natural body substance, may not be addictive. Only widespread testing can answer this question.

Since endorphins were first extracted from animal brains, it is at present prohibitively expensive: $2000 a *treatment,* just as cortisone was very expensive when it was first extracted. Synthesis has brought the price of cortisone within reach of any patient who needs it. Is any of the $7.9 *billion* in Bush's latest War on Drugs plan marked for the synthesis and widespread testing of endorphins? I doubt if many of the congressmen who draft *"tough drug bills"* even know what endorphins are. And the same goes for the so-called drug experts who advise President Bush.

Billions for ineffectual enforcement.

Nothing for effective treatment.

I quote from a reading I have delivered to many receptive university audiences. This is an old number that is once again current and timely. It is called "MOB," for "My Own Business," drawing a line between the Johnsons and the shits:

This planet could be a reasonably pleasant place to live, if everybody could just mind his own business and let others do the same. But a wise old black faggot said to me years ago: "Some people are shits, darling."

I was never able to forget it.

The mark of a hard-core shit is that he has to be RIGHT. He is incapable of minding his own business, because he has no business of his own to mind. He is a professional minder of other people's business.

An example of the genre is the late Henry J. Anslinger, former Commissioner of Narcotics. "The laws must reflect society's disapproval of the addict," he said—a disapproval which he took every opportunity to foment. Such people poison the air we breathe with the blight of their disapproval—southern lawmen feeling their nigger notches, decent church-going women with pinched, mean, evil faces.

"Any form of maintenance is immoral," said Harry, thus rejecting the obvious solution to the so-called drug problem. On the other hand a Johnson minds his own business. He doesn't rush to the law if he smells pot or opium in the hall. Doesn't care about the call-girl on the second floor, or the fags in the back room. But he will give help when help is needed. He won't stand by when someone is drowning or under physical attack, nor when animals are being abused. He figures things like that are everybody's business.

Then along came Ronnie and Nancy, hand in hand, to tell us nobody has the right to mind his own business:

"Indifference is not an option. Only outspoken insistence that drug use will not be tolerated."

Everyone is obliged to become hysterical at the mere thought of drug use, just as office workers in Orwell's *1984* were obliged to scream curses, like Pavlov's frothing dogs, when the enemy leader appeared on screen. And they'd better scream loud and ugly.

William von Raab, former head of US Customs, went even further: "This is a war, and anyone who even *suggests* a tolerant attitude towards drug use should be considered a traitor."

Recollect during the Dexter Manley famous-athlete/cocaine-dealer flap, Eyewitness News was prowling the streets, sticking its mike in people's faces. One horrible biddy stated:

"Well, I think making the money they do, they should serve as an example."

She gets plenty of mike time.

And here a black cat working on some underground cables, straightens up and says, "I think if someone uses drugs, it's his own bus—"

He didn't even get the word out before they jerked the mike away. Freedom of the press to select what they want to hear, and call it the voice of the people.

Urine tests! Our pioneer ancestors would piss in their graves at the thought of urine tests to decide whether a man is competent to do his job. *The measure of competence is performance.* When told that General Grant was a heavy drinker, Lincoln said: "Find out what brand of whiskey he drinks, and distribute it to my other generals."

Doctor William Halsted has been called the "Father of American surgery." A brilliant and innovative practitioner, he introduced antiseptic procedures at a time when, far from donning rubber gloves, surgeons did not even wash their hands, and the death rate from post-operative infection ran as high as 80 percent. Doctor Halsted was a lifelong morphine addict. But he could still hack it and hack it good, and he lost no patients because of his personal habit. In those "good old days," a man's personal habits were *personal* and *private.* Now even a citizen's blood and urine are subject to arbitrary seizure and search.

The world's greatest detective could not have survived a urine test. "Which is it this time, Holmes, cocaine or morphine?"

"Both, Watson—a speed ball."

It is disquieting to speculate what may lurk behind this colossal red herring of the War Against Drugs—a war neither likely to, nor designed to, succeed. One thing is obvious: old, clean money and new, dirty money are shaking hands under the table. And the old tried-and-failed police approach will continue to escalate at the expense of any allocations for treatment and research. In politics, if something doesn't work, that is the best reason to go on doing it. If something looks like it might work, stay well away. Things like that could make waves, and the boys at the top, they don't like waves.

Anslinger's "missionary work," as he called it, has found fertile ground in Malaysia, where there is a mandatory death penalty for possession of a half-ounce or more of heroin or morphine or seven or more ounces of cannabis. (No distinction between hard and soft drugs in Malaysia, it's all "Dadah.") Anyone suspected of trafficking can be held two years without trial. Urine tests are a prerequisite for entry to high schools and universities.

Mahathir Mohamed, the Prime Minister of Malaysia, has launched an all-out radio and TV campaign to create a *"drug-hating personality."* He is said to command widespread support for his drug policies. So did Hitler command support for his anti-semitic program. Just substitute the word "addict" for "Jew," and *Der Stürmer* storms again. *Der Stürmer* was Julius Streicher's anti-Semitic rag, designed to create a Jew-hating personality.

In order to get to the bottom line of any issue, ask yourself: *"Cui bobo?*—Who profits?" According to Michele Sindona's account in Nick Tosches' book *Power on Earth,* the bulk of the world's dirty money is processed in Singapore and Kuala Lumpur, and the sums involved are *trillions of dollars.* Any liberalization of drug laws could precipitate a catastrophic collapse of the black drug market and cut off this salubrious flow of dirty money to the laundries of Malaysia. (Hanging small time pushers/addicts to protect huge Syndicate profits . . . does money come any dirtier?)

And I would be interested to examine the offshore bank accounts of Malaysian officials involved in the fabulously profitable war against drug menace. But that is a job for an investigative reporter like Jack Anderson, a job he is not likely to undertake, since he seems to be in basic sympathy with Malays Prime Minister Mahathir Mohamed.

Interviewing Mohamed on the subject of drugs, Jack Anderson reports that he "spoke with real passion." (And so did Hitler speak with real passion.) In a column entitled, "We Are Losing the War Against Drugs," Anderson speaks of thousands of "stupid and criminal Americans" who persist in using drugs . . . yes, criminal, by act of Congress. With the passage of the Harrison Narcotics Act in 1919, thousands of US citizens— from frugal, hard-working, honest Chinese to old ladies with arthritis and old gentlemen with gout—were suddenly "criminals."

George Will relates the story of a Colombian woman who was detained at Customs until she shit out some cocaine in condoms. He goes on to say: "We should attack demand as well as supply. Life should be made as difficult for users as it was for that woman."

So thousands of suspected users are rounded up and forced to swallow Castor oil in the hope of bringing illegal drugs to light . . .

"Got one!"

"False alarm . . . just a tapeworm."

Fifty years ago, deep in the Ural mountains of Lower Slobbovia, a 13-year old prick named Pavlik Morozov denounced his father to the local authorities as a counter-revolutionary Kulak—had a pig hid in his basement. (A Kulak is a subsistence farmer.) That was when Stalin was starving out the Kulaks to make way for collective farms, which didn't work. Stalin levied an outrageous produce tax, knowing that the farmers would hide their crops, then sent out patrols to search and seize concealed produce and farm animals. At least three million people starved to death in the winters of 1932 and 1933, and that's a conservative estimate.

Little Pavliki was hacked to stroganoff by the outraged neighbors—good job and all. *Thus perish all talking assholes.*

"His name must not die!" sobbed Maxim Gorky, his hearty voice contracted by painful emotion. So Pavliki became a folk hero. Got a street in Moscow named after him, and a statue to commemorate his heroic act. He should have been sculpted with the head of a rat. And the village of Gerasimovka is a fucking shrine, drawing legions of youthful pilgrims to the home of Pavlik Morozov.

"Dirty little *Stukach*."

That's Ruski for "rat"—a word designed to *spit* out.

It is happening here. *Lawrence Journal-World,* October 29, 1986: "Girl, 10, Reports Mother's Drug Use." It was the fourth time that a California girl had turned in her parents for alleged drug abuse since August 13th. And Reagan's Attorney General Ed Meese said that management has the obligation and responsibility for surveillance of problem areas in the workplace, such as locker rooms and above all, toilets, *and the toilets in the nearby taverns,* to prevent drug abuse.

I am an old-fashioned man: I don't like informers. It looks like Meese and Reagan, and now Bush, intend to turn the United States into a nation of mainstream rats.

Well, as Mohamed says, one has to give up a measure of freedom to achieve a blessed drug-free state, at which point the narcs will wither away. Sure, like the KGB withered away in Russia.

Unfortunately, my own most "paranoid" fantasies in recent years have not even come close to the actual menace now posed by anti-drug hysteria, if current polls are even approximately accurate. According to a survey conducted recently by the *Washington Post* and ABC News, 62 percent of Americans would be willing to give up "a few freedoms we have in this country" to significantly reduce illegal drug use; 55 percent said they favored mandatory drug tests for *all* Americans; 67 percent said all high school students should be regularly tested for drugs; 52 percent said they would agree to let police search homes of suspected drug dealers without a court order, even if houses "of people like you were sometimes searched by mistake"; 67 percent favored allowing police to stop cars at random and search for drugs, "even if it means that the cars of people like you are sometimes stopped and searched"; and fully *83 percent* favored encouraging people to report drug users to police, "even if it means telling police about a *family member* who uses drugs."

President Bush said in his television address not long ago: "Our outrage against drugs unites us as a nation!"

A nation of what? *Snoops and informers?*

Take a look at the knee-jerk, hard-core shits who react so predictably to the mere mention of drugs with fear, hate and loathing. Haven't we seen these same people before in various contexts? Storm troopers, lynch mobs, queer-bashers, Paki-bashers, racists— are these the people who are going to revitalize a "drug-free America"?

The emphasis on police action rather than treatment has persisted and accelerated. The addict seeking treatment today will find long waiting lists and often prohibitive costs. And the treatment is old-fashioned withdrawal, with a very high incidence of relapse. In all the television and newspaper talk about drugs, I have yet to hear a mention of the possible role of endorphins in such therapy, or any other innovative medical approach.

The dominant policy of police enforcement has nothing but escalating addiction rates (and ballooning appropriations) to recommend it. Americans used to pride themselves on doing a good job, and doing it right. Hysteria never solved any problem. If something clearly and demonstrably *does not work,* why go on doing it? It's downright un-American.

Now this: an excellent, level-headed anthology, covering the spectrum of drugs in common use. Artaud, Cocteau, Baudelaire and Huxley are included, of course; and here you have James Lee's *Underworld of the East,* a refreshing departure from the repentant whine of cured addicts. "The life of a drug addict can be one of unsurpassed happiness," Lee asserts, "if the user has knowledge and self-control . . ." "A Hashish House in New York" is a tour-de-force of 19th century purple prose, admonishing the reader of the terrible fate that may await those who die addicted to drugs, condemned to hover over living users in the vain hope of relieving incarnate withdrawal. And there's more. This is good material to re-read in the 90s, an antidote to knee-jerk hysteria. This book belongs on the shelf of every Johnson in America.

My advice to the young is: Just Say No to Drug Hysteria!

Introduction

John Strausbaugh

THESE MATERIALS FOCUS almost exclusively on writings by and about people using drugs before the 1960s. Before, that is, the modern era of drug use and drug hysteria. No Tim Leary proselytizing. No Studio 54 anecdotes from the 1970s, no tales of cocaine-huffing yuppies in the 1980s, nothing about crack dealing in the 1990s.

You can read all that elsewhere. It's practically all you can read about drug use. America has a short memory. Media and politicians focus our attention on today's top stories. It's not hard to forget that popular drug use was *not* invented by hippies. That in fact drug use has been a constant in American history for many decades, in Western civilization for centuries, and stretches back to the earliest traces of human consciousness.

This is not necessarily a "pro-drugs" book. It's not precisely an anti-anti-drug book, either. It is, to borrow a phrase from William S. Burroughs, an anti-drug *hysteria* book. Because drug hysteria, like racial hysteria, political hysteria, sex hysteria, or money hysteria, preys on ignorance and limits public discourse to levels of simple-minded cant. Manufactured panic is a poor basis for social policy. When a society panics, freedom of choice is always curtailed, rights are limited. Given the current climate, we felt it was time to present other sides of the "drug debate," other voices and opinions from the past that shouldn't be forgotten.

The notion of a "right to get high" doesn't play very well these days. Neither does the idea that getting high can be good for you. Yet the truth is, everybody gets high. Everybody gives in to the basic human need to get beyond the mundane, to escape everyday life. Some people do it by prayer. Some dance till they drop. Some spin. Some run or exercise until their endorphins boost them into a euphoric state. Some meditate. Some do yoga. Some rent a lot of videos. People fast, beat themselves, chant, handle snakes, abstain from sleep, pierce their bodies. Some people drink prodigious amounts of coffee to get a buzz, and others smoke tobacco. And some do drugs and alcohol.

I've opted to use the term "getting high" as the most innocent catch-all to cover this range of activities inducing ecstatic, euphoric, inebriated, intoxicated, visionary, and altered states of consciousness. Our language is rich in terms for these actions and states, terms both vernacular and official, but almost all are used with very specific associations, and all are laden with implied value judgments. When we drink alcohol we may become "inebriated" or "intoxicated," but we're not said to enter a "visionary" or "altered" state of consciousness. Similarly, drugs used to alter the mind are "narcotics," a law enforcement term weighted with bad connotations, while drugs dispensed by doctors to alter mood or depress mental activity are "pharmaceuticals." When we disapprove of someone's use of drugs we say they are "popping pills." When we approve they are "taking their medicine."

As a catch-all, the term "getting high" has some advantages. It's common vernacular, not officialese or legalese, and it covers a variety of states of consciousness. And, to the extent that it carries an implied value judgment, it's one of the few general terms that suggests a positive attitude.

No known culture has ever deployed such a vast pharmacopoeia of substances for getting high, getting healthy, or just plain coping as modern Western civilization has. But in every culture, in all epochs, people have gotten high. There's strong evidence that as long as humans have been conscious, they have sought to alter their consciousness. Getting high through the use of drugs is a part of virtually every culture on the planet, with only a few exceptions. (And just for the record, getting high is not limited to humans. Cats get high. Apes get high. Goats get high. Pigs, birds, raccoons, chickens, cattle, and donkeys get high. It seems that any organism with enough consciousness to be aware of the opportunity to alter it, does.)

A lot of history often winds up being overlooked or intentionally dropped in drug hysterical discourse. The "drug problem" is hardly new. Distilled spirits have been used since at least the ninth century. The ancient pre-Hindu text of the *Rig-Veda* contains references to a psychoactive drug called soma apparently in use over two thousand years before the Christian era. In some of their rites the ancient Greeks used a mind-altering drug they called *kykeon*. Indigenous American cultures have long used the sacred mushroom, tobacco, and peyote, which they continue to use today. Tobacco provided the economic impetus for the settling of the first colonies in Virginia and Maryland. Opium and laudanum use in Europe goes back at least to the Renaissance. Morphine, isolated from opium in the early 1800s, was in wide use by the middle of that century, as were chloroform and ether. Hashish was all the rage among Paris intellectuals in the 1840s; use of it and of marijuana in Europe go back as far as the earliest European contacts with

Near and Far Eastern cultures, certainly by the Middle Ages. The stimulative use of coca was known in Europe from the time of the conquistadors, and in the 1880s Sigmund Freud, among many others, became an ardent fan, personally and professionally, of its alkaloid derivative, cocaine.

America experienced its first "drug era" in the years between the Civil War and the development of modern pharmaceuticals in the 1910s and 1920s. Substances such as opium, cocaine, and heroin were very frequently used as ingredients in patent medicines and as panaceas for everything from a cough or toothache to dyspepsia and fatigue to nervousness and depression. The Harrison "Narcotics" Act of 1914 and the Eighteenth Amendment–Prohibition–which Congress passed in 1917 and which was enacted in 1920, coincided with the development of new, "safer" drugs and a period of outward public abstemiousness. Prohibition also gave rise to the marijuana craze of the 1920s and 1930s. Psychedelics such as LSD became "the problem children" (Dr. Albert Hofmann's coinage) of the 1950s and 1960s, which brings us to the second "drug era" of the 1960s and beyond.

Why have people in all cultures in all times gotten high? Aldous Huxley and Charles Baudelaire believed that people have an innate need to experience the Other, the Beyond, the Something Else Out There, what Baudelaire called the Thirst for the Infinite. Many psychologists agree: humans have an inherent drive to alter their consciousness. And this is what forms the essential link between a Christian visionary like Francis of Assisi, a Hindu fakir, a native American peyote shaman, and a scientific mystic like Huxley. A number of the writings collected in this book record the searches made by such diverse figures for visionary states.

Humanity's long history of drug use is of course not a rationale or excuse for drug *abuse*. Brutal, destructive, or stupid actions cannot be excused on the basis of long-standing practice. But neither does the compulsive abuse of *some* drugs by *some* people constitute a sensible rationale for creating general hysteria about *all* drugs (and by extension any instance of getting high). Nor should the fact that certain drugs can cause destructive behavior in some people necessarily serve as a basis for denying the positive effects getting high can have for other people.

Just as getting high is common to all cultures, its regulation is common too, although different cultures approach it in various ways and with vastly different measures of control. For example, many cultures have sought to limit the use of intoxicants and mind-altering substances to formal, communal occasions. "Drug use" in these societies is a sacred act, part of specific religious rituals distinctly removed from everyday life. In the non-European Americas there's a time and place and ritual motivation set aside for eating peyote or sacred mushrooms. Indiscriminate or recreational use of a "sacred" drug is viewed as an antisocial act. Often these drugs are "controlled substances" in that their harvesting, preparation, and use are all subject to the authority of a religious leader or shaman.

Some anthropologists and ethnologists believe that modern American culture has difficulties with drugs and alcohol precisely because it has no ritual context with which to control and moderate their use. To the extent that ours is a religious culture, it is mostly Puritan Protestant, with a strong minority presence of Roman Catholicism. It's a tradition that frowns severely on getting high in any way–even getting high within a religious, ritual context, even without the use of drugs. The ecstatic santeria rituals or the euphorias achieved by charismatic Christians (Protestant or Catholic) are considered outre, primitive, highly suspect, perhaps diabolical–and in some cases, as in the snake handling of certain fundamentalist Protestant sects, are illegal.

Lacking a ritual, traditional, communal means for moderating such behavior, our culture has resorted to public disapprobation and legal action. As behavioral control tools, they've never been terribly effective. Politicians may declare a war on getting high and civic and religious leaders condemn it; the means of getting high may be banned or priced out of reach and the full weight of public hysteria mobilized against the "pusher," the "user," and the "addict"–and still people will get high. There are more antidrug laws today than ever before, more attempts at interdiction, prevention, and detection, and a ubiquitous environment of communications media continuously warning and cajoling and condemning and surveilling, yet more people today get high than ever before.

United States presidents and politicians have been declaring wars on getting high for a long, long time. On the face of it, it's the longest and most inept war ever fought, assuming its supporters have been serious. George Washington bought his election to the Virginia House of Burgesses in 1758 by providing the electorate with 144 gallons of liquor, even while publicly speaking against its use by the working masses.

Ulysses S. Grant's drinking habit is legendary, and in his last years, stricken with cancer of the mouth after a lifetime of heavy cigar smoking, he was prescribed daily injections of morphine, swabbed his sores with cocaine, and drank the coca extract *Thé Mariani* to alleviate the pain. In his memoirs he extolled the "wonderful amount of relief" the drugs gave him, though acknowledging that "the tendency is to take more than there is any necessity and oftener." It is likely that Grant was egged on to use cocaine by his publisher, Mark Twain. If Grant lived long enough and had enough stamina to complete his deathbed memoirs, Twain stood to make a small fortune. Twain himself admitted to having been tempted by the lure of profit from cocaine early in his life. At the age of nineteen he went to New Orleans with the idea of catching a boat to Brazil to become a cocaine trader. All that stopped him was the fact that at the time it was not possible to sail from New Orleans to Brazil.

President Chester A. Arthur was noted for his love of alcohol and narcotics. Grover Cleveland drank heavily, used ether and cocaine, and his wife, Frances, appeared in ads for a pharmaceutical company. While publicly supporting Prohibition, Warren Harding and even the supposedly abstemious Herbert Hoover drank bootleg liquor behind closed doors in the White House. John F. Kennedy was rumored to indulge in occasional recreational drug use, although it's never been substantiated, and he was most certainly a great lover of tobacco. Reagan was given morphine after undergoing colon surgery and was reported to have enjoyed it.

In the nineteenth century politicians sought to pinch the flow of drugs into the United States chiefly through economic measures such as import taxes. In 1906 the Pure Food and Drug Act required that the ingredients in patent medicines be listed on the labels. As a result, manufacturers were forced to flag the presence of cocaine and opium for the interested consumer. In 1909 the importation or possession of opium became illegal. Its price consequently shot up, and people switched to newer drugs like morphine and heroin.

The Harrison Act of 1914 was the legal watershed from which all subsequent drug laws have descended. It banned over-the-counter sales of narcotics and instigated a pattern of underground and criminal drug trade which continues to this day. As time went on, subsequent laws such as the Marihuana Act of 1937 prohibited some drugs specifically not covered by the Harrison Act. New drugs were developed and eventually banned, like LSD, which was outlawed in 1967. But some drugs with powerful political and economic clout—tobacco, for instance—remained completely legal until very recently. Prohibition, which lasted from 1920 to 1933, was a failed attempt to make criminals of everyone who took a drink, although numerous residual elements of prohibition remain today in the form of blue laws, dry areas, state-controlled liquor stores, and heavy taxation.

The Comprehensive Drug Abuse Prevention and Control Act, which Nixon signed in 1970, replaced all previous drug laws and included the infamous Controlled Substances Act, which ranked drugs according to their potential addictiveness. Completely lacking in medical substantiation, it was a conservative reaction against the hippies and college students, who were demanding an end to the Vietnam War, and ethnic urban minorities, who were threatening open rebellion. Marijuana and psychedelics were classified with heroin as belonging to the most dangerous, or "Schedule 1," substances, while cocaine and opium (not fads at that time) were considered to be less dangerous "Schedule 2" drugs. The crackdown on cocaine came later, in direct response to its booming popularity in the 1970s and 1980s. Reagan professed a national dedication once again to the war on drugs, as has Bush. Indeed, the Bush regime has pressed the war on more fronts than any previous administration, using drugs as an excuse to wage actual war on small nations, to violate the privacy and dignity of individual citizens through odious drug testing procedures and McCarthyesque antidrug oaths, and to foster a level of hysteria and panic among the public rarely achieved before. The war on drugs in the 1980s and 1990s represents just one of many facets of a remarkably repressive backlash to 1960s' and 1970s' liberalism, a jihad launched by conservative control freaks that includes a war on the poor, a war on women, a war on workers, a war on sex, a war on education, a war on artists . . .

The war on getting high is one issue in a larger, long struggle in America over the issue of mind control. It is now well documented that attempts by the CIA to utilize certain drugs for mind controlling occurred at the same time that the U.S. government was ostensibly devoting immense resources to curtail drug traffic and use.

Free minds mean problems. Insurgent or rebellious imagination means problems. The effect of corporate/political/media axis activities in the late twentieth century has been not only to control the imagination but to make it passive and receptive and docile–an open channel for media and advertising and propaganda, a receptor of prepackaged dreams (TV, movies) and lowest-common-denominator fantasies (revenge fantasies of international politics, the fantasy of knowing and sharing the lifestyles of the rich and famous).

In the last twenty years the all-pervasive, all-invasive communications-infotainment media have escorted American minds farther and farther into a total fantasy environment: national and international politics as TV, with TV actors acting like politicians acting like TV heroes; public discourse as TV and rehearsed radio talk shows called "town meetings" with discussants acting like citizens of a fantasized community. Public opinion directed by weeks of deep hypnopsych implants *(This is what we think. This is what you think. This is what you think. This is what you think.)* and then publicly affirmed by the opinion "poll" *(Tell us, what do you think?).* Real sex and real joy in the real world as dangerous, life-threatening perversions to be sublimated into the polymorphous fantasy realm of an advertainment environment throbbing with unfulfilled desires (because the fulfilled consumer is not a buying customer). Advertainment that has transcended the simplistic, now laughably kitsch level of commodities brandished as objective symbols of basic desires *(This is what you want.)* and which instead now probes the deepest realms of anxiety and apprehension *(This is who you ought to be.).* And all of it overtly or covertly selling a corporate-political party line that often seeks to stir the masses of consumer-citizens at the crudest levels of hysteria and paranoia: fear of other nations and cultures, fear of strangers and "others," fear of other genders or sexual modalities, fear of crime, fear of economic disaster, fear of, fear of, fear of.

As a strategy for societal control, hysteria is neither new nor limited to the issue of drugs. In the 1980s a false hysteria over missing children was drummed up to incite panic about strangers and sex. Child abduction was portrayed as epidemic; an impression was given that children by the thousands were being snatched off the streets by monstrous child-porn snuff-film perverts. The faces of missing children appeared on the news every evening, confronted us every morning as we poured milk into our (ahem) coffee. All despite overwhelming documentation showing that the vast majority of child abductions–statistically speaking, all verifiable cases of child abductions–were being carried out by the estranged or divorced *parents* of the child in question.

There are many similar examples of such trumped-up hysteria–about sex, about strangers and outsiders of all types, about artists and other "degenerates," about Commies (until very recently), about our jobs, and on and on. It's hardly coincidental that so much hysteria and paranoia have been whipped up on so many fronts at a time when the "nuclear family"—a term that has itself become a mordant, malevolent joke in the "nuclear age"—has been disintegrating. With divorce rates skyrocketing, home-and-hearth life has become a quaint old saw; children are rebelling, growing up too fast, becoming too "sophisticated" about sex, drugs, and the dubious realities of consumer culture. Not to mention the fact that birthrates are falling among dominant whites and booming among the poor, nonwhite (soon not-to-be) "minority" members of our unwillingly multicultural society. You bet "our" children are missing. You bet we want them back. Back to Timmy and Lassie, back to Beaver Cleaver. (Whose very name insidiously, comically—unconsciously?—evoked "our" mythic pioneer past, in an age when the height of fashion for little white boys was a Davy Crockett coonskin cap. Lost white American youth—skinners of coons, cleavers of beavers.)

Predictably, in the hysteria over "drug use" very little is said about the "drug use" of the corporate/government/media axis. That is, about the way it makes out of drugs an issue to excuse yet another wave of armed corporate colonization in Latin America; the way it uses drugs as a pretext for invading the privacy of individual citizens and workers, forcing them to prove that they're *not* taking drugs (contrary to the fundamentally American concept of presuming innocence until one is proven guilty), coercing them into signing loyalty oaths to a drug-free government, then selling them T-shirts that proudly (and ignorantly, and ninety-nine times out of a hundred less than truthfully) proclaim a "Drug-Free Body." *(This is what you want. This is who you ought to be.)*

Very little is said about how all the laws, all the police actions both domestic and international, cannot stop people from getting high but only make outlaws out of them for doing it. About how all the laws have created a vast criminal industry in the development and distribution of drugs, while an equally large and fully legal drug industry operated by the pharmaceutical/medical/psychiatric axis—the most effective dope pusher ever—makes dope addicts of enormous sectors of our population. Far more people become addicted to the downers and stress relievers and mood levelers legally prescribed by doctors and shrinks than will ever become "addicted" to LSD. The role of medical and psychiatric professionals in the history of drug use has been long and murky, and they turn up again and again in this book. Although they're the modern descendants of shamans, or "medicine men," they seem most comfortable when dispensing drugs as a method to contain emotions, repress imagination, and control behavior, rather than to open the mind or the spirit.

Corporate conservatives who have dominated American culture over the last few decades have found it very convenient to identify drug use as a major cause of crime and social disintegration in urban communities. It is much more tolerable and useful for them to have the infotainment media focus on drugs rather than the less tangible and uncomfortably pervasive issues of poverty, lack of hope, etc., etc. as the major cause of crime in our cities. Lack of hope is not easily captured in a three-minute news segment, and it doesn't allow for the presentation of a clear image of the villain. News is a reporter–typically a middle-aged white male–entering a poor urban area, usually in the safety of a police prowl car and, often using hi-tech surveillance equipment from a secure distance, catching young "ethnic" males copping a deal on a desolate city street corner. The footage is reminiscent of a PBS nature program furtively capturing with an infrared camera the nocturnal habits of some exotic and largely unknowable species of rare animal. This tactic of distancing the criminal drug user/dealer as some sort of other species was not invented by TV. Similar strategies are evident in some of the stories in this volume, in which intrepid newshounds sneak into the forbidden demimondes of hashish addicts, etc. It's not new, and it's not news, either, but it's very effective in reinforcing the fantasy that getting high is something that "they" do, while many Americans, thanking God and the president, proudly wearing Drug-Free T-shirts, settle down for the weekend with another stack of videotapes and a six-pack.

Prior to the 1960s drug use was commonly portrayed as a subcultural aberration; drug users were a criminal and sick minority, an underground of hepcats, decadents, foreign elements, hoods, and hookers. Then in the 1960s, with the advent of the hippie drug culture, it seemed an entire generation of white, well-educated youth was smoking pot and dropping acid. Everyone got high; by the 1970s "recreational drug use" began to seem as unremarkable a pastime as a game of badminton. In the 1990s it's hard even to remember those times.

The materials collected here were written by a number of widely divergent drug users, describing a range of experiences with a variety of drugs. A recurrent theme in these writings is the use of drugs to achieve visionary states of awareness. Many of those who address this concept are artists who explored uncharted mental states, seeking experiences that would enrich their work. Consciously entering altered states of perception very like the mental state of schizophrenia, they wagered the Nietzschean gamble with their sanity and came back to report to us what they saw there.

Of the writings collected here, only Witciewicz's is a direct dispatch from "the other side," written while in an altered state. Others, such as Baudelaire and Cocteau, experienced their richest periods of artistic inspiration during the years of their heaviest drug use. Baudelaire regretted having to depend on drugs and alcohol to achieve his "artificial paradise." He believed that a great poet should be able to enter paradise unaided, but that didn't stop him from using help. Cocteau eventually decided the gamble was too risky and kicked his opium habit in a series of long and agonizing clinical cures. Antonin Artaud, perhaps the biggest gambler included here, plunged into that other state of consciousness never to return.

Several native American views on the use of peyote for spiritual and religious purposes are presented here as well. Since its establishment as a religion at the beginning of the twentieth century, the native American church has had a rocky time with courts and other arms of the government at both the local and federal levels. Governments have vacillated for decades between prosecuting the native American church's use of peyote and tolerating it under the religious freedoms guaranteed by the First and Fourteenth Amendments. In 1978 Congress passed the Native American Religious Freedom Act, ostensibly to protect the native American church as one of many Indian religious customs. But by 1990 a conservative Supreme Court was determined to close up the last remaining loophole permitting legal use of psychedelics, and it handed down rulings effectively allowing nationwide banning of the church's peyote ceremonies.

Entries by Aldous Huxley and R. Gordon Wasson are fascinating documents from the era of psychedelic experimentation in the 1950s. Huxley, who first took mescaline in 1953, over the next ten years was one of the world's most eloquent proponents of the psychological and spiritual benefits of psychedelics. Included in this volume is an article he wrote for the family magazine *The Saturday Evening Post* in 1958.

Wasson's article appeared in a 1957 issue of *Life* magazine. (The same issue included a notice of Senator Joe McCarthy's death from acute hepatitis in Wisconsin, a very upbeat article about President Ngo Dinh Diem, "the tough miracle man of Vietnam," and a story on a new drug, AET, thought to give "complete protection from the devastating effects of radiation sickness.") Wasson was a vice-president of J. P. Morgan and Company, one of the world's largest banking firms. He was also deeply interested in mystical religious experiences and became convinced that Western civilization could benefit from learning the secrets of the somalike drugs used by many other civilizations. Beginning in 1953, as the article reports, he traveled several times to Mexico to experience sacred mushrooms firsthand.

Sigmund Freud and Albert Hofmann are prime examples of the scientific and medical professional—one almost wants to say medicine man—experimenting with drugs. In 1860 the alkaloid coca extraction called cocaine was isolated. By 1884 the possibility of using cocaine as a local anesthetic was discovered. Further medical testing of cocaine in 1884 was spurred partly by enthusiastic pronouncements made by the young, ambitious Dr. Freud, who had narrowly missed out on discovering its anesthetic properties himself. He had read reports of successful experiments using cocaine to cure morphine addiction, and his tests on a patient and friend, Ernst von Fleischl-Maxrow, seemed positive enough for him to proclaim its wonders in a widely circulated paper entitled "On Cocaine."

The medical and psychiatric communities were galvanized at first, and testing was widespread that year. But in the space of a year there came a flood of disturbing reports that morphine addicts had been turned into cocaine addicts and of surgical patients having bad physical reactions. The fact that many of the people on whom cocaine was tested were themselves physicians or physicians' friends and loved ones no doubt fueled the medical community's panic. Freud was widely denounced and forced to defend himself with the retracting evident in a paper he published just three years later, "Craving for and Fear of Cocaine." His last published paper on cocaine, it went unheeded. Cocaine's dispensation for psychiatric care was hastily abandoned, even by Freud–not, sadly enough, before his friend Fleischl experienced horrific toxic psychoses from the huge doses of cocaine he was taking. (Cocaine's use as a local anesthetic continued until the less-chancy procaine, known commercially as Novocain, was developed in 1904.)

Freud's personal use of cocaine nevertheless continued until at least 1895. He had begun, like so many past and future drug pioneers, by testing it on himself, and he found that he liked it. He liked it a lot. His private letters and thinly veiled comments in some later published papers clearly demonstrate his fondness for the drug as a euphoric and stimulant. Given that cocaine had come to be considered the "third scourge of mankind" (after alcohol and morphine), it is no wonder that his professional ambitions dictated discretion.

The story of Dr. Hofmann's discovery in a Sandoz laboratory in 1943 of LSD-25's psychoactive properties is well known. While Hofmann never approved of the recreational tripping that became so popular in the 1960s, he collaborated with Huxley, Wasson, and others in personal LSD explorations such as the genteel session described in this book. It's clear that, research aside, Hofmann thoroughly enjoyed his experiences with LSD and other psychedelics, and the purpose of many of his trips seems to have been as much recreational as scientific or spiritual. In 1988, fifty years after his discovery of LSD, Dr. Hofmann lent his name and blessings to the Albert Hofmann Foundation, making a small and quiet effort to clear psychedelics' reputation and win new respectability for "the scientific study of human consciousness."

Many other perspectives are presented here as well. People doing drugs just for the fun of it or out of curiosity. People hooked on drugs and others simply unwilling to give them up. People extolling the virtues of one drug or another and a few classic examples of drug hysteria. Each is unique, interesting, and instructive in its own way.

New York City
October 1990

from **The Underworld of the East**

J a m e s   S .   L e e

Libertine, iconoclast, lay philosopher, avid explorer of the "underworld," and lifelong experimenter with many drugs, James Lee was a twenty-two-year-old engineer in London when, in 1894, he sailed off to run a coal-mining operation "situated on the borders of Assam and the wild hill country of the savage Nagas and Sing-phoos." Finding it difficult to adjust to the tropical lifestyle, on the recommendation of a local physician Lee took up the use of "morphia" to cure his ills. This same physician, Dr. Babu, suggested Lee inject cocaine when his reliance on morphine became too much for the fledgling user. Thence forward, Lee enthusiastically embarked on a career of experimentation that led him all over the East and into the sometimes dark but always fascinating recesses of his mind.

About Drugs

Before commencing with my story in its proper order, I will say a few words about the drug habit generally.

During the thirty years in which I was a constant user of drugs of many kinds, various people, including some doctors, and chemists, have asked me how it was that I was able to continue in the habit for so long a time, and use such large quantities of drugs, and still remain in good health.

This true story of my experiences will explain the reason, and also may show the drug habit in an entirely new aspect.

It is now many years since I gave up using all drugs, but during the thirty years with which this story deals, I have used morphia, cocaine, hashish, opium, and a good many other drugs, both singly and in combination.

The doses which I became able to take, after so many years of the habit, may seem almost impossible, yet it is a fact that I have increased my dose gradually, until I could inject eighty grains of pure cocaine a day; sufficient to kill many persons, if divided amongst them.

At other times when I favored morphia, I have injected as much as ten grains per day, although the medical dose is a quarter of a grain.

My arms, shoulders and chest, are a faint blue color, which, if magnified, reveals the marks of thousands of tiny punctures; hypodermic syringe marks.

Many years I have searched the jungles of the Far East for new drugs; testing strange plants, bulbs, and roots, making extracts, and then testing them first on animals, and in some cases on myself, and I will describe later some of the strange effects produced; particularly in the case of one drug, which I will call "The Elixir of Life."

If some of the things I describe are horrible, they are nevertheless true. What strange sights may a man not see during seven years in a country like China, if he goes to look for them below the surface? It is a country of camouflage and hidden ways. Innocent looking junks, quietly floating down the rivers and canals, may be really sumptuously furnished gambling dens and drug haunts, where orgies of many kinds are carried on. No European, unless he is introduced by a trusted Chinese, will ever have the entry to these places.

The life of a drug taker can be a happy one, far surpassing that of any other; or it can be one of suffering and misery; it depends on the user's knowledge. The most interesting period will only be reached after many years, and then only if perfect health has been retained; using several kinds of drugs (for one drug alone spells disaster), and increasing the doses in a carefully thought out system; a system which was first made known to me by the Indian doctor who initiated me into the drug habit.

Waking visions will then begin to appear when under the influence of very large doses, and it is these visions which are so interesting.

I have sat up through the night taking drugs until the room has been peopled with spirits. They may be horrible, grotesque, or beautiful, according to the nature of the drugs producing them. Strange scenes have been enacted before my eyes; scenes which were very real and lifelike, and which I will describe later.

When the Dangerous Drug Act came into force I gave up using all drugs, because the danger and risk of obtaining them was too great. The paltry quantities, about which the authorities make such a fuss, were of no use to me, and I was able to give them up without any trouble or suffering, owing to my experiments and discoveries.

This story will be as a message of hope to all drug addicts. The cure is easy, but not by the method generally adopted, that of gradually reducing the dose; a method which will only cause intense suffering, and sometimes even death.

[Lee goes to Northern India and begins work as an engineer in the coal mine. He narrowly avoids a mine explosion and two attacks by a man-eating tiger. Working in the mine, which he likens to a "wound" in the earth, he begins to develop a kind of Gaia theory, depicting the earth as a living creature and the miners as parasites boring into her flesh.]

I Learn to Inject Morphia

Beautiful places in the tropics, I have heard, are often unhealthy, and this I found was one of them, and it was not long before I got a touch of malaria.

Malaria causes an absolutely rotten feeling, with headache and all the rest of it, so one day I when I had an attack rather worse than usual, I sent over to the hospital for the Indian doctor or "Babu," who was in charge there.

He was a fat and jolly Hindu of about forty years of age. After feeling my pulse and taking my temperature, he said, speaking through his nose like most Babus do, "Yes, sir. You have a little fever, but I will soon cure you."

Then he called Abdul to bring a glass of water, and taking a little case out of his pocket, he opened it and took out a small syringe; the first hypodermic syringe I had ever seen. Withdrawing the glass plunger, he selected a tabloid from a small tube and dropped it in the syringe, replaced the plunger and drew the syringe three-quarters full of water. Placing a hollow needle on the end of the syringe, he first shook it until the tabloid was dissolved, and then injected the contents into my arm. I will never forget that first injection; the beautiful sensation of ease and comfort; the luxurious dreamy feeling of indolence and happiness which immediately ensued. Every distressing symptom of the fever had disappeared, and I only wanted to sit still in my chair. I was simply purring with content. The voice of the Dr. Babu, who was a great talker, was like a gentle murmur, and I saw him through a pleasant haze.

I must have sat there for hours after he had gone, and it was growing dark, and Abdul came in with the lamp, and commenced laying the table for dinner. It was the first meal that I had really enjoyed for some days, and that night I slept well, and awakened fresh next morning.

As the day wore on, I felt not quite so well, rather tired and a little depressed, and I thought that perhaps I required a little more of the medicine the Babu had given me the day before, also I felt that I would like to have another dose, so I went over to the hospital and saw the Babu. He greeted me with a pleasant smile, and made no trouble about giving me another injection.

"What sort of medicine is this, doctor?" I asked him.

"It is morphia," he said, "the most useful medicine in the world."

The word morphia meant little to me then. Of course I had heard about morphia addicts, but I thought that I was quite capable of controlling any impulse I might have of making a habit of it, and I thought a few doses could not make much difference; moreover, the second dose seemed to be even more potent than the first; no doubt he had given me a larger one.

I even persuaded the doctor to give me a syringe and a tube of ¼-grain tabloids.

After a time I found myself looking forward to the afternoon when the day's work was over, and I could take a larger dose and lay dreaming rosy dreams; meanwhile I had got in a supply of tabloids from Calcutta.

There were only day dreams it is true, for I had not yet reached the stage where visions appear while asleep, much less that stage which extremely few drug addicts ever reach, the time when absolutely life-like visions appear while awake. This stage can never be reached on morphia alone.

After a few months of regular indulgence in morphia I began to feel that to get the same results I had to increase my dose and also that the effect wore more quickly.

Also, I found that my digestive system was getting out of order, and I was becoming so costive that no opening medicine had much effect. The latter symptom was causing me considerable inconvenience, and I was getting scared. I was using now about 4 grains a day, injected a grain at a time; instead of the ¼ dose as at first, yet the effect was not so pleasant.

I decided that the drug habit was getting too great a hold on me, and that the time had come when I must give it up; never expecting any difficulty in doing so.

I had heard that morphia users broke themselves of the habit generally by reducing their dose a little every day, until they had given it all up.

I smile at my ignorance now, but then it seemed quite simple, so I started.

Next day I took my usual supply of morphia for the day: 4 grains, and mixed it in a small vial containing six syringes full of water, viz. 120 minims. I now drew up into the syringe one tenth of the mixture (12 minims) and threw it away replacing it by this quantity of water.

Next day I felt all right. "Hurrah, it is easy."

The second day I threw away 24 minims and added only 18 minims of water, thus reducing the quantity of liquid per injection from 20 minims to 19 minims; the mixture also being not so strong.

Now I did not feel so good. I found my thoughts constantly turning to morphia, and going over again the pleasant sensation I had experienced. This seemed to emphasize my present state. I really felt uncomfortable and rather irritable, and I kept thinking what a pleasure it would be to take a thumping big dose.

Pride and fear made me stick to my intention, and persevere with this so-called system, until I had reduced my consumption of morphia to ½ grain a day. Beyond this I could not possibly go. I was suffering terribly; I could not sleep, nor sit still, and I was on the fidget all the time. I had a horrible toothache, and I was jumpy and nervous. I could not get a wink of sleep at night, for I would be up half a dozen times walking about the room, as I had cramps in my feet and legs, which I could not keep in one position while lying in bed for than a minute, before they began to ache again.

I felt wretched in the extreme, and I think that the worst symptom of all was the horrible feeling of depression and gloom–so terrible that it defies description. Moreover, I found that every reduction of the dose increased the sufferings, not only in proportion, but probably four-fold, and I had a tolerable idea that what I was suffering then would be only a fraction of what I would suffer when I got down to the quarter of a grain.

I could not stand it any longer, and I injected a whole grain dose.

Can anyone possibly describe the sensation of relief I felt? I think not; no words possibly could do so. It was simply Heavenly, and that is all I can say. I was now thoroughly scared, because I was back on my 1 grain dose, and soon I even began to feel that I would like to increase it.

I decided to see the Dr. Babu, so I went over to the hospital, where I found he was attending to the outpatients.

I went into his room and waited, and began to think.

I had often noticed a peculiar look in his eyes, when I met him. Sometimes I noticed that the pupils were mere pin points, while at other times they were so large as to almost fill his iris. Moreover, I had noticed that sometimes he would be calm and dreamy in his manner, while again he would be full of life and energy. His moods appeared to change in many different ways.

I remembered the peculiar smile on his face when I told him that I was going to gradually reduce my dose of morphia until I had given it up.

He had enquired two or three times how I was getting on, and each time I had told him of my success he had smiled. I wondered why he had not told me how difficult morphia was to give up; so when he came in I tackled him about it.

"Sir," he said, "morphia is a very strange medicine, it is both Heaven and Hell. It is very difficult to give up, but it can be done."

Morphia should not be used by anyone for longer than a few months, he told me, because by that time it will begin to lose its pleasant effect, and it will also begin to affect the health, because the action of the drug is continually in one direction.

He told me that he used many kinds of drugs, each in turn; changing over from one to another, using them sometimes singly, and at other times in combination, so that no one drug ever got too great a hold on him. Each time he changed over, the drug he had been using regained all its old potency and charm when commenced again.

I complained about the binding effect of the morphia.

"Yes," he said, "that is one of the principal reasons why the long use of morphia alone is so destructive to health. Its deadening effect on the bowels and the digestion. Although purgatives are of little use, and, moreover, are dangerous to a morphia addict, there is one sure remedy."

Then he gave me my first dose of cocaine.

I found the effect extremely pleasant, although I only had a beginner's dose, ½ grain. It was stimulating, and exhilarating, producing a feeling of well being; of joy and good spirits. Large doses will produce great self-confidence, and absolutely banish every feeling of self-consciousness in the most difficult situations, in fact it will make the user glory in becoming conspicuous.

Cocaine in large doses also has another effect, which I will not describe here, and this effect is considerably increased when certain other drugs are mixed with it. It is a strange fact that although cocaine, in itself, is not an opening medicine when used by any other person, the effect is immediate when taken by a morphia addict whose bowels have become inoperative.

Following the Dr. Babu's instructions, I first mixed up an ounce solution containing 1 grain of morphia to each 20 minims of water, and another of a 5 per cent solution of cocaine.

Starting with 20 minims of the morphia solution, injected three times a day, i.e. 3

grains of morphia a day, I reduced the dose by 1 minim each day, and added 1 minim of the cocaine solution, until in twenty days I was using no morphia at all, only cocaine.

I experienced no inconvenience at all, or craving for morphia, only increased pleasure.

My health improved, and I became so full of life and energy, and good spirits, that everyone noticed the change in me. No one suspected that I had been using morphia, they had put the change in me, from the health and spirits which I had when I first arrived, to the listless and dreamy state I had been in for some time, to malaria.

The increased brilliance of my eyes due to cocaine, appeared only to be an excessive state of good health and vitality.

I now experienced even greater pleasure from the indulgence in cocaine, than I had experienced when commencing to use morphia; and the fact that I had been able to give up the latter so easily, filled me with pride, because in the last week or two I had read a good deal about the drug habit. I was studying a book by an Indian writer, which the Babu had lent me.

It is true that I was now using cocaine, instead of morphia, but then cocaine is much easier to give up than morphia. The deprivation does not cause such distressing and terrible symptoms.

I had not yet discovered the perfect cure for all drug habits, this was to come later, but just out of curiosity I tried a beginner's dose of morphia again, and I found that it had regained all the potency and effect that it had when I was first introduced to it.

Cocaine, I found, banished all desire for sleep, and as loss of proper sleep is one of the reasons why the drug quickly ruins the health, I saw the doctor about it.

I had become very friendly with him, and perhaps because I treated him differently from the way most Europeans treated the educated Indian in those days–by affecting to consider them as inferiors–he imparted to me knowledge about many strange drugs, and their effects. He had devoted many years to the study of this subject, and it was due to him that I first got my great idea, with which I will deal in succeeding chapters.

He next initiated me into the art of smoking opium in the Chinese fashion, and I found that a few pipes of this, smoked just before retiring, procured me a refreshing and sound sleep, which is essential to the cocaine addict, but is so seldom obtained.

The opium is smoked in a manner which has been so often described in books that I will not say much about it here. Opium has the appearance of thick black treacle before it is cooked on a skewer, over a small spirit lamp until it becomes of the consistency of cobblers' wax. This is then rolled into a pellet the size of a large pea, and stuck on the pipe bowl with the skewer. When the latter is withdrawn there remains a small hole through the center of the pellet.

The pipe, which is a hollow bamboo, is then held over the flame and the smoke sucked into the lungs.

The effect is extremely soothing and sleep-producing, more so than any other drug, and it is a mistake to think that it produces dreams. When once the smoker is asleep, it is a sound and dreamless sleep.

It is preceded by a very pleasant, dreamy state, in which the imagination is very active, and everything appears beautiful, so that even an ugly woman would appear charming.

I found that I could vary my dose of cocaine very considerably, and occasionally I would have a regular binge and then bring myself back to normal with the aid of a little morphia injected.

I was again in fine health and spirits, and I was becoming more interested in my surroundings.

No one suspected that I was using drugs, for there was nothing about my manner to indicate my habit, especially as during the day I used only small doses.

The Dr. Babu was a jolly old soul and fond of female society, and frequently when I went over to his bungalow of an evening, I would find him entertaining some of the prettiest girls in the settlement, and sometimes he had "Nautch Wallahs," i.e. professional dancing girls, giving an exhibition. Sometimes, also, there were other entertainments which I will not describe.

In those days I was very young and shy, and many things easily shocked me.

I found cocaine became more and more fascinating as the doses were increased and time went on. The small doses such as are taken by a beginner, will produce only a remarkable increase of mental and bodily vigor, with a feeling of great strength, but without any intoxication, but if the dose is considerably increased, a kind of intoxication which is quite different from that produced by drink will ensue, a kind of intoxication which I will endeavor to describe later on.

Strange Waking Dreams

I was now using fairly large quantities of cocaine, often tempered with morphia, and smoking a little opium every night.

The morphia and cocaine, of course, I injected, and I soon found that the punctures of the needle left red spots, which sometimes would inflame, and even, as in one instance, cause a sore, and it was the latter that caused me to mention it to the Doctor Babu.

He looked at my arm, and then told me a few truths that I did not know before, nor had ever thought of.

Like most Babus, he spoke slowly, in copy book English, with a slight nasal accent, choosing his words carefully.

"Do you know, sir, that every time you obtain a puncture in the flesh by means of a hypodermic needle, you introduce into the internal portion of the body considerable agglomerations of bacteria."

I listened to his lecture, and understood from it, that I should only use an all-glass syringe, which should be boiled frequently and put away in sterilizing solution, while a second one was being used. The needles, of which I required several, should be kept in solution, and the points never touched with the fingers before using, and also that the place where the injection was going to be made should be first wiped with cotton wool dipped in spirits of wine.

All this was most important (he informed me) in a case where so many injections are constantly being used, otherwise a minute portion of septic matter would be introduced into the system each time. It was this, he informed me, that was one of the causes for quickly undermining the health of drug injectors. Their system becomes poisoned by septic matter. Many germs are introduced with each injection.

A single drug, used by itself, cannot be continued with for so long as a combination of two or more drugs. The former will quickly ruin the health, because the action is always in one direction.

No wonder the drug habit is considered so deadly, and makes so many mental and physical wrecks.

A person uses cocaine only for several months, or a year say. He uses it continuously without any other drug to correct its action from always being in the same direction. He is in a constant state of exhilaration and stimulation of the nervous system. He hardly ever sleeps because cocaine banishes sleep, neither does he ever feel hungry, because one of the attributes of this drug is to banish hunger.

He soon becomes like a living skeleton, although appearing to be full of life and energy to the last, but it is false energy; just the effort of the cocaine, using up his nervous energy at a greater rate than his system is making it.

Soon a complete collapse must occur.

It is the same with morphia, only the result is brought about in the reverse direction. The morphia user lives in a pleasant, dreamy state, of soothing comfort and reduced heart's action, which in time gradually makes him almost dead to everything in the world but morphia.

A confirmed morphia addict of long standing loses all sex instinct and feeling; although this is not permanent, it returns when the drug is given up, or if cocaine is substituted.

Cocaine, on the other hand, will, in time, if used entirely alone, produce a kind of sex mania.

In after years I have come in contact with thousands of drug addicts in India, China, Japan, the Malay Archipelago and other parts of the world, where I have specially sought them out.

The popularity of the various drugs differs with the country, but opium heads all the others, followed by cocaine, morphia, hashish, ganja, bhang, etc.

Then there are various kinds of liquor which are almost like drugs. Spirits of wine, absinthe, sumsu or rice spirit, arack, made from raisins, and aniseed, and many others.

There are also secret drugs known only to a few in China, drugs which are terrible in their after-effects, but which are more alluring than any of those mentioned. I do not give the names of them here.

For the sore place on my arm, the Babu mixed up some cocaine into a paste and applied it, informing me that this drug is the finest healer known, only it is nearly always used in a solution, which is too weak.

Under his instructions, I now started to use drugs scientifically.

I watched my bodily condition carefully, and corrected at once any adverse symptoms.

Had I a headache on some rare occasion? I removed it at once with a mixture of morphia and cocaine.

A little fever which was natural in this climate and affected every European, I could remove in a few minutes, just as I could remove any kind of pain.

Suppose I was feeling too wakeful to sleep, then a few pipes of opium would send me into a sound, dreamless sleep. Any tendency towards worry, or that commonplace feeling of being dissatisfied with things, could be banished in a few minutes.

Drugs alone could do this, if rightly used, but unfortunately, they are hardly ever used so.

All these narcotic drugs, which are commonly known as Dangerous Drugs, are really a gift of God to mankind. Instead of them doing him harm, they should really be the means of preserving his health, and making his life a state of continual happiness.

I was now able to use large quantities of any particular drug for a time without it harming my health in the slightest, in fact I seemed to benefit by it in every way.

If I had been taking heavy doses of cocaine for some time, living in a state of mental exhilaration and stimulation of every bodily faculty, then I knew that I must I must reverse, and give the nervous system a perfect rest, under the soothing influence of the morphia; and obtain long sound sleeps, with the aid of opium. Moreover, these alternative drugs were equally fascinating, It would be difficult to say that one was more so than another, and the contrast in their action made each one seem more attractive than the last.

The appetite must not be neglected. The stomach will digest enormous quantities of food perfectly, under certain forms of stimulation, if only the nervous energy at the moment is sufficient.

Morphia and brandy together will produce a voracious appetite, and it is a fact that I have eaten a meal at midnight, consisting of three-quarters of a pound of cheese with pickles, half a pound of roast pork, a small loaf of bread and butter and three or four cups of coffee and brandy. Afterwards I have slept soundly and felt fresh and well next morning.

Think of the amount of nutriment the system will obtain from such a meal, enjoyed and perfectly digested.

The study of the effects of the different drug combinations became for me a fascinating hobby, and when I tried "hashish," I found it to be the strangest drug of all. I will tell the reader something about it later, also about "ganja" and "bhang."

One of the finest effects felt after a dose of cocaine, is a marvellous clearness of vision, and a feeling of perfect well being and happiness. Any tired feeling will be instantly banished and replaced by a feeling of great strength and power. The brain will become powerfully stimulated and clear in thought.

Further doses will produce a peculiar kind of intoxication and extreme fertility of the imagination.

If morphia is added, the thoughts will become calmer and even more fertile, and waking dreams will occur; dreams which are marvelously clear.

Thoughts passed through my mind with an amazing sequence, and problems appeared, only to be immediately solved.

[Lee moves on to a new job in Sumatra.]

I Go to the Malay Archipelago

I was making preparations for my voyage home, and the giving up of drugs on the way.

At the present time I had no regular dose, or fixed time of taking, such as is the custom of most drug users. For days, sometimes, I would use just the minimum combination of drugs, which would make me feel just right, with perfect comfort in mind and body; then I would have a regular binge with some particular drug, selecting one which I had not been using much for some time, so that it would have all its finer effects.

Not being able to smoke opium or hashish on the voyage, I would have to cut them out.

The first thing to be done was to cut out all drugs, except cocaine and morphia injections, and these I gradually wangled, until I was using an equal quantity of each.

In a bottle, I mixed up 12 grains of morphia and 12 grains of cocaine with 480 minims of distilled water. This was six days' supply of four injections per day, using 20 minims per injection. The syringe was graduated with the number of minims, in lines on the glass barrel.

For some days before leaving I was using the mixture, and the day's supply was of course 2 grains of morphia and 2 grains of cocaine.

I was leaving Mulki in India for the time being, intending to send for her when I got out to some other country.

I found a small hut for her, in a place about sixty miles away.

I sold my furniture to a new arrival, and said "Good-bye" to my friends, then set off for Calcutta and home; first making arrangements for Mulki's support.

I had come to be very fond of her. Not only was she beautiful in appearance, but she was beautiful in disposition. She had not learned to use drugs, although she had begged many times for me to allow her, and I was afraid that when I was away she would start with opium, as everywhere around there were natives using it.

The voyage home to England was not marked by any unusual incident, except that there was a young medical student on board, who shared my cabin.

Soon he discovered that I was using drugs, and he gave me a lecture on the terrible consequences of the habit. I asked him if he had ever taken any himself, and he confessed that he had not, and that he was going on what he had heard.

Shortly afterwards I missed my syringe.

I did not mention it to him, I just quietly observed, and soon I had more than a suspicion where the syringe had gone to.

However, this did not trouble me, because I had syringes of all kinds in my main baggage; syringes of the best makes, ranging in size from 20 minims, up to 60 minims.

After I had got settled down on board, I started my system in earnest.

I was using 2 grains of morphia, and 2 grains of cocaine per day, as before mentioned.

Without any trouble, I easily got down to 1 grain of each.

Now I mixed up 6 grains of each drug in separate bottles; each with 240 minims of water, and still keeping to the four injections per day, I started by drawing up into the syringe 9 minims of morphia, and 10 minims of cocaine.

Next day the morphia was reduced by another minim and so on until the fourth day my dose was 6 minims of morphia and 10 minims of cocaine.

Now I was beginning to feel slightly the need of a little more morphia.

Instead of taking more, I started reducing the cocaine 1 minim per day until on the eighth day my injection consisted of 6 minims of each drug.

Now I felt that I was getting enough morphia again.

Decreasing the cocaine, had the same effect as though I had increased the morphia.

This may be difficult to believe, yet it is true. The explanation is, that these two drugs are in a certain way antidote to each other, yet when taken together, they both seem to act independently, and one gets the full effect of each drug.

When I had got down to 5 minims of each drug per injection, I marked time for three days.

I was now getting half a grain of each drug per day.

I now commenced afresh, but instead of reducing the quantity of the liquid, I kept to the 10 minims per injection, first mixing up some fresh drugs, as it is not good to keep them mixed long.

Now for four days I added to the morphia solution, an equivalent quantity of distilled water every time I injected, that is to say:

Every time I drew out 5 minims of solution, I added afterwards 5 minims of water. The total quantity of liquid always remained the same in the bottle, but it was getting gradually weaker, and the dilution was taking place on a diminishing scale, as it should do.

Soon the mixture became pretty weak, and I stopped adding more water, and concentrated on reducing the actual number of minims used, until I was down to 5 minims of mixture (¼ syringe full) per injection, and then I recommenced diluting as before.

A few weeks after my arrival in England, I was able to stop using drugs entirely.

I admit that at the end I had a little craving, but it was nothing really, and I was getting freer of it every day. Still, I decided that the system was not perfect, and I meant to continue experimenting and searching, until I found a cure which was fool proof and easy.

I have seen, in China, many years later, opium smokers trying to give up the habit.

They would start by getting a cylindrical pot made of hard wood, and ¾ in. inside diameter, and of sufficient length to hold their day's supply.

Every day they would file a little off the length of the pot.

This kind of system is no good; the craving becomes intense, and few have the will power to carry it out.

In England I had the chance of more than one good position, because I had good technical qualifications, with practical experience also. I wanted to get out to the Malay Archipelago or China to continue my experiments, and to make a study of the drug habit in these countries, so did not accept any work in England.

After about three months, I got a position as engine-wright for the coal mining concern in the Island of Sumatra, in the Malay Archipelago.

The salary was only 18 pounds per month, but I would have accepted anything, to be able to get out there.

The voyage out to Singapore in the Glen line Glen Farg was uneventful. I had not used any drugs at all for over four months. I was in perfect health, but I longed to start using drugs again, because I found that it was the only way to be really happy; to get away from the deadly sameness of life in this world.

Arriving at Singapore, the first thing I did, was to visit a chemist and buy some ½-grain tabloids of both morphia and cocaine. Later I sent an order off to England for 6 doz. tubes (864) of 1-grain tabloids of morphia. Cocaine I could buy in plenty locally, as well as other drugs.

Morphia was more difficult to get; that is, the kind I required; in tabloids made by a certain famous firm for injection purposes.

I put up at the Hotel de la Paix along with some of the ship's passengers; a small but very comfortable place. After getting settled down, and having a good dinner, I took my first dose of drugs, ½ grain of cocaine, and ⅛ grain of morphia injection.

Life immediately took on a fresh meaning. I was in a happy carefree world again. All small difficulties and doubts, which life is full of, were gone, and I felt that no happening whatever could be a hurt.

I spent a happy time in Singapore during the next two days before leaving for Sumatra.

Singapore was in a state of excitement, because the Americans had just captured Manila, and most of the Manila-bound boats and passengers were held up.

First buying as large a stock of drugs as I could get in Singapore, I went aboard the small Chinese steamer, which took me across the straits, the whole journey including several hours up the Indragiri River, taking about twenty-four hours.

When I arrived at my disembarkation place, I thought that I had come to the most miserable place I had ever seen. It was at the mouth of a small tributary called the Tjenako.

The place consisted of a large bamboo platform, built on piles in the river, and on it stood a single wood and bamboo one-story building. It was a house and store belonging to a Chinaman.

There was no dry land to be seen anywhere, only trees standing out of the water on both sides, where the river banks should have been.

For miles around me, the whole country was under water. There were, of course, no roads or railways, and the only traffic consisted of a few Malay sampans going up or down the river. This was the only shop within a day's journey by sampan, and then the only things sold appeared to be rice, salt fish and opium, with a few Malay requirements, which the old Chinaman supplied in return for rubber.

He had an assistant and a coolie to whom he mostly left the work, while he spent nearly all his time smoking opium and sleeping.

I became very friendly with him later,. but this time I just saw him for a few minutes, when the company's manager, an Englishman, who had come to meet me in a small steam branch launch, introduced me.

Almost immediately we proceeded up the main river Indragiri, to visit Ringat, where the Dutch Resident lived. Some Malay coolies were being taken there to be birched for trying to escape. They were contract laborers.

After being introduced to the Resident and his assistant we were conducted to a large room, half office and half sitting-room, where we were given tea.

Presently in came one of the prisoners in charge of three native police, and after a few words, which I did not understand then, from the Resident, the Malay was held down by two of the men, while the other applied a rattan.

The victim was screaming and foaming at the mouth, while we were supposed to be drinking tea and having a friendly talk. It was a nasty experience and it nearly turned me sick.

We left after the coolies had been birched and a batch of about a dozen new Malays who had come in with me from Singapore, had been signed on at the Resident's.

Back at Kwala Tjenako again.

The company was a newly-incorporated Dutch concern.

Coal had been found in the higher lands, about six days' journey by sampan, up the small tributary, the Tjenako, an uncharted river, passing through virgin jungle.

It was proposed to build a light railway from the coal field, to a site about halfway, where a loading wharf would be built and the coal would be there loaded into lighters and towed to the mouth of the Tjenako; then out along the broad Indragiri river, on to Singapore.

The Tjenako was so obstructed by snags and sandbanks that only flat-bottomed sampans could get up it to the site of the coal bed. It was proposed to clear the river up to the loading wharf, which would be the terminus of the railway.

The manager proceeded upstream to headquarters, Pia Tarantang, where the coal was, and left me at the Kwala with a dozen coolies to build a small jetty and a store. This was to act as a receiving station for landing stores, and also the hundreds of Malay and Chinese coolies who would arrive from time to time from Singapore, for work on the railway, and the mine.

I was left alone on the Towler, the Chinaman's jetty, and I surveyed the scene.

A single rickety bamboo jetty with a plaited bamboo platform for a top, and a wooden structure, half shed and half bungalow built on it.

The muddy river flowed silently and swiftly always in one direction, and there was jungle everywhere, but no dry land.

Not twenty feet behind the store was the jungle, unknown, and almost impenetrable. Practically all of this district was unknown to the white man, and even the river, Tjenako, was not shown on the map.

The Malays that were with me were some of the old hands, and one spoke a little English.

They camped on the jetty, and the Towler gave me a room in his store to live in. It contained a massive carved blackwood bed with canopy, the whole covered with Chinese dragons and curious carvings. There was nothing else in the room, and through the cracks in the floor I could see the river running underneath.

The bathroom consisted of two large tree trunks, floating in the stream, and connected together by a platform. There was a square hole in the floor, for an obvious reason.

In The Jungles of Sumatra

Towler was a Chinaman of about thirty-five of age, although he looked to be sixty. He was wizened and shrunken, and he spent most of his time in the little room behind his store, smoking pipe after pipe of opium. In the mornings he would be fairly normal, and then he would be bewailing his fate, and cursing opium.

"Banya Sussa Tuan," he would say, "Tida mow Mukan, Tida mow Binni, Tida buli buong aya," meaning that he did not want to eat, he did not want a wife, nor could he empty his bowels.

He would be groaning and pitying himself all the morning, then in the afternoon, when he had got all stretched out on his mat, with the opium pipe by his side and several pipes smoked, he would be as jolly as could be. Life was beautiful again.

Often did I join him, and smoke his opium, and listen to his stories of China. I meant to go there some time.

The Malays would take the sampans, and go off into the jungle in search for timber for the building of the jetty and store, and as it was not necessary for me to go with them, I left them to it; they knew how to go on. I was keeping my eyes open and learning. I had already learned sufficient Malay, one of the simplest languages in the world, to make myself understood, as I had studied it on the voyage out. I could not yet understand when spoken to.

Towler had tried to give opium up more than once, and had failed, and now he was hopeless. He had sent his Malay girl away because he had no more use for her, he told me, and although he lived well off, with a large store in Singapore, he lived here for opium. A living death.

I introduced him to some of my drugs, and soon he was like a new man; full of life and happiness; another wife. He ordered her as he would a bale of goods–by letter. He was never tired of thanking me for what I had done for him.

A difficulty which had to be overcome, I found, was the water. There was none but that from the muddy river, and although it was all right for drinking after it had settled, it was no good for injections.

Luckily I had some distilled water, and later, I constructed a small apparatus for making my own, so as to get it freshly distilled.

The building and the jetty were now completed, and I took leave of Towler, and proceeded up the river towards my destination; seven days' journey.

The sampan was a large affair, having a covered portion at the back, under which I sat on my mattress.

The deck was boarded over, and on it lived the coolies I was taking back with me, and the three sampan men who poled the boat up stream, against the tide. My boy did the cooking on deck on a little charcoal stove.

I was now fairly started on drugs again; I was using large quantities of all kinds, as I sat in my little shelter while the coolies poled the boat.

At night we tied up to the bank and after cooking and eating their rice, the coolies would stretch themselves out on deck and wrap themselves up in a sarong beside the smoke of the fire.

I was alone, with my drugs and my thoughts.

The night was cool, like most nights here, and the trees were simply alive with monkeys of all shapes and sizes. This was the home of the Orang-Utan, and the jungle abounded in more and greater variety of wild animals than any country in the world. A sportsman's paradise, but few know of it.

Tonight, sitting alone in my covered cabin, I had nothing to do but think. Through the open sides I saw swift-running water, on which the moonlight was shining, turning to patches of silver the ripples wherever there was an obstruction, and showing in feathery outline the outer foliage of the dark jungle.

I wondered what this place would be like a million years hence. What was it like a hundred million years ago?

News travelled in this country in a mysterious way. I had let it be known that I would pay for curious specimens of plants, and natives passing down river often brought me specimens, as they knew that I would pay in opium.

I had just had a very peculiar plant brought me. The decoction I made from it

I first tried on some rats I kept for the purpose; great, voracious creatures, that would eat anything.

I next tried a small dose on myself, without any effects except a slight intoxication, and a feeling of lightness and increased energy. Taking a larger dose next time I found that it had a very curious effect.

At first it made me quite drunk, as far as my movements were concerned, but clear mentally, and later when I tried it in combination with cocaine injected, I had a very peculiar experience which I will try to describe.

A Strange Waking Vision

Sitting on my mattress under the grass roof of the sampan I was journeying down the Tjenako with the stream; gliding swiftly along, without any effort from the two coolies who were sprawled on deck. Only the steersman, with his long oar, at the stern, was standing, and my Chinese boy was busy with the clay stove, cooking my evening meal; a chicken curry.

The sun had set, and the jungle was beginning to fall into shadow; soon it would be dark, and we would pull into the river edge for the night. Already the steersman was looking round for a sandy shoal, on which he could run the sampan.

I had been steadily taking the new drug during the afternoon, and I was intoxicated in an entirely new and strange manner. I had a voracious appetite, and would enjoy my curry. Afterwards I would start with cocaine injections. I meant to have a regular binge, and I was looking forward to some new experience in the Spirit World.

"Would it be a vision which was beautiful, or would it be something horrible? No matter, even the latter would be interesting, and I was no longer scared; no matter what I saw."

It was now quite dark, and the sampan was moored on a sand bank near the edge of the jungle, the coolies being stretched out on deck. They were completely enveloped in their spare sarongs, and looked like corpses stretched out. Their heads were wrapped in cloths.

The smoke from the wood fire forward, drifted through my shelter; it was rather pleasant than otherwise.

I started with ½ grain of cocaine, and in ten minutes 1 grain more, then gradually increased the strength of the injections to about 2 grains, continuing these every quarter of an hour or twenty minutes.

This method prevents any undue shock on the heart, which would occur if an extra large does was taken at once.

When I felt my breathing accelerating too much, I corrected it with a small dose of morphia, mixed with my next injection.

Soon I was Absolute, All powerful; nothing was impossible to me, it seemed. I wished to get some more drugs out of my box, and I willed the box to come to me. I saw the box moving towards me slowly and distinctly, until it was there beneath my hand; yet when I stretched out to open it the box was not there, it was back where it was at first.

I cannot explain how this happened, it may have been a case of perfect self-hypnosis, and when I stretched out my hand the condition was temporarily interrupted; just as on other occasions similar to the present, I have willed a door to close, and have seen it moving distinctly, until it was closed, and then when I have got up from my seat and walked towards it, I have found it still open.

I continued injecting cocaine, with an occasional dose of the new drug.

My cabin had become the size of a large room, and the whole of the space was peopled with living shapes; some of them were beautiful, and some horrible, while others were merely grotesque.

There were no animals or reptiles among them, all were humans. They floated about all around me; each one was alive, and the expression of their eyes was intense; they seemed to tell me some great secret.

Spirit-like faces and forms of many nations, and of all periods; men and women of noble and beautiful appearance passed before me. Their faces only seemed to be alive, for although they approached or receded, I could distinguish no movement of their limbs. Further in the background were others, whose faces and forms were ghastly and horrible, like denizens of a lower world.

As time went on, these latter types seemed to be increasing in number and getting closer, and the beautiful ones were receding and their number getting less.

Slowly approaching me and getting nearer every minute, were a group of Indian lepers. Their appearance was revolting, and would be terrifying, were it not that I was interested, and that I knew they were only visions.

I had seen many lepers, in the flesh, but never had I seen such awful sights as these before me now.

Some of them had hardly any face left; there were only holes where their noses should be, and what flesh there was left on their faces, was of a pinkish white color, livid, with here and there a patch of their natural brown color, where the flesh was not diseased. There was a pinkish white powder on the surface of the skin, which indicated the disintegration or corruption of the flesh.

Their eyes fixed on me with an unwinking stare, which seemed to be full of malice and hate.

They were so close to me now that they seemed to be almost touching me, and I shrank back, and then they were gone.

I now stopped taking any more cocaine, or the other drug, and started smoking some hashish.

I must have dozed for a minute or so, for I remembered nothing in the interval. When I opened my eyes I was sitting in a large dimly-lighted room.

There was a musty smell of corruption and death, and a faint sound of running water.

Along one wall, arranged and laid out on marble or stone slabs, were many corpses. Some lay peaceful in death, while others were bloated and swollen; with starting eyes, and a horrible intensity of expression; while some had started to decay, and I now saw that it was on these that the water was dripping.

As I looked, I saw that they all were rising into a sitting position, although I could see no distinct movement of their limbs. Now they were off the slabs, and were facing me; they were moving towards me.

I looked towards the end of the room, and saw that the wall appeared to be receding, and there were more slabs. Soon the wall had disappeared in the distance, and as far as the eye could see, there was slab after slab, each with its corpse rising and coming towards me.

The first one, which was nearest, was swollen and becoming decayed in parts. It was that of a drowned man who had been in the water a long time, and had been partly eaten in places.

It was now quite close, almost touching me, when it began to swell and increase in size, until almost everything else was blotted out.

The smell was becoming overpowering, and the light was growing dim, when with an effort of will I started up, and the whole scene disappeared, and I was back in the sampan, sitting on my mattress.

As soon as I relaxed, familiar objects again commenced to disappear. I no longer saw the cabin, the boat, or the sleeping coolies stretched on the deck.

The space around me seemed to be filled with faintly luminous globes, which some curious instinct told me were the souls of unborn children, waiting for their turn to be born. Everything around me seemed to be weird and unreal.

The trees in the jungle alongside assumed grotesque shapes, and faces peered out at me from the foliage.

The moon, which had risen, shed an unearthly light on the branches, which, as I looked, took the shapes of animals or reptiles.

If I shut my eyes, I heard the sound of what seemed to be the continuous ringing of bells in the distance. I was living through years of time, and former periods of my life returned, and I lived them again, not only as a memory but actually, with every long-forgotten detail returning with startling clearness.

I must have slept, for when I opened my eyes it was broad daylight, and the boat was in motion.

I was lying on my mattress, and as I looked out, I saw my boy making morning coffee.

I was little the worse for my last night's experience; a slight headache, which I easily removed at once with an injection of morphia.

Every detail of my experience was clearly remembered, and I thought over each detail. It is true that many times I had lived former periods of my life over again, but so far I had never been able to take on another personality, and go back and live in earlier periods of the world's history, but the time was to come; but many years later.

As time went on, the experiences seemed to become more and more realistic.

The new drug, I decided, had a more curious effect than even hashish, and I was preparing a large stock of it in a more concentrated form.

I had bought a proper laboratory evaporating pan. I first boiled the roots until there was a thick brown liquor, and then I evaporated this in the pan, until there remained a dry sediment, which I collected and made into a powder, and stored in bottles and sealed, labelling it No.1.

[Lee visits Singapore.]

I was now confining my drug indulgence almost entirely to morphia, having a proper rest, lounging and dreaming the days away.

Every time I changed over to morphia, it had regained its original charm and potency. I was its master; it was my servant.

Although it is a drug which, beyond all others, one must be on their guard of, I was using it singly. But not for long; soon I would begin to combine it with others. Never again would I allow it to affect my health, or use it long enough to impair its fine effect. Always was I using large quantities of drugs, but in combinations, increasing and decreasing them systematically, and changing their nature. Only thus could life be made a happiness beyond description.

The drug habit was prevalent among all classes in Singapore.

It was chiefly opium that was used, the Chinese smoking it, and the Indians and Malays often eating it.

Not much cocaine was used except in the Red Light quarters, and many Europeans drugged secretly, but in a very crude and timid manner.

Opium has a very powerful and pungent smell when cooked and smoked, and practically every street in the Chinese quarter smelled strongly of it. In fact one could see through the open doors of the Chinese shops and houses men lying smoking the drug.

Most of the women in Malay Street used both opium and cocaine.

I visited many of the better class Chinese houses. The room where the smoking was done was generally furnished with massive blackwood furniture, beautifully carved with dragons and grotesque figures, and the bed was a tremendously heavy affair, with canopy and curtains of silk. The mattress was part of the bed, being woven fiber, and the pillows were small and hard.

The opium pipe, lamp and tools stood on a lacquered tray on the center of the mattress.

They generally rationed themselves to a fixed daily allowance. This means to say that they had become slaves to opium. This daily allowance being a fixed quantity, must soon become of just sufficient effect to bring them to a normal condition.

Without it they were irritable and uncomfortable until the time came for their smoke.

[Lee returns to the jungles of Sumatra.]

I Discover the Elixir of Life

I was still having many strange plants and roots brought to me by the Malays from the interior, and I had collected many myself, but so far I had not found anything special.

I had certainly found some which might be useful. One which produced a violent perspiration, and another which would slow the heart's action, and lower the temperature–producing a sensation of cold.

Then I discovered the perfect antidote.

One evening as I was sitting on my platform or verandah facing the river, some strange native Malays arrived in a sampan. They were people belonging further inland, and they had brought me some plants and roots, in the hope that I would take them in exchange for opium.

Most of them were no use, I had had them before; but there were one or two that I decided to try.

One plant in particular I was struck with. It was a plant carrying many pods, which were full of seed.

Later on I collected the seed and boiled them for a long time.

The decoction I obtained I strained off and found to be of a dark brown color, with a strong aromatic flavor when applied to the tongue.

I next evaporated the liquor in the evaporating, leaving a sediment.

From this I prepared a dry powder, very concentrated in strength.

I tried a little of it on my rats, mixed in their food, and carefully took note of the results.

As nothing happened which I could notice, I continued to give it to them for a few days, and then, as they seemed quite well and healthy, I took a little myself.

If you have ever experimented on yourself with some new kind of medicine from which you were hoping to get results, and waited for its first effects to to appear, you will have some slight idea of my sensations.

In your case you have the knowledge that what you are taking has been tried before, and that at least you are not likely to suffer any ill effects.

In my case, I was trying an unknown drug; a very small quantity it is true, but still I had no idea what its effect would be, and I was waiting, imagining all kinds of sensations.

Finally I came to the conclusion that I could not be sure that it had had any effect at all.

Next day, I took a larger dose.

Now I was sure that the drug had some effect on me, but I could not exactly define what it was. I felt different somehow; more sedate and deliberate in my thoughts and actions, perhaps, with a great calm and peaceful feeling.

The following day I took a little larger dose, about a grain of the powder, and then the effect was quite noticeable. The effect was not like morphia, because it did not produce that delightful dreamy feeling of luxurious ease, in which the imagination is extremely fertile, through a pleasant kind of haze.

Neither had it the fascinating exhilarating effect of cocaine, nor the grotesque distorting and intoxicating effect of hashish. It was unlike any other drug that I knew of. It simply produced a feeling of great vitality, the absolute perfection of mental and bodily health.

It was only after taking it on several occasions that I discovered its real properties.

It was when I decided to try it in conjunction with cocaine, and for this purpose I first injected ½ grain of the latter, and continued with 1-grain doses until I was well under the influence of the drug.

Now I mixed a grain of the new drug, which I will call No. 2, and drank it.

An amazing thing happened.

In almost the time it takes a person to feel the effects of a glass of whiskey I was in a normal condition again; just as though I had never had any cocaine or any other drug.

I was just normal in every respect.

I took note of my heart beats, my respirations, and my temperature, and they were just right; also the dilution of the pupils had disappeared.

The drug had entirely nullified the effect of the cocaine. Again next day I tried it with morphia, and I found it act in the same way, although I had to take a second dose. It did not seem to have so much power over morphia.

Its effect with hashish was even more powerful and complete than with cocaine.

Since then I have tried it with wines and spirits, and even absinthe, which I used for some time in later years.

Not only would this drug remove all forms of intoxication, exhilaration, and narcotic effects, but it would remove pain of most kinds. It would reduce the temperature if too hot, produce a feeling of warmth when too cold, and remove fatigue.

It seemed to have the power of bringing the bodily condition back to normal in every case, and producing a feeling of perfect happiness and content.

Of course cocaine will remove pain, if injected locally where the pain is, but the effect does not last long.

Morphia injected will make the body so comfortable that most pain will disappear, and the effect is lasting, but not permanent.

I intended to obtain more of these plants, and prepare as large a stock of this drug No. 2 as I could, putting it up in sealed for future use. I did not know how long I might be in Sumatra.

[Lee and Mulki travel to England. Then Lee returns to India.]

Mulki had never been in England before, and she was delighted with it, specially with the shops, in which she spent hours having them show her a great part of their stock without any intention of buying, as she had already bought a good outfit. She seemed to think it quite in order to go and examine all the pretty things they had. Whenever she saw anything she liked in a shop window, she would go in and ask to see it. It was a great excitement. Her beautiful face drew a great deal of attention wherever she went, and her childish chatter in pidgin English, which had now become a mixture of the Indian and Chinese varieties, sounded very quaint.

One day, when we were visiting the British Museum, we came to a case containing the weapons, dress, and other things pertaining to the "Nagas;" she became quite excited at the incident, and started explaining in her quaint English all about them to a young fellow with a girl, who were gazing in the case.

Soon more people stopped and listened, and very soon she had a crowd round. Her tongue never stopped. I was gradually edging to the outskirts as I hate being in the public gaze, but Mulki was right in her element.

Suddenly she stopped and looked round for me, and called out my name, and seeing me hid in the background, she pushed her way through. She would have me explain to the crowd all about the "Nagas," but I managed to escape with her.

She had not the slightest particle of shyness, and sometimes in a bus she would address perfect strangers, and hold forth about some subject or other, gradually embracing the whole bus full of people in her talk.

She would ask them the most intimate questions about themselves and family. She made instant friendships, and everyone seemed to like her.

Important events occurred in England about that time, Queen Victoria died, and the South African War came to an end.

Mulki cried a great deal when the great White Queen died. The Queen had talked to her in London.

It happened that we were lodging at the house of a musician employed at the Palace, and Mulki had many times begged him to take her to see the Queen.

One day he took her to the Palace, in the hope that she might get a glimpse of the Queen if lucky.

Queen Victoria, wheeled in a chair and accompanied by some Indian retainers, happened to pass near where Mulki was standing, and the Queen saw her and sent one of the Indians to bring her across.

Queen Victoria spoke to her in Hindustani, and asked all particulars. She talked quite a while with the Queen, who finally ordered one of the attendants to give Mulki a five-shilling piece, and told her to make it into a brooch.

Shortly after this Mulki was in St. Thomas's Hospital with liver abscess.

The Underworld of the Ports

We were living in Sheffield at the time when I got my opportunity for a third trip abroad. I had been about a year acting as chief draughtsman for a firm of Consulting Engineers in High Street. All this time I had been keeping my eyes open for a chance to get out to the Far East again, specially China. It was a country of which I had read so many strange things, I wanted to see them for myself; to delve below the surface, and to find out all I could about the drug habit there, the greatest drug using country in the world.

I was getting fed up with life in England. There was too much sameness about it; a place where there is little real freedom, and where one had to do just as the next fellow did. To wear the same kind of clothes with a collar and tie, and talk about football and horse racing, or be considered no sport; making conversation for the sake of talking, whether one had anything to say or not; to be considered shabby if there was no crease in one's trousers and one preferred comfortable well worn clothes. These were just some of the things that I found irksome.

As the opportunity of getting to China did not seem to occur, and I had a chance of going to India again, I took it, chiefly owing to Mulki's persuasions.

I had been constantly using drugs all this time. I found that I could use large quantities of an evening, and more at weekends, without showing any trace next day, owing to the drug I had brought home from Sumatra.

I forget the name of the P. & O. steamer that I went out to Calcutta on, but at the station, after I had taken leave of Mulki, who was remaining in England until I got settled down and sent for her, a young fellow got into the carriage. Probably he had seen my labeled luggage, for he got into conversation and soon made it known that he was traveling out to Calcutta on the same boat.

At Tilbury he was met by a stout, horsey-looking individual, whom he introduced as his agent, and the latter, after talking a few minutes, said, "Well, your luggage is all on board, and the charge is 1 pound 15." The young man, who had previously informed me that his name was Mr. Wilson, felt in his pocket and produced a wad of notes, and after going through them discovered that he had nothing less than 50-pound, which the horsey-looking one could not change.

Mr. Wilson appeared to consider a moment, wrinkling his brow at the inconvenience of the situation, and turning to me asked if I could change it for him. I could not and said so. Then a bright idea struck him.

"I hardly like to ask you," he said, "but if you will pay the man, I can give it to you when we get on board."

Unfortunately I had nothing less than a 50-pound note myself, a strange coincidence, and I told him so, and the last I saw of them, they were going to seek change somewhere else.

"Tell the steward that my luggage is in the gangway, will you," he said.

"Certainly I will," I replied. "By the way, what is the number of your cabin, then the steward can have the luggage put in for you."

Mr. Wilson appeared to hesitate, and I said, "I suppose you are not in with me, No. 127."

It was a strange coincidence again, we were both to be in the same cabin, and we shook hands on it. He had a poker face, and I could not tell whether or not he knew that I was pulling his leg.

At Naples I went ashore with three other young fellows to see the sights, hiring a guide for the day to show us around. After seeing many, including cathedrals, museums and the cemeteries of which the guide seemed very proud, someone suggested a drink.

Whether any of the party had added any private instructions or not, I cannot say, but I had my suspicions.

He led us up a staircase in what looked like a private house. It struck me as being strange, but as I am always ready to learn anything that I can which seems to be out of the ordinary, I thought I would wait and see.

We went into a large room on the first floor and sat down; I was just starting to en-quire of the guide, when a door at one side opened, and a tall, blond Continental girl came out, and after a glance round, seated herself, to my astonishment, on my knee.

She was quickly followed by several other girls, dark and fair, of various nationalities, who followed her example with regard to my friends.

Drinks were brought out, and soon the party became a merry one, the girls speaking quaint English, which easily identified their nationality, Slav, Latin or Saxon.

The young lady sitting near me took a small tube out of her satchel and shook out a little pellet, which she dropped into her drink.

"What is that?" I asked.

"I have got a leetle cold, I take the medicine."

I took the tube out of her hand, and looked at it; I saw that it was labeled co-caine, ¼ grain.

We had been knocking round for some hours, and I was feeling ready for a dose of any one of my favorite drugs, so I said,

"Is this for a cold?" and being answered, I took out four of the ¼-grain tabloids, and put them in my mouth, immediately taking a drink.

My action seemed to cause a sensation, for she talked excitedly in Italian to the oth-ers. They all watched me, with scared faces, but a grain of cocaine taken by the mouth was only a very small dose for me, I could easily have taken more. After a while, when, in answer to her inquiries, I told her that the medicine did not seem to have much ef-fect, she seemed astonished.

We spent a very pleasant afternoon there, with songs and dancing, etc.

We went ashore at Port Said, in those days a sink of iniquity which, for its size, rivaled any place in the world for beastliness of the worst kind. Here we did not require a guide, as it was a small place and I had been ashore before, but one tried to force himself on us.

He said his name was John Ferguson, from Aberdeen, although he was an Egyptian with a face as black as my boots. He even offered to fight any of us for half a crown, when we refused to employ him otherwise.

We walked along with John dancing behind us, shaking his fist and gradually reducing the stake, until he came down to a shilling. One of the party was about to fight him for nothing.

"Wait a bit," I said. "We don't want to have a row here, or we might end up in some foul-smelling and verminous jail and lose our passage, I know a better way."

Presently we came to a large Egyptian cigarette store that I knew, and going in we bought some cigarettes and explained the case to the manager. The latter said a few words to an assistant, and we had the pleasure of seeing John seized by the coat collar and booted several times.

Arab boys followed us, offering to take us to see the Can Can and worse things, and many shop windows had horribly indecent photographs exposed for sale.

The place seemed to be overrun with guides and touts, all eager to conduct us to questionable places; alongside of which, the Can Can is a mild and innocent spectacle. The outskirts of the place were swarming with Arab girls.

We started off back for the ship, to find that coaling was going on. It was being taken in at both sides, and when viewed from a little distance the whole ship seemed to be enveloped in clouds of coal dust.

When we arrived on board we found coal dust floating in clouds about the deck. All the ports and companion doors, and even the passage and corridor doors were closed, and the air down below, in the saloons and cabins, was stifling, besides being stale and full of ship's smells, as these very soon become manifest below unless there is constant ventilation. The smell was chiefly of hot paint.

A few passengers were still on board, some in the smoke room with the doors shut, and a few hanging about disconsolately on deck, watching the coaling, and at the same time getting coal dust in their eyes and ears, and on their clothes.

Soon we were in the Suez Canal and then on to Aden and Colombo, where we went ashore.

Arrived at the jetty we proceeded along along the main street, past the Grand Oriental Hotel, and the Bristol Hotel further along, but on the opposite side of the road.

The scene was a very animated one. Natives of many different countries passed to and fro; Sinhalese men who might be mistaken in some cases for women, with their long hair oiled on their heads and fastened with tortoiseshell combs, and their colored sarongs or cloths wrapped around their waists, looking almost like skirts. Indians in white or colored turbans and white dhoties wrapped between their legs. Malays and Chinese in their own distinctive costumes. Also in this part of the town there were many Europeans in the streets in white linen suits and sun helmets.

It was the business quarter of the town and there were many European shops and offices.

We called a gharri, and told the man to drive round Colombo.

Presently we left the European quarter of the town behind, and passed along through the native quarter.

Here the scene was very picturesque; no slums like there are to be seen in many Eastern towns.

The roads were lined with tall coconut palms and other tropical trees, forming a pleasant shady avenue; native houses, grass and bamboo-built structures, generally standing under some palm trees; picturesque little self-contained structures in their own little bamboo-fenced compounds.

Strange-looking clumsy bullock carts, drawn by two small hump-backed oxen passed now and then along the vividly green, grass-covered lanes.

Very few Europeans were to be seen here, but hundreds of natives everywhere.

Here came a man with Elephantiasis of the legs; his legs and feet for all the world like those of an elephant, the foot, ankle and calf being the same width right up, and the size of an elephant's foot. Further on we met a man with the disease in a different part of the body. Imagine what a sensation would be created if a man was seen walking down the Strand pushing a wheelbarrow in front of him in which rested an unmentionable part of his body swollen to such a size that only with the aid of a wheelbarrow could he get along.

Beautiful, sweet-smelling plantations of cinnamon and other spices met the eye, and almost every little native compound was almost hidden by fruit trees of all descriptions. Truly a lovely place is Colombo. It is said that sometimes when the wind is in the right direction, passing ships can smell the spices and fruits, which grow so profusely in the island, from twenty miles away.

Leaving Colombo, we turned north, and soon the ship was steaming slowly up the Hooghly, that treacherous passage of water that winds and twists its way among the many small islands of the Sundabunds, between the Bay of Bengal and Calcutta.

A Hooghly pilot was in charge, an important person, for the lives of everyone on board were in his keeping. Many a fine steamer in the past has got caught in the treacherous quicksands, and slowly sunk out of sight below the river bed.

Those of the passengers who had never been in India before were scanning the islands with much interest as they passed; islands of virgin jungle, the haunt of tigers and other wild animals, mysterious, menacing. What cruelties are perpetrated in its hidden recesses, where the law of the wild reigns supreme.

We steamed on, slowly and cautiously, and then we arrived at Garden Reach, opposite Calcutta.

Again I could smell the odor of baked clay, and again I was at Spencer's Hotel in a roof bedroom, looking out over the great city.

Strange Thoughts and Visions

With the first few injections of cocaine, tempered with a little morphia, my thoughts became very clear, and my imagination very fertile, while at the same time remaining sensible and reasonable.

As I continued to take more and more of the drug my thoughts became more fantastic, and I seemed to be living them in actual fact.

Later, by continuing the injections about every twenty minutes, visions began to appear, and I actually saw what I was thinking about.

By now introducing hashish and minute additions of one or two other drugs, the visions which I saw, and the thoughts which accompanied them, began to change in character, and became grotesque and fantastic.

I started off by turning my thoughts to the mystery of the universe.

I felt that no reasonable person who had studied the things around him, and who had used his brains, could doubt the existence of God; perhaps not the God we have created in our minds, but a great intelligence, the Absolute and Ultimate of all power and knowledge.

The wonderful order and design of everything in nature throughout the whole universe impressed my reasoning faculties with the conviction that there must be a Creator. Order does not come out of Chaos by itself. When we see a watch or some wonderful piece of machinery, our reason tells us that there must have been a watchmaker or an engineer, so that when we contemplate the wonderful system of everything in nature the mind immediately deduces the Creator.

Is it reasonable to think that the design just happened?

I have read Atheist works in which the writer points to the many terrible disasters and happenings which take place in the world, such as wars, shipwrecks, explosions, etc., and argues that if there is a God he must either be cruel or unable to prevent them.

We have no knowledge of what purpose is served by these things, or even that they are calamities really in the Absolute, or that the victim has really suffered any injury on the whole.

They are assuming that this life here will be the only one, but for all we know there may be many stages, and many worlds which we have to pass through.

As I became more under the influence of the drug, I seemed to be able to see into the future, to know and follow the progress of humanity.

I realized that the Church, and religion generally, was an influence for the good, and at present it was following the natural Law of Evolution. Its atoms and units were scattered and isolated, but they were concentrating, and coming together, and one religion would join up with another, until eventually there would be only one–the true one. The teaching of mankind to do right to his fellow man.

What teaching could be of more benefit to humanity if followed by all? The evil qualities of the human race would die out, and the world would be a beautiful place to live in.

Science and religion are coming closer together, and the time will come when they will be reconciled one to the other.

I saw the time when the profession of religion would become the most honored one in the world, and then its ministers would teach people the true meaning of the word sin: "The doing of an injury or an injustice to another."

My faculties were now so powerfully stimulated that I could hear the tiniest sound, even the buzzing of a fly's wings as it flew across the room; or I could work out complicated problems in mathematics mentally, remembering, and even seeing, each previous figure.

As time went on, my thoughts began to change, and visions began to appear before me; visions which at the time I believed were always there, but could only be seen by one whose mental and nervous system was powerfully stimulated by drugs or otherwise.

Small luminous globes, which I believed were the souls of unborn children waiting to be born, floated before me. There were spirits hovering round, materializing before my eyes and then disappearing; spirits which I seemed to know were the souls of those dead who, while in the flesh, were neither too good nor too bad for this earth, and were therefore destined to be born here again, and also of those whose lives were cut short before their time, either by accident or design.

Scenes from many periods of the world's history, passed before me, even to the time of prehistoric man.

These were massive creatures of enormous strength, which some curious instinct told me was due to the long hair which covered their bodies, each hair being a conductor which attracted the sun's magnetic rays and passed it into the body, producing vital energy.

"When Delilah cut off Sampson's hair, he lost his strength."

A wraith-like cloud, a luminous shape arose out of the ground before me. It was constantly changing shape; it was an intelligence which had the power of guiding my thoughts, and communicating with me without spoken words. I felt that there was something evil about it; something which was now beginning to produce a horrible sensation of fear and repulsion in me.

I sought to know what it was, and then I knew.

It was trying to draw my soul away. It was the evil spirit of the earth which takes the souls of the wicked–those which are too earthly–down below into the internal fires, for cleansing and purifying.

Only by suffering or being actually in contact with much suffering, can the chief qualities of goodness be learnt–pity, charity, mercy.

It was enveloping me, trying to suffocate me, or to stop the beating of my heart. It was changing into a gigantic flame, and I knew fear.

My fear passed, and I suddenly knew that it could not hurt me, yet I started up and moved away, and it was gone.

I tell this experience just as I remember it in detail, simply to show the strange manner in which drugs, if enough are used, can act on the imagination.

The sensations and imaginations produced are legion, and are never twice the same.

[In 1906 Lee is posted to Shanghai.]

Shanghai is a city where enormous quantities of cocaine, morphia and opium were used (I am speaking of the year 1906–7), specially cocaine, which could be bought from the Chinese chemists by the sixteen ounce bottle.

I soon became friendly with one or two well-to-do Chinese who used drugs, and who knew the underworld of the city thoroughly, so that soon I had the entry of places of which very few Europeans had any idea of the existence.

There was a gambling house situated not far from Nanking Road. It was a highly respectable-looking building, but even so, it had come under suspicion, and had been raided, I believe, more than once, but never had anything suspicious been found.

On each occasion several people, mostly Chinese, and all apparently friends, had been found sitting round a table drinking tea; whereas one minute before a game of "Fan Tan" had been in full operation for high stakes.

How was this done?

The place was fitted up mechanically for a quick change.

The table on which the gambling was being done was suspended from the ceiling by four wires, running through the ceiling into the room above; apparently a private apartment. The table had no legs, and the underside of it exactly matched the ceiling, fitting into a recess, so that when drawn up quickly by mechanical means with all evidence of the game, it couldn't be distinguished from the surrounding ceiling.

Even the pattern of the underside of the table matched the ceiling, and looked like an ornamental center-piece.

The tea table was always in the room, ready set out with tea pots and cups, etc., and at each corner of the table stood an ornament on which the gambling table rested when it came down from the ceiling. The winding apparatus was set in motion by simply pressing a button.

Outside of the settlement, in Chinese territory, practically any kind of vice can be carried on, as the British, or rather the European powers, had no authority.

There were many places in Shanghai where gambling was carried on, especially on the rivers and creeks, about which I will have something to say later.

Among my Chinese acquaintances, was one whom I will call "Wong." He was a merchant in a large way of business; well educated and speaking English perfectly, having been at one of the Universities in England.

He was a confirmed opium smoker and cocaine sniffer, and he knew the underworld of Shanghai and many of the treaty ports thoroughly.

I wished to see and learn everything that was new and strange, therefore I went about with him a good deal on secret excursions.

One night Mr. Wong said to me: "Let us go to the pictures."

I was not particularly interested, but as he seemed to want to go, I agreed, so we called a couple of rickshaws, and started to ride along Nanking Road. After proceeding some distance, I called him and said, "Here, there are no cinemas along this way as far as I know. Where are we going?"

"There is a new place out 'Bubbling Well' way," he said.

I thought it strange, because it is a district of fine houses chiefly, many of them mansions. Still I did not say anything more; he appeared to know all about it.

After driving more than a mile out, we turned into the grounds of a large private house, or what seemed so.

"What place is this?" I said. "It does not look much like a cinema."

"Wait a bit," replied Mr. Wong.

The entrance hall was like the hall of a large private house and was sumptuously furnished. A well-dressed man, who appeared to be either a Greek or Turk or some similar nationality, came out and shook hands with Mr. Wong, who introduced me, and I noticed that Mr. Wong handed the other two ten dollar notes.

We were led into a small room, in which there were several people, mostly Chinese, although there were one or two foreigners of both sexes there. Here, drinks and drugs of all kinds were being served by an attendant at stiff prices. Presently we were conducted to a large room which was fitted up as a Cinema Hall.

It was almost in darkness, but I could see about twenty or thirty people sitting on comfortably upholstered seats.

There was a picture being shown at the moment, and when I looked at the screen I got a shock.

The picture was horribly lewd, not just ordinarily suggestive, but absolutely as lewd as it is possible to make, and it had evidently been prepared by a past master in this kind of thing.

After the film was finished, the lights were put on, and Mr. Wong left me and went over to some friends.

I could see that there were a good few ladies among the audience, and one of them, a young woman of some continental nationality who spoke English with an accent, came and sat down beside me, first asking for my permission with a wide smile, which exposed three or four gold teeth. She evidently took this as an introduction, for she continued the conversation.

Another picture, even worse than the last one, was put on the screen, after which the young lady moved away to another seat, probably thinking that I was no sport.

Upstairs there was dancing, and other things going on, and there was one room in which several people were smoking opium.

The house itself stood in large grounds of its own, with a wide carriage drive up to the door.

I noticed, however, that the big iron gates at the entrance were kept locked, and had to be opened by a porter in a small lodge, and it was a fair distance from the gates to the front door. No doubt there would be electric signals from the lodge to the house . . .

The Chinese City

One day Mr. Wong took me to see the Chinese city. This is quite distinct and some distance from Shanghai proper.

It is an old walled Chinese city; a place of smells and narrow courts, where horrible punishments are inflicted and carried out in public, at the will of the Chinese Mandarin governing it.

At the time of which I am writing, there were places in it where a European would not be alive five minutes unless he was accompanied by a Chinaman who was known.

Here the fumes of opium smoking met one at every turn. They issued from the open doors of houses and shops, and the very air seemed to be flavored with a faint smell of burning opium.

The narrow streets and passages, so narrow that there was just room for two people to pass each other, were full of beggars and hideous mutilations, and distorted limbs, and lepers who were hardly recognizable as human beings, might frequently be seen.

Mr. Wong led the way up one of these narrow passages, the middle of which was an open drain or channel, littered with garbage and refuse, so that we had to crowd close to one side to prevent ourselves falling in.

About half way along the passage we turned in at an open doorway, and into a dimly-lighted room or cellar, containing a great variety of strange looking stuff, most of which smelt powerfully.

Passing through this place, we came to another room behind, in which there was sitting an old Chinaman.

After a little talk in Chinese from Mr. Wong, the old man led the way up some stairs, which were somewhat like a wide ladder, into a room above.

When my eyes became accustomed to the dim light of the place, I saw that we were in a large room entirely bare of furniture. On the boards of the floor were stretched, alongside of each other, about a dozen grass mats, and on most of them there was a Chinese coolie.

Some of them were already lying insensible like dead bodies, while others were still smoking opium.

Some were filthy and in rags, and I noticed that some were quite young boys, although there were old men too.

"This is how the poor coolie smokes his opium," said Mr. Wong. "Each man, for the sum of ten cents, is given a mat to lie on, and the use of a pipe, lamp, and skewer, and a little opium smeared thinly on a kind of thick green leaf. The opium is not pure opium, it is called 'Tye.'"

It is a mixture of opium and the leavings or residue of opium which has already been smoked by more fortunate or more wealthy individuals.

"The very poor among the customers, who are unable even to afford the ten cents, may purchase for a few cash (a fraction of a cent) a pellet of 'Tye' which they swallow."

Discussing the matter with Mr. Wong, we came to the conclusion that one in every four of the male population of China used opium in some form or other.

This was before the Chinese Government issued the order for the discontinuation of opium smoking, with the death penalty for disobedience.

There are some terrible punishments in China for the Chinese, and I think "Ling Hi" is the worst. It means, "The death of a thousand cuts," and the penalty is carried out in public.

The victim is fastened by the feet on to a pedestal, and the executioner, who is an expert at his business, can snip off an eyelid or a lip with one stroke of the sword, or knife. The object is to get in the whole thousand cuts before the condemned dies, and the executioner first proceeds to put in about two hundred cuts on the chest, back and arms; just cutting through the skin in a herring bone pattern.

After the ears, nose, lips, and eyes have been cut out, near the end of the execution, the final cut is given, and the head falls.

It is possible, however, for the executioner to make a slip with his sword and finish the execution much earlier, if he receives a substantial bribe from the friends of the condemned.

Mr. Wong led the way along another passage or street of rather a better class, and stopped before a shop which seemed to deal in food stuff chiefly, but which later I found dealt in other things.

We entered the shop, and Mr. Wong said a few words to the proprietor, who invited us to be seated and offered us tea. Leaving us for a while, we waited patiently for about ten minutes when we were conducted upstairs to a room.

Sitting on a long form of peculiar pattern there were several little Chinese girls, whose ages seemed to vary from about twelve to sixteen or seventeen years.

They were painted, and dressed in gorgeous costumes, and their feet displayed in front of them, as this was an important point.

"If you are requiring a female servant or housekeeper," said Mr. Wong, "you can buy any of these, from about a hundred dollars upwards. She will then become your property until she is twenty, after which the contract will be finished."

I was not thinking of buying any one of them, and there were some beauties amongst them, but I wanted to learn all I could about the matter.

"Suppose that I bought one of them, and then she ran away," I said, "I suppose I would lose the money?"

"There is no fear of that," said Mr. Wong; "besides where could she run to? Moreover, the proprietor would guarantee to get her back or refund a proportion of the money paid. It would not be wise to run away, and the girl knows that," said Mr. Wong, and I thought that I understood his meaning.

I learnt that many Chinamen, and even others, make these purchases.

Female children have little or no value in China; in fact many thousands are dipped in the canals and creeks and drowned at birth, and then buried in the countryside. A girl is only a source of expense, and without earning capacity in the country districts, and only a few who are good looking can be sold when they reach the age of ten years or so.

To have a son is to make provision for one's old age, because a Chinaman will work his fingers to the bone to provide for his parents, whom he venerates.

The girls sat in a row, with a shy expression and downcast eyes, all except one, a little girl of about twelve or thirteen, with rather a cheeky countenance.

Every time I looked, I met her eyes staring at me, and for this reason perhaps I looked a few times, as I felt her eyes on my face all the time.

"You likee me?" she said. "Me velly good girl. Talkee Englis allesame white girl. Makee sing song too much good. You buy?"

"How old you belong?" I asked.

"Me no savee. Plenty small feet," she said, sticking her foot out.

Although she was a pretty little thing, when I saw her foot, a cold feeling went down my back. "You no likee stop this side?" I asked.

"Likee this side allitee, me fear too much bad Chinamans makee buy me."

"You no fear me buy?" I said.

"No fear. Me likee you. You velly good."

I felt extremely sorry for this poor little girl, and for a long time after I felt sad.

What would be her ultimate destination?

What do these girls do when they reach the age of twenty and afterwards? There are no pensions, doles, institutions, or charities here. Most of them have no families or relations that they remember or know of. Many don't even know what part of China they were born in.

We made our excuses and left, and I was glad to get back into French town, which is not far from the Chinese city. We had a good dinner at the house of a friend of Mr. Wong.

There we talked and smoked opium until late. The conversation of really well educated Chinamen is very interesting. Most of them know the whole history of their country for 3,000 years back, and many legends extending for many thousands of years earlier than this. Legends which may even be true.

Mr. Wong informed me that there are records to prove that once, many thousands of years ago, Japan and China were all one country, with Japan as the sea coast. As the great mountains and volcanoes now in Japan rose, the land on the other side sank and became the strip of sea in between the two countries.

Visions

I sat in my bedroom one evening as the sun was going down; I was testing a new combination of drugs.

The room was on the first floor, and the large French windows which opened on to the veranda were open. The house was set back from the roadway, and between it and the house were some large trees with many branches and think foliage.

From time to time I would glance at these trees, because the first indication of the vision stage approaching would be that faces and figures would appear to be among the branches.

Always would visions appear at some distance away at the commencement and then gradually become nearer as time went on, and as I continued taking more drugs.

I had found, by means of several tests, that the visions would always disappear, no matter kind they were, nor by what drugs produced, when I took sufficient of the No. 2 drug. Then I would be normal in every way. Otherwise the vision stage advanced gradually, starting with a wonderfully fertile imagination, a sensation of being within touch of everything in the world, or even in the universe; the power of seeming to know almost anything I wished to know.

It is true that afterwards many of my thoughts appeared strange, grotesque, or absurd, but this did not make them any less real and interesting at the time experienced.

Strange new thoughts came into my mind, and problems which before seemed impossible to solve now seemed easy.

The advance of civilization. Why does civilization advance or increase, and not decrease?

I saw that it does so in accordance with the Law of Evolution. Knowledge accumulates and concentrates, just as units or atoms come together and concentrate.

There is a definite connection between the earth's gravitation and the advance of civilization.

The intensity of the gravitation depends on the earth's mass. It has been shown that millions of tons of meteorites, star dust, and nebulous matter fall on to the earth every year; also the sun is transferring some of its mass to the earth in the form of heat, therefore the earth's mass, and consequently its gravitation, is increasing.

To resist this increased gravitation, every part of our bodies must gradually be getting stronger. The heart, the lungs and every organ in our bodies, including our brains, meet with greater resistance to their action, so the strength and quality of each must increase, and the only way this can occur is by the cells or atoms of the body increasing in number and coming closer together.

Every single piece of knowledge we possess may be likened to a unit or atom, and when these atoms of knowledge accumulate and concentrate in accordance with the

Evolutionary Law, civilization advances.

Prehistoric man had no consideration for any other person but himself, he was an isolated unit. But as evolution went on, mankind gradually became more and more connected and bound up with each other so that in time the human race will become perfect, and the welfare of all will be considered by each, knowing that the welfare of every other person will mean the welfare of himself.

Science, religion, sport, trade, etc., are not so distinctly separated as formerly, each are making more and more use of the other, and in many branches there is already a connection–sport to trade, trade to science, and science to religion.

Velocities of travel are increasing, which means that distances are decreasing, and every part of the earth is coming closer together, if we measure distance by a time factor, which is the correct way. Fifty years ago a journey to Australia took months to perform, whereas now it can be made in a few days.

I continued taking more drugs, and as time went on the room became full of ghost-like shapes, which gradually grew clearer and more distinct; then for the first time during all my years of drug-taking experiences the visions were animated. No longer did they simply float past me as before, their movements were perfectly natural and life-like. Although the figures appeared luminous or slightly transparent, so that I could see the background of the room through them, I was not conscious of this, unless I specially looked for it.

The walls of the room began to recede, until they finally disappeared, and I lost all sense of personality, until I was just an intelligence with the power to observe and think. Time and space had no confining limits for me; I could live many lives, in many different places and periods. My condition was like a perfect and unique form of self-hypnosis.

I could experience anything I wished. I willed it to thunder, and I heard the crash distinctly. For lightning, and I saw the flash. I could sit in the "circus," and see the games, and gladiatorial contests as they took place in the time of Nero.

I could see a close-up view of the sun; the waves of molten white hot matter rolling and leaping to a height of a hundred miles between the crest and hollow, sending off tongues of flame and blue heat, leaping up to a height of two hundred thousand miles in a few minutes of time. Flames, each one of which could entirely envelop a hundred globes like our earth.

There was a point beyond which I could not go; a point which, when reached, the visions would be at a maximum state of clearness, and any further drugs would cause them to become blurred and dim. When this point was reached I slept.

from **"The Poem of Hashish"**

Charles Baudelaire

Charles Baudelaire's passionate melancholy arose from the severest of dilemmas. He believed that the will to preserve the spirit is our saving grace—it is our human task—though to our never-ending folly we often refuse to exercise this will. Deeply interested in altered states of consciousness, as a user of opium and hashish, as well as absinthe, he understood better than most the double-edged sword of their intoxications. Man confronts his double nature as angel *and* demon while under the influence of drugs. Intimately familiar with the horrible passions and magnificent vices of the human soul, in his essay excerpted here, originally titled "On the Artificial Ideal: Hashish" (1858), Baudelaire condemns the man who forfeits his will for momentary, illusory spiritual elevation.

What is Hashish?

Marco Polo's accounts, like those of other early explorers, have been unjustly made fun of; they have been verified by scholars and deserve to be believed. I shall not repeat the story of the Old Man of the Mountain, who used to administer hashish (whence Hashishins or Assassins) to his younger disciples when he wanted to give them an idea of paradise; he then put them in a garden of exquisite delights in order to give them a glimpse, so to speak, of the rewards for passive and unthinking obedience. Concerning the secret society of the Hashishins, the reader can consult [other scholarly sources]. Herodotus describes how the Scythians gathered piles of hemp seeds on which they threw stones heated in a fire. It was like a steam bath, but perfumed as was never a Greek sweating-room, and so keen was their pleasure that they cried aloud for joy.

Hashish, in point of fact, comes to us from the Orient; the stimulating properties of hemp were well known in ancient Egypt, and its use under different names is widespread in India, Algeria, and Arabia. But much nearer home, we have before our eyes curious examples of the intoxicating effects of emanations from plants. Not only do children who have been playing and rolling around in piles of cropped lucern often experience strange giddiness, but it is well known that during the hemp harvest both male and female workers experience similar effects; it is as though a miasma rises from the crop, subtly disturbing the brain. The harvester's mind spins, and is sometimes oppressed with dreams. At times the limbs become weak and refuse to function. We have heard of attacks of sleep-walking amongst Russian peasants, due, it is said, to the use of hempseed oil in preparing food. Who is not familiar with the extraordinary behavior of hens that have eaten hemp seed, and the impetuous and fiery spirit of the horses at weddings or patronal festivals, dosed by the peasants for the steeple-chase with hemp seed, sometimes sprinkled with wine?

However, French hemp is not suitable for making hashish, or at least, judging by repeated experiments, it does not produce a drug of a strength comparable to hashish. Hashish or Indian hemp, cannabis indica, is a plant of the nettle family (Urticaceae), closely resembling the hemp plant of our climate but not as tall. It possesses quite extraordinary intoxicating properties, which have in recent years attracted the attention of scientists and people of society in France. It is more or less highly prized depending on its country of origin; Bengalese is most highly rated by enthusiasts; however varieties from Egypt, Constantinople, Persia and Algeria have the same properties, although they are less strong.

Hashish (herb or grass, i.e. grass par excellence, as though in the one word *grass* the Arabs had tried to define the source of every immaterial pleasure) is given different names according to its composition and method of preparation in the country where it is harvested; in India–bhang; in Africa–teriaki; in Algeria and Arabia–majoon. The time of year for harvesting is not a matter of indifference; it is when the plant is in flower that it is most potent. This is why only the flowering tops are used in the various preparations we shall be mentioning.

The oily extract of hashish as prepared by the Arabs is obtained by boiling the tops of the green plant in butter with a little water. When all the moisture has evaporated the mixture is strained, yielding a substance that looks like a greenish-yellow ointment and smells unpleasantly of hashish and rancid butter. In this form it is used in little pellets of two to four grams; but because of its repulsive odor, which increases with time, the Arabs disguise the extract in sweetmeats.

The most commonly used of these confections, dawamesk, is a mixture of extract, sugar, and various flavorings, such as vanilla, cinnamon, pistachio, almond or musk. Sometimes even a little Spanish fly is added, but this is to achieve effects that have nothing in common with those usually created by hashish. In this form hashish is not at all disagreeable, and can be taken in doses of fifteen, twenty or thirty grams, either in a wafer of unleavened bread or in a cup of coffee.

The experiments conducted by Smith, Gastinel and Decourtive were aimed at discovering the active principle of hashish. In spite of their efforts, little is yet known of its chemical composition; but its properties are generally attributed to a resinous substance present in the considerable proportion of approximately ten per cent. To obtain the resin, the dried plant is ground to a coarse powder and washed several times in alcohol, which is then reduced by boiling; the alcohol is evaporated off until the residue reaches a firm consistency; this residue is treated with water, which dissolves the unwanted gummy matter and leaves one with the pure resin.

The product is soft, dark green in color, and has the characteristic smell of hashish to a very high degree. Five, ten or fifteen centigrams are enough to produce surprising results. The resin can be taken in chocolate or ginger sweets. However, its effects, like those of dawamesk and the oily extract, vary considerably in kind and strength depending on the individual's physical and emotional susceptibility. What is more, the result varies in the same individual. Sometimes he experiences immoderate and irresistible mirth, sometimes a sense of well-being and fullness of life, and at other times he falls into an uneasy dream-filled sleep. However, there are phenomena which recur fairly regularly, especially among people of similar temperament and education; there is a kind of unity in the variety that makes it possible for me to compose the monograph concerning intoxication.

In Constantinople, Algeria, and even in France, some people smoke hashish mixed with tobacco; but then the effects in question occur only in a very attenuated and so to speak sluggish form. I have heard that an essential oil has recently been distilled from hashish that seems to have much more potent qualities than any of the preparations known up to now; but it has not been fully enough studied for me to talk with any certainty about its effects. It is presumably unnecessary to add that tea, coffee and alcohol can help, to a greater or lesser extent, to hasten the onset of this mysterious intoxication.

The Theater of the Seraphim

What does one experience? What does one see? Marvelous things, of course? Extraordinary spectacles? Is it very beautiful? Very dreadful? Very dangerous? These are the ordinary questions, asked with a mixture of curiosity and dread, by the ignorant of the adept. It is like a childish impatience to know, like that of people who have never left their fireside, when they find themselves face to face with a man who has returned from faraway and unknown lands. They imagine hashish intoxication as a prodigious country, a vast theater of magic and conjuring, where everything is miraculous and unforeseen. But that is a prejudice, a complete misunderstanding. And, since for the generality of readers and questioners the word *hashish* includes the idea of a strange and bewildering world, the expectation of tremendous dreams (it would be better to say hallucinations, which are moreover less frequent than people think), I shall immediately note the important difference separating the effects of hashish from the phenomenon of sleep. In sleep, the adventurous voyage of every night, there is something positively miraculous, a miracle whose punctuality has blunted its mystery. Man's dreams are of two classes. In the first kind, full of his ordinary life, his preoccupations, desires, and vices mix in a more or less bizarre way with objects glimpsed during the day, which are carelessly attached to the vast canvas of his memory. This is the natural dream; it is man himself. But the other kind of dream! The absurd, unexpected dream, with neither rapport nor connection with the character, life, or passions of the dreamer! This dream, which I shall call hieroglyphic, apparently represents the supernatural side of life, and it is precisely because it is absurd that the ancients believed it divine. Because it is inexplicable by natural causes, they attributed to it a cause exterior to man; and even today, not counting the oneiromancers,[1] there is a philosophical school that sees in dreams of this kind sometimes a reproach, sometimes a counsel–in sum, a symbolic and moral tableau, engendered in the very spirit of the man who is sleeping. It is a dictionary that must be studied, a language to which wise men must obtain the key.

In hashish intoxication, there is nothing like this. We never leave the natural dream. The intoxication, in all its duration, will only be, it is true, a vast dream, thanks to the intensity of colors and the rapid succession of ideas; but it will always preserve the particular tonality of the individual. Man has wished to dream, the dream will rule the man, but the dream will surely be the son of its father. The lazy man has searched hard in order to introduce artificially the supernatural into his life and thought, but after all, despite the accidental energy of his sensations, it is only the same man enlarged, the same number raised to a very large power. He is mastered, but his misfortune is that this is only by himself, by the already dominant part of himself: *He wanted to be an angel, he has become a beast,*[2] momentarily very powerful, if one could call power an excessive sensibility, without a governor to moderate or utilize it.

Let the worldly and the ignorant know, those eager to experience exceptional delights, that they will find nothing miraculous in hashish, absolutely nothing but an excess of the natural. The brain and the organs on which hashish operates will show only their ordinary, individual phenomena, enlarged, it is true, in number and energy, but always faithful to their origin. Man will not escape the fate of his physical and moral temperament: the hashish will be, for his familiar impressions and thoughts, an enlarging mirror, but a clear one.

Here is the drug under your very eyes: a bit of green preserves, as large as a nut, smelling peculiarly strong, so much that it raises a kind of repulsion and slight waves of nausea, as of course any fine and even agreeable odor would do, raised to its maximum strength and density. (Allow me to note in passing that this proposition might be reversed, and the most repugnant and revolting odor might perhaps become a pleasure, reduced to its minimum quantity and expansion.) So here is happiness!–filling up a small spoon–happiness with its intoxications, follies, and trifles! You may swallow it without fear, it won't kill you. Your physical organs will not be attacked. Perhaps later too frequent an appeal to its spell will diminish the strength of your will, you may be less human than you are today, but the punishment is so far away, the future disaster so hard to define! What do you risk? Perhaps a bit of nervous fatigue tomorrow. Don't you risk every day far greater punishments for far fewer rewards? So, it's done: you have even, to give it more strength and expansion, mixed your dose of the extract with a cup of black coffee; you have taken care to have an empty stomach, postponing until nine or ten o'clock any substantial meal, in order to give the poison complete freedom of action–the most you can take is a little light soup in an hour's time. You are now sufficiently nourished for a long and singular voyage. The whistle has blown, the sails are set, and you have the strange privilege over ordinary travelers of not knowing where you are going. You have willed it: long live fate!

I assume that you have chosen well the moment for this adventurous expedition. Every perfect debauch needs its perfect leisure. You know moreover that hashish exaggerates not only the individual, but also his circumstance and surroundings. You have no work to do that requires punctuality or exactness, no family or love problems. Take care: Any problem or worry, any memory of work claiming your will or attention at a particular time, will sound a knell across your intoxication and poison your pleasure. Any worry will become an anguish, any problem a torture. All these conditions being observed, if you are in favorable surroundings, such as a picturesque countryside or a poetically furnished room, and if you can even expect a little music, then everything is for the best.

Generally there are three phases of hashish intoxication, rather easy to distinguish, and it is a curious thing to observe in novices the first symptoms of the first phase. You've vaguely heard about the marvelous effects of hashish; your imagination has a preconceived idea that it is some kind of ideal rapture; you long to know whether its reality will be up to your expectation. This is enough to throw you from the very beginning into an anxious state, rather favorable to the invading and conquering spirit of the poison. Most novices, when first trying it, complain about the slowness of its effects: they wait for them with a childish impatience, and the drug doesn't act quickly enough for their liking, so they indulge in blustering incredulity that is very entertaining to the initiates, who know how hashish works. The first effects, like the signs of a gathering storm, appear and multiply in the very midst of this incredulity. There is at first a bit of hilarity, ridiculous and irresistible, which seizes you. This seizure of groundless gaiety, which you are almost ashamed of, happens again and again, cutting across intervals of stupor when you try in vain to recollect yourself. The simplest words, the most trivial ideas, take on a bizarre new aspect: you are even astonished at having found them so simple. Incongruous resemblances and comparisons, impossible to foresee, interminable word games, and comic sketches flow continually from your brain. The demon has invaded you: it is useless to balk at this hilarity, as painful as tickling. From time to time you laugh at yourself, at your silliness and folly, and your friends, if they are there, laugh both at your state and their own; but since they are without malice, you are without rancor.

This gaiety, by turns languid and poignant, the uneasiness in the joy, this insecurity and indecision in the malady, generally last only a rather short time. Soon the relationships between ideas become so vague, the thread linking your conceptions so tenuous, that only your companions can understand you. Furthermore, on this subject, there is no means of verification: they may well believe they understand you, and the illusion is reciprocal. This frolicking about, these outbursts of laughter, which are like explosions, appear to be real madness, or at least the foolishness of a maniac, to anyone not in the same state as you. Likewise prudence and good sense, regularity of thought in any prudent witness who is not intoxicated, amuses you as a special kind of dementia. Your roles are inverted: his self-control pushes you to the limits of irony. Isn't it a mysteriously comic situation when a man is pushed into incomprehensible gaiety because of some-one who is not in the same situation as himself? The fool takes pity on the wise man, and from that time the idea of his superiority begins to dawn on the horizon of his intellect. Soon it will grow, swell, and burst like a meteor.

I was witness to a scene of this kind that had gone on for a long while, whose grotesque feature was only intelligible for those who knew, at least by observing others, the effects of the substance and the enormous difference in pitch it creates between two supposedly equal intelligences. A famous musician, who knew nothing of the effects of hashish, who perhaps had never even heard of it, arrives in the middle of a party where several people have taken some. They try to make him understand its marvelous effects. He smiles graciously and complacently at these prodigious accounts, as if he would gladly pretend for several minutes. His doubts are quickly guessed by those wits sharpened by poison, and their laughter wounds him. These outbursts of joy, these word games, these altered faces, irritate him and make him declare, earlier perhaps than he would have wished, "This is a bad imitation of an artist, and moreover it must be rather tiring for those who have undertaken it." This comedy lights up all these wits like a flash of lightning. Their joy is redoubled. "This imitation may seem good to you, but not to me," he says. "It only has to seem good to us," egotistically replies one of the patients. Not knowing whether he is dealing with real madmen or merely with people faking madness, the man thinks the wisest thing to do is to leave, but someone should lock the door and hide the key. Someone else, kneeling before him, asks him pardon in the name of society, and tells him insolently, but tearfully, that despite his spiritual inferiority, which might excite some pity, everyone is filled with a deep friendship for him. So he resigns himself to stay, and even agrees, at their insistence, to play a little music. But the sounds of the violin, spreading in the room like a new contagion, grip first one patient, then another. There are deep hoarse sighs, sudden sobs, rivers of silent tears. Horrified, the musician stops, and going up to one who in his bliss is making the most noise, asks him if he is suffering, and what can be done to comfort him. One of the onlookers, a practical man, suggests lemonade and fruit juices. But the patient, ecstasy in his eyes, looks at them both with an ineffable scorn. Imagine wanting to cure a man sick from too much life, sick from joy!

As one sees by this anecdote, kindness holds a rather important place in the sensations caused by hashish: a soft, lazy, mute kindness, deriving from the sharpening of the nerves. In support of this observation, a person told me of an adventure that had happened to him in this state of rapture, and since he had kept a very exact memory of his sensations, I can perfectly understand his grotesque and inexplicable embarrassment at the difference of pitch and level I am speaking of. I don't remember whether this man was having his first or second hashish experience. Had he taken too strong a dose, or had the hashish produced, with no other apparent assistance (this happens frequently) much stronger effects? He told me that across his supreme enjoyment at feeling full of life and genius, came a sudden meeting with an object of terror. At first overcome by the beauty of his sensations, he became quickly horrified. He asked himself what would become of his intelligence and his organs, if this state, which he took to be supernatural, continued to grow, if his nerves became more and more delicate. Because of the enlarging faculty that the wit of the patient possesses, this fear must be an incredible torture. "I was like a wild horse," he said, "running toward an abyss, wanting to stop, yet not being able to. In effect, it was a terrifying gallop, and my mind, the slave of circumstance, surroundings, accident, and everything implied in the word *chance,* had taken an absolutely ecstatic turn. It is too late, I repeated to myself endlessly in despair. When this feeling ceased, and it seemed to go on for an infinite time though it probably lasted only a few minutes, when I thought I could finally plunge into that bliss, so dear to Orientals, that comes after this furious phase, I was stricken by a new misfortune. A new worry, very trivial and childish, came over me. All of a sudden I remembered that I had been invited to a dinner with important men. I saw myself going through the middle of a careful and discreet crowd, where everyone is master of himself, obliged to conceal my state under the light of numerous lamps. I thought that I had succeeded at it, but then I nearly fainted when I thought of the effort of will I had to make. By some accident or other, the words of the Gospel came surging into my memory, 'Woe to him who brings scandal!' [3] and in wishing to forget them, in trying to forget them, I repeated them endlessly in my mind. My misfortune (and it was a real misfortune) then took on grandiose proportions. I resolved, despite my weakness, to exert myself to go and consult a pharmacist, for I didn't know any antidotes, and I wanted to go with a free spirit into the world, where my work called me. But on the steps of the shop a sudden thought struck me, which stopped me for several instants and made me reflect. I had just seen myself in the mirror of a shop front, and my face had astonished me. The pallor, the sunken lips, the swollen eyes! I shall worry this good man, I said to myself, and for what foolishness! Add to that the sense of ridicule that I wanted to avoid, and the fear of finding people in the shop. But my sudden feeling of goodwill toward this unknown pharmacist dominated all my other sentiments. I imagined the man as sensitive as myself at that unhappy instant, and, as I thought that his ear and his soul, like mine, would vibrate at the slightest noise, I resolved to enter the shop on tiptoe. I told myself that I couldn't show too much discretion toward a man whose kindness I was going to beg. And then I told myself to lower my voice as I had the sound of my steps–do you know it, the hashish voice?–grave, profound, guttural, much resembling that of inveterate opium eaters. The result was the contrary of what I wanted. Instead of reassuring the pharmacist, I horrified him. He knew nothing of this 'illness,' he had never even heard of it. Yet he looked at me with a curiosity strongly mixed with suspicion. Did he take me for a fool, a criminal, a beggar? For none of them, no doubt, but all those absurd

ideas crossed my mind. I had to explain to him at length (what a job!) what hemp preserves were and what use was made of them, repeating to him ceaselessly that there was
no danger, that there was no reason for *him* to become alarmed, and that I was only
asking for a means of softening the effects, or of contravening them, frequently mentioning the sincere chagrin I felt at causing him any bother. Finally—understand all the
humiliation for me contained in these words—he simply asked me to leave. This was the
repayment for my exaggerated charity and kindness. I went to my dinner: I scandalized
no one. No one suspected the superhuman efforts I had to make in order to seem like
everyone else. But I shall never forget the tortures of an ultrapoetic intoxication, inhibited by decorum and impeded by an appointment."

Though naturally inclined to sympathize with all pains born in the imagination,
I cannot help laughing at this story. The man who told it to me has not reformed.
He is still seeking in those cursed preserves the stimulus one must find in oneself,
but as he is a prudent, ordered man, a man of the world, he has lessened his doses,
which has allowed him to increase their frequency. Later he will collect the rotten
fruits of his hygiene.

I now return to the regular development of the intoxication. After this first phase of
infantile gaiety, there is a kind of momentary quieting. But new events are soon announced
by a cool sensation in the extremities (that can actually become an intense cold in some
people) and a great weakness in all the limbs: your hands are powerless, and in your head
and all your being you feel a troublesome stupor. Your eyes enlarge, as if they were drawn
out in all directions by an implacable ecstasy. Your face becomes drowned in pallor. Your
lips become thin and drawn into the mouth, with that quick breathing characteristic of
a man enthralled by great plans, oppressed by vast thoughts, or gathering his breath before jumping. The throat closes up, so to speak. The palate is dry with a thirst it would
be infinitely sweet to satisfy, if the delightful laziness were not more agreeable and opposed to the least bodily movement. Deep, hoarse sighs come from your chest, as if your
old body could no longer support the wishes and activity of your new soul. From time to
time a shock runs through you and causes a momentary shudder, like those starts which,
after a day's work or during a troubled night, come just before real sleep.

Before going further, I would like to tell another story about this sensation of coolness, a story that shows just how much the effects, even the purely physical ones, can
vary in different individuals. This time it is a literary man speaking, and I believe we can
find in certain passages of his tale indications of a literary temperament.

"I had taken a moderate dose of the extract," he told me, "and everything was going
well. The attack of unhealthy laughter had lasted only a short time, and I found myself
in that languid and astonished condition that was almost happiness. I saw a tranquil and
carefree evening ahead. Chance unfortunately constrained me to accompany someone
to the theater. I did my duty bravely, resolved to hide my great desire for quiet and immobility. All the cabs in the neighborhood were taken, and I had to resign myself to a

long walk, through the loud street noises, the stupid conversations of the pedestrians, through an ocean of triviality. A slight coolness had already appeared at the ends of my fingers, and soon it became a piercing cold, as if my hands were plunged in a bucket of icy water. But it was not painful: this acute sensation pierced me rather like a delight. Yet it seemed that the cold invaded me more and more throughout the interminable walk. Two or three times I asked the person I was going with if it was really very cold; he replied that on the contrary the temperature was more than warm. Finally at the theater, in the box we had reserved, with three or four hours of rest ahead of me, I thought I had arrived in the promised land. The feelings I had repressed on the way, with all the poor energy at my disposal, at last all came out, and I freely gave myself up to this mute frenzy. The cold increased constantly, and yet I was seeing people lightly dressed, even wearily wiping their brows. The amusing idea struck me that I was a privileged man, alone given the right to be cold at the theater in summer. The cold built up to an alarming point, but above all I was curious to know just how cold it could get. Finally it became so completely and totally cold that all my ideas froze, so to speak: I was a thinking piece of ice; I thought I was a statue carved from a single block of ice, and this mad hallucination stimulated in me such a pride and emotional well-being that I cannot describe them to you. What added to my abominable amusement was my certainty that all the spectators were ignorant of my condition and my superiority over them, and also the happiness of knowing that my friend had not for an instant suspected the bizarre feelings that possessed me. I had my reward for this pretense, and my exceptional pleasure was a real secret.

"Furthermore, I had scarcely entered the box when I was struck with an impression of darkness that seemed somehow connected with the idea of cold. It may well be that these two ideas lent strength to each other. You know that hashish always calls forth grand displays of light, glorious radiance, and showers of liquid gold; every light seems good with hashish, the light that shimmers all at once and that which is fixed at certain points, the candelabras in the drawing rooms, the candles of Mary's month, the rosy avalanches of sunset. It seemed that this miserable glimmer gave off a quite insufficient light to satisfy my insatiable thirst for clarity: I seemed to enter, as I said, a world of shadows, which actually deepened bit by bit, while I was dreaming of polar nights and eternal winter. As to the play (it was in the comic genre), it alone was luminous, though infinitely small and placed far away, as at the end of a huge stereoscope. I won't tell you that I heard the players—you know that that is impossible; from time to time my mind caught up a shred of phrase, and like an expert dancer used it as a trampoline to jump off into faraway reveries. You might think that a drama heard in this fashion might lack logic and sequence, but you are wrong: I discovered a very subtle meaning in the drama which was created by my inattention. Nothing offended me; I was a little like that poet, seeing *Esther* for the first time, who found it entirely natural that Aman should declare his love to the queen. That was, as you can guess, the moment when he throws himself at Esther's feet to ask pardon for his crimes. If every drama were heard according to this method, they would all reach a great beauty, even those of Racine.

"The players seemed extremely small, and surrounded by a precise and careful outline, like Meissen figurines. I not only saw distinctly the most minute details of their costumes, like the designs of the material, the sewing, the buttons, and so forth, but even the line separating the false hairline from the real, the colors and all the tricks of makeup. And these lilliputians were arrayed in a cold magic clarity, like the one a very clear glass gives to an oil painting. When I was finally able to leave this cavern of frozen shadows and when the interior fantasies had gone and I had returned to my old self, I felt a greater tiredness than any long, forced work had ever caused me."

Indeed at this period in the intoxication a new acuteness and a superior delicacy are perceived in all the senses. Smell, sight, hearing, and touch participate equally in this progression. The eyes glimpse the infinite, the ears perceive the faintest sounds from amid the most roaring tumult. Then the hallucinations begin. External objects slowly and successively take on peculiar forms, become deformed and transformed. Then ambiguities occur, doubts, and transpositions of ideas. Sounds put on colors, and colors contain music. One might say that this is only natural, and any poetic brain, in its normal, healthy condition, could easily conceive such analogies. But I have already warned the reader that there is nothing positively supernatural in hashish intoxication. The only thing that happens is that these analogies put on an unaccustomed liveliness; they penetrate, invade, and overcome the spirit in their despotic way. Musical notes become numbers, and if your mind is at all endowed with mathematical aptitude, the melody and harmony, all the while keeping its sensual character, transforms itself into a vast problem in arithmetic, in which numbers engender numbers whose changes and appearances you can follow with inexplicable ease, with an agility equal to the musician's.

It sometimes happens that personality disappears and objectivity, the property of pantheist poets, develops so abnormally in you that your contemplation of exterior objects makes you forget your own existence, and soon you confuse yourself with them. Your eye fixes on a harmonious tree bending in the wind: in a few seconds what would be in a poet's brain only a natural comparison becomes in yours a reality. First you give the tree your passions, your desire, or your melancholy; its shivering and vibration become your own, and soon you are the tree. Likewise, the bird that soars in the sky first represents the age-old desire to soar above human things, but you are already the bird itself. Suppose you are sitting down and smoking. Your attention may rest a bit too long on the bluish clouds coming from your pipe. The idea of a slow, continuous, eternal evaporation takes hold of your mind, and soon you are applying this idea to your own thoughts, your thinking matter. By a singular misunderstanding, a transposition, or an intellectual error, you feel yourself evaporating, and you attribute to your pipe (into which you are stuffed and packed like tobacco) the strange ability to *smoke you*.

Happily, this interminable fantasy has lasted only a minute, and a lucid interval, won with great effort, allows you to examine the clock. But another rush of ideas carries you away: it rolls you around for a minute in its living vortex, and this minute too will be an eternity. For the proportions of time and being are completely upset by the number and intensity of feelings and ideas. One might seem to live several human lives in the space of one hour. Are you not like some fantastic novel that is lived instead of written? There is no longer any equation between the origins of the pleasures and the pleasures themselves, and from this idea comes the blame due to this dangerous experiment in which freedom disappears.

When I speak of hallucinations, I do not mean the word in its strictest sense. There is an important difference between the pure hallucination, which doctors often have the opportunity to study, and the hallucination–or rather the error of the senses, in the mental state caused by hashish. In the first case, the hallucination is sudden, perfect, and inevitable; in addition, it finds neither pretext nor excuse in the world of external objects. The patient sees shapes or hears sounds where none exist. In the second case, the hallucination is progressive, nearly voluntary, and does not become perfect: it only ripens in the action of the imagination. Finally, there is always an excuse for it: a sound will speak, saying distinct things, but there was a sound to begin with. The intoxicated eye of the man on hashish sees strange shapes, but before becoming strange or monstrous these shapes were simple and natural. The energy, the lifelike quality of the hallucination in no way invalidates this original distinction. One kind has its origins in the surroundings and in present time, the other does not.

In order for you better to understand this turbulence of imagination, this dreamlike development and poetic outpouring to which a brain affected by hashish is condemned, I shall tell another story. This time, it is no leisured youth speaking, nor yet a man of letters: It's a woman, a bit mature and curious, of an excitable spirit, who succumbed to the desire to know the poison, and here describes, to another woman, the essential points of her visions. I am transcribing literally:

"However strange and new these sensations might be that I got from my twelve hours of madness (twelve or twenty? I really can't tell), I'll never try it again. The mental excitement is too strong, the resultant fatigue too great; and to tell the truth, I find in this childishness something rather criminal. But I finally gave in to curiosity; and then it was to be a group madness, with old friends, where I saw no great danger in losing a bit of dignity. First of all I must tell you that this wretched hashish is a very tricky substance: Sometimes one feels the intoxication has disappeared, but it's only a false calm. There are moments of rest, but then it starts all over again. So, around ten in the evening, I found myself in one of those momentary states of repose: I thought I'd been delivered from this excess of liveliness that had occasioned me much amusement, true, but not without worry and a bit of fear. I ate my supper with pleasure, as if tired by a long journey. I hadn't eaten till then out of prudence. But before I'd even left the table, my frenzy seized me again, as a cat would a mouse, and the poison began once again to play with my poor brain. Though my own house is only a short distance from our friends', and though there was a carriage at my disposal, I felt so overcome by the desire to dream and to give myself up to this irresistible madness, that I joyfully accepted their offer to put me up until the next day. You know their château, how they have rearranged and refurbished in a modern style the part they live in, but that the part that is not lived in has been left as it was, in its old style and decoration. They decided to improvise for me a bedroom in the old part of the house, and so chose the smallest room, a kind of faded and decrepit boudoir, though quite charming. I must describe it to you carefully, so that you can understand the peculiar vision which affected me and which took up the whole night, so that I had no time to see the hours flying by.

"The room is very small and narrow. Above the molding the ceiling becomes vaulted; the walls are covered with long, narrow mirrors separated with panels painted with country scenes in the rather loose style of the rest of the decor. Exactly at the molding, on each of the four walls, various allegorical figures are represented, some in attitudes of repose, others running or jumping. Above them are several brilliant birds and flowers. Behind the figures a trellis is painted on the wall, which follows naturally the curve of the ceiling. The ceiling is gilt. All the spaces are also gilt, only interrupted by the geometric form of the painted trellis. You can see that this resembles a very large cage, a very beautiful cage for a very large bird. I should add that the night was fine, transparent, and the moon very bright, so bright that after I blew out the candle the whole room remained visible, not lit by the eye of my imagination, as you might think, but illuminated by this lovely night, whose beams picked out all these gildings, mirrors, and varied colors.

"At first I was very amazed to see great spaces spread out before me, beside me, everywhere: clear rivers and verdant scenes were reflected in tranquil waters. You can guess the effect of the panels interspersed with mirrors. Lifting my eyes, I saw a setting sun like fused metal cooling. That was the gold on the ceiling, but the trellis made me think that I was in a kind of cage or house open on all sides, and it was only the bars of my magnificent prison that separated me from all these marvels. At first I laughed at my illusion, but the more I looked at it, the more the magic increased and took on life, transparence, and an absolute reality. From that time the idea of being shut in controlled my mind, without entirely negating, I must say, the varied pleasures I drew from the spectacle around me. I thought of myself as closed away for a long time, perhaps for thousands of years, in this sumptuous cage, in an enchanted countryside, between wondrous horizons. I thought of Sleeping Beauty, of the punishment I had to suffer, and of my future deliverance. Above my head flew the brilliant tropical birds, and because my ear heard the neck bells of the horses on the highway in the distance, these two sensations combined into a unique idea: I thought the birds had a strange coppery song, and that they sang through metallic throats. They were obviously talking about me and enjoying my captivity. Leaping monkeys and grotesque satyrs made fun of me, a prisoner lying immobile. But all the mythological divinities looked at me with a charming smile, as if to encourage me to endure my fate patiently, and their every look was sidelong so as to seize my attention. I concluded that if some ancient faults, some sins I was ignorant of, had necessitated this temporal punishment, yet I could still count on a higher goodness which, even if wisely condemning me, still offered me pleasures more serious than those that filled our youth. You can see that moral considerations were not absent from my dream, but I observed that the pleasure of seeing these brilliant shapes and colors, of believing myself the center of a fantastic drama, frequently absorbed all my other thoughts. This state lasted a very long time. Did it last until morning? I don't know. All of a sudden I saw the morning sun in my room: I was greatly astonished, and despite great efforts of memory it was impossible to know whether I had slept or had patiently endured a delicious insomnia. A while ago it was night, and now it's daytime! The notion of time, or rather the measure of time, being abolished, the whole night was only measurable for me in the multitude of my thoughts. However long it seems to me from here, yet then it seemed to last only a few seconds, or perhaps it never happened at all.

"I haven't even spoken of my fatigue–it was immense. They say that poetic and creative effort resembles what I experienced, though I've always thought that those people whose job is to move us must be endowed with a calm disposition; but if poetic ecstasy resembles that which was contained in a little spoonful of preserves, I think that the public's pleasure must cost the poets dearly, and it's not without a sort of well-being, a prosaic satisfaction, that I finally find myself back to normal, in my intellectual normality, I mean in real life."

This is obviously a reasonable woman, but we shall only use her tale to draw several useful notes to complete our brief description of the main sensations that hashish causes.

She spoke of supper as a pleasure arriving at just the right time, at a time when a momentary calm, which seemed definitive, allowed her to return to real life. But there are, as I have said, intermittent false calms, and often the hashish causes a voracious hunger and almost always an excessive thirst. Often dinner or supper, instead of leading to a long rest, creates a redoubled action, the giddy crisis of which this lady has complained, and which was followed by a series of enchanted visions, lightly touched with fear, to which she with good humor resigned herself. This tyrannical hunger and thirst cannot be sated without a considerable effort. For one feels so above material things that one must develop one's courage to take up a bottle or a fork.

The final crisis caused by the digestion of food is actually very violent: it is impossible to struggle against it. It would be unendurable if it lasted too long and did not soon give way to another phase of the intoxication which in the case just cited became splendid visions, slightly terrifying and at the same time consoling. This state is what the Orientals call *kif*: no longer something roiling and turbulent, it's a calm and immobile blessedness, a glorious resignation. For a long time you haven't been your own master, but you don't bother about it anymore. Pain and the idea of time have disappeared, or if they dare to show themselves again, they are transfigured by the dominating sensation, and are thus, relative to their usual form, what poetic melancholy is to actual pain.

But above all, let us note that in this lady's story (this is why I have transcribed it) the hallucination is a bastard kind, and draws its being from an exterior spectacle: the mind is only a mirror in which the reflected surroundings are transformed in an exaggerated way. Finally, we witnessed what I would willingly call a moral hallucination: the subject thought she was submitting to a punishment, but the female temperament, unsuited to analysis, did not allow her to note the singularly optimistic nature of the hallucination. The Olympian divinities' benevolent regard was poeticized by what was essentially a hashish eater's gloss. I would not say that this lady skirted remorse, but her thoughts, briefly turned to melancholy and regret, became rapidly colored by hope. It is a change we shall again have occasion to observe.

She spoke of the next day's fatigue, and indeed it is great, but it doesn't show up immediately, and when you are obliged to recognize it, it is always with astonishment. For first of all, when you see a new day arising in your life, you experience an incredible well-being—you seem to enjoy a marvelous lightness of spirit. But you are scarcely out of bed when an old remnant of the intoxication catches up with you and slows you down, like the ball and chain of your recent servitude. Your weak legs rather timidly lead you about, and at every instant you are afraid of breaking yourself like some fragile object. A great languor (some people think it doesn't lack charm) seizes your mind and spreads over your faculties like fog over the countryside. And there you are for several more hours, incapable of work, action, or energy. This is the punishment for the unholy prodigality with which you have spent your nervous energy. You have flung your personality to the four winds, and now what trouble you will have in collecting it again and concentrating it!

Translator's Notes:
[1] Those who divine by dreams.
[2] One of the Pensées of Pascal.
[3] Matthew 18:7.

(Translated by John Githens/Andrew C. Kimmens)

General Security: The
Liquidation of Opium

Antonin Artaud

From his invention of the
Theatre of Cruelty to his
confinement in Rodez, one of
the several institutions in
which he spent most of his
last eleven years, Artaud lived
a life of what Western intellect
condescendingly terms social
rebellion. His admirers acclaim
him as a profoundly spiritual
revolutionary in his quest to
break down all restrictive
"civilized" barriers.By participating with the peyote-using
Tarahumara Indians in northern
Mexico, he purposefully
introduced into an everyday
context the need to achieve
altered states of consciousness. The following essay is
art-house Artaud, the litterateur as passionate dissenter,
written about ten years prior
to his flight from Europe
(1925), theatre, and other
"sane" boundaries.

I have the not-dissimulated intention of finishing with this question so we shall no longer be bugged by the so-called dangers of the drug.

My point of view is clearly anti-social.

There is only one reason to attack opium. It is the fear that its use may become general throughout society.

Now this danger is false.

We are born rotten in the body and in the soul, we are congenitally unadapted; by suppressing opium you won't suppress the need for crime, the cancers of the body and of the soul, the propensity for despair, inborn stupidity, hereditary smallpox, the friability of the instincts. You won't be able to stop souls from being predestined for poison, whatever kind it might be: poison of morphine, poison of reading, poison of isolation, poison of onanism, poison of repeated coitus, poison of the rooted weakness of the soul, poison of alcohol, poison of tobacco, poison of anti-sociability. There are souls that are incurable and lost to the rest of society. If you take away from them a means of madness, they will invent ten thousand more. They will create means more subtle, more furious, absolutely *desperate.* Nature herself is anti-social in her soul, and it is not only through an usurpation of powers that the organized social body can react against humanity's *natural* fallout.

Let the lost get lost. We have other, much better, things to do with our time than to attempt an impossible regeneration which, besides, is useless, *hateful and injurious.*

As long as we haven't been able to abolish a single cause of human desperation, we do not have the right to try to suppress the means by which man tries to clean himself of desperation.

For it would be necessary first to get to suppress this natural and hidden impulse, this *plausible* inclination of man which leads him to find a way, which gives him the *idea* that he might look for a means of getting out of his troubles.

And even more, the lost are lost by nature, and all the ideas of moral regeneration won't do anything about it. There is *an innate determinism,* there is an indisputable incurability about suicide, crime, idiocy, madness; there is an invincible cuckoldom of man, a fallout of character; there is a castration of the mind.

Loss of speech exists, the tabes dorsalis exists, and so do syphilitic meningitis, robbery, usurpation. Hell is already of this world and there are men who are unhappy runaways from hell, runaways destined to repeat their escape *eternally.* And enough of this!

Man is miserable, the soul is weak, there are men who shall always get lost. The means for the lost do not matter; *it is not society's business.*

We have shown well, haven't we, that society can do nothing about it, that it is wasting its time, and that it should no longer persist in being rooted in its own stupidity.

And, in short, *injurious.*

For those who dare face the truth, we know, don't we, the results of the suppression of alcohol in the United States.

A superproduction of madness: beer on a diet of ether; alcohol larded with cocaine, which is sold secretly; multiplied drunkenness, a sort of general drunkenness. *In short, the law of the forbidden fruit.*

The same for opium.

This interdiction which multiplies curiosity for the drug and benefits only the pimps of medicine, or journalism and literature. There are people who have built excremental and famous industries out of their pretended indignation against an inoffensive group of the damned of the drug (inoffensive because so small and always– exceptional), this minority of beings damned by the mind, by the soul, by disease.

Oh, how well the umbilical cord of morality is tied in them. Since their mothers they have never, have they, sinned. They are the apostles, the descendants of the ministers of the gospel; we can only ask ourselves where they draw their indignation from and, above all, how much they have felt by such goings-on and, in any case, what their indignation has done for them.

And, besides, this isn't the question.

In reality, this fury against toxics, and the stupid law that follows it:

1) *is without effect against the need for toxics* which, satisfied or not, is innate to the soul and would induce it to resolutely antisocial gestures, *even if the toxics did not exist;*

2) *exasperates the social need for toxics* and changes it into a secret vice;

3) *is harmful to the real disease,* because this is the real question, the vital knot, the danger-point:

Unfortunately for illness, medicine does exist.

All the laws, all the restrictions, all the campaigns against narcotics will only lead to taking from those in pain and human need, who have irreducible rights over the social state, the solvent of their ills, a food more marvelous to them than bread, and the means at last for their repenetration into life.

Better the plague than morphine, yells official medicine, better hell than life. Only idiots like J. P. Liausu (who besides is an ignorant abortion) pretend that it is necessary to let the *sick soak in their illness.*

And this is where all the vulgar pedantry of certain people shows its hand and gives itself free rein: *in the name of the general good!*

Kill yourself, you who are desperate and you who are tortured in body and soul, lose all hope. There is no more relief for you in this world. The world lives on your graves.

And you, lucid madmen, consumptives, cancer-ridden, chronic meningitics, you are the misunderstood. There is a point in you that no doctor will ever understand and it is this point which, for me, saves you and makes you majestic, pure and marvelous: you are outside life, you are above life, you have pains which the ordinary man does not know, you go beyond the normal level and this is why men are against you, you are poisoning their quietude, you are the dissolvers of their stability. You have irrepressible pains, the essence of which is that they are unadaptable to any known state, incomprehensible to words. You have repeated and unceasing pains, insoluble pains, pains beyond thought, pains which are neither in the body nor the soul, *but which belong to both.* And as for me, I participate in your ills, and I ask you: who dares measure the tranquilizer for you? In the name of what superior light, soul to soul, can they understand us, we who are at the very root of knowledge and of clarity. And this on account of our insistence, our persistence in suffering. We, whom pain makes journey into our souls in search of a calm place to cling to, in search of stability in evil, as the others search for it in good—we aren't mad, we're marvelous doctors, we know the necessary dose for the soul, for sensibility, for the marrow, for thought. We want to be left in peace, the sick must be left in peace, we ask nothing of men, we ask only for relief of our ills. We have well evaluated our life, we know how much restriction it contains confronted by others, and especially confronted by ourselves. We know to what willing flabbiness, to what renunciation of ourselves, to what paralysis of subtleties our malady forces us every day. We are not committing suicide right away. Let us be left in peace in the meanwhile.

(Translated by L. Dejardin)

from **Drugs and the Mind**

R o b e r t   S .   d e   R o p p

According to the cover copy on the 1960 Grove Press paperback edition of *Drugs and the Mind*, Robert S. de Ropp was "a biochemist who works on drugs." It's not in fact clear whether or not he experimented on himself, but his fine volume on the historical varieties of intoxication—from ancient herbs to modern pills—was among the first of its kind. Originally published in 1957, his even, succinct narratives introducing the pioneers of drug testing were a welcome incentive to those who desired to explore for themselves the boundaries of perception tested by such intrepid professionals as S. Weir Mitchell and the sex researcher Havelock Ellis.

IT WAS NOT UNTIL THE END of the nineteenth century that Western scientists became aware of the existence of *peyotl* and began to wonder what properties this insignificant cactus possessed to cause the Indians to encompass it with so splendid a halo of veneration. Earliest of these investigators to describe his own experiences was the American physician Weir Mitchell, who swallowed "on the morning of a busy day," one and a half drams of an extract of mescal buttons followed by further doses in the afternoon. By 5:40 P.M. Mitchell found himself "deliciously at languid ease," and observed floating before his eyes luminous star points and fragments of stained glass. Going into a dark room, he settled down to enjoy the performance evoked by the mysterious action of the drug on the cells of his visual cortex.

> The display which for an enchanted two hours followed was such as I find it hopeless to describe in language which shall convey to others the beauty and splendor of what I saw. Stars, delicate floating films of color, then an abrupt rush of countless points of white light swept across the field of view, as if the unseen millions of the Milky Way were to flow in a sparkling river before my eyes . . . zigzag lines of very bright colors . . . the wonderful loveliness of swelling clouds of more vivid colors gone before I could name them.

In his last vision, Mitchell saw the beach of Newport with its rolling waves as "liquid splendors, huge and threatening, of wonderfully pure green, or red or deep purple, once only deep orange, and with no trace of foam. These water hills of color broke on the beach with myriads of lights of the same tint as the wave."

The author considered it totally impossible to find words to describe the colors. "They still linger visibly in my memory, and left the feeling that I had seen among them colors unknown to my experience."

News of the remarkable properties of *peyotl* spread to Europe, where Havelock Ellis, famed for his pioneer studies in the field of human sexual behavior, decided to experiment with this singular drug. Having obtained in London a small sample of mescal buttons, he settled down in his quiet rooms in the Temple and prepared a decoction from three of the buttons which he drank at intervals between 2:30 and 4:30 P.M.

Weir Mitchell found that he could only see the visions with closed eyes and in a perfectly dark room. I could see them in the dark and with almost equal facility, though they were not of equal brilliancy, when my eyes were wide open. I saw them best, however, when my eyes were closed, in a room lighted only by flickering firelight. This evidently accords with the experience of the Indians, who keep a fire burning brightly throughout their mescal rites.

The visions continued with undiminished brilliance for many hours, and as I felt somewhat faint and muscularly weak, I went to bed, as I undressed being impressed by the red, scaly, bronzed, and pigmented appearance of my limbs whenever I was not directly gazing at them. I had not the faintest desire for sleep; there was a general hyperaesthesia of all the senses as well as muscular irritability, and every slightest sound seemed magnified to startling dimensions. I may also have been kept awake by a vague sense of alarm at the novelty of my condition, and the possibility of further developments.

After watching the visions in the dark for some hours I became a little tired of them and turned on the gas. Then I found that I was able to study a new series of visual phenomena to which previous observers had made no reference.

So impressed was Havelock Ellis by his experiences that he persuaded an artist friend to try the drug. After consuming four of the buttons this artist became violently ill. Paroxysmal attacks of pain in the region of the heart were combined with a sense of imminent death while so great was the dread of light and the dilation of the pupils that the eyelids had to be kept more or less closed. The colored visions did indeed begin at this time but so preoccupied was the artist with his other less pleasant sensations that he had little opportunity to enjoy the strange hues he now perceived.

This artist particularly noted the curious dualism, the split of personality, so often observed by those who enter the strange world to which *peyotl* is the key. On returning to the normal state he experienced that sense of unreality which sometimes assails the spectator of a particularly fascinating play who emerges suddenly into the gray light of the everyday world.

As the year continued Havelock Ellis was tempted to use more of his friends as human guinea pigs to unravel the mysteries of the world of *peyotl*. One, a poet, with an interest in mystical matters and a knowledge of various vision-producing drugs, found the effect of *peyotl* mainly unpleasant and decided he much preferred *hashish*. Another poet was particularly impressed by the "sound-colors" which flowed about him as he played the piano. Havelock Ellis himself found that music had a potent effect on his visions. This was particularly true of Schumann's music, especially of his *Waldscenen* and *Kinderscenen*.

After Havelock Ellis, the next student of *peyotl* was the French pharmacologist Alexandre Rouhier, [but] after these studies little further work was carried out on the effects of crude *peyotl*. The chemists, ever on the lookout for new worlds to conquer, had taken the divine plant into their laboratories, bent on determining the nature of those substances that endow it with its vision-provoking properties. The brown malodorous decoction of the mescal buttons was progressively purified and one crystalline compound after another was separated from the crude material. No less than nine alkaloids were finally crystallized, several of which influenced the behavior of experimental animals. Most poisonous of these alkaloids was lophophorine, which, in doses of about 12 milligrams per kilogram body weight, would produce in rabbits violent convulsions of the type seen in sufferers from tetanus or strychnine poisoning. The substance pellotine produced in man a drowsiness suggesting that it might be of use as a sedative. Anhalonidine, on the other hand, had a stimulating effect on the central nervous system.

But of all the substances isolated from this curious cactus the most important and interesting was called mescaline. To this substance and to this substance alone the extraordinary visions of the *peyotl* eater could be attributed. Mescaline is not a complex substance. It belongs to the large and important group of chemicals known as amines, many of which (for instance, adrenalin and nor-adrenalin) have a powerful action on the chemistry of the body. To be more specific, mescaline is a derivative of ammonia (NH_3) in which one of the hydrogens has been replaced by a chain of carbon atoms. Chemically it is 3, 4, 5-trimethoxy phenyl ethylamine, a substance which can be synthesized without too much difficulty so that those who wish to enjoy the *peyotl*-induced visions need not depend on the cactus for their supply of the drug.

With pure mescaline available, investigators of the properties of the drug no longer had to chew the nauseating cactus or swallow revolting decoctions brewed from its buttons. They left such questionable pleasures to the Indians and continued their studies with the purified essence of the sacred plant, either swallowing or injecting the solution into their persons. Research continued vigorously. From the laboratory of Dr. Beringer in Heidelberg emerged a tome, three hundred and fifteen pages in length, a worthy example of German *Wissenschaftlichkeit,* which remains the most massive contribution on the subject to date. Dr. Beringer's subjects generally took their mescaline in the form of an injection, the dose employed being usually 400 milligrams. Their experiences had much in common with those described by Weir Mitchell and Havelock Ellis, but the metaphysical bent of the Teutonic mind, its tendency to seek the ultimate, the infinite, the inexpressible, added to the already rich spectrum of the mescal experience certain deeper hues not noted by the earlier investigators.

The author, however, would not be doing his duty as an impartial reporter if he did not add that even the glamorous world of mescaline has its darker side. Not everyone can enter its colorful kingdom.

Quite apart from the nausea, anorexia, and insomnia, the mescaline visions themselves are by no means always divine.

For this reason it is improbable that mescaline will ever become widely popular as a means of fleeing the drab realities of the ordinary world. The artificial paradise to which it holds the key is too strange a realm to appeal to the average taste and the cost of getting there, in terms of unpleasant physical reactions, would seem excessive. Many, in fact, would agree with William James that the experience is not worth the *Katzenjammer*.

A Brief Oral History of

Benzedrine Use in the U.S.

H e r b e r t   H u n c k e

Historically the image of the legendary Herbert Huncke will survive under the heading Prototypical Beatnik. In his recently published autobio- graphy, *Guilty of Everything*, seventy-five-year-old Huncke laments, "What's become of the enthusiasm, the interest in doing new things, in trying to further mankind or this world of ours?" His evocative tales of life on the road and in the streets as a hobo, hustler, and drug addict are weighted with conviction and told with compassion. An authentic part of American history, they offer a glimpse into a genuine, neglected per- spective on events too often told from a biased distance. Use of Benzedrine on a large scale in this country, Huncke suggests, was as inevitable as mass addiction to tobacco.

G O BACK TO THE 1930S–though it must have been discovered somewhere in the 20s, I'm almost sure–start from say '32, under cover before '33 I know that–Benzedrine was then only known by a few: nurses and doctors, students at universities where they'd come in contact with science types and medical people, and a few oddballs like myself. I grew up in Chicago, so say at the University of Chicago, someone would say, Man, I have to cram for an exam and I'm exhausted–and some- one would know someone who was a nurse with knowl- edge of this new thing Benzedrine–Hey, why don't you get a few Bennies (right away it was 'Bennies')–I'm guess- ing it started to spread like that, students in-the-know. I learned a lot about amphetamine through them.

Soon I learned that a lot of people who weren't of the underworld were piddling around with the stuff–one ex- perience I had was the summer when I took a job as an elevator boy at the Illinois Athletic Club on Michigan Avenue in Chicago. A guy stepped into the elevator one night and asked me to buy him a bottle of pills–I think two dozen, 10 mgs., for about 89¢. This guy was con- sidered a great athlete, and upper crust–I guess he figured I was only going to be there for a short time, and that I wasn't likely to squeal. Me, I could do a bottle of 20–25 in a period of about three days. It was a stimulating thing, as you know, and you could go for long periods doing things you liked without feeling exhausted. I liked to talk, it was a perfect talking drug. One used it to stay up all night and end up at the jazz joints after hours. Life fasci- nated me no end. To end up over into the Black Belt in the South Side of Chicago–there wasn't anything that knocked me out more.

Everyone's complaint about it though, at the beginning, was that it killed the sex drive–so many stopped using it after a short while. But OK! Perseverance corrected that assumption! See, in those days people were uptight about sex, so psychologically, you know, once Bennie kicked in . . . well, it teases you a little. Sure–it kind of encouraged the freakish aspect–so you had to let go, and when you got going you could go for hours and hours. We found that it *helped* the sex drive! So that's how basic sexual discoveries began to come about–letting go in bed, and then afterwards being less embarrassed to talk about it–they just followed their inclinations!

Benzedrine gets to the mind, too–I don't like to separate the mental from the physical, and while I was jumping around I'd start to think about things I'd never thought of before. Although it gave you all this energy, as I say, it didn't make you angry. One would simply pass out the stuff–no one needed to make a buck off it–one wasn't inclined to steal or anything like that–that wasn't the idea at all. You need a Bennie? Here, I have 10, here's 3 or 4–we weren't so paranoid in those days. . . . And I'd travel around with it, too–town to town, popping. I'd leave Chicago and I could still buy without any problem–this was about the mid-30s. Of course I kept myself well groomed at all times, and while people didn't look down on the drug so much yet it always helps to have a good appearance. Once, I ran into Toledo and I had a problem getting some. It was obviously getting more popular and some drugstores were picking up on that. I had to buy caffeine tablets that time, and I suffered from it–I got ill and could not talk well.

If you start to feel trouble, of course you want to know what the trouble is, right? It still wasn't illegal but it had come to the attention of many people because, I think, workers in the industrial areas and truck drivers were buying it more and more to keep alert on their jobs. I remember in the road stops–in the restroom stalls–seeing *George the Bennie King was here,* or things like that.

It was when they got hip to the pills and they became difficult to get that French & Kline–who had a priority claim as Benzedrine manufacturers in the U.S. to the best of my knowledge (they were located in Pennsylvania, if I recall)–well, they switched over to these nasal inhalers. These quickly became a big item in drug counters. It was put into a small metal container–later plastic–stuffed with some kind of gauze and rolled very tightly with not only Benzedrine, but oil of lettuce and menthol and God knows what else. The problem was you not only got hooked on amphets but on this other shit too! We used to share the inhalers, sitting in a cafeteria with a cup of hot coffee–by the time you got up and walked out you'd be a new man! They were very delightful, just euphoric. The world was beautiful.

They didn't last for very long on the streets–they knew they had a problem almost immediately. Anslinger, who'd already ruined the pot scene, got on the ass of Benzedrine and got carried away with this new thing–Oh, we got something else to take care of now! Don't you know there were a lot of payoffs down the line in the process. The cops–who still didn't know what the fuck amphetamine was on into the '50s–didn't mind because after all what was an inhaler when you came down to it.

By 1939–40, when I hit Times Square, Bennies were illegal but there were those of us who still managed. Over on Eighth Ave there were a couple of drugstores tucked away that street people like myself–who hadn't tipped our mits–used to get by.

(as told to Donald Kennison)

A Fundamental Experiment

René Daumal

As Rimbaudian poet
and boy wonder in Paris
between the wars, Daumal
participated in occasional
surrealist exercises, though
his relationships with its self-
appointed leaders were—to
his credit—almost always
contentious. A self-taught
scholar, Daumal was well
versed in the arts, science,
and religious matters. His
narrative on crossing the
threshold of consciousness,
written shortly before his
early death in 1944, displays
his broad knowledge as well
as his unswerving conviction,
which was equaled by
his visionary ideals.

THE SIMPLE FACT OF THE MATTER is beyond telling. In
the eighteen years since it happened, I have often tried
to put it into words. Now, once and for all, I should like
to employ every resource of language I know in giving an
account of at least the outward and inward circumstances.
This 'fact' consists in a certainty I acquired by accident
at the age of sixteen or seventeen; ever since then, the
memory of it has directed the best part of me toward seeking a means of finding it again, and for good.

My memories of childhood and adolescence are deeply
marked by a series of attempts to experience the beyond,
and those random attempts brought me to the ultimate
experiment, the fundamental experience of which I speak.
At about the age of six, having been taught no kind of religious belief whatsoever, I struck up against the stark problem of death. I passed some atrocious nights, feeling my
stomach clawed to shreds and my breathing half throttled
by the anguish of nothingness, the 'no more of anything.'
One night when I was about eleven, relaxing my entire
body, I calmed the terror and revulsion of my organism
before the unknown, and a new feeling came alive in me;
hope, and a foretaste of the imperishable. But I wanted
more, I wanted a certainty. At fifteen or sixteen I began
my experiments, a search without direction or system.

Finding no way to experiment directly on death–on
my death–I tried to study my sleep, assuming an analogy
between the two. By various devices I attempted to enter
sleep in a waking state. The undertaking is not so utterly
absurd as it sounds, but in certain respects it is perilous.
I could not go very far with it; my own organism gave me
some serious warnings of the risks I was running. One
day, however, I decided to tackle the problem of death it-

self. I would put my body into a state approaching as close as possible that of physiological death, and still concentrate all my attention on remaining conscious and registering everything that might take place. I had in my possession some carbon tetrachloride, which I used to kill beetles for my collection. Knowing this substance belongs to the same chemical family as chloroform (it is even more toxic), I thought I could regulate its action very simply and easily: the moment I began to lose consciousness, my hand would fall from my nostrils carrying with it the handkerchief moistened with the volatile fluid. Later on I repeated the experiment in the presence of friends, who could have given me help had I needed it. The result was always exactly the same; that is, it exceeded and even overwhelmed my expectations by bursting the limits of the possible and by projecting me brutally into another world.

First came the ordinary phenomena of asphyxiation: arterial palpitation, buzzings, sounds of heavy pumping in the temples, painful repercussions from the tiniest exterior noises, flickering lights. Then, the distinct feeling: 'This is getting serious. The game is up,' followed by a swift recapitulation of my life up to that moment. If I felt any slight anxiety, it remained indistinguishable from a bodily discomfort that did not affect my mind. And my mind kept repeating to itself: 'Careful, don't doze off. This is just the time to keep your eyes open.' The luminous spots that danced in front of my eyes soon filled the whole of space, which echoed with the beat of my blood—sound and light overflowing space and fusing in a single rhythm. By this time I was no longer capable of speech, even of interior speech; my mind travelled too rapidly to carry any words along with it. I realized, in a sudden illumination, that I still had control of the hand which held the handkerchief, that I still accurately perceived the position of my body, and that I could hear and understand words uttered nearby—but that objects, words, and meanings of words had lost any significance whatsoever. It was a little like having repeated a word over and over until it shrivels and dies in your mouth: you still know what the word 'table' means, for instance, you could use it correctly, but it no longer truly evokes its object. In the same way everything that made up 'the world' for me in my ordinary state was still there, but I felt as if it had been drained of its substance. It was nothing more than a phantasmagoria—empty, absurd, clearly outlined, and necessary all at once. This 'world' lost all reality because I had abruptly entered another world, infinitely more real, an instantaneous and intense world of eternity, a concentrated flame of reality and evidence into which I had cast myself like a butterfly drawn to a lighted candle. Then, at that moment, comes the *certainty;* speech must now be content to wheel in circles around the bare fact.

Certainty of what? Words are heavy and slow, words are too shapeless or too rigid. With these wretched words I can put together only approximate statements, whereas *my certainty* is for me the archetype of precision. In my ordinary state of mind, all that remains thinkable and formulable of this experiment reduces to one affirmation on which I would stake my life: I feel the certainty of the existence of *something else,* a beyond, another world, or another form of knowledge. In the moment just described, I knew directly, I experienced that beyond in its very reality. It is important to repeat that in that new state I perceived and perfectly comprehended the ordinary state of being, the latter being contained within the former, as waking consciousness contains our unconscious dreams, and not the reverse. This last irreversible relation proves the superiority (in the scale of reality or consciousness) of the first state over the second. I told myself clearly: in a little while I shall return to the so-called 'normal state,' and perhaps the memory of this fearful revelation will cloud over; but it is in this moment that I see the truth. All this came to me without words; meanwhile I was pierced by an even more commanding thought. With a swiftness approaching the instantaneous, it thought itself so to speak in my very substance: for all eternity I was trapped, hurled faster and faster toward ever imminent annihilation through the terrible mechanism of the Law that rejected me. 'That's what it is. So that's what it is.' My mind found no other reaction. Under the threat of something *worse,* I had to follow the movement. It took a tremendous effort, which became more and more difficult, but I was *obliged* to make that effort, until the moment when, letting go, I doubtless fell into a brief spell of unconsciousness. My hand dropped the handkerchief, I breathed air, and for the rest of the day I remained dazed and stupefied—with a violent headache.

I shall now try to bring that wordless *certainty* into focus by means of images and concepts. To begin with, it must be understood that this certainty exists on a *higher level of significance* than that of our usual thoughts. We are accustomed to use images or illustrations to signify concepts; for example a drawing of a circle to represent the concept of a circle. In the state I am describing the concept itself is no longer the final term, the thing signified; the concept—or idea in the usual sense of the word—is itself the sign of something higher. Let me recall that at the moment when the *certainty* revealed itself, my ordinary intellectual mechanisms continued to function; images took shape, ideas and judgments formed in my mind, but free from the weight and tangle of words. This last condition accelerated these operations to the speed of simultaneousness that they often have in moments of great danger—as when one falls while mountain climbing for example.

Thus the images and concepts I am going to describe were present at the time of the experiment on a level of reality intermediate between the appearance of our everyday 'exterior world' and the *certainty* itself. A few of these images and concepts, however, grew out of my having written down later a partially coherent account. Such an account was necessary, for as soon as I wanted to relate the experience to anyone, and first of all to myself, I had to use words and therefore to develop certain implicit aspects of these images and concepts.

Even though the two occurred simultaneously, I shall start with the images. They were both visual and auditory. In the first case, they took the form of what seemed a veil or screen of luminous spots, a veil more real than the ordinary 'world,' which I could still make out behind it. A circle, half red and half black, inscribed itself in a triangle colored in the same fashion, with the red half-circle against the black segment of triangle, and vice versa. And all space was endlessly divided thus into circles and triangles inscribed one within another, combining and moving in harmony, and changing into one another in a geometrically inconceivable manner that could not be reproduced in ordinary reality. A sound accompanied this luminous movement, and I suddenly realized it was I who was making it. In fact I virtually *was* that sound; I sustained my existence by emitting it. The sound consisted of a chant or formula, which I had to repeat faster and faster in order to 'follow the movement.' That formula (I give the facts with no attempt to disguise their absurdity) ran something like this: 'Tem gwef tem gwef dr rr rr,' with an accent on the second 'gwef' and with the last syllable blending back into the first; it gave an unceasing pulse to the rhythm, which was, as I have said, that of my very being. I knew that as soon as it began going too fast for me to follow, the unnameable and frightful thing would occur. In fact it was always *infinitely close* to happening, and infinitely remote . . . that is all I can say.

The concepts revolve around a central idea of *identity:* everything is perpetually one and the same. They took the form of spatial, temporal, and numerical diagrams–diagrams that were present at the time but whose separation into these categories naturally came later along with the verbal description.

The space in which these shapes arose was not Euclidean, for it was so constructed that any indefinite extension of a point returned to itself. That is, I believe, what mathematicians call 'curved space.' Transposed into a Euclidian scheme, the movement could be described as follows. Imagine an immense circle whose circumference reaches the infinite and which is perfect and unbroken *except for one point;* subsequently this point expands into a circle that grows indefinitely, extends its circumference to infinity and merges with the original circle, perfect, pure and unbroken except for one point, which expands into a circle . . . and so on unceasingly, and in fact instantaneously, for at each instant the circumference, enlarged to infinity, reappears simultaneously as a *point;* not a central point, that would be too perfect; but an eccentric point that represents at the same time the nothingness of my existence and the disequilibrium that my existence, by its particularity, introduces into the immense circle of the All–the All which perpetually *obliterates me,* reasserting its undiminished integrity. For it is I alone who am *diminished.*

In respect to time, the scheme of things is perfectly analogous. This movement of an indefinite expansion returning to its origin takes place as duration (a 'curved' duration) as well as space: the last movement is forever identical with the first, it all vibrates simultaneously in an instant, and only the necessity of representing all this in our ordinary 'time' obliges me to speak of an infinite *repetition.* What I see I have always seen and shall always see, again and again; everything recommences in identical fashion at each instant, as if the total nullity of my particular existence within the unbroken substance of the Immobile were the cause of a cancerous proliferation of instants.

In respect to *number,* the indefinite multiplication of points, circles, and triangles dissolves the same way, instantaneously, into a regenerated Unity, perfect *except for me;* and this *except for me,* throwing the unity of the All into disequilibrium, engenders an indefinite and instantaneous multiplication, which immediately merges with the uttermost limit, with a regenerated Unity, perfect *except for me* . . . and everything starts all over again, always in the same place, in the same eternal instant, and without producing any true alteration in the nature of the All.

If I continued thus to try to enclose my *certainty* in any sequence of logical categories, I should be reduced to the same absurd expressions: in the category of causality, for example, cause and effect perpetually blending into one another and separating from one another, passing from one pole to the other because of the disequilibrium produced in their substantial identity by the infinitesimal hole which I *am.*

I have said enough to make it clear that the certainty of which I speak is in equal degrees mathematical, experimental, and emotional: a *mathematical* certainty—or rather *mathematico-logical*—as one can understand indirectly in the conceptual description I have just attempted and which can be abstractly stated as follows: the identity of the existence and the non-existence of the finite in the infinite; an *experimental* certainty, not only because it is based on direct vision (that would be observation and not necessarily experimentation), not only because the experiment can be repeated at any time, but because I ceaselessly tested the certainty in my struggle to 'follow the movement' that rejected me, a struggle in which I could only repeat the little chant I had found as my sole response; an *emotional* certainty because in the whole affair—the core of the experiment lies here—it is I who am at stake: I saw my own nothingness face to face, or rather my perpetual annihilation, total but not absolute annihilation: a mathematician will understand me when I describe it as 'asymptote.'

I insist on the triple nature of this certainty in order to anticipate three kinds of incomprehension in the reader. First, I want to keep lazy minds from falling into the illusion of understanding me when they find only a vague sense of the mystery of the beyond to correspond to my mathematical certainty. Second, I want to prevent psychologists and especially psychiatrists from treating my testimony not as testimony at all but as an interesting psychic manifestation worth studying and explaining by what they believe to be their 'psychological science.' It is in order to forestall their attempts that I have insisted on the experimental nature (and not simply the introspective experience) of my certainty. Third, at the very heart of this certainty, the cry: 'It's I, I who am at stake,' should frighten the curious who think they might like to perform the same or a similar experiment. I warn them now, it is a terrifying experience, and if they want more precise information on its dangers, they can ask me in private. I do not mean the physiological dangers (which are very great); for if, in return for accepting grave illness or infirmity, or for a considerable shortening of the span of physical life, one could attain to a *single* certainty, the price would not be too high. I am not speaking, moreover, only of the dangers of insanity or of damage to the mind, which I escaped by extraordinary good luck. The danger is far graver, comparable to what happened to Bluebeard's wife: she opens the door of the forbidden room, and the horrible spectacle sears her innermost being as with a white-hot iron. After the first experiment, in effect, I was 'unhinged' for several days, cut adrift from what is customarily called 'the real.' Everything seemed to me an absurd phantasmagoria, no logic could convince me of anything, and, like a leaf in the wind, I was ready to obey the faintest interior or exterior impulse. This state almost involved me in irreparable 'actions' (if the word still applies), for nothing held any importance for me any longer. I subsequently repeated the experiment several times, always with exactly the same result; or rather I always found the same moment, the same instant eternally coexisting with the illusory unfolding of my life. Having once seen the danger, however, I stopped repeating the test. Nevertheless, several years later I was given an anaesthetic for a minor operation. The identical thing happened: I confronted the same unique instant, this time, it is true, to the point of total unconsciousness.

My certainty, naturally, had no need of exterior confirmation; rather it suddenly cleared up for me the meaning of all kinds of narratives that other men have tried to make of the same revelation. I understood, in effect, that I was not the only one, not an isolated or pathological case in the cosmos. First of all, several of my friends tried the same experiment. For the most part nothing happened except the ordinary phenomena preceding narcosis. Two of them went a little further, but brought back with them only vague recollections of a profound bewilderment. One said it was like the advertisements for a certain aperitif, in which two waiters are carrying two bottles, whose labels show two waiters carrying two bottles, whose labels . . . The other painfully searched his memory in the attempt to explain: 'Ixian, ixian i, ixian, ixian i . . .' It was obviously his version of 'Tem gwef tem gwef dr rr rr . . .' But a third friend experienced exactly the same reality that I had encountered, and we only needed to exchange a look to know we had seen the same thing. It was Roger Gilbert-Lecomte, with whom I was to edit the review, *Le Grand Jeu;* its tone of profound conviction was nothing more than the reflection of the certainty we shared. And I am convinced that this experience determined the direction his life would take as it did mine, even if somewhat differently.

Little by little I discovered in my reading accounts of the same experience, for I now held the key to these narratives and descriptions whose relation to a single and unique reality I should not previously have suspected. William James speaks of it. O.V. de L. Milosz, in his *Letter to Storge,* gives an overwhelming account of it in terms I had been using myself. The famous circle referred to by a medieval monk, and which Pascal saw (but who first saw it and spoke of it?) ceased to be an empty allegory for me; I knew it represented a devouring vision of what I had seen also. And, beyond all this varied and partial human testimony (there is scarcely a single true poet in whose work I did not find at least a fragment of it), the confessions of the great mystics and, still more advanced, the sacred texts of certain religions, brought me an affirmation of the same reality.

Sometimes I found it in its most terrifying form, as perceived by an individual of limited vision who has not raised himself to the level of such perception, who, like myself, has tried to look into the infinite through the keyhole and finds himself staring into Bluebeard's cupboard. Sometimes I encountered it in the pleasing, plentifully satisfying and intensely luminous form that is the vision of beings truly transformed, who can behold that reality face to face without being destroyed by it. I have in mind the revelation of the Divine Being in the *Bhagavad-Gita*, the vision of Ezekiel and that of St. John the Divine on Patmos, certain descriptions in the *Tibetan Book of the Dead (Bardo thôdol)*, and a passage in the *Lankâvatâra-Sûtra*.

Not having lost my mind then and there, I began little by little to philosophize about the memory of this experience. And I would have buried myself in a philosophy of my own if someone had not come along just in time to tell me: 'Look, the door is open–narrow and hard to reach, but a door. It is the only one for you.'

(Translated by Roger Shattuck)

from **Lame Deer:**

Seeker of Visions

John (Fire) Lame Deer
with Richard Erdoes

A full-blooded Sioux, Lame Deer was born on the Rosebud reservation in South Dakota around the turn of the century. Unlike Hollywood images of the stoic and peacefully wise medicine man, Lame Deer was a reckless and violent rebel as a young man—a heavy drinker, a womanizer, an outlaw—and when he wasn't in prison he worked at menial jobs such as rodeo clown. As is clear in his as-told-to autobiography, throughout his eventful life his passionate determination invariably strengthened his fierce will and vision. Eventually, as a Holy Man of the Lakota tribe, he instructed his people from his experiences. After several years of peyote use while a young man, Lame Deer—in his typically atypical fashion— voluntarily gave it up altogether. Not to be outdone by a mere plant, he concluded that his own highly engaged mind and heart were the only stimuli he needed in this life.

I WAS ABOUT TWENTY-ONE YEARS OLD when some men told me, "There's a new, powerful medicine. It's going to whirl you around. It will make you see God." As with the ghost dance, the men who brought us this new medicine were not from our own tribe. One was an Arapaho and the other a Black Foot, a man called Lone Bear.

I wanted to experience this and I went to their first meeting in a lonely shack. Six men were sitting on the floor of an empty room. They had a half-gallon can full of cut-up peyote. The Arapaho and the Black Foot were talking in their language. I couldn't make it out, but I understood what they were trying to say: "Eat this and you will see a new light!" I felt strange taking this new medicine and took only a few tablespoons at first. The peyote was powerful. The drum got into me. The gourd got into me. There were voices coming to me out of that rattle. I was closing my eyes, looking inward, into myself, hunkered down on my haunches, my back against the wall, feeling my bones through my skin. I like the pejuta because it whirled me around. By midnight I was having visions. First I saw a square turning into a circle, into a half moon, into a beaded belt–green and blue–which was spinning around me. I could see myself as if looking down from a high mountain, sitting with the other six men, seeing myself crouching in the corner of that log house.

Suddenly I was back within myself. My eyes were on the logs, which seemed very close by, like looking through a magnifying glass. I saw something crawling out between the chinks. It was a big ant, maybe ten feet high, the biggest ant there ever was, all horns, shiny like a lobster. As the ant grew bigger, the room expanded with it. I saw insects starting to eat me. I got scared and tried to get away but couldn't move. The leader, the road man, could tell that I was seeing something. He knew how. I felt. He whirled his gourd around, shook his fan of feathers at me. I came back to life, back from someplace outside the log house, it seemed to me.

I was confused. I tried to think about somebody I loved, my grandmother, my uncle–but it didn't work. My thoughts were getting away from me like a stampeding herd. I tried to think about white men, about the frog-skin world–and that didn't work. I tried to think about animals but was unable to concentrate. The men had told me, "Eat this and you will see God." I did not see God. I couldn't think in complete words, only in syllables, one syllable at a time.

I made a prayer to the Great Spirit to help me, show me. A sweet smell came up not in my nostrils but in my mind. It wasn't a perfume or a scent from nature. Only I could smell it. I saw a book turn into a rock, the rock turn into a cave. I didn't know what to make of it, but there was something *wakan,* something sacred there. I knew it was good, but it scared me at the same time.

The leader handed me the staff and the gourd. It was my turn to sing, but I didn't know how and they had to pass me by. When the sun finally came up I was exhausted and lightheaded. I was shook up. Something had happened that I could not explain. It would take a long time to think about it.

I became a peyoter for a number of years and went regularly to their meetings, but I did not give myself up wholly to it. I also got myself deeper into our old Sioux beliefs, the spirit world; listened to preachers, herb men and the *yuwipi.* I was slowly forming an idea of where I wanted to go. I could dimly see my place, but I could also see a number of different roads leading up to it and I did not yet know which one to take. So I tried them all, coming to many dead ends.

The police tried to stamp out this new peyote cult, as they had stamped out the ghost dance, not because peyote was a drug–drugs weren't on our mind then–but because it was Indian, a competition to the missionaries. The police didn't like me very much anyhow, aside from the peyote. I had a place in Pine Ridge and another one in Rosebud. At Pine Ridge I kept a girl. We weren't married according to the white man's view. The missionaries called it a common-law arrangement. They didn't allow this at that time and threw you in jail for it. They said, "You can't stay together with a girl unless you are properly married–our way."

I had gone to a peyote meeting and the police came and raided it. They came at twilight. I guess they must have smelled it or somebody had tipped them off. They broke the door open looking for the peyote but couldn't find any. It was kept two miles away from the house and hadn't been brought in yet for the meeting. As they turned the kerosene lamp up, they saw me. At once they forgot about the peyote and took after me. I was a badman in their eyes, a bad example to all the little sheep on the reservation.

The cabin was only a thousand feet away from the border line between the reservations. The Pine Ridge *and* the Rosebud police were in on the raid, but each had to stay on his own side of the line. They were not supposed to cross it. I ran along the boundary, the Rosebud patrol car on one side, the Pine Ridge wagon on the other. They were taking pot shots at me to make me stop, but I knew they weren't trying to hit me; they didn't dare. If the Rosebud police came too close, I jumped across into Pine Ridge territory and the other way round, hopping back and forth across that line like some oversized grasshopper. Just when I was all tuckered out, my heart pounding like mad, I got into the pine hills where their cars couldn't follow me. They got out with their guns drawn, trying to keep up with me, but I lost them in the dark. They arrested my girl friend, but when I completely disappeared they turned her loose. They watched her, put her out as bait. But I wasn't that easy to catch. I lit out for Standing Rock for a while to let things cool down. I had a beautiful nest out there on the prairie for my girl.

I was a peyoter for six years. After that I quit it. I found out that it was not my way. It was a dead end, a box canyon, and I had to find my way out of it. I don't want to talk down this peyote cult. In many Indian tribes they have people believing in this medicine. Grandfather Peyote brings many people together, not only as members of this religion but as Indians, and that is good. Some tribes have had peyote for so long that it has become their main and only religion. Many people have forgotten their old beliefs, which the missionaries stamped out, and only the peyote is left; it is the only Indian belief they know. But for us Sioux it is something fairly new, different from our belief in the Great Spirit and the sacred pipe. Slowly I came to realize that I should not mix up these two beliefs, confuse them with each other. I felt that the time had come for me to choose–the pipe or the peyote. I chose the pipe.

At the time I quit peyote I had found out what a real Sioux vision was like. If you dream, that's no vision. Anybody can dream. And if you take a herb–well, even the butcher boy at his meat counter will have a vision after eating peyote. The real vision has to come out of your own juices. It is not a dream; it is very real. It hits you sharp and clear like an electric shock. You are wide awake and, suddenly, there is a person standing next to you who you know can't be there at all. Or somebody is sitting close by, and all at once you see him also up on a hill half a mile away. Yet you are not dreaming; your eyes are open. You have to work for this, empty your mind for it.

Peyote is for the poor people. It helps to get them out of their despair, gives them something to grab hold of, but I couldn't stop there, I had to go further. Once you have experienced the real thing you will never be satisfied with anything else. It will be all or nothing for you then.

The find-out, it has lasted my whole life. In a way I was always hopping back and forth across the boundary line of the mind.

Seeking the Magic Mushroom

R .   G o r d o n   W a s s o n

This first-person account of Mexican Indian ritualistic use of hallucinogenic mushrooms first appeared in, of all places, the May 13, 1957, issue of *Life* magazine. Its author, Gordon Wasson—son of a minister and vice-president of a bank—was a friend of the Luces, founders of the most popular family magazine in America, who were attracted by the mystique of psychedelics and enthusiastically partook themselves. Wasson and his wife shared an abiding interest in mushrooms of all kinds. Thus it was perhaps inevitable that the Wassons were led to Mexico, the sacred land of "God's flesh," where Gordon Wasson participated in and described the first recorded mushroom trip. On later pilgrimages to the small Oaxacan village of his first experience, Wasson accepted the dubious patronage of the CIA, whose ears pricked up on learning of his happy success in the field of "drug research."

ON THE NIGHT OF JUNE 29–30, 1955, in a Mexican Indian village so remote from the world that most of the people still speak no Spanish, my friend Allan Richardson and I shared with a family of Indian friends a celebration of "holy communion" where "divine" mushrooms were first adored and then consumed. The Indians mingled Christian and pre-Christian elements in their religious practices in a way disconcerting for Christians but natural for them. The rite was led by two women, mother and daughter, both of them *curanderas,* or shamans. The proceedings went on in the Mixeteco language. The mushrooms were of a species with hallucinogenic powers; that is, they cause the eater to see visions. We chewed and swallowed these acrid mushrooms, saw visions, and emerged from the experience awestruck. We had come from afar to attend a mushroom rite but had expected nothing so staggering as the virtuosity of the performing *curanderas* and the astonishing effects of the mushrooms. Richardson and I were the first white men in recorded history to eat the divine mushrooms, which for centuries have been a secret of certain Indian peoples living far from the great world in southern Mexico. No anthropologists had ever described the scene that we witnessed.

I am a banker by occupation and Richardson is a New York society photographer and is in charge of visual education at the Brearley School.

It was, however, no accident that we found ourselves in the lower chamber of that thatch-roofed, adobe-walled Indian home. For both of us this was simply the latest trip to Mexico in quest of the mushroom rite. For me and my wife, who was to join us with our daughter a day later, it was a climax to nearly 30 years of inquiries and research into the strange role of the toadstools in the early cultural history of Europe and Asia.

Thus that June evening found us, Allan Richardson and me, deep in the south of Mexico, bedded down with an Indian family in the heart of the Mixeteco mountains at an altitude of 5,500 feet. We could stay only a week or so: we had no time to lose. I went to the *municipio* or town hall, and there I found the official in charge, the *síndico,* seated alone at his great table in an upper room. He was a young Indian, about 35 years old, and he spoke Spanish well. His name was Filemón. He had a friendly manner and I took a chance. Leaning over his table, I asked him earnestly and in a low voice if I could speak to him in confidence. Instantly curious, he encouraged me. "Will you," I went on, "help me learn the secrets of the divine mushroom?" and I used the Mixeteco name, *'nti sheeto,* correctly pronouncing it with glottal stop and tonal differentiation of the syllables. When Filemón recovered from his surprise he said warmly that nothing could be easier. He asked me to pass by his house, on the outskirts of town, at siesta time.

Allan and I arrived there at about 3 o'clock. Filemón's home is built on a mountain-side, with a trail on one side at the level of the upper story and a deep ravine on the other. Filemón at once led us down the ravine to a spot where the divine mushrooms were grow-ing in abundance. After photographing them we gathered them in a cardboard box and then labored back up the ravine in the heavy moist heat of that torrid afternoon. Not letting us rest Filemón sent us high up above his house to meet the *curandera,* the woman who would officiate at the mushroom rite. A connection of his, Eva Mendez by name, she was a *curandera de primera categoría,* of the highest quality, *una Señora sin mancha,* a woman without stain. We found her in the house of her daughter, who pursues the same vocation. Eva was resting on a mat on the floor from her previous night's perfor-mance. She was middle-aged, and short like all Mixetecos, with a spirituality in her ex-pression that struck us at once. She had presence. We showed our mushrooms to the woman and her daughter. They cried out in rapture over the firmness, the fresh beauty and the abundance of our young specimens. Through an interpreter we asked if they would serve us that night. They said yes.

About 20 of us gathered in the lower chamber of Filemón's house after 8 o'clock that evening. Allan and I were the only strangers, the only ones who spoke no Mixeteco. Only our hosts, Filemón and his wife, could talk to us in Spanish. The welcome accorded to us was of a kind that we had never experienced before in the Indian country. Everyone ob-served a friendly decorum. They did not treat us stiffly, as strange white men; we were of their number. The Indians were wearing their best clothes, the women dressed in their *huipiles* or native costumes, the men in clean white trousers tied around the waist with strings and their best serapes over their clean shirts. They gave us chocolate to drink, some-what ceremonially, and suddenly I recalled the words of the early Spanish writer who had said that before the mushrooms were served, chocolate was drunk. I sensed what we were in for: at long last we were discovering that the ancient communion rite still survived and we were going to witness it. The mushrooms lay there in their box, regarded by everyone respectfully but without solemnity. The mushrooms are sacred and never the butt of the vulgar jocularity that is often the way of the white man with alcohol.

At about 10:30 o'clock Eva Mendez cleaned the mushrooms of their grosser dirt and then, with prayers, passed them through the smoke of resin incense burning on the floor. As she did this, she sat on a mat before a simple altar table adorned with Christian images, the Child Jesus and the Baptism in Jordan. Then she apportioned the mushrooms among the adults. She reserved 13 pair for herself and 13 pair for her daughter. (The mushrooms are always counted in pairs.) I was on tiptoe of expectancy: she turned and gave me six pair in a cup. I could not have been happier: this was the culmination of years of pursuit. She gave Allan six pair too. His emotions were mixed. His wife Mary had consented to his coming only after she had drawn from him a promise not to let those nasty toadstools cross his lips. Now he faced a behavior dilemma. He took the mushrooms, and I heard him mutter in anguish, "My God, what will Mary say!" Then we ate our mushrooms, chewing them slowly, over the course of a half hour. They tasted bad–acrid with a rancid odor that repeated itself. Allan and I were determined to resist any effects they might have, to observe better the events of the night. But our resolve soon melted before the onslaught of the mushrooms.

Before midnight the Señora (as Eva Mendez is usually called) broke a flower from the bouquet on the altar and used it to snuff out the flame of the only candle that was still burning. We were left in darkness and in darkness we remained until dawn. For a half hour we waited in silence. Allan felt cold and wrapped himself in a blanket. A few minutes later he leaned over and whispered, "Gordon, I am seeing things!" I told him not to worry, I was too. The visions had started. They reached a plateau of intensity deep in the night, and they continued at that level until about 4 o'clock. We felt slightly unsteady on our feet and in the beginning were nauseated. We lay down on the mat that had been spread before us, but no one had any wish to sleep except the children, to whom mushrooms are not served. We were never more wide awake, and the visions came whether our eyes were opened or closed. They emerged from the center of the field of vision, opening up as they came, now rushing, now slowly, at the pace that our will chose. They were in vivid color, always harmonious. They began with art motifs, angular such as might decorate carpets or textiles or wallpaper or the drawing board of an architect. Then they evolved into palaces with courts, arcades, gardens–resplendent palaces all laid over with semiprecious stones. Then I saw a mythological beast drawing a regal chariot. Later it was as though the walls of our house had dissolved, and my spirit had flown forth, and I was suspended in mid-air viewing landscapes of mountains, with camel caravans advancing slowly across the slopes, the mountains rising tier above tier to the very heavens. Three days later, when I repeated the same experience in the same room with the same *curanderas,* instead of mountains I saw river estuaries, pellucid water flowing through an endless expanse of reeds down to a measureless sea, all by the pastel light of a horizontal sun. This time a human figure appeared, a woman in primitive costume, standing and staring across the water, enigmatic, beautiful, like a sculpture except that she breathed and was wearing woven colored garments. It seemed as though I was viewing a world of which I was not a part and with which I could not hope to establish contact. There I was, poised in space, a disembodied eye, invisible, incorporeal, seeing but not seen.

The visions were not blurred or uncertain. They were sharply focused, the lines and colors being so sharp that they seemed more real to me than anything I had ever seen with my own eyes. I felt that I was now seeing plain, whereas ordinary vision gives us an imperfect view; I was seeing the archetypes, the Platonic ideas, that underlie the imperfect images of everyday life. The thought crossed my mind: could the divine mushrooms be the secret that lay behind the ancient Mysteries? Could the miraculous mobility that I was now enjoying be the explanation for the flying witches that played so important a part in the folklore and fairy tales of northern Europe? These reflections passed through my mind at the very time that I was seeing the visions, for the effect of the mushrooms is to bring about a fission of the spirit, a split in the person, a kind of schizophrenia, with the rational side continuing to reason and observe the sensations that the other side is enjoying. The mind is attached as by an elastic cord to the vagrant senses.

Meanwhile the Señora and her daughter were not idle. When our visions were still in the initial phases, we heard the Señora waving her arms rhythmically. She began a low, disconnected humming. Soon the phrases became articulate syllables, each disconnected syllable cutting the darkness sharply. Then by stages the Señora came forth with a full-blooded canticle, sung like very ancient music. It seemed to me at the time like an introit to the Ancient of Days. As the night progressed her daughter spelled her at singing. They sang well, never loud, with authority. What they sang was indescribably tender and moving, fresh, vibrant, rich. I had never realized how sensitive and poetic an instrument the Mixeteco language could be. Perhaps the beauty of the Señora's performance was partly an illusion induced by the mushrooms; if so, the hallucinations are aural as well as visual. Not being musicologists, we know not whether the chants were wholly European or partly indigenous in origin. From time to time the singing would rise to a climax and then suddenly stop, and then the Señora would fling forth spoken words, violent, hot, crisp words that cut the darkness like a knife. This was the mushroom speaking through her, God's words, as the Indians believe, answering the problems that had been posed by the participants. This was the Oracle. At intervals, perhaps every half hour, there was a brief intermission, when the Señora would relax and some would light cigarets.

At one point, while the daughter sang, the Señora stood up in the darkness where there was an open space in our room and began a rhythmic dance with clapping or slapping. We do not know exactly how she accomplished her effect. The claps or slaps were always resonant and true. So far as we know, she used no device, only her hands against each other or possibly against different parts of her body. The claps and slaps had pitch, the rhythm at times was complex, and the speed and volume varied subtly. We think the Señora faced successively the four points of the compass, rotating clockwise, but are not sure. One thing is certain: this mysterious percussive utterance was ventriloquistic, each slap coming from an unpredictable direction and distance, now close to our ears, now distant, above, below, here and yonder, like Hamlet's ghost *hic et ubique*. We were amazed and spellbound, Allan and I.

There we lay on our mat, scribbling notes in the dark and exchanging whispered comments, our bodies inert and heavy as lead, while our senses were floating free in space, feeling the breezes of the outdoors, surveying vast landscapes or exploring the recesses of gardens of ineffable beauty. And all the while we were listening to the daughter's chanting and to the unearthly claps and whacks, delicately controlled, of the invisible creatures darting around us.

The Indians who had taken the mushrooms were playing a part in the vocal activity. In the moments of tension they would utter exclamations of wonder and adoration, not loud, responsive to the singers and harmonizing with them, spontaneously yet with art.

On that initial occasion we all fell asleep around 4 o'clock in the morning. Allan and I awoke at 6, rested and heads clear, but deeply shaken by the experience we had gone through. Our friendly hosts served us coffee and bread. We then took our leave and walked back to the Indian house where we were staying, a mile or so away.

From the many mushroom celebrations that I have now witnessed, nine in all, it is clear to me that at least in the Mixeteco country the congregation is indispensable to the rite. Since the congregation, in order to participate, must be brought up in the tradition, any white persons should be greatly outnumbered by the Indians. But this does not mean that the mushrooms lose their potency if not eaten communally. My wife and our daughter Masha, 18, joined us a day after the ceremony that I have described, and on July 5, in their sleeping bags, they ate the mushrooms while alone with us. They experienced the visions too. They saw the same brilliant colors; my wife saw a ball in the Palace of Versailles with figures in period costumes dancing to a Mozart minuet. Again, on August 12, 1955, six weeks after I had gathered the mushrooms in Mexico, I ate them in a dried state in my bedroom in New York, and found that if anything they had gained in their hallucinogenic potency.

It was a walk in the woods, many years ago, that launched my wife and me on our quest of the mysterious mushroom. We were married in London in 1926, she being Russian, born and brought up in Moscow. She had lately qualified as a physician at the University of London. I am from Great Falls, Mont. of Anglo-Saxon origins. In the late summer of 1927, recently married, we spent our holiday in the Catskills. In the afternoon of the first day we went strolling along a lovely mountain path, through woods crisscrossed by the slanting rays of a descending sun. We were young, carefree and in love. Suddenly my bride abandoned my side. She had spied wild mushrooms in the forest, and racing over the carpet of dried leaves in the woods, she knelt in poses of adoration before first one cluster and then another of these growths. In ecstasy she called each kind by an endearing Russian name. She caressed the toadstools, savored their earthy perfume. Like all good Anglo-Saxons, I knew nothing about the fungal world and felt that the less I knew about those putrid, treacherous excrescences the better. For her they were things of grace, infinitely inviting to the perceptive mind. She insisted on gathering them, laughing at my protests, mocking my horror. She brought a skirtful back to the lodge. She cleaned and cooked them. That evening she ate them, alone. Not long married, I thought to wake up the next morning a widower.

These dramatic circumstances, puzzling and painful for me, made a lasting impression on us both. From that day on we sought an explanation for this strange cultural cleavage separating us in a minor area of our lives. Our method was to gather all the information we could on the attitude toward wild mushrooms of the Indo-European and adjacent peoples. We tried to determine the kinds of mushrooms that each people knows, the uses to which these kinds are put, the vernacular names for them. We dug into the etymology, to arrive at the metaphors hidden in their roots. We looked for mushrooms in myths, legends, ballads, proverbs, in the writers who drew their inspiration from folklore, in the clichés of daily conversation, in slang and the telltale recesses of obscene vocabularies. We sought them in the pages of history, in art, in Holy Writ. We were not interested in what people learn about mushrooms from books, but what untutored country folk know from childhood, the folk legacy of the family circle. It turned out that we had happened on a novel field of inquiry.

As the years went on and our knowledge grew, we discovered a surprising pattern in our data: each Indo-European people is by cultural inheritance either "mycophobe" or "mycophile," that is, each people either rejects and is ignorant of the fungal world or knows it astonishingly well and loves it. Our voluminous and often amusing evidence in support of this thesis fills many sections of our new book, and it is there that we submit our case to the scholarly world. The great Russians, we find, are mighty mycophiles, as are also the Catalans, who possess a mushroomic vocabulary of more than 200 names. The ancient Greeks, Celts, and Scandinavians were mycophobes, as are the Anglo-Saxons. There was another phenomenon that arrested our attention: wild mushrooms from earliest times were steeped in what the anthropologists call *mana,* a supernatural aura. The very word "toadstool" may have meant originally the "demonic stool" and been the specific name of a European mushroom that causes hallucinations. In ancient Greece and Rome there was a belief that certain kinds of mushrooms were procreated by the lightning bolt. We made the further discovery that this particular myth, for which no support exists in natural science, is still believed among many widely scattered peoples: the Arabs of the desert, the peoples of India, Persia and the Pamirs, the Tibetans and

Chinese, the Filipinos and the Maoris of New Zealand, and even among the Zapotecs of Mexico. . . . All of our evidence taken together led us many years ago to hazard a bold surmise: was it not probable that, long ago, long before the beginnings of written history, our ancestors had worshipped a divine mushroom? This would explain the aura of the supernatural in which all fungi seem to be bathed. We were the first to offer the conjecture of a divine mushroom in the remote cultural background of the European peoples, and the conjecture at once posed a further problem: what kind of mushroom was once worshipped and why?

Our surmise turned out not to be farfetched. We learned that in Siberia there are six primitive peoples–so primitive that anthropologists regard them as precious museum pieces for cultural study–who use an hallucinogenic mushroom in their shamanistic rites. We found that the Dyaks of Borneo and the Mount Hagen natives of New Guinea also have recourse to similar mushrooms. In China and Japan we came upon an ancient tradition of a divine mushroom of immortality, and in India, according to one school, the Buddha at his last supper ate a dish of mushrooms and was forthwith translated to nirvana.

When Cortez conquered Mexico, his followers reported that the Aztecs were using certain mushrooms in their religious celebrations, serving them, as the early Spanish friars put it, in a demonic holy communion and calling them *teonanacatl*, "God's flesh." But no one at that time made a point of studying this practice in detail, and until now anthropologists have paid little attention to it. We with our interest in mushrooms seized on the Mexican opportunity, and for years have devoted the few leisure hours of our busy lives to the quest of the divine mushroom in Middle America. We think we have discovered it in certain frescoes in the Valley of Mexico that date back to about 400 A.D., and also in the "mushroom stones" carved by the highland Maya of Guatemala that go back in one or two instances to the earliest era of stone carvings, perhaps 1000 B.C.

For a day following our mushroom adventure Allan and I did little but discuss our experience. We had attended a shamanistic rite with singing and dancing among our Mixeteco friends which no anthropologist has ever before described in the New World, a performance with striking parallels in the shamanistic practices of some of the archaic Palaeo-Siberian peoples. But may not the meaning of what we had witnessed go beyond this? The hallucinogenic mushrooms are a natural product presumably accessible to men in many parts of the world, including Europe and Asia. In man's evolutionary past, as he groped his way out from his lowly past, there must have been a moment in time when he discovered the secret of the hallucinatory mushrooms. Their effect on him, as I see it, could only have been profound, a detonator to new ideas. For the mushrooms revealed to him worlds beyond the horizons known to him, in space and time, even worlds on a different plane of being, a heaven and perhaps a hell. For the credulous primitive mind, the mushrooms must have reinforced mightily the idea of the miraculous. Many emotions are shared by men with the animal kingdom, but awe and reverence and the fear of God are peculiar to men. When we bear in mind the beatific sense of awe and ecstasy and caritas engendered by the divine mushrooms, one is emboldened to the point of asking whether they may not have planted in primitive man the very idea of a god.

It is no accident, perhaps, that the first answer of the Spanish-speaking Indian, when I asked about the effect of the mushrooms, was often this: *Le llevan ahí donde Dios está,* "They carry you there where God is," an answer that we have received on several occasions, from Indians in different cultural areas, almost as though it were in a sort of catechism. At all times there have been rare souls–the mystics and certain poets–who have had access without the aid of drugs to the visionary world for which the mushrooms hold the key. William Blake possessed the secret: "He who does not imagine in . . . stronger and better light than his perishing mortal eye can see, does not imagine at all." But I can testify that the mushrooms make those visions accessible to a much larger number. The visions that we saw must have come from within us, obviously. But they did not recall anything that we had seen with our own eyes. Somewhere within us there must lie a repository where these visions sleep until they are called forth. Are the visions a subconscious transmutation of things read and seen and imagined, so transmuted that when they are conjured forth from the depths we no longer recognize them? Or do the mushrooms stir greater depths still, depths that are truly the Unknown?

In each of our successive trips to the Indian peoples of southern Mexico, we have enlarged our knowledge of the use of the divine mushrooms, and as our knowledge has increased, new and exciting questions keep arising. We have found five distinct cultural areas where the Indians invoke the mushrooms, but the usage varies widely in every area. What is needed is a perceptive approach by trained anthropologists in every area, cooperating with mushroom specialists. Of these latter there are in the whole world relatively few: mushrooms are a neglected field in the natural sciences. In this field Professor Roger Heim is known the world over. He is not only a man with vast experience in the field of mushrooms: he is an outstanding scientist in other fields, a man steeped in the humanities, the head of the Muséum National d'Histoire Naturelle in Paris. At an early stage of our inquiries he had lent us his counsel, and in 1956 our progress had been such as to justify him in accompanying us on another field trip. There came with us also a chemist, Professor James A. Moore of the University of Delaware; an anthropologist, Guy Stresser-Péan of the Sorbonne; and once again our loyal friend Allan Richardson as photographer.

This time the immediate problem was to identify the hallucinogenic mushrooms and to command a steady supply of them for laboratory study. This is harder than a layman would think. Though the early Spanish writers wrote about the divine mushrooms four centuries ago, no anthropologist and no mycologist had been sufficiently interested to pursue the problem until our own generation. Those who know these mushrooms are Indians belonging to tribes farthest removed from us culturally, locked in their mountains remote from highways, locked also behind the barrier of their languages. One must win their confidence and overcome their suspicion of white men. One must face the physical discomforts of life and dangers of disease in the Indian villages in the rainy season, when the mushrooms grow. Occasionally a white face is seen in those parts in the dry season, but when the rains come, those rare beings—missionaries, archaeologists, anthropologists, botanists, geologists—vanish. There are other difficulties. Of the seven *curanderos* that by now I have seen take the mushrooms, only two, Eva Mendez and her daughter, were dedicated votaries. Some of the others were equivocal characters. Once we saw a *curandero* take only a token dose of mushrooms, and there was another who ate and served to us a kind of mushroom that had no hallucinogenic properties at all. Had we seen only him, we should have come away thinking that the famed properties of the mushrooms were a delusion, a striking instance of autosuggestion. Do we discover here an effort at deception, or had the dried mushrooms through age lost their peculiar property? Or, much more interesting anthropologically, do some shamans deliberately substitute innocent species for the authentic kinds in a retreat from what is too sacred to be borne? Even when we have won the confidence of a skilled practitioner like Eva, the atmosphere must be right for a perfect performance and there must be an abundance of mushrooms. Sometimes even in the rainy season the mushrooms are scarce, as we have learned from costly experience.

We now know that there are seven kinds of hallucinogenic mushrooms in use in Mexico. But not all the Indians know them even in the villages where they are worshipped, and either in good faith or to make the visitor happy, the *curanderos* sometimes deliver the wrong mushrooms. The only certain test is to eat the mushrooms. Professor Heim and we have thus established beyond challenge the claims of four species. The next best thing is to obtain multiple confirmation from informants unknown to each other, if possible from various cultural areas. This we have done with several additional kinds. We are now certain as to four species, reasonably sure about two other kinds, and inclined to accept the claims of a seventh, these seven belonging to three genera. Of these seven, at least six appear to be new to science. Perhaps in the end we shall discover more than seven kinds.

The mushrooms are not used as therapeutic agents: they themselves do not effect cures. The Indians "consult" the mushrooms when distraught with grave problems. If someone is ill, the mushroom will say what led to the illness and whether the patient will live or die, and what should be done to hasten recovery. If the verdict of the mushroom is for death, the believing patient and his family resign themselves: he loses appetite and soon expires and even before his death they begin preparations for the wake. Or one may consult the mushroom about the stolen donkey and learn where it will be found and who took it. Or if a beloved son has gone out into the world—perhaps as a wetback to the states—the mushroom is a kind of postal service: it will report whether he still lives or is dead, whether he is in jail, married, in trouble or prosperous. The Indians believe that the mushrooms hold the key to what we call extrasensory perception.

Little by little the properties of the mushrooms are beginning to emerge. The Indians who eat them do not become addicts: when the rainy season is over and the mushrooms disappear, there seems to be no physiological craving for them. Each kind has its own hallucinogenic strength, and if enough of one species be not available, the Indians will mix the species, making a quick calculation of the right dosage. The *curandero* usually takes a large dose and everyone else learns to know what his own dose should be. It seems that the dose does not increase with use. Some persons require more than others. An increase in the dose intensifies the experience but does not greatly prolong the effect. The mushrooms sharpen, if anything, the memory, while they utterly destroy the sense of time. On the night that we have described we lived through eons. When it seemed to us that a sequence of visions had lasted for years, our watches would tell us that only seconds had passed. The pupils of our eyes were dilated, the pulse ran slow. We think the mushrooms have no cumulative effect on the human organism. Eva Mendez has been taking them for 35 years, and when they are plentiful she takes them night after night.

The mushrooms present a chemical problem. What is the agent in them that releases the strange hallucinations? We are now reasonably sure that it differs from such familiar drugs as opium, coca, mescaline, hashish, etc. But the chemist has a long road to go before he will isolate it, arrive at its molecular structure and synthesize it. The problem is of great interest in the realm of pure science. Will it also prove of help in coping with psychic disturbances?

My wife and I have traveled far and discovered much since that day 30 years ago in the Catskills when we first perceived the strangeness of wild mushrooms. But what we have already discovered only opens up new vistas for further study. Today we are about to embark on our fifth expedition to the Mexican Indian villages, again seeking to increase and refine our knowledge of the role played by mushrooms in the lives of these remote peoples. But Mexico is only the beginning. All the evidence relating to the primitive beginnings of our own European cultures must be reviewed to see whether the hallucinogenic mushroom played a part there, only to be overlooked by posterity.

from **LSD: My Problem Child**

Albert Hofmann

On April 19, 1943, Dr. Albert Hofmann accidentally experienced the first LSD trip, while experimenting with synthetically derived variations of the ergot alkaloid in his laboratory at Sandoz Pharmaceuticals in Basel, Switzerland. He had been researching this field since the late 1920s, and in the following ten years he was able to synthesize many new lysergic acid derivatives, several of which were of significant medical importance. The twenty-fifth compound in the series, LSD-25, which he believed would act as a respiratory stimulant, Hofmann unknowingly administered to himself during a recrystallizing procedure. Although only a seemingly inconsequential amount fell on his fingers, the incident proved to be a pivotal development in the history of psychoactive substances.

ONE EXPERIMENT, which served as a comparison between LSD and psilocybin, took place in the spring of 1962. The proper occasion for it presented itself at the home of the Jüngers, in the former head forester's house of Stauffenberg's Castle in Wilflingen. My friends, the pharmacologist Professor Heribert Konzett and the Islamic scholar Dr. Rudolf Gelpke, also took part in this mushroom symposium.

The old chronicles described how the Aztecs drank *chocolatl* before they ate *teonanácatl*. Thus Mrs. Liselotte Jünger likewise served us hot chocolate, to set the mood. Then she abandoned the four men to their fate.

We had gathered in a fashionable living room, with a dark wooden ceiling, white tile stove, period furniture, old French engravings on the walls, a gorgeous bouquet of tulips on the table. Ernst Jünger wore a long, broad, dark blue striped kaftan-like garment that he had brought from Egypt; Heribert Konzett was resplendent in a brightly embroidered mandarin gown; Rudolf Gelpke and I had put on housecoats. The everyday reality should be laid aside, along with everyday clothing.

Shortly before sundown we took the drug, not the mushrooms, but rather their active principle, 20 mg psilocybin each. That corresponded to some two-thirds of the very strong dose that was taken by the *curandera* Maria Sabina in the form of *Psilocybe* mushrooms.

After an hour I still noticed no effect, while my companions were already very deeply into the trip. I had come with the hope that in the mushroom inebriation I could manage to allow certain images from euphoric moments of my childhood, which remained in my memory as blissful experiences, to come alive: a meadow covered with chrysanthemums lightly stirred by the early summer wind; the rosebush in the evening light after a rain storm; the blue irises hanging over the vineyard wall. Instead of these bright images from my childhood home, strange scenery emerged, when the mushroom factor finally began to act. Half stupefied, I sank deeper, passed through totally deserted cities with a Mexican type of exotic, yet dead splendor. Terrified, I tried to detain myself on the surface, to concentrate alertly on the outer world, on the surroundings. For a time I succeeded. I then observed Ernst Jünger, colossal in the room, pacing back and forth, a powerful, mighty magician. Heribert Konzett in the silky lustrous housecoat seemed to be a dangerous, Chinese clown. Even Rudolf Gelpke appeared sinister to me, long, thin, mysterious.

With the increasing depth of inebriation, everything became yet stranger. I even felt strange to myself. Weird, cold, foolish, deserted, in a dull light, were the places I traversed when I closed my eyes. Emptied of all meaning, the environment also seemed ghostlike to me whenever I opened my eyes and tried to cling to the outer world. The total emptiness threatened to drag me down into absolute nothingness. I remember how I seized Rudolf Gelpke's arm as he passed by my chair, and held myself to him, in order not to sink into dark nothingness. Fear of death seized me, and illimitable longing to return to the living creation, to the reality of the world of men. After timeless fear I slowly returned to the room. I saw and heard the great magician lecturing uninterruptedly with a clear, loud voice, about Schopenhauer, Kant, Hegel, and speaking about the old Gäa, the beloved little mother. Heribert Konzett and Rudolf Gelpke were already completely on the earth again, while I could only regain my footing with great effort.

For me this entry into the mushroom world had been a test, a confrontation with a dead world and with the void. The experiment had developed differently from what I had expected. Nevertheless, the encounter with the void can also be appraised as a gain. Then the existence of the creation appears so much more wondrous.

Midnight had passed, as we sat together at the table that the mistress of the house had set in the upper story. We celebrated the return with an exquisite repast and with Mozart's music. The conversation, during which we exchanged our experiences, lasted almost until morning.

Ernst Jünger has described how he had experienced this trip, in his book *Annäherungen–Drogen und Rausch* [Approaches–drugs and inebriation] (published by Ernst Klett Verlag, Stuttgart, 1970), in the section "Ein Pilz-Symposium" [A mushroom symposium]. The following is an extract from the work:

As usual, a half hour or a little more passed in silence. Then came the first signs: the flowers on the table began to flare up and sent out flashes. It was time for leaving work; outside the streets were being cleaned, like on every weekend. The brush strokes invaded the silence painfully. This shuffling and brushing, now and again also a scraping, pounding, rumbling, and hammering, has random causes and is also symptomatic, like one of the signs that announces an illness. Again and again it also plays a role in the history of magic practices . . .

By this time the mushroom began to act; the spring bouquet glowed darker. That was no natural light. The shadows stirred in the corners, as if they sought form. I became uneasy, even chilled, despite the heat that emanated from the tiles. I stretched myself on the sofa, drew the covers over my head.

Everything became skin and was touched, even the retina—there the contact was light. This light was multicolored; it arranged itself in strings, which gently swung back and forth; in strings of glass beads of oriental doorways. They formed doors, like those one passes through in a dream, curtains of lust and danger. The wind stirred them like a garment. They also fell down from the belts of dancers, opened and closed themselves with the swing of the hips, and from the beads a rippling of the most delicate sounds fluttered to the heightened senses. The chime of the silver rings on the ankles and wrists is already too loud. It smells of sweat, blood, tobacco, chopped horse hairs, cheap rose essence. Who knows what is going on in the stables?

It must be an immense palace, Mauritanian, not a good place. At this ballroom flights of adjoining rooms lead into the lower stratum. And everywhere the curtains with their glitter, their sparkling, radioactive glow. Moreover, the rippling of glassy instruments with their beckoning, their wooing solicitation: "Will you go with me, beautiful boy?" Now it ceased, now it repeated, more importunate, more intrusive, almost already assured of agreement.

Now came forms—historical collages, the *vox humana,* the call of the cuckoo. Was it the whore of Santa Lucia, who stuck her breasts out of the window? Then the play was ruined. Salome danced; the amber necklace emitted sparks and made the nipples erect. What would one not do for one's Johannes? [1]—damned, that was a disgusting obscenity, which did not come from me, but was whispered through the curtain .

The snakes were dirty, scarcely alive, they wallowed sluggishly over the floor mats. They were garnished with brilliant shards. Others looked up from the floor with red and green eyes. It glistened and whispered, hissed and sparkled like diminutive sickles at the sacred harvest. Then it quieted, and came anew, more faintly, more forward. They had me in their hand. "There we immediately understood ourselves."

Madam came through the curtain: she was busy, passed by me without noticing me. I saw the boots with the red heels. Garters constricted the thick thighs in the middle, the flesh bulged out there. The enormous breasts, the dark delta of the Amazon, parrots, piranhas, semiprecious stones everywhere.

Now she went into the kitchen—or are there still cellars here? The sparkling and whispering, the hissing and twinkling could no longer be differentiated; it seemed to become concentrated, now proudly rejoicing, full of hope.

It became hot and intolerable; I threw the covers off. The room was faintly illuminated; the pharmacologist stood at the window in the white mandarin frock, which had

served me shortly before in Rottweil at the carnival. The orientalist sat beside the tile
stove; he moaned as if he had a nightmare. I understood; it had been a first round, and
it would soon start again. The time was not yet up. I had already seen the beloved little
mother under other circumstances. But even excrement is earth, belongs like gold to
transformed matter. One must come to terms with it, without getting too close.

These were the earthy mushrooms. More light was hidden in the dark grain
that burst from the ear, more yet in the green juice of the succulents on the glow-
ing slopes of Mexico. . . .[2]

The trip had run awry–possibly I should address the mushrooms once more. Yet
indeed the whispering returned, the flashing and sparkling–the bait pulled the fish
close behind itself. Once the motif is given, then it engraves itself, like on a roller each
new beginning, each new revolution repeats the melody. The game did not get beyond
this kind of dreariness.

I don't know how often this was repeated, and prefer not to dwell upon it. Also, there
are things which one would rather keep to oneself. In any case, midnight was past . . .

We went upstairs; the table was set. The senses were still heightened and the Doors
of Perception were opened. The light undulated from the red wine in the carafe; a froth
surged at the brim. We listened to a flute concerto. It had not turned out better for the
others: How beautiful, to be back among men. Thus Albert Hofmann . . .

The orientalist on the other hand had been in Samarkand, where Timur rests in a
coffin of nephrite. He had followed the victorious march through cities, whose dowry
on entry was a cauldron filled with eyes. There he had long stood before one of the
skull pyramids that terrible Timur had erected, and in the multitude of severed heads
had perceived even his own. It was encrusted with stones.

A light dawned on the pharmacologist when he heard this: Now I know why you were
sitting in the armchair without your head–I was astonished; I knew I wasn't dreaming.

I wonder whether I should not strike out this detail since it borders on the area of
ghost stories.

The mushroom substance had carried all four of us off, not into luminous heights,
rather into deeper regions. It seems that the psilocybin inebriation is more darkly colored in the majority of cases than the inebriation produced by LSD. The influence of
these two active substances is sure to differ from one individual to another. Personally,
for me, there was more light in the LSD experiments than in the experiments with the
earthy mushroom, just as Ernst Jünger remarks in the preceding report.

Another LSD Session

The next and last thrust into the inner universe together with Ernst Jünger, this time
again using LSD, led us very far from everyday consciousness. We came close to the ultimate door. Of course this door, according to Ernst Jünger, will in fact only open for

us in the great transition from life into the hereafter.

This last joint experiment occurred in February 1970, again at the head forester's house in Wilflingen. In this case there were only the two of us. Ernst Jünger took 0.15 mg LSD, I took 0.10 mg. Ernst Jünger has published without commentary the log book, the notes he made during the experiment, in *Approaches,* in the section "Nochmals LSD" [LSD once again]. They are scanty and tell the reader little, just like my own records.

The experiment lasted from morning just after breakfast until darkness fell. At the beginning of the trip, we again listened to the concerto for flute and harp by Mozart, which always made me especially happy, but this time, strange to say, seemed to me like the turning of porcelain figures. Then the intoxication led quickly into wordless depths. When I wanted to describe the perplexing alterations of consciousness to Ernst Jünger, no more than two or three words came out, for they sounded so false, so unable to express the experience; they seemed to originate from an infinitely distant world that had become strange; I abandoned the attempt, laughing hopelessly. Obviously, Ernst Jünger had the same experience, yet we did not need speech; a glance sufficed for the deepest understanding. I could, however, put some scraps of sentences on paper, such as at the beginning: "Our boat tosses violently." Later, upon regarding expensively bound books in the library: "Like red-gold pushed from within to without–exuding golden luster." Outside it began to snow. Masked children marched past and carts with carnival revelers passed by in the streets. With a glance through the window into the garden, in which snow patches lay, many-colored masks appeared over the high walls bordering it, embedded in an infinitely joyful shade of blue: "A Breughel garden–I live *with* and *in* the objects." Later: "At present–no connection with the everyday world." Toward the end, deep, comforting insight expressed: "Hitherto confirmed on my path." This time LSD led to a blessed approach.

I am often asked what has made the deepest impression upon me in my LSD experiments, and whether I have arrived at new understandings through these experiences.

Of greatest significance to me has been the insight that I attained as a fundamental understanding from all of my LSD experiments: what one commonly takes as "the reality," including the reality of one's own individual person, by no means signifies something fixed, but rather something that is ambiguous–that there is not only one, but that there are many realities, each comprising also a different consciousness of the ego.

One can also arrive at this insight through scientific reflections. The problem of reality is and has been from time immemorial a central concern of philosophy. It is, however, a fundamental distinction, whether one approaches the problem of reality rationally, with the logical methods of philosophy, or if one obtrudes upon this problem emotionally, through an existential experience. The first planned LSD experiment was therefore so deeply moving and alarming, because everyday reality and the ego experiencing it, which I had until then considered to be the only reality, dissolved, and an unfamiliar ego experienced another, unfamiliar reality. The problem concerning the innermost self also appeared, which, itself unmoved, was able to record these external and internal transformations.

Reality is inconceivable without an experiencing subject, without an ego. It is the product of the exterior world, of the sender and of a receiver, an ego in whose deepest self the emanations of the exterior world, registered by the antennae of the sense organs, become conscious. If one of the two is lacking, no reality happens, no radio music plays, the picture screen remains blank.

If one continues with the conception of reality as a product of sender and receiver, then the entry of another reality under the influence of LSD may be explained by the fact that the brain, the seat of the receiver, becomes biochemically altered. The receiver is thereby tuned into another wavelength than that corresponding to normal, everyday reality. Since the endless variety and diversity of the universe correspond to infinitely many different wavelengths, depending on the adjustment of the receiver, many different realities, including the respective ego, can become conscious. These different realities, more correctly designated as different aspects of *the* reality, are not mutually exclusive but are complementary, and form together a portion of the all-encompassing, timeless, transcendental reality, in which even the unimpeachable core of self-consciousness, which has the power to record the different egos, is located.

The true importance of LSD and related hallucinogens lies in their capacity to shift the wavelength setting of the receiving "self," and thereby to evoke alterations in reality consciousness. This ability to allow different, new pictures of reality to arise, this truly cosmogonic power, makes the cultish worship of hallucinogenic plants as sacred drugs understandable.

What constitutes the essential, characteristic difference between everyday reality and the world picture experienced in LSD inebriation? Ego and the outer world are separated in the normal condition of consciousness, in everyday reality; one stands face-to-face with the outer world, it has become an object. In the LSD state the boundaries between the experiencing self and the outer world more or less disappear, depending on the depth of the inebriation. Feedback between receiver and sender takes place. A portion of the self overflows into the outer world, into objects, which begin to live, to have another, a deeper meaning. This can be perceived as a blessed, or as a demonic transformation imbued with terror, proceeding to a loss of the trusted ego. In an auspicious case, the new ego feels blissfully united with the objects of the outer world and consequently also with its fellow beings. This experience of deep oneness with the exterior world can even intensify to a feeling of the self being one with the universe. This condition of cosmic consciousness, which under favorable conditions can be evoked by LSD or by another hallucinogen from the group of Mexican sacred drugs, is analogous to spontaneous religious enlightenment, with the *unio mystica*. In both conditions, which often last only for a timeless moment, a reality is experienced that exposes a gleam of the transcendental reality, in which universe and self, sender and receiver, are one.[3]

Gottfried Benn, in his essay "Provoziertes Leben" [Provoked life] (in *Ausdruckswelt,* Limes Verlag, Wiesbaden, 1949), characterized the reality in which self and world are separated, as "the schizoid catastrophe, the Western entelechy neurosis." He further writes:

> . . . In the southern part of our continent this concept of reality began to be formed. The Hellenistic-European agonistic principle of victory through effort, cunning, malice, talent, force, and later, European Darwinism and "superman," was instrumental in its formation. The ego emerged, dominated, fought; for this it needed instruments, material, power. It had a different relationship to matter, more removed sensually, but closer formally. It analyzed matter, tested, sorted: weapons, object of exchange, ransom money. It clarified matter through isolation, reduced it to formulas, took pieces out of it, divided it up. [Matter became] a concept which hung like a disaster over the West, with which the West fought, without grasping it, to which it sacrificed enormous quantities of blood and happiness; a concept whose inner tension and fragmentations it was impossible to dissolve through a natural viewing or methodical insight into the inherent unity and peace of prelogical forms of being . . . instead the cataclysmic character of this idea became clearer and clearer . . . a state, a social organization, a public morality, for which life is economically usable life and which does not recognize the world of provoked life, cannot stop its destructive force. A society, whose hygiene and race cultivation as a modern ritual is founded solely on hollow biological statistics, can only represent the external viewpoint of the mass; for this point of view it can wage war, incessantly, for reality is simply raw material, but its metaphysical background remains forever obscured.[4]

As Gottfried Benn formulates it in these sentences, a concept of reality that separates self and the world has decisively determined the evolutionary course of European intellectual history. Experience of the world as matter, as object, to which man stands opposed, has produced modern natural science and technology–creations of the Western mind that have changed the world. With their help human beings have subdued the world. Its wealth has been exploited in a manner that may be characterized as plundering, and the sublime accomplishment of technological civilization, the comfort of Western industrial society, stands face-to-face with a catastrophic destruction of the environment. Even to the heart of matter, to the nucleus of the atom and its splitting, this objective intellect has progressed and has unleashed energies that threaten all life on our planet.

A misuse of knowledge and understanding, the products of searching intelligence, could not have emerged from a consciousness of reality in which human beings are not separated from the environment but rather exist as part of living nature and the universe. All attempts today to make amends for the damage through environmentally protective measures must remain only hopeless, superficial patchwork, if no curing of the "Western entelechy neurosis" ensues, as Benn has characterized the objective reality conception. Healing would mean existential experience of a deeper, self-encompassing reality.

The experience of such a comprehensive reality is impeded in an environment rendered dead by human hands, such as is present in our great cities and industrial districts. Here the contrast between self and outer world becomes especially evident. Sensations of alienation, of loneliness, and of menace arise. It is these sensations that impress themselves on everyday consciousness in Western industrial society; they also take the upper hand everywhere that technological civilization extends itself, and they largely determine the production of modern art and literature.

There is less danger of a cleft reality experience arising in a natural environment. In field and forest, and in the animal world sheltered therein, indeed in every garden, a reality is perceptible that is infinitely more real, older, deeper, and more wondrous than everything made by people, and that will yet endure, when the inanimate, mechanical, and concrete world again vanishes, becomes rusted and fallen into ruin. In the sprouting, growth, blooming, fruiting, death, and regermination of plants, in their relationship with the sun, whose light they are able to convert into chemically bound energy in the form of organic compounds, out of which all that lives on our earth is built; in the being of plants the same mysterious, inexhaustible, eternal life energy is evident that has also brought us forth and takes us back again into its womb, and in which we are sheltered and united with all living things.

We are not leading up to a sentimental enthusiasm for nature, to "back to nature" in Rousseau's sense. That romantic movement, which sought the idyll in nature, can also be explained by a feeling of humankind's separation from nature. What is needed today is a fundamental reexperience of the oneness of all living things, a comprehensive reality consciousness that ever more infrequently develops spontaneously, the more the primordial flora and fauna of our mother earth must yield to a dead technological environment.

The notion of reality as the self juxtaposed to the world, in confrontation with the outer world, began to form itself, as reported in the citation from Benn, in the southern portion of the European continent in Greek antiquity. No doubt people at that time knew the suffering that was connected with such a cleft reality consciousness. The Greek genius tried the cure, by supplementing the multiformed and richly colored, sensual as well as deeply sorrowful Apollonian world view created by the subject/object cleavage, with the Dionysian world of experience, in which this cleavage is abolished in ecstatic inebriation. Nietzsche writes in *The Birth of Tragedy:*

> It is either through the influence of narcotic potions, of which all primitive peoples
> and races speak in hymns, or through the powerful approach of spring, penetrating
> with joy all of nature, that those Dionysian stirrings arise, which in their

intensification lead the individual to forget himself completely. . . . Not only does the bond between man and man come to be forged once again by the magic of the Dionysian rite, but alienated, hostile, or subjugated nature again celebrates her reconciliation with her prodigal son, man.

The Mysteries of Eleusis, which were celebrated annually in the fall, over an interval of approximately 2,000 years, from about 1500 B.C. until the fourth century A.D., were intimately connected with the ceremonies and festivals in honor of the god Dionysus. These Mysteries were established by the goddess of agriculture, Demeter, as thanks for the recovery of her daughter Persephone, whom Hades, the god of the underworld, had abducted. A further thank offering was the ear of grain, which was presented by the two goddesses to Triptolemus, the first high priest of Eleusis. They taught him the cultivation of grain which Triptolemus then disseminated over the whole globe. Persephone, however, was not always allowed to remain with her mother, because she had taken nourishment from Hades, contrary to the order of the highest gods. As punishment she had to return to the underworld for a part of the year. During this time, it was winter on the earth, the plants died and were withdrawn into the ground, to awaken to new life early in the year with Persephone's journey to earth.

The myth of Demeter, Persephone, Hades, and the other gods, which was enacted as a drama, formed, however, only the external framework of events. The climax of the yearly ceremonies, which began with a procession from Athens to Eleusis lasting several days, was the concluding ceremony with the initiation, which took place in the night. The initiates were forbidden by penalty of death to divulge what they had learned, beheld, in the innermost, holiest chamber of the temple, the *telesterion* (goal). Not one of the multitude that were initiated into the secret of Eleusis has ever done this. Pausanias, Plato, many Roman emperors like Hadrian and Marcus Aurelius, and many other known personages of antiquity were party to this initiation. It must have been an illumination, a visionary glimpse of a deeper reality, an insight into the true basis of the universe. That can be concluded from the statements of initiates about the value, about the importance of the vision. Thus it is reported in a Homeric Hymn: "Blissful is he among men on Earth, who has beheld that! He who has not been initiated into the holy Mysteries, who has had no part therein, remains a corpse in gloomy darkness." Pindar speaks of the Eleusinian benediction with the following words: "Blissful is he, who after having beheld this enters on the way beneath the Earth. He knows the end of life as well as its divinely granted beginning." Cicero, also a famous initiate, likewise put in first position the splendor that fell upon his life from Eleusis, when he said: "Not only have we received the reason there, that we may live in joy, but also, besides, that we may die with better hope."

How could the mythological representation of such an obvious occurrence, which runs its course annually before our eyes–the seed grain that is dropped into the earth, dies there, in order to allow a new plant, new life, to ascend into the light—prove to be such a deep, comforting experience as that attested by the cited reports? It is traditional knowledge that the initiates were furnished with a potion, the *kykeon,* for the final ceremony. It is also known that barley extract and mint were ingredients of the *kykeon. Religious scholars and scholars of mythology, like Karl Kerényi, from whose book on the Eleusinian Mysteries (Rhein-Verlag, Zürich, 1962) the preceding statements were taken, and with whom I was associated in relation to the research on this mysterious potion,*[5] are of the opinion that the *kykeon* was mixed with an hallucinogenic drug.[6] That would make understandable the ecstatic-visionary experience of the Demeter-Persephone myth, as a symbol of the cycle of life and death in both a comprehensive and timeless reality.

When the Gothic king Alarich, coming from the north, invaded Greece in 396 A.D. and destroyed the sanctuary of Eleusis, it was not only the end of a religious center, but it also signified the decisive downfall of the ancient world. With the monks that accompanied Alarich, Christianity penetrated into the country that must be regarded as the cradle of European culture.

The cultural-historical meaning of the Eleusinian Mysteries, their influence on European intellectual history, can scarcely be overestimated. Here suffering humankind found a cure for its rational, objective, cleft intellect, in a mystical totality experience, that let it believe in immortality, in an everlasting existence.

This belief had survived in early Christianity, although with other symbols. It is found as a promise, even in particular passages of the Gospels, most clearly in the Gospel according to John, as in Chapter 14: 16–20. Jesus speaks to his disciples, as he takes leave of them:

> And I will pray the Father, and he shall give you another Comforter, that he may abide with you forever;
> *Even the Spirit of truth;* whom the world cannot receive, because it seeth him not, neither knoweth him: but ye know him; for he dwelleth with you, and shall be in you.
> I will not leave you comfortless: I will come to you. Yet a little while, and the world seeth me no more; but ye see me: because I live, ye shall live also.
> *At that day ye shall know that I am in my Father, and ye in me, and I in you.*

This promise constitutes the heart of my Christian beliefs and my call to natural-scientific research: we will attain to knowledge of the universe through the spirit of truth, and thereby to understanding of our being one with the deepest, most comprehensive reality, God.

Ecclesiastical Christianity, determined by the duality of creator and creation, has, however, with its nature-alienated religiosity largely obliterated the Eleusinian-Dionysian legacy of antiquity. In the Christian sphere of belief, only special blessed men have attested to a timeless, comforting reality, experienced in a spontaneous vision, an experience to which in antiquity the elite of innumerable generations had access through the initiation at Eleusis. The *unio mystica* of Catholic saints and the visions that the representatives of Christian mysticism–Jakob Boehme, Meister Eckhart, Angelus Silesius, Thomas Traherne, William Blake, and others–describe in their writings, are obviously essentially related to the enlightenment that the initiates to the Eleusinian Mysteries experienced.

The fundamental importance of a mystical experience, for the recovery of people in Western industrial societies who are sickened by a one-sided, rational materialistic world view, is today given primary emphasis, not only by adherents to Eastern religious movements like Zen Buddhism, but also by leading representatives of academic psychiatry. Of the appropriate literature, we will here refer only to the books of Balthasar Staehelin, the Basel psychiatrist working in Zürich.[7] They make reference to numerous other authors who deal with the same problem. Today a type of "metamedicine," "metapsychology," and "metapsychiatry " is beginning to call upon the metaphysical element in people, which manifests itself as an experience of a deeper, duality-surmounting reality, and to make this element a basic healing principle in therapeutic practice.

In addition, it is most significant that not only medicine but also wider circles of our society consider the overcoming of the dualistic, cleft world view to be a prerequisite and basis for the recovery and spiritual renewal of occidental civilization and culture. This renewal could lead to the renunciation of the materialistic philosophy of life and the development of a new reality consciousness.

As a path to the perception of a deeper, comprehensive reality, in which the experiencing individual is also sheltered, meditation, in its different forms, occupies a prominent place today. The essential difference between meditation and prayer in the usual sense, which is based upon the duality of creator-creation, is that meditation aspires to the abolishment of the I-you-barrier by a fusing of object and subject, of sender and receiver, of objective reality and self.

Objective reality, the world view produced by the spirit of scientific inquiry, is the myth of our time. It has replaced the ecclesiastical-Christian and mythical-Apollonian world view.

But this ever broadening factual knowledge, which constitutes objective reality, need not be a desecration. On the contrary, if it only advances deep enough, it inevitably leads to the inexplicable, primal ground of the universe: the wonder, the mystery of the divine–in the microcosm of the atom, in the macrocosm of the spiral nebula; in the seeds of plants, in the body and soul of people.

Meditation begins at the limits of objective reality, at the farthest point yet reached by rational knowledge and perception. Meditation thus does not mean rejection of objective reality; on the contrary, it consists of a penetration to deeper dimensions of reality. It is not escape into an imaginary dream world; rather it seeks after the comprehensive truth of objective reality, by simultaneous, stereoscopic contemplation of its surfaces and depths.

It could become of fundamental importance, and be not merely a transient fashion of the present, if more and more people today would make a daily habit of devoting an hour, or at least a few minutes, to meditation. As a result of the meditative penetration and broadening of the natural-scientific world view, a new, deepened reality consciousness would have to evolve, which would increasingly become the property of all humankind. This could become the basis of a new religiosity, which would not be based on belief in the dogmas of various religions, but rather on perception through the "spirit of truth." What is meant here is a perception, a reading and understanding of the text at first hand, "out of the book that God's finger has written" (Paracelsus), out of the creation.

The transformation of the objective world view into a deepened and thereby religious reality consciousness can be accomplished gradually, by continuing practice of meditation. It can also come about, however, as a sudden enlightenment; a visionary experience. It is then particularly profound, blessed, and meaningful. Such a mystical experience may nevertheless "not be induced even by decade-long meditation," as Balthasar Staehelin writes. Also, it does not happen to everyone, although the capacity for mystical experience belongs to the essence of human spirituality.

Nevertheless, at Eleusis, the mystical vision, the healing, comforting experience, could be arranged in the prescribed place at the appointed time, for all of the multitudes who were initiated into the holy Mysteries. This could be accounted for by the fact that an hallucinogenic drug came into use; this, as already mentioned, is something that religious scholars believe.

The characteristic property of hallucinogens, to suspend the boundaries between the experiencing self and the outer world in an ecstatic, emotional experience, makes it possible with their help, and after suitable internal and external preparation, as it was accomplished in a perfect way at Eleusis, to evoke a mystical experience according to plan, so to speak.

Meditation is a preparation for the same goal that was aspired to and was attained in the Eleusinian Mysteries. Accordingly it seems feasible that in the future, with the help of LSD, the mystical vision, crowning meditation, could be made accessible to an increasing number of practitioners of meditation.

I see the true importance of LSD in the possibility of providing material aid to meditation aimed at the mystical experience of a deeper, comprehensive reality. Such a use accords entirely with the essence and working character of LSD as a sacred drug.

Footnotes

[1] Translator's note: "Johannes" here is slang for penis, as in English "Dick" or "Peter."

[2] Jünger is referring to LSD, a derivative of ergot, and mescaline, derived from the Mexican *péyotl* cactus.

[3] The relationship of spontaneous to drug-induced enlightenment has been most extensively investigated by R.C. Zaehner, *Mysticism–Sacred and Profane* (The Clarendon Press, Oxford, 1957).

[4] This excerpt from Benn's essay was taken from Ralph Metzner's translation "Provoked Life: An Essay on the Anthropology of the Ego," which was published in *Psychedelic Review* 1 (1): 47-54, 1963. Minor corrections in Metzner's text have been made by A.H.

[5] In the English publication of Kerényi's book *Eleusis* (Schocken Books, New York, 1977) a reference is made to this collaboration.

[6] In *The Road to Eleusis* by R. Gordon Wasson, Albert Hofmann, and Carl A.P. Ruck (Harcourt Brace Jovanovich, New York, 1978) the possibility is discussed that the *kykeon* could have acted through an LSD-like preparation of ergot.

[7] *Haben und Sein* (1969), *Die Welt als Du* (1970), *Urvertrauen und zweite Wirklichkeit* (1973), and *Die finale Mensch* (1976); all published by Theologischer Verlag, Zürich.

(Translated by Jonathan Ott)

from The Hasheesh Eater:

being passages from The Life

of a Pythagorean

Fitz Hugh Ludlow

The son of a clergyman in a small American town, Fitz Hugh Ludlow (1836–1870) wrote his best-known work when he was nineteen and published it two years later. The book was a curiosity and enjoyed a mild success in the United States and Great Britain. In his preface Ludlow acknowledges his great indebtedness to Thomas De Quincey, who also took very seriously the pursuit of knowledge through drug use. No record of American cannabis use exists predating the accounts of Ludlow and his friend Bayard Taylor, whose reports of hashish use were, in fact, published prior to Ludlow's. Although both cannabis and hashish were generally accessible at the time, Ludlow knew that his habit would outrage proper society, and he published his volume anonymously. His enthusiasm, however, is unbridled in this transcendent, poetic prose.

The Night Entrance

About the shop of my friend Anderson the apothecary there always existed a peculiar fascination, which early marked it out as my favorite lounging-place. In the very atmosphere of the establishment, loaded as it was with a composite smell of all things curative and preventive, there was an aromatic invitation to scientific musing, which could not have met with a readier acceptance had it spoken in the breath of frankincense. The very gallipots grew gradually to possess a charm for me as they sat calmly ranged upon their oaken shelves, looking like a convention of unostentatious philanthropists, whose silent bosoms teemed with every variety of renovation for the human race. A little sanctum at the inner end of the shop, walled off with red curtains from the profane gaze of the unsanative, contained two chairs for the doctor and myself, and a library where all the masters of physic were grouped, through their sheep and paper representatives, in more friendliness of contact than has ever been known to characterize a consultation of like spirits under any other circumstances. Within the limits of four square feet. Pereira and Christison condensed all their stores of wisdom and research, and Dunglison and Brathwaite sat cheek by jowl beside them. There stood the Dispensatory, with the air of a business-like office, wherein all the specifics of the materia medica had been brought together for a scientific conversazione, but, becoming enamored of each other's society, had resolved to stay, overcrowded though they might be, and make an indefinite sitting of it. In a modest niche, set apart like a vestibule from the apartments of the medical gentlemen, lay a shallow case, which disclosed, on the lifting of a cover, the neatly-ordered rank of tweezers, probe, and lancet, which constituted my friend's claim to the confidence of the plethoric community; for, although unblessed with metropolitan fame, he was still no *"Cromwell guiltless of his country's blood."*

Here many an hour have I sat buried in the statistics of human life or the history of the make-shifts for its preservation. Here details of surgical or medical experiment have held me in as complete engrossment as the positions and crises of romance; and here especially, with a disregard to my own safety which would have done credit to Quintus Curtius, have I made upon myself the trial of the effects of every strange drug and chemical which the laboratory could produce. Now with the chloroform bottle beneath my nose have I set myself careering upon the wings of a thrilling and accelerating life, until I had just enough power remaining to restore the liquid to its place upon the shelf, and sink back into the enjoyment of the delicious apathy which lasted through the few succeeding moments. Now ether was substituted for chloroform, and the difference of their phenomena noted, and now some other exhilarant, in the form of an opiate or stimulant, was the instrument of my experiments, until I had run through the whole gamut of queer agents within my reach.

In all these experiences research and not indulgence was my object, so that I never became the victim of any habit in the prosecution of my headlong investigations. When the circuit of all the accessible tests was completed, I ceased experimenting, and sat down like a pharmaceutical Alexander, with no more drug-worlds to conquer.

One morning, in the spring of 185–, I dropped in upon the doctor for my accustomed lounge.

"Have you seen," said he, "my new acquisitions?"

I looked toward the shelves in the direction of which he pointed, and saw, added since my last visit, a row of comely pasteboard cylinders inclosing vials of the various extracts prepared by Tilden & Co. Arranged in order according to their size, they confronted me, as pretty a little rank of medicinal sharpshooters as could gratify the eye of an amateur. I approached the shelves, that I might take them in review.

A rapid glance showed most of them to be old acquaintances. "Conium, taraxacum, rhubarb–ha! what is this? Cannabis Indica?" "That," answered the doctor, looking with a parental fondness upon his new treasure, "is a preparation of the East Indian hemp, a powerful agent in cases of lockjaw." On the strength of this introduction, I took down the little archer, and, removing his outer verdant coat, began the further prosecution of his acquaintance. To pull out a broad and shallow cork was the work of an instant, and it revealed to me an olive-brown extract, of the consistency of pitch, and a decided aromatic odor. Drawing out a small portion upon the point of my penknife, I was just going to put it to my tongue, when "Hold on!" cried the doctor, "do you want to kill yourself? That stuff is deadly poison." "Indeed!" I replied; "no, I can not say that I have any settled determination of that kind;" and with that I replaced the cork, and restored the extract, with all its appurtenances, to the shelf.

The remainder of my morning's visit in the sanctum was spent in consulting the Dispensatory under the title "Cannabis Indica." The sum of my discoveries there may be found, with much additional information, in that invaluable popular work, Johnston's Chemistry of Common Life. This being universally accessible, I will allude no further to the result of that morning's researches than to mention the three following conclusions to which I came.

First, the doctor was both right and wrong; right, inasmuch as a sufficiently large dose of the drug, if it could be retained in the stomach, would produce death, like any other narcotic, and the ultimate effect of its habitual use had always proved highly injurious to mind and body; wrong, since moderate doses of it were never immediately deadly, and many millions of people daily employed it as an indulgence similarly to opium. Second, it was the hasheesh referred to by Eastern travelers, and the subject of a most graphic chapter from the pen of Bayard Taylor, which months before had moved me powerfully to curiosity and admiration. Third, I would add it to the list of my former experiments.

In pursuance of this last determination, I waited till my friend was out of sight, that I might not terrify him by that which he considered a suicidal venture, and then quietly uncapping my little archer a second time, removed from his store of offensive armor a pill sufficient to balance the ten grain weight of the sanctorial scales. This, upon the authority of Pereira and the Dispensatory, I swallowed without a tremor as to the danger of the result.

Making all due allowance for the fact that I had not taken my hasheesh bolus fasting, I ought to experience its effects within the next four hours. That time elapsed without bringing the shadow of a phenomenon. It was plain that my dose had been insufficient.

For the sake of observing the most conservative prudence, I suffered several days to go by without a repetition of the experiment, and then, keeping the matter equally secret, I administered to myself a pill of fifteen grains. This second was equally ineffectual with the first.

Gradually, by five grains at a time, I increased the dose to thirty grains, which I took one evening half an hour after tea. I had now almost come to the conclusion that I was absolutely unsusceptible of the hasheesh influence. Without any expectation that this last experiment would be more successful than the former ones, and indeed with no realization of the manner in which the drug affected those who did make the experiment successfully, I went to pass the evening at the house of an intimate friend. In music and conversation the time passed pleasantly. The clock struck ten, reminding me that three hours had elapsed since the dose was taken, and as yet not an unusual symptom had appeared. I was provoked to think that this trial was as fruitless as its predecessors.

Ha! what means this sudden thrill? A shock, as of some unimagined vital force, shoots without warning through my entire frame, leaping to my fingers' ends, piercing my brain, startling me till I almost spring from my chair.

I could not doubt it. I was in the power of the hasheesh influence. My first emotion was one of uncontrollable terror–a sense of getting something which I had not bargained for. That moment I would have given all I had or hoped to have to be as I was three hours before.

No pain any where–not a twinge in any fibre–yet a cloud of unutterable strangeness was settling upon me, and wrapping me impenetrably in from all that was natural or familiar. Endeared faces, well known to me of old, surrounded me, yet they were not with me in my loneliness. I had entered upon a tremendous life which they could not share. If the disembodied ever return to hover over the hearth-stone which once had a seat for them, they look upon their friends as I then looked upon mine. A nearness of place, with an infinite distance of state, a connection which had no possible sympathies for the wants of that hour of revelation, an isolation none the less perfect for seeming companionship.

Still I spoke; a question was put to me, and I answered it; I even laughed at a bon mot. Yet it was not my voice which spoke; perhaps one which I once had far away in another time and another place. For a while I knew nothing that was going on externally, and then the remembrance of the last remark which had been made returned slowly and indistinctly, as some trait of a dream will return after many days, puzzling us to say where we have been conscious of it before.

A fitful wind all the evening had been sighing down the chimney; it now grew into the steady hum of a vast wheel in accelerating motion. For a while this hum seemed to resound through all space. I was stunned by it–I was absorbed in it. Slowly the revolution of the wheel came to a stop, and its monotonous din was changed for the reverberating peal of a grand cathedral organ. The ebb and flow of its inconceivably solemn tone filled me with a grief that was more than human. I sympathized with the dirge-like cadence as spirit sympathizes with spirit. And then, in the full conviction that all I heard and felt was real, I looked out of my isolation to see the effect of the music on my friends. Ah! we were in separate worlds indeed. Not a trace of appreciation on any face.

Perhaps I was acting strangely. Suddenly a pair of busy hands, which had been running neck and neck all the evening with a nimble little crochet-needle over a race-ground of pink and blue silk, stopped at their goal, and their owner looked at me steadfastly. Ah! I was found out–I had betrayed myself. In terror I waited, expecting every instant to hear the word "hasheesh." No, the lady only asked me some question connected with the previous conversation. As mechanically as an automaton I began to reply. As I heard once more the alien and unreal tones of my own voice, I became convinced that it was some one else who spoke, and in another world. I sat and listened; still the voice kept speaking. Now for the first time I experienced that vast change which hasheesh makes in all measurements of time. The first word of the reply occupied a period sufficient for the action of a drama; the last left me in complete ignorance of any point far enough back in the past to date the commencement of the sentence. Its enunciation might have occupied years. I was not in the same life which had held me when I heard it begun.

And now, with time, space expanded also. At my friend's house one particular arm-chair was always reserved for me. I was sitting in it at a distance of hardly three feet from the centre-table around which the members of the family were grouped. Rapidly that distance widened. The whole atmosphere seemed ductile, and spun endlessly out into great spaces surrounding me on every side. We were in a vast hall, of which my friends and I occupied opposite extremities. The ceiling and the walls ran upward with a glid-ing motion, as if vivified by a sudden force of resistless growth.

Oh! I could not bear it. I should soon be left alone in the midst of an infinity of space. And now more and more every moment increased the conviction that I was watched. I did not know then, as I learned afterward, that suspicion of all earthly things and per-sons was the characteristic of the hasheesh delirium.

In the midst of my complicated hallucination, I could perceive that I had a dual ex-istence. One portion of me was whirled unresistingly along the track of this tremendous experience, the other sat looking down from a height upon its double, observing, rea-soning, and serenely weighing all the phenomena. This calmer being suffered with the other by sympathy, but did not lose its self-possession. Presently it warned me that I must go home, lest the growing effect of the hasheesh should incite me to some act which might frighten my friends. I acknowledged the force of this remark very much as if it had been made by another person, and rose to take my leave. I advanced toward the cen-tre-table. With every step its distance increased. I nerved myself as for a long pedestrian journey. Still the lights, the faces, the furniture receded. At last, almost unconsciously, I reached them. It would be tedious to attempt to convey the idea of the time which my leave-taking consumed, and the attempt, at least with all minds that have not passed through the same experience, would be as impossible as tedious. At last I was in the street.

Beyond me the view stretched endlessly away. It was an unconverging vista, whose nearest lamps seemed separated from me by leagues. I was doomed to pass through a merciless stretch of space. A soul just disenthralled, setting out for his flight beyond the farthest visible star, could not be more overwhelmed with his newly-acquired con-ception of the sublimity of distance than I was at that moment. Solemnly I began my infinite journey.

Before long I walked in entire unconsciousness of all around me. I dwelt in a mar-velous inner world. I existed by turns in different places and various states of being. Now I swept my gondola through the moonlit lagoons of Venice. Now Alp on Alp towered above my view, and the glory of the coming sun flashed purple light upon the topmost icy pinnacle. Now in the primeval silence of some unexplored tropical forest I spread my feathery leaves, a giant fern, and swayed and nodded in the spice-gales over a river whose waves at once sent up clouds of music and perfume. My soul changed to a veg-etable essence, thrilled with a strange and unimagined ecstasy. The palace of Al Haroun could not have brought me back to humanity.

I will not detail all the transmutations of that walk. Ever and anon I returned from my dreams into consciousness, as some well-known house seemed to leap out into my path, awaking me with a shock. The whole way homeward was a series of such awakings and relapses into abstraction and delirium until I reached the corner of the street in which I lived.

Here a new phenomenon manifested itself I had just awaked for perhaps the twentieth time, and my eyes were wide open. I recognized all surrounding objects, and began calculating the distance home. Suddenly, out of a blank wall at my side a muffled figure stepped into the path before me. His hair, white as snow, hung in tangled elf-locks on his shoulders, where he carried also a heavy burden, like unto the well-filled sack of sins which Bunyan places on the back of his pilgrim. Not liking his manner, I stepped aside, intending to pass around him and go on my way. This change of our relative position allowed the blaze of a neighboring street-lamp to fall full on his face, which had hitherto been totally obscured. Horror unspeakable! I shall never, till the day I die, forget that face. Every lineament was stamped with the records of a life black with damning crime; it glared upon me with a ferocious wickedness and a stony despair which only he may feel who is entering on the retribution of the unpardonable sin. He might have sat to a demon painter as the ideal of Shelley's Cenci. I seemed to grow blasphemous in looking at him, and, in an agony of fear, began to run away. He detained me with a bony hand, which pierced my wrist like talons, and, slowly taking down the burden from his own shoulders, laid it upon mine. I threw it off and pushed him away. Silently he returned and restored the weight. Again I repulsed him, this time crying out, "Man, what do you mean?" In a voice which impressed me with the sense of wickedness as his face had done, he replied, "You shall bear my burden with me," and a third time laid it on my shoulders. For the last time I hurled it aside, and, with all my force, dashed him from me. He reeled backward and fell, and before he could recover his disadvantage I had put a long distance between us.

Through the excitement of my struggle with this phantasm the effects of the hasheesh had increased mightily. I was bursting with an uncontrollable life; I strode with the thews of a giant. Hotter and faster came my breath; I seemed to pant like some tremendous engine. An electric energy whirled me resistlessly onward; I feared for myself lest it should burst its fleshly walls, and glance on, leaving a wrecked frame-work behind it.

At last I entered my own house. During my absence a family connection had arrived from abroad, and stood ready to receive my greeting. Partly restored to consciousness by the naturalness of home-faces and the powerful light of a chandelier which shed its blaze through the room, I saw the necessity of vigilance against betraying my condition, and with an intense effort suppressing all I felt, I approached my friend, and said all that is usual on such occasions. Yet recent as I was from my conflict with the supernatural, I cast a stealthy look about me, that I might learn from the faces of the others if, after all, I was shaking hands with a phantom, and making inquiries about the health of a family of hallucinations. Growing assured as I perceived no symptoms of astonishment, I finished the salutation and sat down.

It soon required all my resolution to keep the secret which I had determined to hold inviolable. My sensations began to be terrific—not from any pain that I felt, but from the tremendous mystery of all around me and within me. By an appalling introversion, all the operations of vitality which, in our ordinary state, go on unconsciously, came vividly into my experience. Through every thinnest corporeal tissue and minutest vein I could trace the circulation of the blood along each inch of its progress. I knew when every valve opened and when it shut; every sense was preternaturally awakened; the room was full of a great glory. The beating of my heart was so clearly audible that I wondered to find it unnoticed by those who were sitting by my side. Lo, now, that heart became a great fountain, whose jet played upward with loud vibrations, and, striking upon the roof of my skull as on a gigantic dome, fell back with a splash and echo into its reservoir. Faster and faster came the pulsations, until at last I heard them no more, and the stream became one continuously pouring flood, whose roar resounded through all my frame. I gave myself up for lost, since judgment, which still sat unimpaired above my perverted senses, argued that congestion must take place in a few moments, and close the drama with my death. But my clutch would not yet relax from hope. The thought struck me, Might not this rapidity of circulation be, after all, imaginary? I determined to find out.

Going to my own room, I took out my watch, and placed my hand upon my heart. The very effort which I made to ascertain the reality gradually brought perception back to its natural state. In the intensity of my observations, I began to perceive that the circulation was not as rapid as I had thought. From a pulseless flow it gradually came to be apprehended as a hurrying succession of intense throbs, then less swift and less intense, till finally, on comparing it with the second-hand, I found that about 90 a minute was its average rapidity. Greatly comforted, I desisted from the experiment. Almost instantly the hallucination returned. Again I dreaded apoplexy, congestion, hemorrhage, a multiplicity of nameless deaths, and drew my picture as I might be found on the morrow, stark and cold, by those whose agony would be re-doubled by the mystery of my end. I reasoned with myself; I bathed my forehead—it did no good. There was one resource left: I would go to a physician.

With this resolve, I left my room and went to the head of the staircase. The family had all retired for the night, and the gas was turned off from the burner in the hall below. I looked down the stairs: the depth was fathomless; it was a journey of years to reach the bottom! The dim light of the sky shone through the narrow panes at the sides of the front door, and seemed a demon-lamp in the middle darkness of the abyss. I never could get down! I sat me down despairingly upon the topmost step.

Suddenly a sublime thought possessed me. If the distance be infinite, I am immortal. It shall be tried. I commenced the descent, wearily, wearily down through my league-long, year-long journey. To record my impressions in that journey would be to repeat what I have said of the time of hasheesh. Now stopping to rest as a traveler would turn aside at a wayside inn, now toiling down through the lonely darkness, I came by-and-by to the end, and passed out into the street.

Under the Shadow of Esculapius

On reaching the porch of the physician's house, I rang the bell, but immediately forgot whom to ask for. No wonder; I was on the steps of a palace in Milan–no (and I laughed at myself for the blunder), I was on the staircase of the Tower of London. So I should not be puzzled through my ignorance of Italian. But whom to ask for? This question recalled me to the real bearings of the place, but did not suggest its requisite answer. Whom shall I ask for? I began setting the most cunning traps of hypothesis to catch the solution of the difficulty. I looked at the surrounding houses; of whom had I been accustomed to think as living next door to them? This did not bring it. Whose daughter had I seen going to school from this house but the very day before? Her name was Julia–Julia–and I thought of every combination which had been made with this name from Julia Domna down to Giulia Grisi. Ah! now I had it–Julia H.; and her father naturally bore the same name. During this intellectual rummage I had rung the bell half a dozen times, under the impression that I was kept waiting a small eternity. When the servant opened the door she panted as if she had run for her life. I was shown up stairs to Dr. H.'s room, where he had thrown himself down to rest after a tedious operation. Locking the door after me with an air of determined secrecy, which must have conveyed to him pleasant little suggestions of a design upon his life, I approached his bedside.

"I am about to reveal to you," I commenced, "something which I could not for my life allow to come to other ears. Do you pledge me your eternal silence?"

"I do; what is the matter?"

"I have been taking hasheesh–Cannabis Indica, and I fear that I am going to die."

"How much did you take?"

"Thirty grains."

"Let me feel your pulse." He placed his finger on my wrist and counted slowly, while I stood waiting to hear my death-warrant. "Very regular," shortly spoke the doctor; "triflingly accelerated. Do you feel any pain?" "None at all." "Nothing the matter with you; go home and go to bed." "But–is there–is there–no–danger of–apoplexy?" "Bah!" said the doctor; and, having delivered himself of this very Abernethy-like opinion of my case, he lay down again. My hand was on the knob, when he stopped me with, "Wait a minute; I'll give you a powder to carry with you, and if you get frightened again after you leave me, you can take it as a sedative. Step out on the landing, if you please, and call my servant."

I did so, and my voice seemed to reverberate like thunder from every recess in the whole building. I was terrified at the noise I had made. I learned in after days that this impression is only one of the many due to the intense susceptibility of the sensorium as produced by hasheesh. At one time, having asked a friend to check me if I talked loudly or immoderately while in a state of fantasia among persons from whom I wished to conceal my state, I caught myself shouting and singing from very ecstasy, and reproached him with a neglect of his friendly office. I could not believe him when he assured me that I had not uttered an audible word. The intensity of the inward emotion had affected the external through the internal ear.

I returned and stood at the foot of the doctor's bed. All was perfect silence in the room, and had been perfect darkness also but for the small lamp which I held in my hand to light the preparation of the powder when it should come. And now a still sublimer mystery began to enwrap me. I stood in a remote chamber at the top of a colossal building, and the whole fabric beneath me was steadily growing into the air. Higher than the topmost pinnacle of Bel's Babylonish temple–higher than Ararat–on, on forever into the lonely dome of God's infinite universe we towered ceaselessly. The years flew on; I heard the musical rush of their wings in the abyss outside of me, and from cycle to cycle, from life to life I careered, a mote in eternity and space. Suddenly emerging from the orbit of my. transmigrations, I was again at the foot of the doctor's bed, and thrilled with wonder to find that we were both unchanged by the measureless lapse of time. The servant had not come.

"Shall I call her again?" "Why, you have this moment called her." "Doctor," I replied solemnly, and in language that would have seemed bombastic enough to any one who did not realize what I felt, "I will not believe you are deceiving me, but to me it appears as if sufficient time has elapsed since then for all the Pyramids to have crumbled back to dust." "Ha! ha! you are very funny to-night," said the doctor; "but here she comes, and I will send her for something which will comfort you on that score, and reestablish the Pyramids in your confidence." He gave the girl his orders, and she went out again.

The thought struck me that I would compare *my time* with other people's. I looked at my watch, found that its minute-hand stood at the quarter mark past eleven, and, returning it to my pocket, abandoned myself to my reflections.

Presently I saw myself a gnome imprisoned by a most weird enchanter, whose part I assigned to the doctor before me, in the Domdaniel caverns, "under the roots of the ocean." Here, until the dissolution of all things, was I doomed to hold the lamp that lit that abysmal darkness, while my heart, like a giant clock, ticked solemnly the remaining years of time. Now, this hallucination departing, I heard in the solitude of the night outside the sound of a wondrous heaving sea. Its waves, in sublime cadence, rolled forward till they met the foundations of the building; they smote them with a might which made the very topstone quiver, and then fell back, with hiss and hollow murmur, into the broad bosom whence they had arisen. Now through the street, with measured tread, an armed host passed by. The heavy beat of their footfall and the griding of their brazen corslet-rings alone broke the silence, for among them all there was no more speech nor music than in a battalion of the dead. It was the army of the ages going by into eternity. A godlike sublimity swallowed up my soul. I was overwhelmed in a fathomless barathrum of time, but I leaned on God, and was immortal through all changes.

And now, in another life, I remembered that far back in the cycles I had looked at my watch to measure the time through which I passed. The impulse seized me to look again. The minute-hand stood half way between fifteen and sixteen minutes past eleven. The watch must have stopped; I held it to my ear; no, it was still going. I had traveled through all that immeasurable chain of dreams in thirty seconds. "My God!" I cried, "I am in eternity." In the presence of that first sublime revelation of the soul's own time, and her capacity for an infinite life, I stood trembling with breathless awe. Till I die, that moment of unveiling will stand in clear relief from all the rest of my existence. I hold it still in unimpaired remembrance as one of the unutterable sanctities of my being. The years of all my earthly life to come can never be as long as those thirty seconds.

Finally the servant reappeared. I received my powder and went home. There was a light in one of the upper windows, and I hailed it with unspeakable joy, for it relieved me from a fear which I could not conquer, that while I had been gone all familiar things had passed away from earth. I was hardly safe in my room before I doubted having ever been out of it. "I have experienced some wonderful dream," said I, "as I lay here after coming from the parlor." If I had not been out, I reasoned that I would have no powder in my pocket. The powder was there, and it steadied me a little to find that I was not utterly hallucinated on every point. Leaving the light burning, I set out to travel to my bed, which gently invited me in the distance. Reaching it after a sufficient walk, I threw myself down.

The Kingdom of the Dream

The moment that I closed my eyes a vision of celestial glory burst upon me. I stood on the silver strand of a translucent, boundless lake, across whose bosom I seemed to have been just transported. A short way up the beach, a temple, modeled like the Parthenon, lifted its spotless and gleaming columns of alabaster sublimely into a rosy air–like the Parthenon, yet as much excelling it as the godlike ideal of architecture must transcend that ideal realized by man. Unblemished in its purity of whiteness, faultless in the unbroken symmetry of every line and angle, its pediment was draped in odorous clouds, whose tints outshone the rainbow. It was the work of an unearthly builder, and my soul stood before it in a trance of ecstasy. Its folded doors were resplendent with the glory of a multitude of eyes of glass, which were inlaid throughout the marble surfaces at the corners of diamond figures from the floor of the porch to the topmost moulding. One of these eyes was golden, like the midday sun, another emerald, another sapphire, and thus onward through the whole gamut of hues, all of them set in such collocations as to form most exquisite harmonies, and whirling upon their axes with the rapidity of thought. At the mere vestibule of the temple I could have sat and drunk in ecstasy forever; but lo! I am yet more blessed. On silent hinges the doors swing open, and I pass in.

I did not seem to be in the interior of a temple. I beheld myself as truly in the open air as if I had never passed the portals, for whichever way I looked there were no walls, no roof, no pavement. An atmosphere of fathomless and soul-satisfying serenity surrounded and transfused me. I stood upon the bank of a crystal stream, whose waters, as they slid on, discoursed notes of music which tinkled on the ear like the tones of some exquisite bell-glass. The same impression which such tones produce, of music refined to its ultimate ethereal spirit and borne from a far distance, characterized every ripple of those translucent waves. The gently slowing banks of the stream were luxuriant with a velvety cushioning of grass and moss, so living green that the eye and the soul reposed on them at the same time and drank in peace. Through this amaranthine herbage strayed the gnarled, fantastic roots of giant cedars of Lebanon, from whose primeval trunks great branches spread above me, and interlocking, wove a roof of impenetrable shadow; and wandering down the still avenues below those grand arboreal arches went glorious bards, whose snowy beards fell on their breasts beneath countenances of ineffable benignity and nobleness.

They were all clad in flowing robes, like God's highpriests, and each one held in his hand a lyre of unearthly workmanship. Presently one stops midway down a shady walk, and, baring his right arm, begins a prelude. While his celestial chords were trembling up into their sublime fullness, another strikes his strings, and now they blend upon my ravished ear in such a symphony as was never heard elsewhere, and I shall never hear again out of the Great Presence. A moment more, and three are playing in harmony; now the fourth joins the glorious rapture of his music to their own, and in the completeness of the chord my soul is swallowed up. I can bear no more. But yes, I am sustained, for suddenly the whole throng break forth in a chorus, upon whose wings I am lifted out of the riven walls of sense, and music and spirit thrill in immediate communion. Forever rid of the intervention of pulsing air and vibrating nerve, my soul dilates with the swell of that transcendent harmony, and interprets from it arcana of a meaning which words can never tell. I am borne aloft upon the glory of sound. I float in a trance among the burning choir of the seraphim. But, as I am melting through the purification of that sublime ecstasy into oneness with the Deity himself, one by one those pealing lyres faint away, and as the last throb dies down along the measureless ether, visionless arms swiftly as lightning carry me far into the profound, and set me down before another portal. Its leaves, like the first, are of spotless marble, but ungemmed with wheeling eyes of burning color.

Before entering on the record of this new vision I will make a digression, for the purpose of introducing two laws of the hasheesh operation, which, as explicatory, deserve a place here. First, after the completion of any one fantasia has arrived, there almost invariably succeeds a shifting of the action to some other stage entirely different in its surroundings. In this transition the general character of the emotion may remain unchanged. I may be happy in Paradise and happy at the sources of the Nile, but seldom, either in

Paradise or on the Nile, twice in succession. I may writhe in Etna and burn unquench-ably in Gehenna, but almost never, in the course of the same delirium, shall Etna or Gehenna witness my torture a second time.

Second, after the full storm of a vision of intense sublimity has blown past the hasheesh-eater, his next vision is generally of a quiet, relaxing, and recreating nature. He comes down from his clouds or up from his abyss into a middle ground of gentle shadows, where he may rest his eyes from the splendor of the seraphim or the flames of fiends. There is a wise philosophy in this arrangement, for otherwise the soul would soon burn out in the excess of its own oxygen. Many a time, it seems to me, has my own thus been saved from extinction.

This next vision illustrated both, but especially the latter of these laws. The temple-doors opened noiselessly before me, but it was no scene of sublimity which thus broke in upon my eyes. I stood in a large apartment, which resembled the Senate-chamber at Washington more than any thing else to which I can compare it. Its roof was vaulted, and at the side opposite the entrance the floor rose into a dais surmounted by a large arm-chair. The body of the house was occupied by similar chairs disposed in arcs; the heavy paneling of the walls was adorned with grotesque frescoes of every imaginable bird, beast, and monster, which, by some hidden law of life and motion, were forever changing, like the figures of the kaleidoscope. Now the walls bristled with hippogriffs; now, from wain-scot to ceiling, toucans and maccataws swung and nodded from their perches amid emer-ald palms; now Centaurs and Lapithae clashed in ferocious tumult, while crater and cyathus were crushed beneath ringing hoof and heel. But my attention was quickly dis-tracted from the frescoes by the sight of a most witchly congress, which filled all the chairs of that broad chamber. On the dais sat an old crone, whose commanding position first engaged my attention to her personal appearance, and, upon rather impolite scrutiny, I beheld that she was the product of an art held in preeminent favor among persons of her age and sex. She was *knit* of purple yarn! In faultless order the stitches ran along her face; in every pucker of her re-entrant mouth, in every wrinkle of her brow, she was a yarny counterfeit of the grandam of actual life, and by some skillful process of stuffing her nose had received its due peak and her chin its projection. The occupants of the seats below were all but reproductions of their president, and both she and they were constantly sway-ing from side to side, forward and back, to the music of some invisible instruments, whose tone and style were most intensely and ludicrously Ethiopian. Not a word was spoken by any of the woolly conclave, but with untiring industry they were all knitting, knit-ting, knitting ceaselessly, as if their lives depended on it. I looked to see the objects of their manufacture. They were knitting old women like themselves! One of the sisterhood had nearly brought her double to completion; earnestly another was engaged in round-ing out an eyeball; another was fastening the gathers at the corners of a mouth; another was setting up stitches for an old woman in petto.

With marvelous rapidity this work went on; ever and anon some completed crone sprang from the needles which had just achieved her, and, instantly vivified, took up the instruments of reproduction, and fell to work as assiduously as if she had been a member of the congress since the world began. "Here," I cried, "here, at last, do I realize the meaning of endless progression!" and, though the dome echoed with my peals of laughter, I saw no motion of astonishment in the stitches of a single face, but, as for dear life, the manufacture of old women went on unobstructed by the involuntary rudeness of the stranger.

An irresistible desire to aid in the work possessed me; I was half determined to snatch up a quartette of needles and join the sisterhood. My nose began to be ruffled with stitches, and the next moment I had been a partner in their yarny destinies but for a hand which pulled me backward through the door, and shut the congress forever from my view.

For a season I abode in an utter void of sight and sound, but I waited patiently in the assurance that some new changes of magnificence were preparing for me. I was not disappointed. Suddenly, at a far distance, three intense luminous points stood on the triple wall of darkness, and through each of them shot twin attenuated rays of magic light and music. Without being able to perceive any thing of my immediate surroundings, I still felt that I was noiselessly drifting toward those radiant and vocal points. With every moment they grew larger, the light and the harmony came clearer, and before long I could distinguish plainly three colossal arches rising from the bosom of a waveless water. The mid arch towered highest; the two on either side were equal to each other. Presently I beheld that they formed the portals of an enormous cavern, whose dome rose above me into such sublimity that its cope was hidden from my eyes in wreaths of cloud. On each side of me ran a wall of gnarled and rugged rock, from whose jutting points, as high as the eye could reach, depended stalactites of every imagined form and tinge of beauty, while below me, in the semblance of an ebon pavement, from the reflection of its overshadowing crags, lay a level lake, whose exquisite transparency wanted but the smile of the sun to make it glow like a floor of adamant. On this lake I lay in a little boat divinely carved from pearl after the similitude of Triton's shelly shallop; its rudder and its oarage were my own unconscious will, and, without the labors of especial volition, I floated as I list with a furrowless keel swiftly toward the central giant arch. With every moment that brought me nearer to my exit, the harmony that poured through it developed into a grander volume and an intenser beauty.

And now I passed out.

Claude Lorraine, freed from the limitations of sense, and gifted with an infinite canvas, may, for aught I know, be upon some halcyon island of the universe painting such a view as now sailed into my vision. Fitting employment would it be for his immortality were his pencil dipped into the very fountains of the light. Many a time in the course of my life have I yearned for the possession of some grand old master's soul and culture in the presence of revelations of Nature's loveliness which I dared not trust to memory; before this vision, as now in the remembrance of it, that longing became a heartfelt pain. Yet, after all, it was well; the mortal limner would have fainted in his task. Alas! how does the material in which we must embody the spiritual cramp and resist its execution! Standing before windows where the invisible spirit of the frost had traced his exquisite algae, his palms and his ferns, have I said to myself, with a sigh, Ah! Nature alone, of all artists, is gifted to work out her ideals!

Shall I be so presumptuous as to attempt in words that which would beggar the palette and the pencil of old-time disciples of the beautiful? I will, if it be only to satisfy a deep longing.

From the arches of my cavern I had emerged upon a horizonless sea. Through all the infinitudes around me I looked out, and met no boundaries of space. Often in after times have I beheld the heavens and the earth stretching out in parallel lines forever, but this was the first time I had ever stood "un-ringed by the azure world," and I exulted in all the sublimity of the new conception. The whole atmosphere was one measureless suffusion of golden motes, which throbbed continually in cadence, and showered radiance and harmony at the same time. With ecstasy vision spread her wings for a flight against which material laws locked no barrier, and every moment grew more and more entranced at further and fuller glimpses of a beauty which floated like incense from the pavement of that eternal sea. With ecstasy the spiritual ear gathered in continually some more distant and unimaginable tone, and grouped the growing harmonies into one sublime chant of benediction. With ecstasy the whole soul drank in revelations from every province, and cried out, "Oh, awful loveliness!" And now out of my shallop I was borne away into the full light of the mid firmament; now seated on some toppling peak of a cloud-mountain, whose yawning rifts disclosed far down the mines of reserved lightning; now bathed in my ethereal travel by the rivers of the rainbow, which, side by side, coursed through the valleys of heaven; now dwelling for a season in the environment of unbroken sunlight, yet bearing it like the eagle with undazzled eye; now crowned with a coronal of prismatic beads of dew. Through whatever region or circumstances I passed, one characteristic of the vision remained unchanged: peace—everywhere godlike peace, the sum of all conceivable desires satisfied.

Slowly I floated down to earth again. There Oriental gardens waited to receive me. From fountain to fountain I danced in graceful mazes with inimitable houris, whose foreheads were bound with fillets of jasmine. I pelted with figs the rare exotic birds, whose gold and crimson wings went flashing from branch to branch, or wheedled them to me with Arabic phrases of endearment. Through avenues of palm I walked arm-in-arm with Hafiz, and heard the hours flow singing through the channels of his matchless poetry. In gay kiosques I quaffed my sherbet, and in the luxury of lawlessness kissed away by drops that other juice which is contraband unto the faithful. And now beneath citron shadows I laid me down to sleep. When I awoke it was morning—actually morning, and not a hasheesh hallucination. The first emotion that I felt upon opening my eyes was happiness to find things again wearing a natural air. Yes; although the last experience of which I had been conscious had seemed to satisfy every human want, physical or spiritual, I smiled on the four plain white walls of my bedchamber, and hailed their familiar unostentatiousness with a pleasure which had no wish to transfer itself to arabesque or rainbows. It was like returning home from an eternity spent in loneliness among the palaces of strangers. Well may I say an eternity, for during the whole day I could not rid myself of the feeling that I was separated from the preceding one by an immeasurable lapse of time. In fact, I never got wholly rid of it.

I rose that I might test my reinstated powers, and see if the restoration was complete. Yes, I felt not one trace of bodily weariness nor mental depression. Every function had returned to its normal state, with the one exception mentioned; memory could not efface the traces of my having passed through a great mystery. I recalled the events of the past night, and was pleased to think that I had betrayed myself to no one but Dr. H. I was satisfied with my experiment.

Ah! would that I had been satisfied! Yet history must go on.

The Hour and Power of Darkness

It may perhaps be not altogether a fanciful classification to divide every man's life into two periods, the locomotive and the static. Restless fluidity always characterizes the childish mind in its healthy state, exemplifying itself in the thousand wayward freaks, hair-breadth experiments, and unanswerable questions which keep the elder portions of a family in continual oscillation between mirth and terror. There is not always a thorough solidification of the mental nature, even when the great boy has learned what to do with his hands, and how to occupy his station at maturer tea-parties with becoming dignity and resignation. No longer, to be sure, does he gratify experimental tendencies by taking the eight-day clock to pieces to look at its machinery; no longer does he nonplus grave aunts and grandmothers with questions upon the causes of his own origination, but the same dynamic propensities exist expanded into a larger and more self-conscious sphere. His restlessness of limb has now become the desire of travel, his investigation into the petty matters of household economy has grown into a thirst for research whose field is the world and whose instruments are the highest faculties of induction.

With some men this state remains unchanged through a long life, but to most of us there comes, sooner or later, a period when the longing for change dies out, and a fixed place and an unalterable condition become the great central ideas of existence. We look back with a wonder that is almost incredulousness upon the time when a ride by railway was the dream of weeks preceding, and try in vain to realize the supernatural freshness which the earth put on when for the first time we discovered that we were near-sighted, and looked through some friend's spectacles. Motion, except for the rare purpose of recreation, becomes an annoyance to us beyond a circumscribed territory, and we have emerged into the static condition of life before we are aware.

Much earlier than the usual period did this become the case with me. A feeble childhood soon exhausted its superfluous activities, and into books, ill health, and musing I settled down when I should have been playing cricket, hunting, or riding. The younger thirst for adventure was quenched by rapid degrees as I found it possible to ascend Chimborazo with Humboldt lying on a sofa, or chase harte-beests with Cumming over muffins and coffee. The only exceptions to this state of imaginative indolence were the hours spent in rowing or sailing upon the most glorious river of the world, and the consciousness that the Hudson rolled at my own door only contributed to settle the conviction that there was no need of going abroad to find beauties in which the soul might wrap itself as in a garment of delight. Even at these seasons exercise was not so much the aim as musing. Many a time, with the handles of my sculls thrust under the side-girders, and the blades turned full to the wind, have I sat and drifted for hours through mountain-shadows, and past glimpses of light that flooded the woody gorges, with a sense of dreamy ecstasy which all the novelties of a new world could never have supplied.

Oh, most noble river, what hast thou not been to me? In childhood thy ripples were the playmates of my perpetual leisure, dancing up the sandy stretches of thy brink, and telling laughing tales of life's beamy spray and sunshine. In after years, the grand prophet of a wider life, thine ebb sang chants to the imperial ocean, into whose pearly palaces thou .vast hastening, and thy flood brought up the resounding history of the infinite surges whence thou hadst returned. It is not thine to come stealing from unnamed fountains of mystery, nor to crown thy sublime mountains with the ruined battlements of a departed age; but more than Nile hath God glorified thee, and Nature hath hallowed thy walls with her own armorial bearings till thou art more reverend than Rhine. On thy guarding peaks Antiquity sits enthroned, asking no register in the crumbling monuments of man, but bearing her original sceptre from the hand of Him who first founded her domain beside thy immortal flow.

Gradually the Hudson came to supply all my spiritual wants. Were I sad, I found sympathy in the almost human murmurs of his waters, as, stretched upon the edge of some rocky headland, I heard them go beating into the narrow caves beneath me, and return sighing, as if defrauded of a hiding-place and a home. Were I merry, the white-caps danced and laughed about my prancing boat, and the wind whistled rollicking glees against my stays. In weariness, I leaped into the stream; his cool hand upbore and caressed me till I returned braced for thought, and renewed as by a plunge into El Dorado. In the Hudson I found a wealth which satisfied all wishes, and my supreme hope was that on his banks I might pass all my life. Thus supplied with beauty, consolation, dreams, all things, every day I became more and more careless of the world beyond, and in my frame grew even *hyperstatic*.

It was in this state that hasheesh found me. After the walk which I last recorded, the former passion for travel returned with powerful intensity. I had now a way of gratifying it which comported both with indolence and economy. The whole East, from Greece to farthest China, lay within the compass of a township; no outlay was necessary for the journey. For the humble sum of six cents I might purchase an excursion ticket over all the earth; ships and dromedaries, tents and hospices were all contained in a box of Tilden's extract. Hasheesh I called the "drug of travel," and I had only to direct my thoughts strongly toward a particular part of the world previously to swallowing my bolus to make my whole fantasia in the strongest possible degree topographical. Or, when the delirium was at its height, let any one suggest to me, however faintly, mountain, wilderness, or market-place, and straightway I was in it, drinking in the novelty of my surroundings in all the ecstasy of a discoverer. I swam up against the current of all time; I walked through Luxor and Palmyra as they were of old; on Babylon the bittern had not built her nest, and I gazed on the unbroken columns of the Parthenon.

Soon after my pedestrian journey through Asia I changed my residence for a while, and went to live in the town of Schenectady. It was here that the remainder of my hasheesh-life was passed, and here, for many days, did I drain alternately cups of super-human joy and as superhuman misery. At Union College, of which I was a resident, I had a few friends to whom I communicated my acquaintance with the wondrous drug which was now becoming a habit with me. Some of them were surprised, some warned me, and as they will most of them be introduced into the narrative which I am writing, I now mention them thus particularly, lest it may be thought strange that, in an ordinary town of small size, there should be found by one man a sufficient number of congenial persons to vary the dramatis personae of a story as mine will be varied.

Having exhausted the supply of hasheesh which I had originally obtained from the shelves of my old lounging-place at the shop of the doctor, I procured a small jar of a preparation of the same drug by another chemist, which, I was told, was much weaker than the former. Late in the evening I took about fifty grains of the new preparation, arguing that this amount was a rational equivalent for the thirty which had before been my maximum dose.

It is impossible, however, to base any calculation of the energy of hasheesh upon such a comparison. The vital forces upon which this most magical stimulant operates are too delicate, too recondite to be treated like material parts in a piece of mechanism whose power of resistance can be definitely expressed by an equation. There are certain nerves, no doubt, which the anatomist and the physician will find affected by the cannabine influence–certain functions over which its essence appears to hold peculiar regency; but we must have proceeded much farther in the science which treats of the connection between matter and mind, must know much more of those imponderable forces which, more delicate than electricity and more mysterious than the magnetic fluid, weave the delicate interacting network that joins our human duality, before we can treat that part of us affected by hasheesh as a constant in any calculation.

There are two facts which I have verified as universal by repeated experiment, which fall into their place here as aptly as they can in the course of my narrative: 1st. At two different times, when body and mind are apparently in precisely analogous states, when all circumstances, exterior and interior, do not differ tangibly in the smallest respect, the same dose of the same preparation of hasheesh will frequently produce diametrically opposite effects. Still further, I have taken at one time a pill of thirty grains, which hardly gave a perceptible phenomenon, and at another, when my dose had been but half that quantity, I have suffered the agonies of a martyr, or rejoiced in a perfect phrensy. So exceedingly variable are its results, that, long before I abandoned the indulgence, I took each successive bolus with the consciousness that I was daring an uncertainty as tremendous as the equipoise between hell and heaven. Yet the fascination employed Hope as its advocate, and won the suit. 2d. If, during the ecstasy of hasheesh delirium, another dose, however small–yes, though it be no larger than half a pea–be employed to prolong the condition, such agony will inevitably ensue as will make the soul shudder at its own possibility of endurance without annihilation. By repeated experiments, which now occupy the most horrible place upon my catalogue of horrible remembrances, have I proved that, among all the variable phenomena of hasheesh, this alone stands unvarying. The use of it directly after any other stimulus will produce consequences as appalling.

But to return from my digression. It was perhaps eight o'clock in the evening when I took the dose of fifty grains. I did not retire until near midnight, and as no effects had then manifested themselves, I supposed that the preparation was even weaker than my ratio gave it credit for being, and, without any expectation of result, lay down to sleep. Previously, however, I extinguished my light. To say this may seem trivial, but it is as important a matter as any which it is possible to notice. The most direful suggestions of the bottomless pit may flow in upon the hasheesh-eater through the very medium of darkness. The blowing out of a candle can set an unfathomed barathrum wide agape beneath the flower-wreathed table of his feast, and convert his palace of sorcery into a Golgotha. Light is a necessity to him, even when sleeping; it must tinge his visions, or they assume a hue as sombre as the banks of Styx.

I do not know how long a time had passed since midnight, when I awoke suddenly to find myself in a realm of the most perfect clarity of view, yet terrible with an infinitude of demoniac shadows. Perhaps, I thought, I am still dreaming; but no effort could arouse me from my vision, and I realized that I was wide awake. Yet it was an awaking which, for torture, had no parallel in all the stupendous domain of sleeping incubus. Beside my bed in the centre of the room stood a bier, from whose corners drooped the folds of a heavy pall; outstretched upon it lay in state a most fearful corpse, whose livid face was distorted with the pangs of assassination. The traces of a great agony were frozen into fixedness in the tense position of every muscle, and the nails of the dead man's fingers pierced his palms with the desperate clinch of one who has yielded not without agonizing resistance. Two tapers at his head, two at his feet, with their tall and unsnuffed wicks, made the ghastliness of the bier more luminously unearthly, and a smothered laugh of derision from some invisible watcher ever and anon mocked the corpse, as if triumphant demons were exulting over their prey. I pressed my hands upon my eyeballs till they ached, in intensity of desire to shut out the spectacle; I buried my head in the pillow, that I might not hear that awful laugh of diabolic sarcasm.

But—oh horror immeasurable! I beheld the walls of the room slowly gliding together, the ceiling coming down, the floor ascending, as of old the lonely captive saw them, whose cell was doomed to be his coffin. Nearer and nearer am I borne toward the corpse. I shrunk back from the edge of the bed; I cowered in most abject fear. I tried to cry out, but speech was paralyzed. The walls came closer and closer together. Presently my hand lay on the dead man's forehead. I made my arm as straight and rigid as a bar of iron; but of what avail was human strength against the contraction of that cruel masonry? Slowly my elbow bent with the ponderous pressure; nearer grew the ceiling—I fell into the fearful embrace of death. I was pent, I was stifled in the breathless niche, which was all of space still left to me. The stony eyes stared up into my own, and again the maddening peal of fiendish laughter rang close beside my ear. Now I was touched on all sides by the walls of the terrible press; there came a heavy crush, and I felt all sense blotted out in darkness.

I awaked at last; the corpse was gone, but I had taken his place upon the bier. In the same attitude which he had kept I lay motionless, conscious, although in darkness, that I wore upon my face the counterpart of his look of agony. The room had grown into a gigantic hall, whose roof was framed of iron arches; the pavement, the walls, the cornice were all of iron. The spiritual essence of the metal seemed to be a combination of cruelty and despair. Its massive hardness spoke a language which it is impossible to embody in words, but any one who has watched the relentless sweep of some great engine crank, and realized its capacity for murder, will catch a glimpse, even in the memory, of the thrill which seemed to say, "This iron is a tearless fiend," of the unutterable meaning I saw in those colossal beams and buttresses. I suffered from the vision of that iron as from the presence of a giant assassin.

But my senses opened slowly to the perception of still worse presences. By my side there gradually emerged from the sulphureous twilight which bathed the room the most horrible form which the soul could look upon unshattered—a fiend also of iron, white hot and dazzling with the glory of the nether penetralia. A face that was the ferreous incarnation of all imaginations of malice and irony looked on me with a glare, withering from its intense heat, but still more from the unconceived degree of inner wickedness which it symbolized. I realized whose laughter I had heard, and instantly I heard it again. Beside him another demon, his very twin, was rocking a tremendous cradle framed of bars of iron like all things else, and candescent with as fierce a heat as the fiend's.

And now, in a chant of the most terrific blasphemy which it is possible to imagine, or rather of blasphemy so fearful that no human thought has ever conceived of it, both the demons broke forth, until I grew intensely wicked merely by hearing it. I still remember the meaning of the song they sang, although there is no language yet coined which will convey it, and far be it from me even to suggest its nature, lest I should seem to perpetuate in any degree such profanity as beyond the abodes of the lost no lips are capable of uttering. Every note of the music itself accorded with the thought as symbol represents essence, and with its clangor mixed the maddening creak of the forever-oscillating cradle, until I felt driven into a ferocious despair. Suddenly the nearest fiend, snatching up a pitchfork (also of white-hot iron), thrust it into my writhing side, and hurled me shrieking into the fiery cradle. I sought in my torture to scale the bars; they slipped from my grasp and under my feet like the smoothest icicles. Through increasing grades of agony I lay unconsumed, tossing from side to side with the rocking of the dreadful engine, and still above me pealed the chant of blasphemy, and the eyes of demoniac sarcasm smiled at me in mockery of a mother's gaze upon her child.

"Let us sing him," said one of the fiends to the other, "the lullaby of Hell." The blasphemy now changed into an awful word-picturing of eternity, unveiling what it was, and dwelling with raptures of malice upon its infinitude, its sublimity of growing pain, and its privation of all fixed points which might mark it into divisions. By emblems common to all language rather than by any vocal words, did they sing this frightful apocalypse, yet the very emblems had a sound as distinct as tongue could give them. This was one, and the only one of their representatives that I can remember. Slowly they began, "To-day is father of to-morrow, to-morrow hath a son that shall beget the day succeeding." With increasing rapidity they sang in this way, day by day, the genealogy of a thousand years, and I traced on the successive generations, without a break in one link, until the rush of their procession reached a rapidity so awful as fully to typify eternity itself; and still I fled on through that burning genesis of cycles. I feel that I do not convey my meaning, but may no one else ever understand it better!

Withered like a leaf in the breath of an oven, after millions of years I felt myself tossed upon the iron floor. The fiends had departed, the cradle was gone. I stood alone, staring into immense and empty spaces. Presently I found that I was in a colossal square, as of some European city, alone at the time of evening twilight, and surrounded by houses hundreds of stories high. I was bitterly athirst. I ran to the middle of the square, and reached it after an infinity of travel. There was a fountain carved in iron, every jet inimitably sculptured in mockery of water, yet dry as the ashes of a furnace. "I shall perish with thirst," I cried. "Yet one more trial. There must be people in all these immense houses. Doubtless they love the dying traveler, and will give him to drink. Good friends! water! water!" A horribly deafening din poured down on me from the four sides of the square. Every sash of all the hundred stories of every house in that colossal quadrangle flew up as by one spring. Awakened by my call, at every window stood a terrific maniac. Sublimely in the air above me, in front, beside me, on either hand, and behind my back, a wilderness of insane faces gnashed at me, glared, gibbered, howled, laughed horribly, hissed, and cursed. At the unbearable sight I myself became insane, and, leaping up and down, mimicked them all, and drank their demented spirit.

A hand seized my arm—a voice called my name. The square grew lighter—it changed—it slowly took a familiar aspect, and gradually I became aware that my room-mate was standing before me with a lighted lamp. I sank back into his arms, crying "Water! water, Robert! For the love of heaven, water!" He passed across the room to the wash-stand, leaving me upon the bed, where I afterward found he had replaced me on being awakened by hearing me leap frantically up and down upon the floor. In going for the water, he seemed to be traveling over a desert plain to some far-off spring, and I hailed him on his return with the pitcher and the glass as one greets his friend restored after a long journey. No glass for me! I snatched the pitcher, and drank a Niagara of refreshment with every draught. I reveled in the ecstasy of a drinker of the rivers of Al Ferdoos.

Hasheesh always brings with it an awakening of perception which magnifies the smallest sensation till it occupies immense boundaries. The hasheesh-eater who drinks during his highest state of exaltation almost invariably supposes that he is swallowing interminable floods, and imagines his throat an abyss which is becoming gorged by the sea. Repeatedly, as in an agony of thirst I have clutched some small vessel of water and tipped it at my lips, I have felt such a realization of an overwhelming torrent that, with my throat still charred, I have put the water away, lest I should be drowned by the flow.

With the relighting of the lamp my terrors ceased. The room was still immense, yet the iron of its structure, in the alembic of that heavenly light, had been transmuted into silver and gold. Beamy spars, chased by some unearthly graver, supported the roof above me, and a mellow glory transfused me, shed from sunny panels that covered the walls. Out of this hall of grammarye I suddenly passed through a crystal gate, and found myself again in the world outside. Through a valley carpeted with roses I marched proudly at the head of a grand army, and the most triumphant music pealed from all my legions. In the symphony joined many an unutterable instrument, bugles and ophicleides, harps and cymbals, whose wondrous peals seemed to say, "We are self-conscious; we exult like human souls." There were roses every where—roses under foot, roses festooning the lattices at our sides, roses showering a prodigal flush of beauty from the arches of an arbor overhead. Down the valley I gained glimpses of dreamy lawns basking in a Claude Lorraine sunlight. Over them multitudes of rosy children came leaping to throw garlands on my victorious road, and singing paeans to me with the voices of cherubs. Nations that my sword had saved ran bounding through the flowery walls of my avenue to cry "Our hero—our savior," and prostrate themselves at my feet. I grew colossal in a delirium of pride. I felt myself the centre of all the world's immortal glory. As once before the ecstasy of music had borne me from the body, so now I floated out of it in the intensity of my triumph. As the last cord was dissolved, I saw all the attendant splendors of my march fade away, and became once more conscious of my room restored to its natural state.

Not a single hallucination remained. Surrounding objects resumed their wonted look, yet a wonderful surprise broke in upon me. In the course of my delirium, the soul, I plainly discovered, had indeed departed from the body. I was that soul utterly divorced from the corporeal nature, disjoined, clarified, purified. From the air in which I hovered I looked down upon my former receptacle. Animal life, with all its processes, still continued to go on; the chest heaved with the regular rise and fall of breathing, the temples throbbed, and the cheek flushed. I scrutinized the body with wonderment; it seemed no more to concern me than that of another being. I do not remember, in the course of the whole experience I have had of hasheesh, a more singular emotion than I felt at that moment. The spirit discerned itself as possessed of all the human capacities, intellect, susceptibility, and will–saw itself complete in every respect; yet, like a grand motor, it had abandoned the machine which it once energized, and in perfect independence stood apart. In the prerogative of my spiritual nature I was restrained by no objects of a denser class. To myself I was visible and tangible, yet I knew that no material eyes could see me. Through the walls of the room I was able to pass and repass, and through the ceiling to behold the stars unobscured.

This was neither hallucination nor dream. The sight of my reason was preternaturally intense, and I remembered that this was one of the states which frequently occur to men immediately before their death has become apparent to lookers-on, and also in the more remarkable conditions of trance. That such a state is possible is incontestably proved by many cases on record in which it has fallen under the observation of students most eminent in physico-psychical science.

A voice of command called on me to return into the body, saying in the midst of my exultation over what I thought was my final disenfranchisement from the corporeal, "The time is not yet." I returned, and again felt the animal nature joined to me by its mysterious threads of conduction. Once more soul and body were one.

from **Movers and Shakers:**

Intimate Memories, volume III

M a b e l   D o d g e   L u h a n

Lover to John Reed and hostess of legendary "Evenings" in New York's Greenwich Village and "At Homes" at the ornate Villa Curonia, in Florence, attended by dozens of notable figures such as D. H. Lawrence, Amy Lowell, Carl Van Vechten, and Gertrude Stein, Mabel Dodge (later Mabel Dodge Luhan) was a *salonneuse* extraordinaire. Her elite bohemianism was typical of wealthy turn-of-the-century Americans who chose to live a step lower than proper society. When a friend suggested that she and her friends try peyote, Dodge agreed, apparently out of a combination intrigue and boredom. The casual escapade might have become a disaster had Dodge not been determined to have, if nothing else, a good story to tell later on.

D URING THE SPRING OF 1914 in one of the intervals when Reed was away, I had a strange experience with my friends. Bobby Jones had returned from Germany and was staying in one of the rooms in the back end of the apartment on Ninth Street, Andrew was in and out all the time, and Genevieve Onslow was staying for a few days in the other end of the apartment, too. Genevieve had returned from China and was on her way home to Chicago. She was in a highly stimulated mood—full of a mystical elation, and scraps of Chinese philosophy fell from her occasionally.

"If you *want* to do a thing, Mabel, don't do it, but if you *feel* to do it, do it," she would exclaim. But I didn't know what she meant.

The Hapgoods had a cousin staying with them, Raymond Harrington. He had been living among the Indians in Oklahoma doing ethnological research. He looked rather strange and had sunken eyes and an intense expression. I had never seen any Indians, but I told the Hapgoods that I thought he looked like one and they agreed.

Now Raymond told us about a peculiar ceremony among the Indians he lived with that enabled them to pass beyond ordinary consciousness and see things as they are in Reality. He said they used an Indian medicine called *peyote* in the ceremony, and sang all night long. He told us that the Indians that belonged to the Peyote Cult were the most sober and industrious of all, that they made better beadwork and seemed to be able to recover old designs through their use of the stuff and to become imbued with a nobility and a religious fervor greater than those who didn't use it.

We were all most curious about it and begged him to tell us more. When I pressed him, I found he actually had some *peyote* with him; then of course I said we must all try it. But he was grave and said it was not a thing to play with, that if we would go through with it seriously he would try to reconstruct the ceremony for us and give us an opportunity of experiencing the magnificent enhancement and enlargement of consciousness possible only through its power. It was not like hashish or any other drug, he said. In fact, it was not a drug at all, but a marvelous vehicle of the Indian life enabling one to be more deeply and wholly and concisely what one inherently was when not inhibited and overlaid by the limitations of the senses we used every day.

We were all thrilled.

Certain things were necessary to the ceremony, Raymond said We must have a green arrow, some eagle feathers, a fire, the Mountain of the Moon, and the Peyote Path. All these he must procure or simulate to compose the structure of the experience. Then there would have to be singing. The singing must never cease all through the ritual. One or another of us must always be singing, taking up the song as another left off. And we must enter the event after fasting, and continue all night until the morning star arose, when we could break our fast with fruit juice and then eat.

Raymond himself was very serious as he told us about it, almost somber, seeming wholly a convert to the practice. We grew serious too, and tried to carry it all out as he desired. We decided to ask Max Eastman and Ida to come because Ida was a friend of Genevieve's; and we were to have Andrew, Bobby, the Hapgoods, and Terry.

Terry was a grand anarchist, possessing a beautiful skeleton, a splendid head with noble features, a great quantity of iron gray hair and Irish blue eyes. He was a literal I.W.W. and a true anarchist. When he was a young man he passed up the capitalistic system and swore he would never take a job or do a day's work under it, and he had carried out his vow. He was incredibly poor, thin to starvation, for he was nearly always hungry, but he never did an hour's work for anyone or "earned" a dollar. He was a splendid talker, a dreamer, a poet, a man. Wonderful Terry! Mukerji has written of him in *Caste and Outcast*. In that book he was Jerry, one of Mukerji's two companions in San Francisco; but Mukerji had not the depth to reach, himself, to Terry's deep levels.

Raymond went out and found a green branch to make the arrow, and he found the eagle feathers. For a "fire" he laid a lighted electric bulb on the floor with my Chinese red shawl over it, and for the Mountain of the Moon–I forget what he did about that–but the Peyote Path was a white sheet folded into a narrow strip, running towards the east along the floor.

The evening we were to engage ourselves to experiment with consciousness, none of us ate any dinner. We, at Raymond's order, had dressed in our best, and the room had been thoroughly cleaned beforehand. Everything had to be tuned up a little for this, evidently–all of the accessories and surroundings must be of the finest and cleanest, the most shining. Like Church, I thought to myself.

At nine o'clock we extinguished the lights and sat on the floor in a crescent shape with the Peyote Path running eastward out of our midst. Raymond, who constituted himself the Chief, sat at the foot of the path behind the fire, an arrow in one hand, and a few lovely eagle feathers in the other. The *peyote* lay in a little heap in the center of the space before him. It looked like small, dried-up buttons with shriveled edges, and it had a kind of fur on the upper side.

Raymond told us to just take it and chew it, as many as we liked—but, once we began the Ceremony, to beware of stopping before it was over, when the Morning Star should rise. He looked so somber sitting there cross-legged that I was filled to bursting with sudden laughter. I was thrilled and excited and amused.

Suddenly Raymond seized a piece of the peyote and popped it into his mouth and began to sing. At last he raised his chin and began to howl like a dog, as it seemed to me. I looked covertly at the others.

The mere presence of that *peyote* seemed already to have emphasized the real nature in us all. I was laughing, but Neith looked down at the fire, distantly grave and withdrawn, beautiful and strange. Hutch appeared rather boyish, like a boy in church who lowers his head and peeps over his prayer book at another boy. Bobby's face was simulating a respectful attention, while it hid his thoughts. Ida looked more like a superior lioness than ever, cynical and intolerant; Max grinned amiably, complacent and friendly to anything, and Terry seemed more remote than the others–as he contemplated. the end of his cigarette (for cigarettes were *de rigueur* and, in fact, compulsory, I believe).

Genevieve Onslow's frog-like eyes were brilliant and intense. Her thin face looked like parchment. Andrew's brows twitched as he gave and yet did not give himself to the occasion; a half smile played over his sulky lips, but it was an irritated smile. Only I seemed to myself to be just exactly as usual, unaffected by anything and observant of it all.

Raymond chewed on his *peyote* and sang his song that was like the howl of a dog. He swung the tempo faster and motioned to us to begin.

Then we all, in our different fashions, reached out and took the *peyote* and put it into our mouths, and began to chew upon it. But it was bitter! Oh, how it was bitter! I chewed for a little while and watched the others. They all seemed to be chewing away, too. Everybody chewed.

But after a while, as I swallowed the bitter saliva, I felt a certain numbness coming over me in my mouth and limbs. But it was only over my body. My brain was clearly filled with laughter! Laughter, laughter, laughter at all the others there. Laughter, and at the same time a canny, almost smug discretion took possession of me.

When Raymond had chewed up his first *peyote,* and the others had all chewed theirs, he, still singing, handed his green arrow to the one who sat on his right hand, and motioned him to sing, and motioned to us all to take another *peyote* with him.

Raymond's unfortunate neighbor didn't know how to sing Indian songs. Raymond, with an urgently anxious look on his face, continued to sing himself, as he beckoned the other to sing. Evidently he *must* sing–it was frightfully important.

Raymond impressed this need so acutely that Hutch (it was Hutch!) actually lifted up his voice–and popping a *peyote* into his mouth, sat with the green arrow in a hieratical pose, and howled in a disjointed and unrhythmical way that, however, did not seem unpleasant to Raymond. It was evidently not so much the *way* you did a thing, it was that you *did* it, that counted.

Presently, I raised a *peyote* to my mouth, made a movement with my lips and, prudently, I secreted it deeper into the palm of my hand. Shaking with ghoulish laughter, I held it until my first move to take it was forgotten, and then I thrust it behind me on the floor. But the others chewed and chewed on their second *peyote,* and each of them had sunk just a little deeper into themselves–had become a trifle *more* themselves. . . .

Useless to describe the slow inward progress of the *peyote.* On the surface everything remained the same. Forgetting self-consciousness in a deepened being, each one sang in his turn. Some time after the second *peyote,* Max and Ida got up and left almost unnoticed. My one and only taste had started me laughing and the laughter endured. Everyone seemed ridiculous to me–utterly ridiculous and immeasurably far away from me. Far away from me, several little foolish human beings sat staring at a mock fire and made silly little gestures. Above them I leaned, filled with an unlimited contempt for the facile enthrallments of humanity, weak and petty in its activities, bound so easily by a dried herb, bound by its notions of everything–anarchy, poetry, systems, sex and society.

Bobby! Look at Bobby's beard! Like a Persian miniature of a late period, not well drawn, inexpressive, he rolled subjugated eyes, increasingly solemn as he viewed the changing colors unrolling before him. And Hutch! Good heavens! Hutch looked like a Lutheran Monk! Genevieve stared continually at a spot on the rug before her, her eyes enormous now, the whites showing all around them in an appalled revelation of something.

But Terry! Almost I stopped laughing when I looked at Terry, for he had increased in stature. His head was huge, and clear cut, every bone in his face, as he looked with a terrible intensity of Seeing at the lighted end of his cigarette. No, I could not laugh at Terry. He frightened me a little.

Another thing that was noticeable was the eerie effect upon everyone's expression from the dim light of the "fire," that electric globe smoldering under the red shawl. It reminded me of the ghastly results we used to procure as children by having two of us stare fixedly at each other, while another turned the gas jet up and then lowered it; continuing thus, we were able to induce the most devilish expressions, with deathly shades of color that fluctuated with the varying light. So now, although the light was fixed, though dim, it seemed that various and strange changes came over the faces before me.

The night wore on, and a more and more peculiar atmosphere enclosed us. The songs kept up–monotonous and outlandish, and gradually my laughter wore itself out and I grew weary and longed to leave. For me to long to leave was but a signal for my departure, for I was an impatient soul–undisciplined. I began to whisper and make signs, nodding my head towards my bedroom, and most of the others, I discovered, were as ready as I to go. As inconspicuously as possible, then, the Hapgoods, Bobby and Andrew and I rose–and stood–looking at the others.

But the others were oblivious. Harrington, Terry and Genevieve continued, their fixedness of attention upon other worlds than ours. They were lost to us. They did not see us or take any notice of us at all. We crept off to bed, I to my white room at the far end of the suite, the Hapgoods, Andrew and Bobby out through the kitchen to the little bedrooms beyond in the Ninth Street part of the apartment.

After I was in bed I lay still and listened. The weird song from the front room came only in a faraway, muffled fashion through my closed door. I visualized the scene I had left, the darkened room, the "fire," the Peyote Path, and the Mountain of the Moon. I saw, in my mind's eye, the three people sitting there absorbed, unheeding, lost.

And my mind grew angry all of a sudden. Very angry! To think that that was going on there in my house and *I could not stop it* if I wanted to! Until this thought came to me, I had not particularly, wanted to stop it, but as soon as I did think of it, it frightened me by its intensity. It was not so much that something was going on, but that something was going on *in my house* that I could not stop even if I wanted to. And instantly, because this was the case, I wanted terribly to stop it. I *must* stop it! But how?

Nothing could reach those entranced people. They were gone! Gone into the *peyote* world and I did not know how to follow them and bring them back. I grew more and more angry and more in a panic than ever before in my life, except, perhaps, that time at Aunt Clarissa's on Staten Island.

How could I stop that thing?

I began to throw all my attention into praying, with the fullest concentration and passion of which I was capable–praying to It–to that Force in which I believed and which I thought I knew how to contact.

"Oh, Great Force, hear me! Stop that thing in there! *Stop it! Stop it!*" I breathed my whole being into my prayer.

And as I prayed I heard in the distance–further away than than the muffled chant–a sound of steps, of hobbling, hasty steps, and the tap of a cane, coming nearer and nearer through the silent house. I held my breath. The hurried steps came nearer and nearer–they were coming from the other end of the house. I recognized them. Only Andrew sounded like that. I had summoned him. Let anyone, who doubts these possibilities, try once with power and passion to invoke the Force that lies about us.

I lay scarcely breathing now and waited for him to carry out my prayer, and I heard him stamp as though in a fury, past my door, through the dining room and the next room, to where I knew the three others sat cross-legged and oblivious on the floor, enwrapped in another consciousness than his.

I listened to him "stop" that thing. I heard him trampling heavily about, uttering short, angry words; I heard the windows thrown up, and I heard–what was that?–something like a dreadful cry of anguish. An instant's silence, and then a tapping at my door.

I turned on the electric light and I jumped out of bed and rushed to open it a crack. Genevieve stood there. Her face gleamed almost phosphorescent, her large eyes, showing the whites all round them, glared at me.

"Mabel!" she gasped. "Oh, Mabel! It is *terrible,*" and she was gone.

I flung on a dressing gown and ran out. Andrew was lurching around the room with a furious face–looking like an avenging angel, striking his cane into the red shawl that lay in a heap, at the white sheet that had been the "path," and at the few *peyotes* that were scattered, now, about the floor.

Terry sat gazing fixedly at the end of his cigarette–but Harrington looked about him dazed and horrified.

"Stop, man! That is terribly dangerous!" he said over and over as I came in.

When Andrew saw me, he cried:

"After I got to bed I suddenly felt I couldn't stand having this thing going on any more! *I had* to break it up."

"Where is Genevieve?" I cried.

But she was gone.

While I went to call Hutch and Neith and tell them what had happened, Harrington sat like a haunted, helpless creature in a corner of a sofa and Terry, moved now to the little room off the drawing room, sat serene and attentive, always gazing at the end of his cigarette.

Genevieve was gone. There was no doubt about that. We hunted the rooms for her, but she had fled like a phantom out of the apartment, down the stairs and out–out–

Where?

And now we entered upon the second phase of that crazy night. The thought of Genevieve out in the windy streets of the city was unthinkable, the condition she was in–unaccountable for herself–unable to explain anything–not even knowing where she was–it frightened us all. We didn't know where to look for her–where to go first should one of us start out after her.

I saw Hutch fumbling on his hands and knees behind a chair and went to look closer and ask what on earth he was doing. He gave me a queer look. He was gathering up bits of *peyote*–whole ones and the broken ones I had thrust behind me.

"If the *Police* should come in here and find this . . ."

Police! Heavens, I *was* scared!

Harrington, muttering to himself in a corner, seemed not to be with us at all–no more did Terry, sitting alone and smiling down at his cigarette. Hutch and Neith and I and Andrew–we were the only ones to deal with the situation and we hadn't the remotest idea where to begin.

A sharp ring at the telephone startled us all. I ran to answer it and it was Max.

"Genevieve is here," he said. "We heard her crying under the window."

"How *is* she?" I cried.

"Well, I don't know. We will put her to bed and see you in the morning."

The sickening light of dawn began to creep into the rooms and show up the strange disorder about us. Furniture displaced, the red shawl, and the white sheet lying on the floor. And two men with white faces with us, but not of us.

The fear about Genevieve somewhat allayed, we turned back to the *peyote*–that most mysterious of all the growing things that I had ever encountered.

Hutch, lowering his voice, came up and spoke to me. I noticed he had altered. He appeared diminished and shrunken as though he had lost fifty pounds of flesh. He was pale and he looked awed.

"Mabel," he said, "I have learned tonight something wonderful. I cannot put it into words exactly, but I have found the short cut to the Soul."

"What is it?" I asked

"The death of the flesh," he almost whispered, and I saw from his eyes that the *peyote* in him lent a far deeper significance to the words for him than for me.

"I *saw* it," he went on. "I saw the death of the flesh occur in my body and I saw the Soul emerge from that death."

"I saw no such thing," said Neith, smiling with a beautiful strangeness. "As I sat there, I saw the walls of this house fall away and I was following a lovely river for miles and miles through the most wonderful virginal forest I have ever known." She was elated and enhanced.

"I saw what Sex is," Andrew broke in. "And it is a square crystal cube, transparent and colorless; and at the same time I saw that I was looking at my Soul."

Then Harrington sprang up. In the early cold light of the morning his face was greenish and his eyes stared horrified.

"I can't breathe," he gasped. "My heart–Get me something. Some fruit . . ."

Scared, I ran into the kitchen looking for some oranges When I came back Hutch was bending over him.

"It is like a palpitation," he said.

And Terry sat on–smiling, not hearing or seeing us–just gazing down at his cigarette.

If only the *day* would come," I exclaimed. "And the cook and breakfast and everything!"

Finally we were seated at the table and we were drinking coffee Harrington sat with his head in his hands and sometimes a violent shaking came over him.

"You don't know what you did," he said once to Andrew.

And all this time Terry stayed where he was, never coming near us; serene and immobile, he sat with one long leg crossed over the other and seemed to ponder on illimitable things. We carried some orange juice to him, but he did not see us.

Andrew continued to expostulate and explain his action–almost to himself, it seemed.

"I *had* to do it," he said wonderingly, over and over, and Hutch, not listening to him, repeated his own wonderment in rumpling tones, meditatively:

"Think of it–to learn the way to the Soul–the shortest way . . ."

Our cook looked at us curiously as she served our queer breakfast. I can't imagine what she thought and no one but myself noticed her. It was, as usual, my curse to be aware of all the elements at once.

Then Max and Ida came with Genevieve and left her, not saying much beyond the need to get a doctor for her. Max sort of slipped away quite quickly, but Ida stayed.

Genevieve was just gibbering. She was making curious rapid movements, her eyes rolled in her head, she ran with dreadful haste into her room, Neith and Ida and I after her. She began to pick up one thing and then another.

"I must go!" she cried, not looking at any of us. "I must see father. I have something to tell him." She clasped two little silk Chinese slippers to her breast. "Father always came and sat by me when I went to bed and was frightened," she said, and her words came tumbling with utmost haste from her white lips. "And now I must tell him something." There was a terribly touching quality about her that made one want to cry, but I swallowed this feeling and ran to ask Hutch what to do.

We thought it best to telegraph her father and then to get a doctor for her, so I wired Mr. Onslow:

GENEVIEVE ILL WITH A NERVOUS BREAKDOWN –MABEL DODGE.

To which he replied immediately to Genevieve, saying:

I AM COMING TO MY LITTLE GIRL AS FAST AS POSSIBLE KEEP UP YOUR COURAGE DEAR –FATHER.

Hutch said, "We must call Harry Lorber–he is discreet. He won't talk." And he rang him up.

This East Side Jewish doctor was the friend of all of us and of all the Radicals. He was used to dilemmas. He examined Genevieve carefully. While he was there she seemed not to see him, and kept staring off into a corner of the room. Harry led Hutch and me out of the room and said quizzically:

"Dope, hey?"

"We don't know," replied Hutch, earnestly, "what it is." And he told Harry all that had happened and produced one of the *peyote*s to show him.

"I never heard of it. I wonder if it is anything like *mescal.* That comes from old Mexico. This stuff has a powerful action on the heart and is evidently a hypnotic. A highly strung girl like this might easily be injured by it. I'd like to study this queer-looking little button," he went on, smiling at the thing in his hand. "Evidently Dasburg gave her a terrific shock by breaking in so brusquely upon the dream state it produces."

He was pacing up and down the room, now.

"She must have a nurse," he said. "I know a good girl." And he telephoned her. Then he gave Genevieve some medicine. "Don't let her out of your sight," Harry cautioned the nurse, "and watch her pulse. I'll come back in a couple of hours."

Then he went up to Terry, whom he knew, and spoke to him. Terry looked up for the first time in all that long night and smiled the most illumined smile I have ever seen. His eyes were blue like gentians.

"Harry," he said, "I have seen the Universe, and Man! It is wonderful!" Then he got his hat and just walked out and I don't think I have ever seen him to talk to again.

Genevieve seemed to give up, then. She let us do as we would with her and we established her on a *chaise longue* in the front room She seemed to give up like a child and did not try to go on gathering her things to pack them. She lay there staring and staring out of the window, quiet now, not speaking, nor seeming to see us, and the tears streamed down her face.

"Genevieve," I whispered, "what do you see?"

"God," she replied, never moving her eyes.

"And is it . . . ?"

"It is very, very sad," she said from the depths of her soul.

I left her to the nurse and went to my room, but I hadn't been away more than a few moments when the girl came running in, exclaiming,

"Is she *here?*"

"No! Did you leave her?"

"Only to get her a glass of water. When I came back, she was gone–!"

Heavens! It was too much. With the uncanny, unhesitating certainty of a lunatic, Genevieve had seized her first chance. She was out in the street again. We had lost her, maybe this time for good.

Really, I didn't know where to turn now. For I called Ida and Max and they had seen nothing of her. Besides, instinctively I knew she would not go to them a second time when they had delivered her into our hands and we had held her against her will. Hutch was awfully upset, too.

"We *must* not let this get into the papers," he said, with the journalist's realization of their possibilities. "Yet we may need to notify the police," he went on. "I think I'll call John Collier."

Collier was over at the People's Institute. He was one of the really emancipated people I knew and he had an extraordinarily youthful face that sometimes looked like that of a good child and sometimes was consumed with hate.

It was Hutch who had first told me he was a genius, and I believed that he was. His work was sometimes mixed up with poor people, generally foreigners, whose European cultures he tried to preserve. He was constantly organizing pageants wherein Syrians, Slavs, or Italians could parade dressed in their native costumes and occasionally he pulled off a brilliant innovation such as turning the Public Schools into Recreation Centers and having Play Streets in the heart of the city. He was a reformer–and his friends were reformers. There was something drear about some of them but not about Collier. He had a deep flame in him.

Luther Gulick, who invented the Camp Fire Girls, and Fred Howe, who tried to make Ellis Island human, were his friends, and he knew all the city officials–so I suppose Hutch thought of him on that account, in the dilemma we were in.

We telephoned and he came right over, for the People's Institute was only a short way up the Avenue. He came into the apartment with his green eyes slightly malicious, but always amused, and his untidy hair falling over his brow–a small, *chétif* boyish figure with a great many strings in his hands that we knew he could pull if he wanted to.

Hutch told the strange story over again as briefly as he could. We were in a hurry to get something done. Genevieve was lost and her father had probably started for New York. What should we say to him if he came before we found her?

Collier drew down his thin lips and raised his eyebrows.

"Undoubtedly you could all be indicted under the illicit drug act," he began, in a low voice that could strike terror into his listeners. His method was the kind that first alarms and then allays. He described the worst possibility, then proceeded to remedy it.

"But we didn't know it was a Drug!" exclaimed Hutch, impatiently.

"That doesn't *matter*. It evidently *was* one. A very interesting one, too. I'd like to experiment with it sometime," he continued, pedantically.

"Well, you can't *now*. What do you think we'd better *do*?" queried Hutch. "You know the resources of the town better than I do. Shall we send out a general alarm–or something more discreet?"

"Well, of course I can call up Sheriff Harburger and put him on to it, or I can go to a private Agency and get a couple of good men, but I'm inclined to think the least publicity we give it the better, considering how well-known Mrs. Dodge and this house are. Some cub of a reporter would get hold of the story the minute it goes outside these doors. Someone may have *already* got it!" he went on, brightly, almost hopefully, I thought.

The time was rolling by and it was getting later and later in the day. My feelings were very mixed. I didn't think anything would happen because I didn't feel that certainty I always had inside me before disaster, a kind of realization before the event, of what was to come, that, if I examined it and trusted to it, never deceived me. And yet the talk of these two men was alarming. What bothered me most was that I should be personally implicated in the eyes of my acquaintances with a situation that was ambiguous enough to deserve, even at any angle, the name of a "Dope Party." Horrors!

I had heard of such gatherings and they were the antithesis of all I wished to stand for. The level of my life, at least in my own eyes, was infinitely raised above such sordid sensationalism. The very word "dope" annoyed me, and seemed to cling to me like pitch. I longed to be well out of its circuit–yet there I was, hemmed in, unable to run away and forget the whole disagreeable scrape, obliged to cope with a situation brought upon me by the others, who should have had the thing at *their* house, not mine, I thought. Why should I be the one who would have to bear the brunt of all that might result from their crazy cousin's peculiarities?

Well, it wasn't the first time, nor the last, that my shoulders would support an unexpected and undeserved opprobrium, I went on thinking. I felt more and more aloof, disgusted, bored, and disconnected from the whole thing. Why, I had apparently been the only one who had known enough not to seize the stuff and swallow handfuls of it! And yet there I was probably with a "dope party" staring at me from the pages of all the evening papers.

I felt pretty helpless with the stormy petrel that Collier had turned into and the inefficient and unresourceful Hutch who had no ideas at all when they were really needed.

I don't remember what they finally did, how we found Genevieve, what happened next, or anything about it. I know that every one of the others who had been at the apartment that night talked about it *for years,* and even still continue to do so, that I kept forever hearing echoes of every description about it, some of them of the worst kind. Undoubtedly that legend has encircled the world.

I know I never saw Genevieve again and that she didn't want to see me, and that her family have never had anything but a horror of me, filled with blame and the darkest suspicions, but that I have some strange communications that she sent me after a while from Chicago, composed of symbols and hieroglyphs with a phrase or two interspersed, and that these symbols are among the most ancient known and are found, faintly recognizable, carved on old rocks in the Indian country, though their meaning remains unknown to scholars.

I know, indeed, that that night was another-world night when, undoubtedly, the white apartment with its colored glass was the scene of something more esoteric and indecipherable than it ever housed before or since. But why it should have been brought to pass in *my* rooms, bringing in its train unmerited and hateful "allegations"–that was perhaps the greatest mystery of all, at least to me!

Terry I never saw at close hand, only in the distance at Eugene O'Neill's in Provincetown; Genevieve I never saw, though I had those strange papers from her that she sent while she was still under the influence of the *peyote;* Raymond Harrington, I never saw either, though I have heard of him at the Heye Museum in New York, where the Indian collection of ceremonial regalia connected with *peyote* in the Southwest is the finest to be found anywhere in the world.

from **Really the Blues**

M e z z   M e z z r o w

Milton Mezzrow was an ofay half-cat jazz musician who fell for black blues and spent his life among the people he adopted as his own. Blacks accepted him with open arms —not merely because he supplied the best marijuana on the streets (called the mezz, in his honor). His autobiography,first published in 1946, is a hip tour of mid-century underground culture in the States, from Chicago to New Orleans to Harlem. His tale is full of boho kicks the likes of which Kerouac and Cassady were to pursue a generation later. Mezzrow has been called the "single most important figure in the history of marijuana in America." In this excerpt, Mezz gets high for the first time.

IT WAS THAT FLASHY, SAWED-OFF RUNT of a jockey named Patrick who made a viper out of me after Leon Rappolo failed. Back in the Arrowhead Inn, where I first met Patrick, he told me he was going to New Orleans and would be back one day with some marihuana, real golden-leaf. He asked me did I want some of the stuff, and coming up tough I said sure, bring me some, I'd like to try it. When Patrick marched into the Martinique one night I began to look for the nearest exit, but it was too late. "Hi ya, boy," he said with a grin bigger than he was hisself, "let's you and me go to the can, I got something for you." That men's room might have been a deathhouse, the way I kept curving away from it, but this muta-mad Tom Thumb latched on to me like a ball-and-chain and steered me straight inside.

As soon as we were alone he pulled out a gang of cigarettes and handed them to me. They were as fat as ordinary cigarettes but were rolled in brown wheatstraw paper. We both lit up and I got halfway through mine hoping they would break the news to mother gently, before he stopped me. "Hey," he said, "take it easy, kid. You want to knock yourself out?"

I didn't feel a thing and I told him so. "Do you know one thing?" he said. "You ain't even smokin' it right. You got to hold that muggle so that it barely touches your lips, see, then draw in air around it. Say *tfff, tfff,* only breathe in when you say it. Then don't blow it out right away, you got to give the stuff a chance." He had a tricky look in his eye that I didn't go for at all. The last time I saw that kind of look it was on a district attorney's mug, and it caused me a lot of inconvenience.

After I finished the weed I went back to the bandstand.

Everything seemed normal and I began to play as usual. I passed a stick of gauge around for the other boys to smoke, and we started a set.

The first thing I noticed was that I began to hear my saxophone as though it was inside my head, but I couldn't hear much of the band in back of me, although I knew they were there. All the other instruments sounded like they were way off in the distance; I got the same sensation you'd get if you stuffed your ears with cotton and talked out loud. Then I began to feel the vibrations of the reed much more pronounced against my lip, and my head buzzed like a loudspeaker. I found I was slurring much better and putting just the right feeling into my phrases–I was really coming on. All the notes came easing out of my horn like they'd already been made up, greased and stuffed into the bell, so all I had to do was blow a little and send them on their way, one right after the other, never missing, never behind time, all without an ounce of effort. The phrases seemed to have more continuity to them and I was sticking to the theme without ever going tangent. I felt I could go on playing for years without running out of ideas and energy. There wasn't any struggle; it was all made-to-order and suddenly there wasn't a sour note or a discord in the world that could bother me. I began to feel very happy and sure of myself. With my loaded horn I could take all the fist-swinging, evil things in the world and bring them together in perfect harmony, spreading peace and joy and relaxation to all the keyed-up and punchy people everywhere. I began to preach my millenniums on my horn, leading all the sinners on to glory.

The other guys in the band were giggling and making cracks, but I couldn't talk with my mouthpiece between my lips, so I closed my eyes and drifted out to the audience with my music. The people were going crazy over the subtle changes in our playing; they couldn't dig what was happening but some kind of electricity was crackling in the air and it made them all glow and jump. Every so often I opened my eyes and found myself looking straight into a girl's face right in front of the bandstand, swinging there like a pendulum. She was an attractive, rose-complexioned chick, with wind-blown honey-colored hair, and her flushed face was all twisted up with glee. That convulsed face of hers stirred up big waves of laughter in my stomach, waves that kept breaking loose and spreading up to my head, shaking my whole frame. I had to close my eyes fast to keep from exploding with the joy.

It's a funny thing about marihuana–when you first begin smoking it you see things in a wonderful soothing, easygoing new light. All of a sudden the world is stripped of its dirty gray shrouds and becomes one big bellyful of giggles, a spherical laugh, bathed in brilliant, sparkling colors that hit you like a heatwave. Nothing leaves you cold any more; there's a humorous tickle and great meaning in the least little thing, the twitch of somebody's little finger or the click of a beer glass. All your pores open like funnels, your nerve ends stretch their mouths wide, hungry and thirsty for new sights and sounds and sensations; and every sensation, when it comes, is the most exciting one you've ever had. You can't get enough of anything–you want to gobble up the whole goddamned universe just for an appetizer. Them first kicks are a killer, Jim.

Suppose you're the critical and analytical type, always ripping things to pieces, tearing the covers off and being disgusted by what you find under the sheet. Well, under the influence of muta you don't lose your surgical touch exactly, but you don't come up evil and grimy about it. You still see what you saw before but in a different, more tolerant way, through rose-colored glasses and things that would have irritated you before just tickle you. Everything is good for a laugh; the wrinkles get ironed out of your face and you forget what a frown is, you just want to hold on to your belly and roar till the tears come. Some women especially, instead of being nasty and mean just go off bellowing until hysteria comes on. All the larceny kind of dissolves out of them—they relax and grin from ear to ear, and get right on the ground floor with you. Maybe no power on earth can work out a lasting armistice in that eternal battle of the sexes, but muggles are the one thing I know that can even bring about an overnight order to "Cease firing."

Tea puts a musician in a real masterly sphere, and that's why so many jazzmen have used it. You look down on the other members of the band like an old mother hen surveying her brood of chicks; if one of them hits a sour note or comes up with a bad modulation, you just smile tolerantly and figure, oh well, he'll learn, it'll be better next time, give the guy a chance. Pretty soon you find yourself helping him out, trying to put him on the right track. The most terrific thing is this, that all the while you're playing, really getting off, your own accompaniment keeps flashing through your head, just like you were a one-man band. You hear the basic tones of the theme and keep up your pattern of improvisation without ever getting tangled up, giving out with a uniform sequence all the way. Nothing can mess you up. You hear everything at once and you hear it right. When you get that feeling of power and sureness, you're in a solid groove.

You know how jittery, got-to-be-moving people in the city always get up in the subway train two minutes before they arrive at the station? Their nerves are on edge; they're watching the clock, thinking about schedules, full of that high-powered mile-a-minute jive. Well, when you've picked up on some gauge that clock just stretches its arms, yawns, and dozes off. The whole world slows down and gets drowsy. You wait until the train stops dead and the doors slide open, then you get up and stroll out in slow motion, like a sleepwalker with a long night ahead of him and no appointments to keep. You've got all the time in the world. What's the rush, buddy? Take-it-easy, that's the play, it's bound to sweeten it all the way.

I kept on blowing, with my eyes glued shut, and then a strange thing happened. All of a sudden somebody was screaming in a choked, high-pitched voice, like she was being strangled, "Stop it, you're killing me! Stop! I can't stand it!" When I opened my eyes it seemed like all the people on the dance floor were melted down into one solid, mesmerized mass; it was an overstuffed sardine-can of an audience, packed in an olive-oil trance. The people were all pasted together, looking up at the band with hypnotic eyes and swaying—at first I saw just a lot of shining eyes bobbing lazily on top of a rolling sea of flesh. But off to one side there was discord, breaking the spell. An entertainer, one of the girls who did a couple of vocals and specialized in a suggestive dance routine, was having a ball all to herself. She had cut loose from her partner and was throwing herself around like a snake with the hives. The rhythm really had this queen; her eyes almost jumped out of their sockets and the cords in her neck stood out stiff and hard like ropes. What she was doing with the rest of her anatomy isn't discussed in mixed company.

"Don't do that!" she yelled. "Don't do that to me!" When she wasn't shouting her head off she just moaned way down in her soundbox, like an owl gargling.

Then with one flying leap she sailed up on the bandstand, pulled her dress up to her neck, and began to dance. I don't know if dance is the right word for what she did–she didn't move her feet hardly at all, although she moved practically everything else. She went through her whole routine, bumps and grinds and shakes and breaks, making up new twists as she went along, and I mean twists. A bandstand was sure the wrong place to do what she was trying to do that night. All the time she kept screaming, "Cut it out! It's murder!" but her body wasn't saying no.

It was a frantic scene, like a nightmare walking, and it got wilder because all the excitement made us come on like gangbusters to accompany this palsy-bug routine. Patrick and his gang of vipers were getting their kicks–the gauge they picked up on was really in there, and it had them treetop tall, mellow as a cello. Monkey Pollack stood in the back, moving a little less than a petrified tree, only his big lips shaking like meatballs with the chills, and the Ragtime Cowboy Jew was staring through the clouds of smoke as though he was watching a coyote do a toe-dance. That girl must have been powered with Diesel engines, the way she kept on going. The sweat was rolling down her screwed-up face like her pores were faucets, leaving streaks of mascara in the thick rouge. She would have made a scarecrow do a nip-up and a flip.

The tension kept puffing up like an overstuffed balloon, and finally it broke. There was the sharp crack of pistol shots ringing through the sweat and strain. Fear clamped down over the sea of faces like a mask, and the swaying suddenly stopped.

It was only Mac, our gunplayful cowboy bartender. Whenever he got worked up he would whip out his pistols and fire at the ceiling, catching the breaks in our music The excitement that night was too much for him and to ease his nerves he was taking pot-shots at the electric bulbs, with a slap-happy grin on his kisser. Every time he pulled the trigger another Mazda crossed the Great Divide–he may have been punchy but his trigger finger didn't know about it.

The girl collapsed then, as though somebody had yanked the backbone right out of her body. She fell to the floor like a hunk of putty and lay in a heap, quivering and making those funny noises way down in her throat. They carried her upstairs and put her to bed, and I guess she woke up about six weeks later. Music sure hath charms, all right, but what it does to the savage breast isn't always according to the books.

The bandstand was only a foot high but when I went to step down it took me a year to find the floor, it seemed so far away. I was sailing through the clouds, flapping my free-wheeling wings, and leaving the stand was like stepping off into space. Twelve months later my foot struck solid ground with a jolt, but the other one stayed up there on those lovely soft clouds, and I almost fell flat on my face. There was a roar of laughter from Patrick's table and I began to feel self-conscious and nauseous at the same time. I flew to the men's room and got there just in time. Patrick came in and started to laugh at me.

"What's the matter, kid?" he said. "You not feeling so good?" At that moment I was up in a plane, soaring around the sky, with a buzz-saw in my head. Up and around we went, saying nuts to Newton and all his fancy laws of gravitation, but suddenly we went into a nosedive and I came down to earth, sock. Ouch. My head went spattering off in more directions than a hand grenade. Patrick put a cold towel to my temples and I snapped out of it. After sitting down for a while I was all right.

When I went back to the stand I still heard all my music amplified, as though my ear was built right into the horn. The evening rolled away before I knew it. When the entertainers sang I accompanied them on the piano, and from the way they kept glancing up at me I could tell they felt the harmonies I was inventing behind them without any effort at all. The notes kept sliding out of my horn like bubbles in seltzer water. My control over the vibrations of my tones was perfect, and I got a terrific lift from the richness of the music, the bigness of it. The notes eased out like lava running down a mountain, slow and sure and steaming. It was good.

When you run into hop, Jim, skip and jump. Hop is strictly for hamfats.

Detroit must have been built in a poppy field, there was so much opium going up in smoke in that town. I kept hearing stories from friends about all the hopdogs that lived in Detroit. A musician friend of mine named Mike who kipped in one of these hotels had to mugg with a lot of hophead gangsters who roomed near him, especially with a tough oscar named Frankie Riccardi. This Frankie, a sociable guy with a yen for company, used to drop in on Mike to beat up his chops a while. Mike would have felt happier playing host to a headhunter with his toolkit under his arm.

Frankie Riccardi was always shooting his mouth off to Mike about how great his hop was and how it made our muta look about as strong as ladies' cigars. One day while he was spieling about his dope, Mike called me over to straighten this gunman out with some golden-leaf and lowrate him once and for all. We tipped Frankie off on the routine and he burned up two sticks of gauge real fast, putting on a Samson act, sneering all the time. "These things got as much kick as some corn silk," he said. "Ain't you guys got something real strong, like a malted milk or maybe some farina? *Strunz!*"

Then the tea hit him—all of a sudden he jumped up from his chair and began to squeal like a monkey with his tail cut off. It was really something to see, this bad trigger man running over to the window, tearing at his collar and yelling, "Oh my God, I'm dyin',

I'm dyin' call the doctor! For Christ's sake, get me a doctor!" I felt like asking him didn't he want some more of that farina but my P.A. system blew a tube.

We knew that Frankie's gargling and gagging wasn't exactly a death-rattle. He was just having a stomach attack from over-eating or constipation, and the most he needed was some bicarbonate of soda and a physic, not a croaker. You see, when you get high off of gauge it dries up the saliva in your mouth and your stomach fills up with gas and presses against your ticker, till for the first time in your life you feel every beat your heart is making without looking for it. It's the strangest sensation you ever had since you were old enough to know better, like somebody was using your eardrums for tomtoms. At first you hear your heart beat fast, then it begins to come on slow with loud accentuated beats that confuse you so much you can't hear them at all. That's when the fun begins. It's like there's an alarm clock buried under your ribs, ticking off the seconds and reminding you that the shroud-tailor has designs on you. Then it stops. The next thing you think of is, Lord, I must be dying, I can't hear my heart beat any more. It's really on then.

One of my friends, a fine musician, cornered me one day and we began to discuss our outcome with the tea. I wasn't selling it yet, and we tried to analyze the difference there was between gauge and whisky.

"Man, they can say what they want about us vipers," he said, "but you just dig them lushhounds with their old antique jive, always comin' up loud and wrong, whippin' their old ladies and wastin' up all their pay, and then the next day your head feels like all the hammers in the piano is beatin' out a tune on your brain. Just look at the difference between you and them other cats, that come uptown juiced to the gills, crackin' out of line and passin' out in anybody's hallway. Don't nobody come up thataway when he picks up on some good grass."

I sure knew what he was talking about. The very same thing, that contrast between the lushies and the vipers, had hit me hard way back in Chicago and Detroit, and I told him so.

"Yeah," he said, "and then for instance you take a lot of ofay liquor-heads, when they come up here and pass the jug around. Half of them will say they had enough 'cause some spade just took a drink out of it, and those that do take it will hem and haw, tryin' to rub the top off the bottle so's you can't see them, 'fore they put it to their chops. Now with vipers it's different. You don't have to pass a roach to a viper, he'll take it right out of your hand and go to puffin' on it not even thinkin' about who had it in his chops before. Them Indians must of had some gauge in that pipe of peace that they passed around, at least they had the right idea, ha ha! Now, far as hurtin' anybody is concerned, you know and I know that we can wake up the next day and go on about our business, marihuana or mary-don't-wanna, and that's that. It ain't against the law and you told me they couldn't put it under the Harrison Act because it wasn't habit-forming, so let's carry on from here. We'll both smoke it every day for about two or three months and then one of us'll quit for a while and find out for ourselves what happens."

That's exactly what we did. I was the first one to stop for a trial, and I have yet to find any bad after-effects, outside of a twenty-month jail sentence.

(Before I go any further I want to make one thing clear: I never advocated that anybody should use marihuana, and I sure don't mean to start now. Even during the years when I sold the stuff I never "pushed" it like a salesman pushes vacuum cleaners or Fuller brushes. I had it for anybody who came asking, if he was a friend of mine. I didn't promote it anywhere, and I never gave it to kids, not even to little Frankie Walker. I sold it to grown-up friends of mine who had got to using it on their own, just like I did; it was a family affair, not any high-pressure business. Sort of everybody to their own notion, that was the whole spirit. I laid off five years ago, and if anybody asks my advice today, I tell them straight to steer clear of it because it carries a rap. That's my final word to all the cats: today I know of one very bad thing the tea can do to you–it can put you in jail. 'Nuff said.)

Most of us were getting our tea from some Spanish boys, and one day they showed up with a guy who pushed the stuff in Detroit when I was there. He wasn't selling it any more, but he put us in touch with another cat who kept coming up from Mexico with real golden-leaf, the best that could be had. As soon as we got some of that Mexican bush we almost blew our tops. Poppa, you never smacked your chops on anything sweeter in all your days of viping. It had such a wonderful smell and the kick you got was really out of this world. Guys used to say it tasted like chocolate candy, a brand Hershey never even thought of. I laid it on the cats in the Barbeque, and pretty soon all Harlem was after me to light them up. I wasn't working then and didn't have much money left to gaycat with, but I couldn't refuse to light my friends up. Before I knew it I had to write to our connection for a large supply, because everybody I knew wanted some. "Man, you can be ridin' on rubber in no time with that stuff, and it ain't against the law neither," the cats told me. "Just think how many cats you can make happy," they kept saying. Before I knew it, I was standing on The Corner pushing gauge. Only I did no pushing. I just stood under the Tree of Hope, my pokes full up, and the cats came and went, and so did all my golden-leaf.

Overnight I was the most popular man in Harlem. New words came into being to meet the situation: *the mezz* and *the mighty mezz,* referring, I blush to say, to me and to the tea both; *mezzroll,* to describe the kind of fat, well-packed and clean cigarette I used to roll (this word later got corrupted to *meserole* and it's still used to mean a certain size and shape of reefer, which is different from the so-called panatella); *the hard-cuttin' mezz* and *the righteous bush.* Some of those phrases really found a permanent place in Harlemese, and even crept out to color American slang in general. I was knocked out the other day when I picked up a copy of Cab Calloway's *Hipster's Dictionary* and found *mezz* defined there as "anything supreme, genuine"; and in Dan Burley's *Original Handbook of Harlem Jive* the same word is defined as meaning "tops, sincere"!

Stuff Smith wrote a song, later recorded by Rosetta Howard for Decca under the name of "If You're a Viper," that started out

Dreamed about a reefer five foot long
The mighty mezz but not too strong,
You'll be high but not for long
If you're a viper.

from **An Essay on Hasheesh**

Victor Robinson

Written in the spring of 1910, this essay appeared in a medical journal two years later. For the next ten years it acquired something of a following and was cited in other medical reports as well as in Max Eastman's book *The Sense of Humor.* Robinson, a physician practicing in Harlem, published his monograph in 1925. Hashish, "the winning rival of opium as a producer of visions of paradise," was to Robinson and his friends not only a medical experiment but a delightful experience that did more than merely assuage pain or grief and became a giddy and enlightening diversion. Dr. Robinson seemed to find his true calling in his eloquent descriptions of his intoxicating experiences. Indeed, the essay is so engaging and inviting that its first critics worried it would excessively popularize use of the drug.

MY BROTHER FREDERIC ROBINSON took 25 minims in the presence of some ladies whom he had invited to witness the fun. An hour passed without results. A second hour followed, but–to use the slang of the street–there was nothing doing. The third hour promised to be equally fruitless, and as it was already late in the evening, the ladies said good-by. No sooner did they leave the room, than I heard the hasheesh-laugh. The hemp was doing its work. In a shrill voice my brother was exclaiming, "What foo-oolish people, what foo-oo-ool-ish people to leave just when the show is beginning." The ladies came back. And it was a show. Frederic made Socialistic speeches, and argued warmly for the cause of Woman Suffrage. He grew most affectionate and insisted on holding a lady's hand. His face was flushed, his eyes were half closed, his abdomen seemed uneasy, but his spirit was happy. He sang, he rhymed, he declaimed, he whistled, he mimicked, he acted. He pleaded so passionately for the rights of Humanity that it seemed he was using up the resources of his system. But he was tireless. With both hands he gesticulated, and would brook no interruption.

Peculiar ideas suggested themselves. For instance, he said something was "sheer nonsense," and then reasoned as follows: "Since shears are the same as scissors, instead of sheer nonsense I can say scissors nonsense." He also said, "I will give you a kick in the tickle"–and was much amused by the expression.

At all times he recognized those about him, and remained conscious of his surroundings. When the approach of dawn forced the ladies to depart, Frederic made a somewhat unsavory joke, and immediately exclaimed triumphantly, "I wouldn't have said that if the ladies were here for a million dollars." Someone yawned deeply, and being displeased by the unexpected appearance of a gaping orifice, Frederic melodramatically gave utterance to this Gorky-like phrase: "From the depths of dirtiness and despair there rose a sickly odorous yawn"—and instantly he remarked that the first portion of this sentence was alliterative! Is it not strange that such consciousness and such intoxication can exist in the same brain simultaneously?

The next day he remembered all that occurred, was in excellent spirits, laughed much and easily, and felt himself above the petty things of this world.

On May 19, 1910, this world was excited over the visit of Halley's comet. It is pleasant to remember that the celestial guest attracted as much attention as a political campaign or a game of baseball. On the evening of this day, at 10 o'clock, I gave 45 minims to a court stenographer named Henry D. Demuth. At 11:30 the effects of the drug became apparent, and Mr. Demuth lost consciousness of his surroundings to such an extent that he imagined himself an inhabitant of Sir Edmund Halley's nebulous planet. He despised the earth and the dwellers thereon; he called it a miserable little flea-bite, and claimed its place in the cosmos was no more important than a flea-jump. With a scornful finger he pointed below, and said in a voice of contempt, "That little joke down there, called the earth."

"Victor," he said, "you're a fine fellow, you're the smartest man in Harlem, you've got the god in you, but the best thoughts you write are low compared to the things we think up here." A little later he condescended to take me up with him, and said, "Victor, we're up in the realm now, and we'll make money when we get down on that damned measly earth again; they respect Demuth on earth."

He imitated how Magistrate Butts calls a prisoner to the bar. "Butts," he explained, "is the best of them. Butts—Butts—cigarette-butts." If this irreverent line should ever fall beneath the dignified eyes of His Honor, instead of fining his devoted stenographer for contempt of court, may he bear in his learned mind the fact that under the influence of narcotics men are mentally irresponsible.

By this time Mr Demuth's vanity was enormous. "God, Mark Twain and I are chums," he remarked casually. "God is wise, and I am wise. And to think that people *dictate* to me!"

He imagined he had material for a great book. "I'm giving you the thoughts; slap them down, we'll make a fortune and go whacks. We'll make a million. I'll get half and Vic will get half. With half a million we'll take it easy for a while on this damned measly earth. We'll live till a hundred and two, and then we'll skedaddle didoo. At one hundred and two it will be said of Henry Disque Demuth that he shuffled off this mortal coil. We'll skip into the great idea—hooray! hooray! Take down everything that is signifi*cant*—with an accent on the *cant*—Immanuel Kant was a wise man, and I'm a wise man; I am wise, because I'm wise."

It is to be regretted that in spite of all the gabble concerning the volume that was to make both of us rich, not even one line was dictated by the inspired author. In fact he got no further than the title, and it must be admitted that of all titles in the world, this is the least catchy. It is as follows: "Wise is God; God is Wise."

Later came a variation in the form of a hissing sound which was meant to be an imitation of the whizzing of Halley's comet; there was a wild swinging of the sheets as a welcome to the President; a definition of religion as the greatest joke ever perpetrated; some hasheesh-laughter; and the utterance of this original epigram: Shakespeare, seltzer-beer, be cheerful.

A little later all variations ceased, for the subject became a monomaniac, or at any rate, a fanatic. He became thoroughly imbued with the great idea that the right attitude to preserve towards life is to take all things on earth as a joke. Hundreds and hundreds and hundreds of times he repeated: "The idea of the great idea, the idea of the great idea, the idea of the great idea." No question could steer him out of this track. "Who's up on the comet? Any pretty girls there?" asked Frederic. "The great idea is up there," was the answer.

"Where would you fall if you fell off the comet?"

"I'd fall into the great idea."

"What do you do when you want to eat and have no money?"

"You have to get the idea."

"When will you get married?"

"When I get the idea."

Midnight came, and he was still talking about his great idea. At one o'clock I felt bored. "If you don't talk about anything else except the idea, we'll have to quit," I said.

"Yes," he replied, "we'll all quit, we'll all be wrapped up in the great idea." He took out his handkerchief to blow his nose, remarking, "The idea of my nose." I approached him. "Don't interfere," he cried, "I'm off with the great idea."

I began to descend the stairs. When half way down I stopped to listen. He was still a monomaniac. Had he substituted the word thought or theory or conception or notion or belief or opinion or supposition or hypothesis or syllogism or tentative conjecture, I would have returned. But as I still heard only the idea of the great idea, I went to bed.

In the morning his countenance was ashen, which formed a marked contrast to its extreme redness the evening before. He should have slept longer, but I thought of the duties to be performed for Judge Butts, and determined to arouse him, although I knew my touch would cast him down from the glorious Halley's comet to the measly little flea-bite of an earth, besides jarring the idea of the great idea.

So I shook him, but instead of manifesting anger, he smiled and extended his hand cordially, as if he had not seen me for a long time. The effects of the drug had not entirely disappeared, and his friends at work thought him drunk, and asked with whom he had been out all night. Mr. Demuth was in first-class spirits, he bubbled over with idealism, and felt a contempt for all commercial transactions. He was the American Bernard Shaw, and looked upon the universe as a joke of the gods. While adding some figures of considerable importance—as salaries depended upon the results—a superintendent passed. Mr. Demuth pointed to the column that needed balancing, and asked, "This is all a joke, isn't it?" Not appreciating the etiology of the query, the superintendent nodded and passed on.

There yet remains my own case. On March 4, 1910, I came home, feeling very tired. I found that some Cannabis indica which I had expected had arrived. After supper, while finishing up an article, I began to debate with myself whether I should join the hasheesh-eaters that night. The argument ended in my taking 20 minims at 9 o'clock. I was alone in the room, and no one was aware that I had yielded to temptation. An hour later I wrote in my memoranda book: Absolutely no effect. At 10:30, I completed my article, and entered this note: No effect at all from the hemp. By this time I was exhausted, and being convinced that the hasheesh would not act, I went to bed in disappointment. I fell asleep immediately.

I hear music. There is something strange about this music. I have not heard such music before. The anthem is far away, but in its very faintness there is a lure. In the soft surge and swell of the minor notes there breathes a harmony that ravishes the sense of sound. A resonant organ, with a stop of sapphire and a diapason of opal, diffuses endless octaves from star to star. All the moonbeams form strings to vibrate the perfect pitch, and this entrancing unison is poured into my enchanted ears. Under such a spell, who can remain in bed? The magic of that melody bewitches my soul. I begin to rise horizontally from my couch. No walls impede my progress, and I float into the outside air. Sweeter and sweeter grows the music, it bears me higher and higher, and I float in tune with the infinite—under the turquoise heavens where globules of mercury are glittering.

I become an unhindered wanderer through unending space. No air-ship can go here, I say. I am astonished at the vastness of infinity. I always knew it was large, I argue, but I never dreamed it was as huge as this. I desire to know how fast I am floating through the air, and I calculate that it must be about a billion miles a second.

I am transported to wonderland. I walk in streets where gold is dirt, and I have no desire to gather it. I wonder whether it is worth while to explore the canals of Mars, or rock myself on the rings of Saturn, but before I can decide, a thousand other fancies enter my excited brain.

I wish to see if I can concentrate my mind sufficiently to recite something, and I succeed in correctly quoting this stanza from a favorite poem which I am perpetually re-reading:

Come into the garden, Maud,
For the black bat, night, has flown,
Come into the garden, Maud,
I am here at the gate alone;

And the woodbine spices are wafted abroad,
  And the musk of the rose is blown.

It occurs to me that it is high honor for Tennyson to have his poetry quoted in heaven.

I turn, I twist, I twirl. I melt, I fade, I dissolve. No diaphanous cloud is so light and airy as I. I admire the ease with which I float. My gracefulness fills me with delight. My body is not subject to the law of gravitation. I sail dreamily along, lost in exquisite intoxication.

New scenes of wonder continually unravel themselves before my astonished eyes. I say to myself that if I could only record one one-thousandth of the ideas which come to me every second, I would be considered a greater poet than Milton.

I am on the top of a high mountain-peak. I am alone–only the romantic night envelops me. From a distant valley I hear the gentle tinkling of cow-bells. I float downwards, and find immense fields in which peacocks' tails are growing. They wave slowly, to better exhibit their dazzling ocelli, and I revel in the gorgeous colors. I pass over mountains and I sail over seas. I am the monarch of the air.

I hear the songs of women. Thousands of maidens pass near me, they bend their bodies in the most charming curves, and scatter beautiful flowers in my fragrant path. Some faces are strange, some I knew on earth, but all are lovely. They smile, and sing and dance. Their bare feet glorify the firmament. It is more than flesh can stand. I grow sensual unto satyriasis. The aphrodisiac effect is astonishing in its intensity. I enjoy all the women of the world. I pursue countless maidens through the confines of heaven. A delicious warmth suffuses my whole body. Hot and blissful I float through the universe, consumed with a resistless passion. And in the midst of this unexampled and unexpected orgy, I think of the case reported by the German Dr. Reidel, about a drug-clerk who took a huge dose of hasheesh to enjoy voluptuous visions, but who heard not even the rustle of Aphrodite's garment, and I laugh at him in scorn and derision.

I sigh deeply, open my eyes, and find myself sitting with one foot in bed, and the other on my desk. I am bathed in warm sweat which is pleasant. But my head aches, and there is a feeling in my stomach which I recognize and detest. It is nausea. I pull the basket near me, and await the inevitable result. At the same time I feel like begging for mercy, for I have traveled so far and so long, and I am tired beyond limit, and I need a rest. The fatal moment approaches, and I lower my head for the easier deposition of the rising burden. And my head seems monstrously huge, and weighted with lead. At last the deed is done, and I lean back on the pillow.

I hear my sister come home from the opera. I wish to call her. My sister's name is Ellen. I try to say it, but I cannot. The effort is too much. I sigh in despair. It occurs to me that I may achieve better results if I compromise on Nell, as this contains one sylla ble instead of two. Again I am defeated. I am too weary to exert myself to any extent, but

I am determined. I make up my mind to collect all my strength, and call out: Nell. The result is a fizzle. No sound issues from my lips. My lips do not move. I give it up. My head falls on my breast, utterly exhausted and devoid of all energy.

Again my brain teems. Again I hear that high and heavenly harmony, again I float to the outposts of the universe and beyond, again I see the dancing maidens with their soft yielding bodies, white and warm. I am excited unto ecstasy. I feel myself a brother to the Oriental, for the same drug which gives him joy is now acting on me. I am conscious all the time, and I say to myself in a knowing way with a suspicion of a smile: All these visions because of 20 minims of Cannabis indica. My only regret is that the trances are ceaseless. I wish respite, but for answer I find myself floating over an immense ocean. Then the vision grows so wondrous, that body and soul I give myself up to it, and I taste the fabled joys of paradise. Ah, what this night is worth!

The music fades, the beauteous girls are gone, and I float no more. But the black rubber covering of my typewriter glows like a chunk of yellow phosphorus. By one door stands a skeleton with a luminous abdomen and brandishes a wooden sword. By the other door a little red devil keeps guard. I open my eyes wide, I close them tight, but these spectres will not vanish. I know they are not real, I know I see them because I took hasheesh, but they annoy me nevertheless. I become uncomfortable, even frightened. I make a superhuman effort, and succeed in getting up and lighting the gas. It is two o'clock. Everything is the way it should be, except that in the basket I notice the remains of an orange–somewhat the worse for wear.

I feel relieved, and fall asleep. Something is handling me, and I start in fright. I open my eyes and see my father. He has returned from a meeting at the Academy of Medicine, and surprised at seeing a light in my room at such a time, has entered. He surmises what I have done, and is anxious to know what quantity I have taken. I should have answered, with a wink, *quantum sufficit,* but I have no inclination for conversation; on hearing the question repeated, I answer, "Twenty minims." He tells me I look as pale as a ghost, and brings me a glass of water. I drink it, become quite normal, and thus ends the most wonderful night of my existence.

In the morning my capacity for happiness is considerably increased. I have an excellent appetite, the coffee I sip is nectar, and the white bread ambrosia. I take my camera, and walk to Central Park. It is a glorious day. Everyone I meet is idealized. The lake never looked so placid before. I enter the hot-houses, and a gaudy-colored insect buzzing among the lovely flowers fills me with joy. I am too languid to take any pictures; to set the focus, to use the proper stop, to locate the image, to press the bulb–all these seem Herculean feats which I dare not even attempt. But I walk and walk, without apparent effort, and my mind eagerly dwells on the brilliant pageantry of the night before. I do not wish to forget my frenzied nocturnal revelry upon the vast dome of the broad blue heavens. I wish to remember forever, the floating, the mercury-globules, the peacock-feathers, the colors, the music, the women. In memory I enjoy the carnival all over again.

"For the brave Meiamoun," writes Theophile Gautier, "Cleopatra danced; she was apparelled in a robe of green, open at either side; castanets were attached to her alabaster hands. . . . Poised on the pink tips of her little feet, she approached swiftly to graze his forehead with a kiss; then she recommenced her wondrous art, and flitted around him, now backward-leaning, with head reversed, eyes half-closed, arms lifelessly relaxed, locks uncurled and loose-hanging like a bacchante of Mount Maenalus; now again active, animated, laughing, fluttering, more tireless and capricious in her movements than the pilfering bee. Heart-consuming love, sensual pleasure, burning passion, youth inexhaustible and ever-fresh, the promise of bliss to come–she expressed all. . . . The modest stars had ceased to contemplate the scene; their golden eyes could not endure such a spectacle; the heaven itself was blotted out, and a dome of flaming vapor covered the hall."

But for me a thousand Cleopatras caroused–and did not present me a vase of poison to drain at a draught. Again I repeated to myself: "And all these charming miracles because of 20 minims of *Fluidextractum Cannabis Indicae, U.S.P.*"

By the afternoon I had so far recovered as to be able to concentrate my mind on technical studies. I will not attempt to interpret my visions psychologically, but I wish to refer to one aspect. Spencer, in *Principles of Psychology,* mentions hasheesh as possessing the power of reviving ideas. I found this to be the case. I spoke about air-ships because there had been a discussion about them at supper; I quoted from Tennyson's *Maud* because I had been re-reading it; I saw mercury-globules in the heavens because that same day I had worked with mercury in preparing mercurial plaster; and I saw the peacock-tails because a couple of days previous I had been at the Museum of Natural History and had closely observed a magnificent specimen. I cannot account for the women.

All poets–with the possible exception of Margaret Sangster–have celebrated Alcohol, while Rudyard Kipling has gone so far as to solemnize delirium tremens; B. V. has glorified Nicotine; DeQuincey has immortalized Opium; Murger is full of praise for Caffeine; Dumas in *Monte Cristo* has apotheosized hasheesh, Gautier has vivified it in *Club des Hachicins,* Baudelaire has panegyrized it in *Artificial Paradises,* but as few American pens have done so, I have taken it upon myself to write a sonnet to the most interesting plant that blooms:

Near Punjab and Pab, in Sutlej and Sind,
Where the cobras-di-capello abound,
Where the poppy, palm and the tamarind,
With cummin and ginger festoon the ground–
And the capsicum fields are all abloom,
From the hills above to the vales below,
Entrancing the air with a rich perfume,

There too does the greenish Cannabis grow:
Inflaming the blood with the living fire,
Till the burning joys like the eagles rise,
And the pulses throb with a strange desire,
While passion awakes with a wild surprise:–
O to eat that drug, and to dream all day,
Of the maids that live by the Bengal Bay!

from **The Diary of Anaïs Nin,**

1947–1955, volume V

A n a ï s   N i n

Anaïs Nin's deeply reflective writings touched on the most intimate of subjects and were precisely targeted probes into her own psyche. After hearing reports of the newly synthesized hallucinogenic chemical LSD from friends of a similar intellectually curious bent, she decided to experiment. Intending to write about its effects on her consciousness, perhaps to everyone's surprise but her own, she discovered that although she somewhat enjoyed the vision-inducing aspects of the drug, she was not all that impressed and consequently did not further pursue use of such chemicals. The fiery ways of the flesh seemed more desirable than the power—however imaginative—of fantasies.

I HAD JUST READ ALDOUS HUXLEY'S *The Doors of Perception* but it did not impress me as much as Gil Henderson's talk about the visionary effects of LSD. He had participated in an experiment with Dr. Oscar Janiger. He painted an American Indian doll before taking LSD and then again after the ingestion of the drug, and the difference between them was astonishing. The first version was rigid and photographic. The second impressionistic, emotional. Gil asked me if I wanted to participate in an experiment because Dr. Janiger was hoping a writer would be more articulate about the experience. There were to be two other subjects there, a biologist from UCLA and another painter. Gil would be my sober pilot, that is, a person who has taken LSD before and now stands by to help one and guide one if necessary.

It seemed strange to be coming to a psychiatrist's office for such an adventure. Dr. Janiger took Gil and me into his private office, which was lined with books and very dark. I had little time to form an impression of him, for he immediately dispensed a number of blue pills, five or eight, I do not remember, with a glass of water. Then he conducted us to the waiting room, where the biologist sat already with a pad on his knee, pen in hand.

At first everything appeared unchanged. But after a while, perhaps twenty minutes, I noticed first of all that the rug was no longer flat and lifeless, but had become a field of stirring and undulating hairs, much like the movement of the sea anemone or a field of wheat in the wind. Then I noticed that doors, walls, and windows were liquefying. All rigidities disappeared. It was as if I had been plunged to the bottom of the sea, and everything had become undulating and wavering. The door knobs were no longer door knobs, they melted and undulated like living serpents. Every object in the room became a living, mobile breathing world. I walked away, into a hallway opening into several small rooms. On the way there was a door leading to the garden. Gil opened it. The dazzle of the sun was blinding, every speck of gold multiplied and magnified. Trees, clouds, lawns heaved and undulated too, the clouds flying at tremendous speed. I ceased looking at the garden because on the plain door now appeared the most delicate Persian designs, flowers, mandalas, patterns in perfect symmetry. As I designed them they produced their matching music. When I drew a long orange line, it emitted its own orange tone. My body was both swimming and flying. I felt gay and at ease and playful. There was perfect connection between my body and everything that was happening. For example, the colors in the designs gave me pleasure, as well as the music. The singing of mockingbirds was multiplied, and became a whole forest of singing birds. My senses were multiplied as if I had a hundred eyes, a hundred ears, a hundred fingertips. The murals which appeared were perfect, they were Oriental, fragile, and complete, but then they became actual Oriental cities, with pagodas, temples, rich Chinese gold and red altars, and Balinese music. The music vibrated through my body as if I were one of the instruments and I felt myself becoming a full percussion orchestra, becoming green, blue, orange. The waves of the sounds ran through my hair like a caress. The music ran down my back and came out of my fingertips. I was a cascade of red-blue rainfall, a rainbow. I was small, light, mobile. I could use any method of levitation I wished. I could dissolve, melt, float, soar. Wavelets of light touched the rim of my clothes, phosphorescent radiations. I could see a new world with my middle eye, a world I had missed before. I caught images behind images, the walls behind the sky, the sky behind the infinite. The walls became fountains, the fountains became arches, the domes skies, the sky a flowering carpet, and all dissolved into pure space. I looked at a slender line curving over into space which disappeared into infinity. I saw a million zeros on this line, curving, shrinking in the distance, and I laughed and said: "Excuse me, I am not a mathematician. How can I measure the infinite?" To Dr. Janiger, who was passing by, I said: "Without being a mathematician I understood the infinite." He did not seem impressed. I saw his face as a Picasso, with a slight asymmetry. It seemed to me that one of his eyes was larger, and this eye was prying into my experience, and I turned away. Gil was sometimes there, but now I became aware that he was a child, that he had a big round face with a grin. Now I was standing on the rim of a planet, alone. I could hear the fast rushing sound of the planets rotating in space. Then I was moving among them and I realized a certain skill would be necessary to handle this new means of transportation. The image of myself standing in space and trying to get my "space legs" amused me. I wondered who had been there before me and whether I would return to earth. The solitude distressed me for the first time, the sense of distance, so I asked Gil very vehemently: "Are you sure that I will find my way back?" Gil answered reasonably: "Of course, I found my way back. I'm here." He asked me if there was anything I wanted, a glass of water or a sandwich. I answered: "I want a pagoda." And after a while I added: "I realize this is an unreasonable request." I returned to my starting point. I was standing in front of an ugly door, but as I looked closer it was not plain or green but it was a Buddhist temple, a Hindu column, a Moroccan ceiling, gold spires being formed and re-formed as if I were watching the hand of a designer at work. I was designing red spirals which unfurled until they formed a rose window or a mandala with edges of radium. As each design was born and arranged itself, it dissolved and the next one followed without confusion. Each form, each line emitted its equivalent in music in perfect accord with the design. An undulating line emitted a sustaining undulating melody, a circle had corresponding musical notations, diaphanous colors, diaphanous sounds, a pyramid created a pyramid of ascending notes, and vanishing ones left only an echo. These designs were preparatory sketches for entire Oriental cities. I saw the temples of Java, Kashmir, Nepal, Ceylon, Burma, Cambodia, in all the colors of precious stones illumined from within. Then the outer forms of the temples dissolved to reveal the inner chapels and shrines. The reds and golds inside the temples created an intricate musical orchestration like Balinese music. Two sensations began to torment me: one that it was happening too quickly and that I would not be able to remember it, another that I would not be able to tell what I saw, it was too elusive and too overwhelming. The temples grew taller, the music wilder, it became a tidal wave of sounds with gongs and bells predominating. Gold spires emitted a long flute chant. Every line and color was constantly breathing and mutating.

It was then I began to experience difficulties in breathing. I felt immensely cold, and very small in my cape, as if I had undergone an Alice in Wonderland metamorphosis. I told Gil I could not breathe, and he took me to the doctor. The doctor calmed me with words. I had asked for oxygen. He suggested I lie down and cover myself well. Gil was seated near me, grinning. I asked him if he had had difficulties breathing. I still had the impression I had been among the planets. I remembered the illustration from Saint-Exupéry's *Little Prince,* the child standing all alone on the edge of the planet. I lay down and covered myself. I was smoking a cigarette. I looked at the curtains of the room and they turned to a gauzy gold. The whole room became filled with gold, as if by a strong sun. The walls turned to gold, the bedcover was gold, my whole body was becoming GOLD, liquid gold, scintillating, warm gold. I WAS GOLD. It was the most pleasurable sensation I had ever known, like an orgasm. It was the secret of life, the alchemist's secret of life. From the feeling of intense cold, as if I were chloroformed, of loss of gravity of the legs, and diminution in size, I passed to the sensation of being gold. Suddenly I was weeping, weeping. I could feel the tears and I saw the handkerchief in my hand. Weeping to the point of dissolution. Why should I be weeping? I could see Gil smiling, and realized the absurdity of weeping when traveling through space. As soon as the concept of absurdity struck me, the comic spirit appeared again. It was another Anaïs, not the one which was lying down weeping, but a small, gay, light Anaïs, very lively, very restless and mobile. The comic spirit of Anaïs was aware of Gil's predicament: "Poor Gil, you are out with an ordinary weepy female! What a ridiculous thing to spoil a voyage through space by weeping. But before we go on, I want to explain to you why women weep. IT IS THE QUICKEST WAY TO REJOIN THE OCEAN. You liquefy, become fluid, flow back into the ocean where the colors are more beautiful." The comic spirit of Anaïs shook herself jauntily and said: "Let's stop this weeping. Everything is more wonderful under water (than in space?). It is alive and it breathes." Space was lonely, and empty, a vast desert. After the feeling of GOLD I had a feeling of danger. My world is so beautiful, so beautiful, but so fragile. I was pleading for protection of this evanescent beauty. I thought I was the quickest mind alive and the quickest with words, but words cannot catch up with these transformations, metamorphoses. They are beyond words, beyond words. . . The Oriental cities vanished and the infinite appeared again, but now it was bordered on each side by celestial gardens of precious stones on silver and gold stems. Temptation not to pursue the infinite, but to enjoy the gardens. Space is definitely without sensuous appeal.

The comic spirit of Anaïs stood aside and laughed at so much Russian-opera extravaganza. But the other Anaïs maintained her pose as a Balinese dancer with legs slightly bent, the tips of the fingers meeting in a symbolic gesture of pleading. I could feel the weight of the brocade.

I watched a shoreline of gold waves breaking into solid gold powder and becoming gold foam, and gold hair, shimmering and trembling with gold delights. I felt I could capture the secret of life because the secret of life was metamorphosis and transmutation, but it happened too quickly and was beyond words. Comic spirit of Anaïs mocks words and herself. Ah, I cannot capture the secret of life with WORDS.

Sadness.

The secret of life was BREATH. That was what I always wanted words to do, to BREATHE. Comic spirit of Anaïs rises, shakes herself within her cape, gaily, irresponsibly, surrenders the abstruse difficulties. NOW I KNOW WHY THE FAIRY TALES ARE FULL OF JEWELS.

After my experience with LSD I began to examine whether it was an unfamiliar world, inaccessible except to the chemical alterations of reality.

I found the origin of most of the images either in my work or in literary works by other writers.

In *House of Incest*, written in 1935, objects become liquefied and I describe them as seen through water. There is a reference to Byzantium and I was brought up on volumes of *Voyages Autour du Monde*, which had images of Cambodia, Thailand, Bali, India, and Japan, and which remained forever in my memory. I have listened to countless recordings of Balinese music, tapes made by Colin McFee.

Images of split selves appear in *House of Incest*.

The image of loneliness on another planet is derived from my frequent reading of

The Little Prince by Antoine de Saint-Exupéry.

In *House of Incest* there is mention of crystals, precious stones: "The muscovite like a bride, the pyrite, the hydrous silica, the cinnabar, the azurite of benefic Jupiter, the malachite, all crushed together, melted jewels, melted planets."

The sensation of becoming gold is one I had many times when sunbathing on the sand; the sun's reflection came through my closed eyelids, and I felt myself becoming gold.

I could find correlations all through my writing, find the sources of the images in past dreams, in reading, in memories of travel, in actual experience, such as the one I had once in Paris when I was so exalted by life that I felt I was not touching the ground, I felt I was sliding a few inches away from the sidewalk.

Therefore, I felt, the chemical did not reveal an unknown world. What it did was to shut out the quotidian world as an interference and leave you alone with your dreams and fantasies and memories. In this way it made it easier to gain access to the subconscious life. But obviously, by way of writing, reveries, waking dreams, and night dreams, I had visited all those landscapes. The drug added a synthesis of color, sound, image, a simultaneous fusion of all the senses which I had constantly aspired to in my writing and often achieved.

I reached the fascinating revelation that this world opened by LSD was accessible to the artist by way of art. The gold sun mobile of Lippold could create a mood if one were receptive enough, if one let the image penetrate the body and turn the body to gold. All the chemical did was to remove resistance, to make one permeable to the image, and to make the body receptive by shutting out the familiar landscape which prevented the dream from invading us.

What has happened that people lose contact with such images, visions, sensations, and have to resort to drugs which ultimately harm them?

They have been immured, the taboo on dream, reverie, visions, and sensual receptivity deprives them of access to the subconscious. I am grateful for my natural access. But when I discuss this with Huxley, he is rather irritable: "You're fortunate enough to have a natural access to your subconscious life, but other people need drugs and should have them."

This does not satisfy me because I feel that if I have a natural access others could have it too. How did I reach this? Difficult to retrace one's steps. Can you say I had a propensity for dreaming, a faculty for abstracting myself from the daily world in order to travel to other places? What I cannot trace [is] the origin of seemed natural tendencies which I allowed to develop, and which I found psychoanalysis encouraged and trained. The technique was accessible to those willing to accept psychoanalysis as a means of connecting with the subconscious. I soon recognized its value. My faith in it is unshaken. But then there is also the appetite for what nourishes such a rich underground life: learning color from the painters, movement from the dancers, music from musicians. They train your senses, they sensitize the senses. It was the banishment of art which brought on a culture devoid of sensual perception, of the participation in the senses, so that experience did not cause the "highs," the exaltations, the ecstasies they caused in me. The puritans killed the senses. English culture killed emotion. And now it was necessary to dynamite the concrete lid, to "blow the mind" as the LSD followers call it. The source of all wonder, aliveness, and joy was feeling and dreaming, and being able to fulfill one's dreams.

Even the art of reading, lost to America, was a constant nourishing source which revealed countries I wanted to see, people I wanted to know, experiences I wanted to have. How cruelly the weight of ordinary life, *la condition humaine,* weighed upon America, with everything forcing you to live in the prosaic, the shabby, the practical, the quotidian, the down-to-earth, the mediocrity of political life, the monstrosities of history via the media, because they believed this was contact with life, and it was the very thing which destroyed the contact with life.

So the drugs, instead of bringing fertile images which in turn can be shared with the world (as the great painters, great poets, great musicians shared their abundance with the unfertile ones, enriched undernourished lives), have instead become a solitary vice, a passive dreaming which alienates the dreamer from the whole world, isolates him, ultimately destroys him. It is like masturbation. The one who wrestles his images from experience, from his smoky dreams, to create, is able then to build what he has seen and hungered for. It does not vanish with the effects of the chemical. The knowledge gained without the drugs, as, for example, my feeling for color learned from watching the painters when I was posing for them, is a permanent acquisition. It became part of my being, it was applicable to my travels, to my image of people. It was or became a new faculty, part of my sensory perception, available, but the effort I made to learn was also the strengthening of the ability to create with a sense of color, to create houses, clothes, visions of cities, enjoyment of color not only as a passing, ephemeral, vanishing dream, *but as reality.* And that is the conflict. The drug effect does not strengthen the desire to turn the dream, the vision, into reality. It is passive.

I have to go on in my own way, which is a disciplined, arduous, organic way of integrating the dream with creativity in life, a quest for the development of the senses, the vision, the imagination as dynamic elements with which to create a new world, a new kind of human being. Seeking wholeness not by dreaming alone, by a passive dreaming that drugs give, but by an active, dynamic dreaming that is connected with life, interrelated, makes a harmony in which the pleasures of color, texture, vision are a creation in reality, which we can enjoy with the *awakened* senses. What can be more wonderful than the carrying out of our fantasies, the courage to enact them, embody them, live them out instead of depending on the dissolving, dissipating, vanishing quality of the drug dreams.

I will not be just a tourist in the world of images, just watching images passing by which I cannot live in, make love to, possess as permanent sources of joy and ecstasy.

from "The Turning-point of My Life"

Mark Twain

In 1910 *Harper's Bazaar* invited several prominent authors to write about the "turning point" of their lives. Ever skeptical, Mark Twain questioned the premise of such a dubious exercise and offered a humorous history lesson on one of history's most "celebrated" turning points: Caesar's decision to cross the Rubicon. Naturally, Twain did not focus on Caesar himself but on the anonymous stranger who took the first step, thus "casting the die" for the future of the species. At the heart of his essay is an intriguing what-if story in which Twain describes how his own fate was thrust upon him as a result of an event that did not come to pass: a plan to export the miraculous Amazonian coca plant throughout the world.

TO ME, THE MOST IMPORTANT FEATURE of my life is its literary feature. I have been professionally literary something more than forty years. There have been many turning-points in my life, but the one that was the last link in the chain appointed to conduct me to the literary guild is the most *conspicuous* link in that chain. *Because* it was the last one. It was not any more important than its predecessors. All the other links have an inconspicuous look, except the crossing of the Rubicon; but as factors in making me literary they are all of the one size, the crossing of the Rubicon included.

I know how I came to be literary, and I will tell the steps that led up to it and brought it about.

The crossing of the Rubicon was not the first one, it was hardly even a recent one; I should have to go back ages before Caesar's day to find the first one. To save space I will go back only a couple of generations and start with an incident of my boyhood. When I was twelve and a half years old, my father died. It was in the spring. The summer came, and brought with it an epidemic of measles. For a time, a child died almost every day. The village was paralyzed with fright, distress, despair. Children that were not smitten with the disease were imprisoned in their homes to save them from the infection. In the homes there were no cheerful faces, there was no music, there was no singing but of solemn hymns, no voice but of prayer, no romping was allowed, no noise, no laughter, the family moved spectrally about on tiptoe, in a ghostly hush. I was a prisoner. My soul was steeped in this awful dreariness—and in fear. At some time or other every day and every night a sudden shiver shook me to the marrow, and I said to myself, "There, I've got it! and I shall die." Life on these miserable terms was not worth living, and at last I made up my mind to get the disease and have it over, one way or the other. I escaped from the house and went to the house of a neighbor where a playmate of mine was very ill with the malady. When the chance offered I crept into his room and got into bed with him. I was discovered by his mother and sent back into captivity. But I had the disease; they could not take that from me. I came near to dying. The whole village was interested, and anxious, and sent for news of me every day; and not only once a day, but several times. Everybody believed I would die; but on the fourteenth day a change came for the worse and they were disappointed.

This was a turning-point of my life. (Link number one.) For when I got well my mother closed my school career and apprenticed me to a printer. She was tired of trying to keep me out of mischief, and the adventure of the measles decided her to put me into more masterful hands than hers.

I became a printer, and began to add one link after another to the chain which was to lead me into the literary profession. A long road, but I could not know that; and as I did not know what its goal was, or even that it had one, I was indifferent. Also contented.

A young printer wanders around a good deal, seeking and finding work; and seeking again, when necessity commands. N. B. Necessity is a *Circumstance;* Circumstance is man's master—and when Circumstance commands, he must obey; he may argue the matter—that is his privilege, just as it is the honorable privilege of a falling body to argue with the attraction of gravitation—but it won't do any good, he must *obey*. I wandered for ten years, under the guidance and dictatorship of Circumstance, and finally arrived in a city of Iowa, where I worked several months. Among the books that interested me in those days was one about the Amazon. The traveler told an alluring tale of his long voyage up the great river from Para to the sources of the Madeira, through the heart of an enchanted land, a land wastefully rich in tropical wonders, a romantic land where all the birds and flowers and animals were of the museum varieties, and where the alligator and the crocodile and the monkey seemed as much at home as if they were in the Zoo. Also, he told an astonishing tale about *coca,* a vegetable product of miraculous powers, asserting that it was so nourishing and so strength-giving that the native of the mountains of the Madeira region would tramp up hill and down all day on a pinch of powdered coca and require no other sustenance.

I was fired with a longing to ascend the Amazon. Also with a longing to open up a trade in coca with all the world. During months I dreamed that dream, and tried to contrive ways to get to Para and spring that splendid enterprise upon an unsuspecting planet. But all in vain. A person may *plan* as much as he wants to, but nothing of consequence is likely to come of it until the magician *Circumstance* steps in and takes the matter off his hands. At last Circumstance came to my help. It was in this way. Circumstance, to help or hurt another man, made him lose a fifty-dollar bill in the street; and to help or hurt me, made me find it. I advertised the find, and left for the Amazon the same day. This was another turning-point, another link.

Could Circumstance have ordered another dweller in that town to go to the Amazon and open up a world-trade in coca on a fifty-dollar basis and been obeyed? No, I was the only one. There were other fools there–shoals and shoals of them–but they were not of my kind. I was the only one of my kind.

Circumstance is powerful, but it cannot work alone; it has to have a partner. Its partner is man's *temperament*–his natural disposition. His temperament is not his invention, it is *born* in him, and he has no authority over it, neither is he responsible for its acts. He cannot change it, nothing can change it, nothing can modify it–except temporarily. But it won't stay modified. It is permanent, like the color of the man's eyes and the shape of his ears. Blue eyes are gray in certain unusual lights; but they resume their natural color when that stress is removed.

A Circumstance that will coerce one man will have no effect upon a man of a different temperament. If Circumstance had thrown the bank-note in Caesar's way, his temperament would not have made him start for the Amazon. His temperament would have compelled him to do something with the money, but not that. It might have made him advertise the note–and wait. We can't tell. Also, it might have made him go to New York and buy into the Government, with results that would leave Tweed nothing to learn when it came his turn.

Very well, Circumstance furnished the capital, and my temperament told me what to do with it. Sometimes a temperament is an ass. When that is the case the owner of it is an ass, too, and is going to remain one. Training, experience, association, can temporarily so polish him, improve him, exalt him that people will think he is a mule, but they will be mistaken. Artificially he *is* a mule, for the time being, but at bottom he is an ass yet, and will remain one.

By temperament I was the kind of person that *does* things. Does them, and reflects afterward. So I started for the Amazon without reflecting and without asking any questions. That was more than fifty years ago. In all that time my temperament has not changed, by even a shade. I have been punished many and many a time, and bitterly, for doing things and reflecting afterward, but these tortures have been of no value to me: I still do the thing commanded by Circumstance and Temperament, and reflect afterward. Always violently. When I am reflecting, on those occasions, even deaf persons can hear me think.

I went by the way of Cincinnati, and down the Ohio and Mississippi. My idea was to take ship, at New Orleans, for Para. In New Orleans I inquired, and found there was no ship leaving for Para. Also, that there never had *been* one leaving for Para. I reflected. A policeman came and asked me what I was doing, and I told him. He made me move on, and said if he caught me reflecting in the public street again he would run me in.

After a few days I was out of money. Then Circumstance arrived, with another turning-point of my life–a new link. On my way down, I had made the acquaintance of a pilot. I begged him to teach me the river, and he consented. I became a pilot.

from "Über Coca"
("On Cocaine")

Sigmund Freud

Having suddenly become intrigued with cocaine as a possible miracle drug to cure specific infirmities, the father of psychoanalysis began to administer the extract to himself in what was, at first, a series of self-experiments. Freud gradually became a habitual user of cocaine and in 1884 published a paper, excerpted here, reporting its positive effects on both mind and body. He reluctantly recanted his medical enthusiasm for the drug in "Craving for and Fear of Cocaine," in 1887, after its ill effects had become frequently apparent on the upper class patients on whom he and other physicians had attempted to demonstrate its curative properties. Freud privately believed, however, that his own psyche was strong enough to withstand the hazards of cocaine and continued to use the drug throughout his life.

The Effect of Coca on the Healthy Human Body

I have carried out experiments and studied, in myself and others, the effect of coca on the healthy human body; my findings agree fundamentally with Mantegazza's description of the effect of coca leaves.[1]

The first time I took 0.05g. of *cocaïnum muriaticum* in a 1% water solution was when I was feeling slightly out of sorts from fatigue. This solution is rather viscous, somewhat opalescent, and has a strange aromatic smell. At first it has a bitter taste, which yields afterwards to a series of very pleasant aromatic flavors. Dry cocaine salt has the same smell and taste, but to a more concentrated degree.

A few minutes after taking cocaine, one experiences a sudden exhilaration and feeling of lightness. One feels a certain furriness on the lips and palate, followed by a feeling of warmth in the same areas; if one now drinks cold water, it feels warm on the lips and cold in the throat. On other occasions the predominant feeling is a rather pleasant coolness in the mouth and throat.

During this first trial I experienced a short period of toxic effects, which did not recur in subsequent experiments. Breathing became slower and deeper and I felt tired and sleepy; I yawned frequently and felt somewhat dull. After a few minutes the actual cocaine euphoria began, introduced by repeated cooling eructation. Immediately after taking the cocaine I noticed a slight slackening of the pulse and later a moderate increase.

I have observed the same physical signs of the effect of cocaine in others, mostly people of my own age. The most constant symptom proved to be the repeated cooling eructation. This is often accompanied by a rumbling which must originate from high up in the intestine; two of the people I observed, who said they were able to recognize movements of their stomachs, declared emphatically that they had repeatedly detected such movements. Often, at the outset of the cocaine effect, the subjects alleged that they experienced an intense feeling of heat in the head. I noticed this in myself as well in the course of some later experiments, but on other occasions it was absent. In only two cases did coca give rise to dizziness. On the whole the toxic effects of coca are of short duration, and much less intense than those produced by effective doses of quinine or salicylate of soda; they seem to become even weaker after repeated use of cocaine.

Mantegazza refers to the following occasional effects of coca: temporary erythema, an increase in the quantity of urine, dryness of the conjunctiva and nasal mucous membranes. Dryness of the mucous membrane of the mouth and of the throat is a regular symptom which lasts for hours. Some observers (Marvaud, Collan) report a slight cathartic effect. Urine and feces are said to take on the smell of coca. Different observers give very different accounts of the effect on the pulse rate. According to Mantegazza, coca quickly produces a considerably increased pulse rate which becomes even higher with higher doses; Collan, too, noted an acceleration of the pulse after coca was taken, while Rossier, Demarle, and Marvaud experienced, after the initial acceleration, a longer lasting retardation of the pulse rate. Christison noticed in himself, after using coca, that physical exertion caused a smaller increase in the pulse rate than otherwise; Reiss disputes any effect on the pulse rate. I do not find any difficulty in accounting for this lack of agreement; it is partly owing to the variety of the preparations used (warm infusion of the leaves, cold cocaine solution, etc.), and the way in which they are applied,[2] and partly to the varying reactions of individuals. With coca this latter factor, as Mantegazza has already reported, is in general of very great significance. There are said to be people who cannot tolerate coca at all; on the other hand, I have found not a few who remained unaffected by 5cg, which for me and others is an effective dose.

The psychic effect of *cocaïnum muriaticum* in doses of 0.05–0.10g consists of exhilaration and lasting euphoria, which does not differ in any way from the normal euphoria of a healthy person. The feeling of excitement which accompanies stimulus by alcohol is completely lacking; the characteristic urge for immediate activity which alcohol produces is also absent. One senses an increase of self-control and feels more vigorous and more capable of work; on the other hand, if one works, one misses that heightening of the mental powers which alcohol, tea, or coffee induce. One is simply normal, and soon finds it difficult to believe that one is under the influence of any drug at all.[3] This gives the impression that the mood induced by coca in such doses is due not so much to direct stimulation as to the disappearance of elements in one's general state of well-being which cause depression. One may perhaps assume that the euphoria resulting from good health is also nothing more than the normal condition of a well-nourished cerebral cortex which "is not conscious" of the organs of the body to which it belongs.

During this stage of the cocaine condition, which is not otherwise distinguished, appear those symptoms which have been described as the wonderful stimulating effect of coca. Long-lasting, intensive mental or physical work can be performed without fatigue; it is as though the need for food and sleep, which otherwise makes itself felt peremptorily at certain times of the day, were completely banished. While the effects of cocaine last one can, if urged to do so, eat copiously and without revulsion; but one has the clear feeling that the meal was superfluous. Similarly, as the effect of coca declines it is possible to sleep on going to bed, but sleep can just as easily be omitted with no unpleasant consequences. During the first hours of the coca effect one cannot sleep, but this sleeplessness is in no way distressing.

I have tested this effect of coca, which wards off hunger, sleep, and fatigue and steels one to intellectual effort, some dozen times on myself; I had no opportunity to engage in physical work.

A very busy colleague gave me an opportunity to observe a striking example of the manner in which cocaine dispels extreme fatigue and a well justified feeling of hunger; at 6:00 P.M. this colleague, who had not eaten since the early morning and who had worked exceedingly hard during the day, took 0.05g of *cocaïnum muriaticum*. A few minutes later he declared that he felt as though he had just eaten an ample meal, that he had no desire for an evening meal, and that he felt strong enough to undertake a long walk.

This stimulative effect of coca is vouched for beyond any doubt by a series of reliable reports, some of which are quite recent.

By way of an experiment, Sir Robert Christison—who is seventy-eight years old—tired himself to the point of exhaustion by walking fifteen miles without partaking of food. After several days he repeated the procedure with the same result; during the third experiment he chewed two drams of coca leaves and was able to complete the walk without the exhaustion experienced on the earlier occasions; when he arrived home, despite the fact that he had been for nine hours without food or drink, he experienced no hunger or thirst, and woke the next morning without feeling at all tired. On yet another occasion he climbed a 3000-foot mountain and arrived completely exhausted at the summit; he made the descent upon the influence of coca, with youthful vigor and no feeling of fatigue.

Clemens and J. Collan have had similar experiences—the latter after walking for several hours over snow; Mason calls coca "an excellent thing for a long walk"; Aschenbrandt reported recently how Bavarian soldiers, weary as a result of hardships and debilitating illnesses, were nevertheless capable, after taking coca, of participating in maneuvers and marches. Moréno y Maïz was able to stay awake whole nights with the aid of coca; Mantegazza remained for forty hours without food. We are, therefore, justified in assuming that the effect of coca on Europeans is the same as that which the coca leaves have on the Indians of South America.

The effect of a moderate dose of coca fades away so gradually that, in normal circumstances, it is difficult to define its duration. If one works intensively while under the influence of coca, after from three to five hours there is a decline in the feeling of well-being, and a further dose of coca is necessary in order to ward off fatigue. The effect of coca seems to last longer if no heavy muscular work is undertaken. Opinion is unanimous that the euphoria induced by coca is not followed by any feeling of lassitude or other state of depression. I should be inclined to think that after moderate doses (0.05–0.10g) a part at least of the coca effect lasts for over twenty-four hours. In my own case, at any rate, I have noticed that even on the day after taking coca my condition compares favorably with the norm. I should be inclined to explain the possibility of a lasting gain in strength, such as has often been claimed for coca by the totality of such effects.

It seems probable, in the light of reports which I shall refer to later, that coca, if used protractedly but in moderation, is not detrimental to the body. Von Anrep treated animals for thirty days with moderate doses of cocaine and detected no detrimental effects on their bodily functions. It seems to me noteworthy—and I discovered this in myself and in other observers who were capable of judging such things—that a first dose or even repeated doses of coca produce no compulsive desire to use the stimulant further; on the contrary, one feels a certain unmotivated aversion to the substance. This circumstance may be partly responsible for the fact that coca, despite some warm recommendations, has not established itself in Europe as a stimulant.

The effect of large doses of coca was investigated by Mantegazza in experiments on himself. He succeeded in achieving a state of greatly increased happiness accompanied by a desire for complete immobility; this was interrupted occasionally, however, by the most violent urge to move. The analogy with the results of the animal experiments performed by von Anrep is unmistakable. When he increased the dose still further he remained in a *sopore beato:* His pulse rate was extremely high and there was a moderate rise in body temperature; he found that his speech was impeded and his handwriting unsteady; and eventually he experienced the most splendid and colorful hallucinations, the tenor of which was frightening for a short time, but invariably cheerful thereafter. This coca intoxication, too, failed to produce any state of depression, and left no sign whatsoever that the experimenter had passed through a period of intoxication. Moréno y Maïz also experienced a similar powerful compulsion to move after taking fairly large doses of coca. Even after using 18 drams of coca leaves Mantegazza experienced no impairment of full consciousness. A chemist who attempted to poison himself by taking l.5g of cocaine became sick and showed symptoms of gastroenteritis, but there was no dulling of the consciousness.

The Therapeutic Uses of Coca

It was inevitable that a plant which had achieved such a reputation for marvelous effects in its country of origin should have been used to treat the most varied disorders and illnesses of the human body. The first Europeans who became aware of this treasure of the native population were similarly unreserved in their recommendation of coca. On the basis of wide medical experience, Mantegazza later drew up a list of the therapeutic properties of coca, which one by one received the acknowledgment of other doctors. In the following section I have tried to collate the recommendations concerning coca, and, in doing so, to distinguish between recommendations based on successful treatment of illnesses and those which relate to the psychological effects of the stimulant. In general the latter outweigh the former. At present there seems to be some promise of widespread recognition and use of coca preparations in North America, while in Europe doctors scarcely know them by name. The failure of coca to take hold in Europe, which in my opinion is unmerited, can perhaps be attributed to reports of unfavorable consequences attendant upon its use, which appeared shortly after its introduction into Europe; or to the doubtful quality of the preparations, their relative scarcity and consequent high price. Some of the evidence which can be found in favor of the use of coca has been proved valid beyond any doubt, whereas some warrants at least an unprejudiced investigation. Merk's [sic] cocaine and its salts are, as has been proved, preparations which have the full or at least the essential effects of coca leaves.

a) Coca as a stimulant.

The main use of coca will undoubtedly remain that which the Indians have made of it for centuries: it is of value in all cases where the primary aim is to increase the physical capacity of the body for a given short period of time and to hold strength in reserve to meet further demands—especially when outward circumstances exclude the possibility of obtaining the rest and nourishment normally necessary for great exertion. Such situations arise in wartime, on journeys, during mountain climbing and other expeditions, etc.—indeed, they are situations in which the alcoholic stimulants are also generally recognized as being of value. Coca is a far more potent and far less harmful stimulant than alcohol, and its widespread utilization is hindered at present only by its high cost. Bearing in mind the effect of coca on the natives of South America, a medical authority as early as Pedro Crespo (Lima, 1793) recommended its use by European navies; Neudörfer (1870), Clemens (1867) and Surgeon-Major E. Charles recommended that it should be adopted by the armies of Europe as well; and Aschenbrandt's experiences should not fail to draw the attention of army administrators to coca. If cocaine is given as a stimulant, it is better that it should be given in small effective doses (0.05–0.10g) and repeated so often that the effects of the doses overlap. Apparently cocaine is not stored in the body; I have already stressed the fact that there is no state of depression when the effects of coca have worn off.

At present it is impossible to assess with any certainty to what extent coca can be expected to increase human mental powers. I have the impression that protracted use of coca can lead to a lasting improvement if the inhibitions manifested before it is taken are due only to physical causes or to exhaustion. To be sure, the instantaneous effect of a dose of coca cannot be compared with that of a morphine injection; but, on the good side of the ledger, there is no danger of general damage to the body as is the case with the chronic use of morphine.

Many doctors felt that coca would play an important role by filling a gap in the medicine chest of the psychiatrists. It is a well-known fact that psychiatrists have an ample supply of drugs at their disposal for reducing the excitation of nerve centers, but none which could serve to increase the reduced functioning of the nerve centers. Coca has consequently been prescribed for the most diverse kinds of psychic debility—hysteria, hypochondria, melancholic inhibition, stupor, and similar maladies. Some successes have been reported: for instance, the Jesuit, Antonio Julian (Lima, 1787) tells of a learned missionary who was freed from severe hypochondria; Mantegazza praises coca as being almost universally effective in improving those functional disorders which we now group together under the name of neurasthenia; Fliessburg reports excellent results from the use of coca in cases of "nervous prostration"; and according to Caldwell, it is the best tonic for hysteria.

E. Morselli and G. Buccola carried out experiments involving the systematic dispensation of cocaine, over a period of months, to melancholics. They gave a preparation of cocaine, as prescribed by Trommsdorf, in subcutaneous injections, in doses ranging from 0.0025–0.10g per dose. After one or two months they confirmed a slight improvement in the condition of their patients, who became happier, took nourishment, and enjoyed regular digestion.[4]

On the whole, the efficacy of coca in cases of nervous and psychic debility needs further investigation, which will probably lead to partially favorable conclusions. According to Mantegazza coca is of no use, and is sometimes even dangerous, in cases of organic change and inflammation of the nervous system.

b) The use of coca for digestive disorders of the stomach.

This is the oldest and most firmly founded use of coca, and at the same time it is the most comprehensible to us. According to the unanimous assertions of the oldest as well as the most recent authorities (Julian, Martius, Unanué, Mantegazza, Bingel, Scrivener,[5] Frankl, and others) coca in its most various forms banishes dyspeptic complaints and the disorders and debility associated therewith, and after protracted use results in a permanent cure. I have myself made a series of such observations.

Like Mantegazza[6] and Frankl, I have experienced personally how the painful symptoms attendant upon large meals—viz a feeling of pressure and fullness in the stomach, discomfort and a disinclination to work—disappear with eructation following small doses of cocaine (0.025–0.05). Time and again I have brought such relief to my colleagues; and twice I observed how the nausea resulting from gastronomic excesses responded in a short time to the effects of cocaine, and gave way to a normal desire to eat and a feeling of bodily well-being. I have also learned to spare myself stomach troubles by adding a small amount of cocaine to salicylate of soda.

My colleague, Dr. Josef Pollak, has given me the following account of an astonishing effect of cocaine, which shows that it can be used to treat not merely local discomfort in the stomach but also serious reflex reactions; one must therefore assume that cocaine has a powerful effect on the mucous membrane and the muscular system of this organ.

"A forty-two-year-old, robust man, whom the doctor knew very well, was forced to adhere most strictly to a certain diet and to prescribed mealtimes; otherwise he could not avoid the attacks about to be described. When traveling or under the influence of any emotional strain he was particularly susceptible. The attacks followed a regular pattern: They began in the evening with a feeling of discomfort in the epigastrium, followed by flushing of the face, tears in the eyes, throbbing in the temples and violent pain in the forehead, accompanied by a feeling of great depression and apathy. He could not sleep during the night; toward morning there were long painful spasms of vomiting which lasted for hours. Round about midday he experienced some relief, and on drinking a few spoonfuls of soup had a feeling 'as though the stomach would at last eject a bullet which had lain in it for a long time.' This was followed by rancid eructation, until, toward evening, his condition returned to normal. The patient was incapable of work throughout the day and had to keep to his bed.

"At 8:00 PM on the tenth of June the usual symptoms of an attack began. At ten o'clock, after the violent headache had developed, the patient was given 0.075g *cocaïnum muriaticum*. Shortly thereafter he experienced a feeling of warmth and eructation, which seemed to him to be 'still too little.' At 10:30 a second dose of 0.075g of cocaine was given; the eructations increased; the patient felt some relief and was able to write a long letter. He alleged that he felt intensive movement in the stomach; at twelve o'clock, apart from a slight headache, he was normal, even cheerful, and walked for an hour. He could not sleep until 3:00 AM, but that did not distress him. He awoke the next morning healthy, ready for work, and with a good appetite."

The effect of cocaine on the stomach—Mantegazza assumes this as well—is twofold: stimulation of movement and reduction of the organ's sensitivity. The latter would seem probable not only because of the local sensations in the stomach after cocaine has been taken but because of the analogous effect of cocaine on other mucous membranes. Mantegazza claims to have achieved the most brilliant successes in treatments of gastralgia and enteralgia, and all painful and cramping afflictions of the stomach and intestines, which he attributes to the anesthetizing properties of coca. On this point I cannot confirm Mantegazza's experiences; only once, in connection with a case of gastric catarrh, did I see the sensitivity of the stomach to pressure disappear after the administration of coca. On other occasions I have observed myself, and also heard from other doctors, that patients suspected of having ulcers or scars in the stomach complained of increased pain after using coca; this can be explained by the increased movement of the stomach.

Accordingly, I should say that the use of coca is definitely indicated in cases of atonic digestive weakness and the so-called nervous stomach disorders; in such cases it is possible to achieve not merely a relief of the symptoms but a lasting improvement.

c) Coca in cachexia.

Long-term use of coca is further strongly recommended—and allegedly has been tried with success—in all diseases which involve degeneration of the tissues, such as severe anemia, phthisis, long-lasting febrile diseases, etc.; and also during recovery from such diseases. Thus McBean noted a steady improvement in cases of typhoid fever treated with coca. In the case of phthisis, coca is said to have a limiting effect on the fever and sweating. Peckham reports with regard to a case of definitely diagnosed phthisis that after fluid extract of coca had been used for seven months there was a marked improvement in the patient's condition. Hole gives an account of another rather serious case in which chronic lack of appetite had led to an advanced condition of emaciation and exhaustion; here, too, the use of coca restored the patient to health. R. Bartholow observed, in general, that coca proved useful in treating phthisis and other "consumptive processes." Mantegazza and a number of other authorities attribute to coca the same invaluable therapeutic quality: that of limiting degeneration of the body and increasing strength in the case of cachexia.

One might wish to attribute such successes partly to the undoubted favorable effect of coca on the digestion, but one must bear in mind that a good many of the authors who have written on coca regard it as a "source of savings"; i.e., they are of the opinion that a system which has absorbed even an extremely small amount of cocaine is capable, as a result of the reaction of the body to coca, of amassing a greater store of vital energy which can be converted into work than would have been possible without coca. If we take the amount of work as being constant, the body which has absorbed cocaine should be able to manage with a lower metabolism, which in turn means a smaller intake of food.

This assumption was obviously made to account for the, according to von Voit, unexplained effect of coca on the Indians. It does not even necessarily involve a contradiction of the law of conservation of energy. For labor which draws upon food or tissue components involves a certain loss, either in the utilization of assimilated food or in the conversion of energy into work; this loss could perhaps be reduced if certain appropriate steps were taken. It has not been proved that such a process takes place, however. Experiments designed to determine the amount of urine eliminated with and without the use of coca have not been altogether conclusive; indeed, these experiments have not always been conducted in such conditions that they could furnish conclusive results. Moreover, they seem to have been carried out on the assumption that the elimination of urine—which is known not to be effected by labor—would provide a measure of metabolism in general. Thus Christison noted a slight reduction in the solid components of his urine during the walks on which he took coca; Lippmann, Demarle, Marvaud, and more recently Mason similarly concluded from their experiments that the consumption of coca reduces the amount of urine elimination. Gazeau, on the other hand, established an increase of urine elimination of 11–24% under the influence of coca. A better availability of materials already stored in the body explains, in his opinion, the body's increased working power and ability to do without food when under the influence of coca. No experiments have been carried out with regard to the elimination of carbon dioxide.

Voit proved that coffee, which also rated as a "source of savings," had no influence on the breakdown of albumen in the body. We must regard the conception of coca as a "source of savings" as disproven after certain experiments in which animals were starved, both with and without cocaine, and the reduction of their body weight and the length of time they were able to withstand inanition were observed. Such experiments were carried out by Cl. Bernard, Moréno y Maïz, Demarle, Gazeau, and von Anrep. The result was that the animals to which cocaine had been administered succumbed to inanition just as soon—perhaps even sooner—than those which had received no cocaine. The starvation of La Paz—an experiment carried out by history itself, and reported by Unanué—seems to contradict this conclusion, however, for the inhabitants who had partaken of coca are said to have escaped death by starvation. In this connection one might recall the fact that the human nervous system has an undoubted, if somewhat obscure, influence on the nourishment of tissues; psychological factors can, after all, cause a healthy man to lose weight.

The therapeutic quality of coca which we took as our argument at the outset does not, therefore, deserve to be rejected out of hand. The excitation of nerve centers by cocaine can have a favorable influence on the nourishment of the body afflicted by a consumptive condition, even though that influence might well not take the form of a slowing down of metabolism.

I should add here that coca has been warmly praised in connection with the treatment of syphilis. R.W. Taylor claims that a patient's tolerance of mercury is increased and the mercury cachexia kept in check when coca is administered at the same time. J. Collan recommends it as the best remedy for *stomatitis mercurialis* and reports that Pagvalin always prescribes it in conjunction with preparations of mercury.

d) Coca in the treatment of morphine and alcohol addiction.

In America the important discovery has recently been made that coca preparations possess the power to suppress the craving for morphine in habitual addicts, and also to reduce to negligible proportions the serious symptoms of collapse which appear while the patient is being weaned away from the morphine habit. According to my information (which is largely from the *Detroit Therapeutic Gazette*), it was W.H. Bentley who announced, in May 1878, that he had substituted coca for the customary alkaloid in the case of a female morphine addict. Two years later, Palmer, in an article in the *Louisville Medical News*, seems to have aroused the greatest general interest in this treatment of morphine addiction; for the next two years "*Erythroxylon coca* in the opium habit" was a regular heading in the reports of the *Therapeutic Gazette*. From then on information regarding successful cures became rarer: whether because the treatment became established as a recognized cure, or because it was abandoned, I do not know. Judging by the advertisements of drug dealers in the most recent issues of American papers, I should rather conclude that the former was the case.

There are some sixteen reports of cases in which the patient has been successfully cured of addiction; in only one instance is there a report of failure of coca to alleviate morphine addiction, and in this case the doctor wondered why there had been so many warm recommendations for the use of coca in cases of morphine addiction. The successful cases vary in their conclusiveness. Some of them involve large doses of opium or morphine and addictions of long standing. There is not much information on the subject of relapses, as most cases were reported within a very short time of the cure having been effected. Symptoms which appear during abstention are not always reported in detail. There is especial value in those reports which contain the observation that the patients were able to dispense with coca after a few weeks without experiencing any further desire for morphine. Special attention is repeatedly called to the fact that morphine cachexia gave way to excellent health, so that the patients were scarcely recognizable after their cure. Concerning the method of withdrawal, it should be made clear that in the majority of cases a gradual reduction of the habitual dose of the drug, accompanied by a gradual increase of the coca dose, was the method chosen; however, sudden discontinuation of the drug was also tried. In the latter case Palmer prescribes that a certain dose of coca should be repeated as often during the day as the desire for morphine recurs.[7] The daily dose of coca is lessened gradually until it is possible to dispense. with the antidote altogether. From the very beginning the attacks experienced during abstinence were either slight or else became milder after a few days. In almost every case the cure was effected by the patient himself, whereas the cure of morphine addiction without the help of coca, as practiced in Europe, requires surveillance of the patient in a hospital.

I once had occasion to observe the case of a man who was subjected to the type of cure involving the sudden withdrawal of morphine, assisted by the use of coca; the same patient had suffered severe symptoms as a result of abstinence in the course of a previous cure. This time his condition was tolerable; in particular, there was no sign of depression or nausea as long as the effects of coca lasted; chills and diarrhea were now the only permanent symptoms of his abstinence. The patient was not bedridden, and could function normally. During the first days of the cure he consumed 3dg of *cocaïnum muriaticum* daily, and after ten days he was able to dispense with the coca treatment altogether.

The treatment of morphine addiction with coca does not, therefore, result merely in the exchange of one kind of addiction for another—it does not turn the morphine addict into a *coquero*; the use of coca is only temporary. Moreover, I do not think that it is the general toughening effect of coca which enables the system weakened by morphine to withstand, at the cost of only insignificant symptoms, the withdrawal of morphine. I am rather inclined to assume that coca has a directly antagonistic effect on morphine, and in support of my view I quote the following observations of Dr. Josef Pollak on a case in point:

"A thirty-three-year-old woman has been suffering for years from severe menstrual migraine which can be alleviated only by morphia injections. Although the lady in question never takes morphia or experiences any desire to do so when she is free of migraine, during the attacks she behaves like a morphine addict. A few hours after the injection she suffers intense depression, biliousness, attacks of vomiting, which are stopped by a second morphine injection; thereupon, the symptoms of intolerance recur, with the result that an attack of migraine, along with all its consequences, keeps the patient in bed for three days in a most wretched condition. Cocaine was then tried to combat the migraine, but the treatment proved unsuccessful. It was necessary to resort to morphine injections. But as soon as the symptoms of morphine intolerance appeared, they were quickly relieved by 1 dg of cocaine, with the result that the patient recovered from her attack in a far shorter time and consumed much less morphine in the process."

Coca was tried in America for the treatment of chronic alcoholism at about the same time as it was introduced in connection with morphine addiction, and most reports dealt with the two uses conjointly. In the treatment of alcoholism, too, there were cases of undoubted success, in which the irresistible compulsion to drink was either banished or alleviated, and the dyspeptic complaints of the drinkers were relieved. In general, however, the suppression of the alcohol craving through the use of coca proved to be more difficult than the suppression of morphomania; in one case reported by Bentley the drinker became a *coquero*. One need only suggest the immense economic significance which coca would acquire as a "source of savings" in another sense, if its effectiveness in combating alcoholism were confirmed.

e) Coca and asthma

Tschudi and Markham report that by chewing coca leaves they were spared the usual symptoms of the so-called mountain sickness while climbing in the Andes; this complex of symptoms includes shortness of breath, pounding of the heart, dizziness, etc. Poizat reports that the asthmatic attacks of a patient were arrested in every case by coca. I mention this property of coca because it appears to admit of a physiological explanation. Von Anrep's experiments on animals resulted in early paralysis of certain branches of the vagus; and altitude asthma, as well as the attacks characteristic of chronic bronchitis, may be interpreted in terms of a reflex excitation originating in the pulmonary branches of the vagus. The use of coca should be considered for the treatment of other vagus neuroses.

f) Coca as an aphrodisiac.

The natives of South America, who represented their goddess of love with coca leaves in her hand, did not doubt the stimulative effect of coca on the genitalia. Mantegazza confirms that the *coqueros* sustain a high degree of potency right into old age; he even reports cases of the restoration of potency and the disappearance of functional weaknesses following the use of coca, although he does not believe that coca would produce such an effect in all individuals. Marvaud emphatically supports the view that coca has a stimulative effect; other writers strongly recommend coca as a remedy for occasional functional weaknesses and temporary exhaustion; and Bentley reports on a case of this type in which coca was responsible for the cure.

Among the persons to whom I have given coca, three reported violent sexual excitement which they unhesitatingly attributed to the coca. A young writer, who was enabled by treatment with coca to resume his work after a longish illness, gave up using the drug because of the undesirable secondary effects which it had on him.

g) Local application of coca.

Cocaine and its salts have a marked anesthetizing effect when brought in contact with the skin and mucous membrane in concentrated solution; this property suggests its occasional use as a local anesthetic, especially in connection with affections of the mucous membrane. According to Collan, Ch. Fauvel strongly recommends cocaine for treating diseases of the pharynx, describing it as *"le tenseur par excellence des chordes vocales."* Indeed, the anesthetizing properties of cocaine should make it suitable for a good many further applications.

Footnotes

[1] Like Aschenbrandt (*Deutsche med. Wochenschrift*, Dec., 1883) I used the hydrochloric preparation of cocaine as described by Merk [sic] in Darmstadt. This preparation may be bought in Vienna in Haubner's Engelapotheke am Hof at a price which is not much higher than Merk's [sic], but which must, nevertheless, be regarded as very high. The management of the pharmacy in question is trying, as they have been kind enough to inform me, to lower the price of the drug by establishing new sources of supply.

² For the results obtained from subcutaneous injections see Morselli's and Buccola's work.

³ Wilder's account of the effects of cocaine on himself coincide most closely with my own observations (*Detroit Therapeutic Gazette*. Nov., 1882).

⁴ Their assertions about the physiological effects of cocaine accord with those of Mantegazza. They observed, as an immediate effect of cocaine injections, dilation of the pupils, temperature heightened by up to 1.2 degrees quickening of the pulse and respiration. There is never an attack of sickness.

⁵ *Loc. cit.* "an excellent tonic in weakness of the stomach."

⁶ Mantegazza's exhaustive medical case-histories impress me as being thoroughly credible.

⁷ *T[herapeutic] G[azette]*, July 1880. The preparation used was mostly the fluid extract, manufactured by Parke, Davis and Co.

(Translated by Steven A. Edminster/Fredrick C. Redlich)

A Hashish-House in New York

H. H. Kane

Subtitled "The Curious
Adventures of an Individual
Who Indulged in a Few
Pipefuls of the Narcotic
Hemp," the following story,
although written as fictional
reportage, describes an actual
location in New York City.
Like Paris, late-nineteenth-
century New York was—for
those who knew where to
look—an exotic city of bohemian privileges, and hashish
use was not uncommon.
At first skeptical about the
existence of such places, the
narrator is escorted into a
labyrintine "hemp retreat,"
from which he emerges
having encountered a vivid,
undeniable truth.

AND SO YOU THINK that opium-smoking as seen in
the foul cellars of Mott Street and elsewhere is the
only form of narcotic indulgence of any consequence
in this city, and that hashish, if used at all, is only smoked
occasionally and experimentally by a few scattered individuals?"

"That certainly is my opinion, and I consider myself
fairly well informed."

"Well, you are far from right, as I can prove to you if
you care to inform yourself more fully on the subject. There
is a large community of hashish smokers in this city, who
are daily forced to indulge their morbid appetites, and I
can take you to a house uptown where hemp is used in
every conceivable form, and where the lights, sounds, odors,
and surroundings are all arranged so as to intensify and en-
hance the effects of this wonderful narcotic."

"I must confess that I am still incredulous."

"Well, if it is agreeable to you, meet me at the Hoffman
House reading-room tomorrow night at ten o'clock, and
I think I shall be able to convince you."

The above is the substance of a conversation that
took place in the lobby of a downtown hotel between
the writer of these lines and a young man about thirty-
eight years of age, known to me for some years past as
an opium-smoker. It was through his kindness that I
had first gained access to and had been able to study up
the subject of opium-smoking. Hence I really antici-
pated seeing some interesting phases of hemp indulgence, and was not disappointed.

The following evening at precisely ten o'clock I met
the young man at the Hoffman House, and together we
took a Broadway car uptown, left it at Forty-second Street,

and walked rapidly toward the North River,[1] talking as we went.

"'You will probably be greatly surprised at many things you will see tonight," he said, "just as I was when I was first introduced into the place by a friend. I have travelled over most of Europe, and have smoked opium in every *joint* in America, but never saw anything so curious as this, nor experienced any intoxication so fascinating yet so terrible as that of hashish."

"Are the habitués of this place of the same class as those who frequent the opium-smoking dives?"

"By no means. They are about evenly divided between Americans and foreigners; indeed, the place is kept by a Greek, who has invested a great deal of money in it. All the visitors, both male and female, are of the better classes, and absolute secrecy is the rule. The house has been opened about two years, I believe, and the number of regular habitués is daily on the increase."

"Are you one of the number?"

"I am, and find the intoxication far pleasanter and less hurtful than that from opium. Ah! here we are."

We paused before a gloomy-looking house, entered the gate, and passed up the steps. The windows were absolutely dark, and the entranceway looked dirty and desolate. Four pulls at the bell, a pause, and one more pull were followed by a few moments' silence, broken suddenly by the sound of falling chain, rasping bolt, and the grinding of a key in the lock. The outer door was cautiously opened, and at a word from my companion we passed into the vestibule. The outer door was carefully closed by someone whom I could not distinguish in the utter darkness. A moment later the inner door was opened, and never shall I forget the impression produced by the sudden change from total darkness to the strange scene that met my eyes. The dark vestibule was the boundary line separating the cold, dreary streets and the ordinary world from a scene of Oriental magnificence.

A volume of heavily scented air, close upon the heels of which came a deadly sickening odor, wholly unlike anything I had ever smelled, greeted my nostrils. A hall lamp of grotesque shape flooded the hall with a subdued violet light that filtered through crenated disks of some violet fabric hung below it. The walls and ceilings, if ever modern, were no longer so, for they were shut in and hung by festoons and plaits of heavy cloth fresh from Eastern looms. Tassels of blue, green, yellow, red, and tinsel here and there peeped forth, matching the curious edging of variously colored bead-work that bordered each fold of drapery like a huge procession of luminous ants, and seemed to flow into little phosphorescent pools wherever the cloth was caught up. Queer figures and strange lettering, in the same work, were here and there disclosed upon the ceiling cloth.

Along one side of the hall, between two doors, were ranged huge tubs and pots of majolica-like ware and blue-necked Japanese vases, in which were plants, shrubs, and flowers of the most exquisite color and odor. Green vines clambered up the walls and across the ceiling, and catching their tendrils in the balustrades of the stairs (which were also of curious design), threw down long sprays and heavy festoons of verdure.

As my companion, who had paused a moment to give me time to look about me, walked toward the far end of the hall, I followed him, and passed into a small room on the right, where, with the assistance of a colored servant, we exchanged our coats, hats, and shoes for others more in keeping with our surroundings. First a long plush gown, quilted with silk down the front, and irregularly ornamented in bead and braid with designs of serpents, flowers, crescents, and stars, was slipped on over the head. Next a tasselled smoking-cap was donned, and the feet incased in noiseless list slippers. In any other place or under any other circumstances I should have felt ridiculous in this costume, but so in keeping was it with all I had seen, and so thoroughly had I seemed to have left my every-day self in the dark vestibule, that I felt perfectly at home in my strange dress. We next crossed the hall to a smaller room, where a young man, apparently a Frenchman, furnished us, on the payment of two dollars each, with two small pipes and a small covered bronze cup, or urn, filled with a dry green shrub, which I subsequently learned was *gunjeh* (the dried tops and leaves of the hemp plant), for smoking. My friend, on the payment of a further sum, obtained a curious little box which contained some small black lozenges, consisting of the resin of hemp, henbane, crushed datura seeds, butter, and honey, and known in India as *Majoon,* amongst the Moors as *El Mogen.*

Passing from this room we ascended the richly carpeted stairs, enarbored by vines, and paused upon a landing from which three doors opened. Upon one a pink card bore Dryden's line, "Take the good the gods provide thee." The knob turned by my friend's hand allowed the door to swing open, and, welcomed by a spice breeze from India, we were truly in paradise.

"This," he said, in a whisper, "is the public room, where anyone having pipe or lozenge, and properly attired, may enter and indulge—eat, smoke, or dream, as best suits him."

Wonder, amazement, admiration, but faintly portray my mental condition. Prepared by what I had already seen and experienced for something odd and Oriental, still the magnificence of what now met my gaze far surpassed anything I had ever dreamed of, and brought to my mind the scenes of the *Arabian Nights,* forgotten since boyhood until now. My every sense was irresistibly taken captive, and it was some moments before I could realize that I really was not the victim of some dream, for I seemed to have wholly severed my connection with the world of today, and to have stepped back several centuries into the times of genii, fairies, and fountains—into the very heart of Persia or Arabia.

Not an inharmonious detail marred the symmetry of the whole. Beneath, my feet sank almost ankle-deep into a velvet carpet—a sea of subdued colors. Looked at closely, I found that the design was that of a garden: beds of luxurious flowers, stars and crescents, squares and diamond-shaped plots, made up of thousands of rare exotics and richly colored leaves. Here a brook, edged with damp verdure, from beneath which peeped coy violets and tiny bluebells; there a serpentine gravelled walk that wound in and out amongst the exquisite plants, and everywhere a thousand shrubs in bloom or bud. Above, a magnificent chandelier, consisting of six dragons of beaten gold, from whose eyes and throats sprang flames, the light from which, striking against a series of curiously set prisms, fell shattered and scintillating into a thousand glancing beams that illuminated every corner of the room. The rows of prisms being of clear and variously colored glass, and the dragons slowly revolving, a weird and ever-changing hue was given to every object in the room.

All about the sides of the spacious apartment, upon the floor, were mattresses covered with different-colored cloth, and edged with heavy golden fringe. Upon them were carelessly strewn rugs and mats of Persian and Turkish handicraft, and soft pillows in heaps. Above the level of these divans there ran, all about the room, a series of huge mirrors framed with gilded serpents intercoiled, effectually shutting off the windows. The effect was magnificent. There seemed to be twenty rooms instead of one, and everywhere could be seen the flame-tongued and fiery-eyed dragons slowly revolving, giving to all the appearance of a magnificent kaleidoscope in which the harmonious colors were ever blending and constantly presenting new combinations.

Just as I had got thus far in my observations I caught sight of my friend standing at the foot of one of the divans, and beckoning to me. At the same moment I also observed that several of the occupants of other divans were eying me suspiciously. I crossed to where he was, esteeming it a desecration to walk on such a carpet, and, despite my knowledge to the contrary, fearing every moment to crush some beautiful rose or lily beneath my feet. Following my friend's example, I slipped off my list foot-gear, and half reclined beside him on the divan and pillows, that seemed to reach up and embrace us. Pulling a tasselled cord that hung above our heads, my friend spoke a few words to a gaudily turbaned colored servant who came noiselessly into the room in answer to his summons, disappeared again, and in a moment returned bearing a tray, which he placed between us. Upon it was a small lamp of silver filigree-work, two globelike bowls, of silver also, from which protruded a long silver tube and a spoonlike instrument. The latter, I soon learned, was used to clean and fill the pipes. Placing the bronze jar of hashish on the tray, my friend bade me lay my pipe beside it, and suck up the fluid in the silver cup through the long tube. I did so, and found it delicious.

"That," said he, "is tea made from the genuine coca leaf. The cup is the real *mate* and the tube a real *bombilla* from Peru.[2] Now let us smoke. The dried shrub here is known as *gunjeh,* and is the dried tops of the hemp plant. Take a little tobacco from that jar and mix with it, else it will be found difficult to keep it alight. These lozenges here are made from the finest Nepaul resin of the hemp, mixed with butter, sugar, honey, flour, pounded datura seeds, some opium, and a little henbane, or hyoscyamus. I prefer taking these to smoking, but, to keep you company, I will also smoke tonight. Have no fear. Smoke four or five pipefuls of the *gunjeh,* and enjoy the effect. I will see that no harm befalls you."

Swallowing two of the lozenges, my guide filled our pipes, and we proceeded to smoke, and watch the others. These pipes, the stems of which were about eighteen inches in length, were incrusted with designs in varicolored beads, strung on gold wire over a ground of some light spirally twisted tinsel, marked off into diamond-shaped spaces by thin red lines. From the stem two green and yellow silken tassels depended. A small bell-shaped piece of clouded amber formed the mouthpiece, while at the other end was a small bowl of red clay scarcely larger than a thimble. As I smoked I noticed that about two-thirds of the divans were occupied by persons of both sexes, some of them masked, who were dressed in the same manner as ourselves. Some were smoking, some reclining listlessly upon the pillows, following the tangled thread of a hashish reverie or dream. A middle-aged woman sat bolt-upright, gesticulating and laughing quietly to herself; another with lacklustre eyes and dropped jaw was swaying her head monotonously from side to side. A young man of about eighteen was on his knees, praying inaudibly; and another man, masked, paced rapidly and noiselessly up and down the room, until led away somewhere by the turbaned servant.

As I smoked, the secret of that heavy, sickening odor was made clear to me. It was the smell of burning hashish. Strangely enough, it did not seem to be unpleasant any longer, for, although it rather rasped my throat at first, I drew large volumes of it into my lungs. Lost in lazy reverie and perfect comfort, I tried to discover whence came the soft, undulating strains of music that had greeted me on entering, and which still continued. They were just perceptible above the silvery notes of a crystal fountain in the centre of the room, the falling spray from which plashed and tinkled musically as it fell from serpents' mouths into a series of the very thinnest huge pink shells held aloft by timid hares. The music seemed to creep up through the heavy carpet, to ooze from the walls, to flurry, like snowflakes, from the ceiling, rising and falling in measured cadences unlike any music I had ever heard. It seemed to steal, now softly, now merrily, on tiptoe into the room to see whether we were awake or asleep, to brush away a tear, if tear there was, or gambol airily and merrily, if such was our humor, and then as softly, sometimes sadly, to steal out again and lose itself in the distance. It was just such music as a boatful of fairies sailing about in the clear water of the fountain might have made, or that with which an angel mother would sing its angel babe to sleep. It seemed to enter every fibre of the body, and satisfy a music-hunger that had never before been satisfied. I silently filled my second pipe, and was about to lapse again into a reverie that had become delightfully full of perfect rest and comfort, when my companion, leaning toward me, said:

"I see that you are fast approaching Hashishdom. Is there not a sense of perfect rest and strange, quiet happiness produced by it?"

"There certainly is. I feel supremely happy, at peace with myself and all the world, and all that I ask is to be let alone. But why is everything so magnificent here? Is it a whim of the proprietor, or an attempt to reproduce some such place in the East?" I asked.

"Possibly the latter; but there is another reason that you may understand better later. It is this: the color and peculiar phases of a hashish dream are materially affected by one's surroundings just prior to the sleep. The impressions that we have been receiving ever since we entered, the lights, odors, sounds, and colors, are the strands which the deft fingers of imagination will weave into the hemp reveries and dreams, which seem as real as those of everyday life, and always more grand. Hashish eaters and smokers in the East recognized this fact, and always, prior to indulging in the drug, surrounded themselves with the most pleasant sounds, faces, forms, etc."

"I see," I answered, dreamily. "But what is there behind those curtains that I see moving now and again?" The heavy curtains just opposite where we lay seemed to shut in an alcove.

"There are several small rooms there," said my companion, "shut off from this room by the curtains you see move. Each is magnificently fitted up, I am told. They are reserved for persons, chiefly ladies, who wish to avoid every possibility of detection, and at the same time enjoy their hashish and watch the inmates of this room."

"Are there many ladies of good social standing who come here?"

"Very many. Not the cream of the *demi-monde,* understand me, but *ladies.* Why, there must be at least six hundred in this city alone who are *habituées.* Smokers from different cities, Boston, Philadelphia, Chicago, and especially New Orleans, tell me that each city has its hemp retreat, but none so elegant as this."

And my companion swallowed another lozenge and relapsed into dreamy silence. I too lay back listlessly, and was soon lost in reverie, intense and pleasant. Gradually the room and its inmates faded from view; the revolving dragons went swifter and more swiftly, until the flaming tongues and eyes were merged into a huge ball of flame, that, suddenly detaching itself with a sharp sound from its pivot, went whirling and streaming off into the air until lost to sight in the skies. Then a sudden silence, during which I heard the huge waves of an angry sea breaking with fierce monotony in my head. Then I heard the fountain; the musical tinkle of the spray as it struck upon the glass grew louder and louder, and the notes longer and longer, until they merged into one clear, musical bugle note that woke the echoes of a spring morning, and broke sharp and clear over hill and valley, meadowland and marsh, hilltop and forest. A gayly caparisoned horseman, bugle in hand, suddenly appeared above a hillcrest. Closely following, a straggling group of horsemen riding madly. Before them a pack of hounds came dashing down the hillside, baying deeply. Before them I, the fox, was running with the speed of desperation, straining every nerve to distance or elude them. Thus for miles and miles I ran on until at last, almost dead with fright and fatigue, I fell panting in the forest. A moment more and the cruel hounds would have had me, when suddenly a little field-mouse appeared, caught me by the paw, and dragged me through the narrow entrance to her nest. My body lengthened and narrowed until I found myself a serpent, and in me rose the desire to devour my little preserver, when, as I was about to strike her with my fangs, she changed into a beautiful little fairy, tapped my ugly black flat head with her wand, and as my fangs fell to earth I resumed my human shape. With the parting words, "Never seek to injure those who endeavor to serve you," she disappeared.

Looking about I found myself in a huge cave, dark and noisome. Serpents hissed and glared at me from every side, and huge lizards and ugly shapes scrambled over the wet floor. In the far corner of the cave I saw piles of precious stones of wondrous value that glanced and sparkled in the dim light. Despite the horrid shapes about me, I resolved to secure some, at least, of these precious gems. I began to walk toward them, but found that I could get no nearer—just as fast as I advanced, so fast did they seem to recede. At last, after what seemed a year's weary journey, I suddenly found myself beside them, and falling on my knees, began to fill my pockets, bosom, even my hat. Then I tried to rise, but could not: the jewels weighed me down. Mortified and disappointed, I replaced them all but three, weeping bitterly. As I rose to my feet it suddenly occurred to me that this was in no way real—only a hashish dream. And, laughing, I said, "You fool, this is all non-sense. These are not real jewels; they only exist in your imagination." My real self argu-ing thus with my hashish self, which I could see, tired, ragged, and weeping, set me to laughing still harder, and then we laughed together—my two selves. Suddenly my real self faded away, and a cloud of sadness and misery settled upon me, and I wept again, throw-ing myself hysterically upon the damp floor of the cave.

Just then I heard a voice addressing me by name, and looking up, I saw an old man with an enormous nose bending over me. His nose seemed almost as large as his whole body. "Why do you weep, my son?" he said; "are you sad because you can not have all these riches? Don't, then, for some day you will learn whoso hath more wealth than is needed to minister to his wants must suffer for it. Every farthing above a certain rea-sonable sum will surely bring some worry, care, anxiety, or trouble. Three diamonds are your share; be content with them. But, dear me, here I am again neglecting my work! Here it is March, and I'm not half through yet!"

"Pray what is your work, venerable patriarch?" I asked; "and why has the Lord given you such a huge proboscis?"

"Ah! I see that you don't know me," he replied. "I am the chemist of the earth's bow-els, and it is my duty to prepare all the sweet and delicate odors that the flowers have. I am busy all winter making them, and early in the spring my nymphs and apprentices de-liver them to the Queen of the Flowers, who in turn gives them to her subjects. My nose is a little large because I have to do so much smelling. Come and see my laboratory."

His nose a little large! I laughed until I almost cried at this, while following him.

He opened a door, and entering, my nostrils met the oddest medley of odors I had ever smelled. Everywhere workmen with huge noses were busy mixing, filtering, distill-ing, and the like.

"Here," said the old man, "is a batch of odor that has been spoiled. Mistakes are fre-quent, but I find use for even such as that. The Queen of Flowers gives it to disobedient plants or flowers. You mortals call it asafoetida. Come in here and see my organ;" and he led the way into a large rocky room, at one end of which was a huge organ of curious construction. Mounting to the seat, he arranged the stops and began to play.

Not a sound could be heard, but a succession of odors swept past me, some slowly, some rapidly. I understood the grand idea in a moment. Here was music to which that of sound was coarse and earthly. Here was a harmony, a symphony, of odors! Clear and sharp, intense and less intense, sweet, less sweet, and again still sweeter, heavy and light, fast and slow, deep and narcotic, the odors, all in perfect harmony, rose and fell, and swept by me, to be succeeded by others.

Irresistibly I began to weep, and fast and thick fell the tears, until I found myself a little stream of water, that, rising in the rocky caverns of the mountain, dashed down its side into the plain below. Fiercely the hot sun beat upon my scanty waters, and like a thin gray mist I found myself rising slowly into the skies, no longer a stream. With other clouds I was swept away by the strong and rapid wind far across the Atlantic, over the burning sand wastes of Africa, dipping toward the Arabian Sea, and suddenly falling in huge raindrops into the very heart of India, blossoming with poppies. As the ground greedily sucked up the refreshing drops I again assumed my form.

Suddenly the earth was rent apart, and falling upon the edge of a deep cavern, I saw far below me a molten, hissing sea of fire, above which a dense vapor hung. Issuing from this mist, a thousand anguished faces rose toward me on scorched and broken wings, shrieking and moaning as they came.

"Who in Heaven's name are these poor things?"

"These," said a voice at my side, "are the spirits, still incarnate, of individuals who, during life, sought happiness in the various narcotics. Here, after death, far beneath, they live a life of torture most exquisite, for it is their fate, ever suffering for want of moisture, to be obliged to yield day by day their life-blood to form the juice of poppy and resin of hemp in order that their dream, joys, hopes, pleasures, pains, and anguish of past and present may again be tasted by mortals."

As he said this I turned to see who he was, but he had disappeared. Suddenly I heard a fierce clamor, felt the scrawny arms of these foul spirits wound about my neck, in my hair, on my limbs, pulling me over into the horrible chasm, into the heart of hell, crying, shrilly, "Come! thou art one of us. Come! come! come!" I struggled fiercely, shrieked out in my agony, and suddenly awoke, with the cold sweat thick upon me.

"Are you, then, so fond of it that nothing can awaken you? Here have I been shaking and pulling you for the past five minutes. Come, rouse yourself; your dreams seem to be unpleasant."

Gradually my senses became clearer. The odors of the room, the melodies of early evening, the pipe that had fallen from my hand, the faces and forms of the hemp-smokers, were once more recognized.

My companion wished me to stay, assuring me that I would see many queer sights before morning, but I declined, and after taking, by his advice, a cup of Paraguay tea (coca leaf), and then a cup of sour lemonade, I passed downstairs, exchanged my present for my former dress, returned my pipe, and left the house.

The dirty streets, the tinkling car-horse bell, the deafening "Here you are! twenty sweet oranges for a quarter!" and the drizzling rain were more grateful by far than the odors, sounds, and sights, sweet though they were, that I had just left. Truly it was the cradle of dreams rocking placidly in the very heart of a great city, translated from Bagdad to Gotham.

Footnotes:

[1] Another name for the Hudson River.

[2] There is some confusion here. Maté is a tea made from a hollylike South American tree, *Ilex paraguayensis*, also called "Paraguay tea." No drink is made from coca leaves, *Erythroxylon coca*. A bombilla is simply a reed, used here as a straw.

The Peyote Plant and Ceremony

James Mooney,
U.S. Bureau of Ethnology

One of the earliest non-native American participant-observers of the peyote ceremony was James Mooney, who was sent to Indian Territory (now Oklahoma) in the late nineteenth century by the Smithsonian's newly organized Bureau of American Ethnology to study the Ghost Dance movement. While documenting this phenomenon, Mooney also became involved in the peyote religion. He participated in all-night ceremonies and eventually published the first objective written account of peyote rituals in the United States. With his first-hand knowledge, he became an ardent supporter of peyotism, actively advocating the legalization of what in 1918 became the Native American Church. The following article was written in 1896 for a medical journal as a testimonial to the medicinal and therapeutic value of peyote.

ABOUT FIVE YEARS AGO, while making investigations among the Kiowa Indians on behalf of the Bureau of Ethnology, the attention of the writer was directed to the ceremonial use of a plant for which were claimed wonderful medical and psychologic properties. So numerous and important are its medical applications, and so exhilarating and glorious its effect, according to the statements of the natives, that it is regarded as the vegetable incarnation of a deity, and the ceremonial eating of the plant has become the great religious rite of all the tribes of the southern plains.

The plant is a small cactus, having the general size and shape of a radish, and covered on the exposed surface with the characteristic cactus prickles. . . . In each language it has a different name, usually referring to the prickles. Among the Kiowas it was *señi;* among the Comanches, *wokowi;* with the Mescaleros, *ho;* and with the Tarahumaris, *hikori.* The traders of the Indian Territory commonly call it mescal, although it must not be confounded with another mescal in Arizona, the *Agave,* from which the Apaches prepare an intoxicating drink. The local Mexican name upon the Rio Grande is *peyote* or *pellote,* from the old Aztec name *peyotl.*

The use of the plant for medical and religious purposes is probably as ancient as the Indian occupancy of the region over which it grows. There is evidence that the ceremonial rite was known to all the tribes from the Arkansas to the valley of Mexico, and from the Sierra Madre to the coast. . . .

In proportion as the plant was held sacred by the Indians, so it was regarded by the early missionaries as the direct invention of the devil, and the eating of the peyote was made a crime equal in enormity to the eating of human flesh. From the beginning it has been condemned without investigation, and even under the present system severe penalties have been threatened and inflicted against Indians using it or having it in their possession. Notwithstanding this, practically all the men of the Southern Plains tribes eat it habitually in the ceremony, and find no difficulty in procuring all they can pay for. In spite of its universal use and the constant assertion of the Indians that the plant is a valuable medicine and the ceremony a beautiful religious rite, no agency physician, post surgeon, missionary, or teacher—with a single exception—has ever tested the plant or witnessed the ceremony.

A detailed account of mythology, history and sacred ritual in connection with the peyote would fill a volume. Such an account, to be published eventually by the Bureau of Ethnology, the writer is now preparing, as the result of several years of field study among the Southern Plains tribes. As this article is intended primarily for medical readers, the ceremonial part will be but briefly noted here.

The ceremony occupies from twelve to fourteen hours, beginning about 9 or 10 o'clock and lasting sometimes until nearly noon the next day. Saturday night is now the time usually selected, in deference to the white man's idea of Sunday as a sacred day and a day of rest. The worshippers sit in a circle around the inside of the sacred tipi, with a fire blazing in the cent[er]. The exercises open with a prayer by the leader, who then hands each man four peyotes, which he takes and eats in quick succession, first plucking out the small tuft of down from the cent[er]. In eating, the dry peyote is first chewed in the mouth, then rolled into a large pellet between the hands and swallowed, the man rubbing his breast and the back of his neck at the same time to aid the descent. After this first round the leader takes the rattle, while his assistant takes the drum, and together they sing the first song four times, with full voices, at the same time beating the drum and shaking the rattle with all the strength of their arms. The drum and rattle are then handed to the next couple, and so the song goes on round and round the circle—with only a break for the baptismal ceremony at midnight, and another for the daylight ceremony—until perhaps 9 o'clock the next morning. Then the instruments are passed out of the tipi, the sacred foods are eaten, and the ceremony is at an end. At midnight a vessel of water is passed around, and each takes a drink and sprinkles a few drops upon his head. Up to this hour no one has moved from his position, sitting crosslegged upon the ground and with no support for his back, but now any one is at liberty to go out and walk about for a while and return again. Few, however, do this, as it is considered a sign of weakness. The sacred food at the close of the ceremony consists of parched corn in sweetened water; rice or other boiled grain; boiled fruit, usually now prunes or dried apples; and dried meat pounded up with sugar. Every person takes a little of each, first taking a drink of water to clear his mouth.

After midnight the leader passes the peyote around again, giving to each man as many as he may call for. On this second round I have frequently seen a man call for ten and eat them one after the other as rapidly as he could chew. They continue to eat at intervals until the close. There is much spitting, and probably but little of the juice is swallowed. Every one smokes handmade cigarettes, the smoke being regarded as a sacred incense. At intervals some fervent devotee will break out into an earnest prayer, stretching his hands out towards the fire and the sacred peyote the while. For the rest of the time, when not singing the song and handling the drum or rattle with all his strength, he sits quietly with his blanket drawn about him and his eyes fixed upon the sacred peyote in the cent[er], or perhaps with his eyes shut and apparently dozing. He must be instantly ready, however, when his turn comes at the song, or to make a prayer at the request of some one present, so that it is apparent the senses are always on the alert and under control of the will.

There is no preliminary preparation, such as by fasting or the sweat-bath, and supper is eaten as usual before going in. The dinner, which is given an hour or two after the ceremony, is always as elaborate a feast as the host can provide. The rest of the day is spent in gossiping, smoking, and singing the new songs, until it is time to return home. They go to bed at the usual time, and are generally up at the usual time the next morning. No salt is used in the food until the day after the ceremony.

As a rule, only men take part in the regular ceremony, but sick women and children are brought in, and, after prayers for their recovery, are allowed to eat one or more peyotes prepared for them by the priest.

Briefly stated, it may be said that the Indians regard the peyote as a panacea in medicine, a source of inspiration, and the key which opens to them all the glories of another world. They consider it particularly effective in hemorrhage and consumptive diseases. For this reason the returned students from the East, who almost inevitably acquire consumption in the damp eastern climate, are usually among the staunchest defenders of the ceremony, having found by experience that the plant brings them relief.

A marked instance is the case of my Kiowa interpreter, Paul Setkopti, a man now forty-two years of age. Twenty years ago, at the close of the last unsuccessful outbreak of these tribes, he was one of sixty warriors sent as prisoners of war to Fort Marion, Florida. Here, being young and unusually intelligent, he attracted the notice of a benevolent lady from the North who taught him English and finally secured permission to take him with her to her home in New York State, where she undertook to educate him to go back as a missionary and physician to his people. But he had already contracted consumption in Florida, and during nearly the whole of his four years in New York he was stretched upon a sick-bed, racked with cough and frequent hemorrhages, until at last, as there seemed no chance for life, he was sent back, at his request, to die among his own people. He arrived completely prostrated; and, being strongly urged by his Indian friends, he ate a few peyotes—with such speedy relief from the cough that he continued the practice. That was thirteen years ago, and he is still alive and in fairly good health, although he spits constantly, has occasional hemorrhages, and is not strong enough for hard labor. His mind is keen, however, and he makes an excellent interpreter, faithful above the average. He is a leader in the ceremony, and defends it in eloquent English, because, as he says, the peyote keeps him alive. He never misses an opportunity to be present at the ceremony if he can reach the place in time. It is particularly to be noted that this man, after years of training and education in a refined home for the special purpose of making him a Christian missionary and a physician in his tribe, has become an apostle of the proscribed peyote rite, on account of his personal experience of the virtues of the plant.

On one occasion, when I was present alone in a camp where they were preparing to eat peyote that night, he rode in late in the evening, through a cold drizzling rain, and told me that he had been eating peyote the previous night at a camp about twenty miles away, and hearing that they were going to eat in our camp that night and that I had no interpreter with me, he had come to stay with me and explain the ceremony. I tried my best to get him to go to bed and not to lose two nights' sleep, in addition to the exposure in the rain in his weakened condition, but all I could get for reply was: "I will stay with you." I finally persuaded him to lie down at least until he should hear the drum. On hearing the signal, about 11 o'clock at night, he came into the tipi and bent over the fire to warm himself, when he was seized with such a fit of coughing that it seemed as if his lungs would be torn to pieces. I again tried to persuade him to go back to bed, but he said: "No; I shall eat peyote, and soon I shall be all right." He then took and ate four peyotes, stepped into his place, and when it was his turn then and throughout the night sang his song like the others, and came out as fresh as they in the morning, after two consecutive nights without sleep. There was no more coughing after eating the first four peyotes.

The Indians frequently use the peyote in decoction, without any ritual, for fevers, headaches, and breast pains, and it is sometimes used in the same way by the Mexicans of the lower Rio Grande. I have also seen an Indian eat one between meals as a sort of tonic appetizer. The habit never develops into a mania, but is always under control.

As to its effect upon age or condition, I have seen a twelve-year-old boy, at his first initiation, eat six peyotes and sit through the long night ceremony, without any worse result than a sleepiness which came over him after dinner, so that he slept all that afternoon and night until the next morning. I have seen a tottering old man, who had been a priest of the ceremony for half a century, led into the tipi by the hand like a child, eat his four peyotes, and then take the rattle and sing the song in a clear voice, and repeat it as often as his turn came until morning, when he came out with the rest, so little fatigued that he was able to sit down and answer intelligently all the questions I asked. Imagine a white man of eighty years of age sitting up in a constrained position, without sleep, all night long and nearly all morning, and then being in condition to be interviewed.

As to the mental effect of the habitual use of the plant, it may be sufficient to say that the great high priest of the rite among the Comanches is Zuanah [Quanah Parker], the half-[blood] chief of the tribe, and any who know him at home or in Washington will admit that there is no more shrewd or capable business man in the Southwest. On one occasion I was with him when he sat up all night leading the ceremony, eating perhaps thirty peyotes. Coming out in the morning, he found two cattlemen awaiting him on important business, which occupied him and his white secretary all that afternoon; next day he was up before daylight ready for an early breakfast before starting for Texas to conclude the deal. This after eating a large quantity of the cactus and losing a night's sleep; and Zuanah is entirely too smart a man to attend to business when his brain is not in working order.

On every occasion when I have been present at the ceremony I have carefully observed the participants, sometimes as many as thirty at a time, to note the after-effects, but have seen no indication of a reaction that day or afterward. They unanimously declare that there is no reaction; which agrees with my own experience. After sitting twelve or fourteen hours in a constrained position, each in turn enacting his part several times in the course of the night, and eating from ten to possibly fifty peyotes apiece, they come out bright and cheerful, eat their dinner with good appetite, and afterward sing, smoke and gossip until it is time to return home. There is no sign of fatigue or any abnormal physical or mental condition, unless it be the tendency to continue singing the songs in an undertone and beating time with the finger for a rattle for hours afterward. I am unable to say whether this is the effect of the plant or is due to pure fondness for the songs; probably it is a result of both these influences. Once after the ceremony I found myself involuntarily beating time to a song that had particularly struck my fancy. I think, however, that this was largely because I wanted to learn the song, as immediately after coming out from the tipi I had spent some time posing and photographing the company, which I could hardly have done without full control of my faculties and movements.

I know from experience that the peyote is a powerful stimulant and enables one to endure great physical strains without injurious reaction; in which respect it seems to differ from all other known stimulants. During my first all-night attendance at the ceremony I ate none, as I did not feel sure that I could keep my brain clear for observation otherwise, and the result was that from cold, numbness and exhaustion I was hardly able to stand upon my feet when it was over. Since then I have always taken three or four, and have been able to take note of all that occurred throughout the night, coming out in the morning as fresh as at the start to make pictures of the men, afterward writing, reading, or talking with my friends until bedtime. I have never felt the full mental effect of the plant, having eaten only small quantities at a time, and keeping my mind constantly tense and alert for observation. I am probably also less sensitive to such influences, from long familiarity with Indian ceremonies. I have experienced enough, however, to be satisfied that what the Indians say of the mental effect is true.

from **Mescal: The "Divine" Plant and Its Psychological Effects**

Heinrich Klüver

A flurry of research activity involving peyote and its synthetic equivalent, mescaline, arose around the turn of the century, peaking in the late 1920s, conducted primarily by S. Weir Mitchell in the United States, Havelock Ellis in England, Louis Lewin and Karl Beringer in Germany, and Alexandre Rouhier in France. Dr. Beringer, an associate of Jung and Hesse, published his 315-page text *Der Meskalinrausch (Mescaline Inebriation)* in 1927. The following year, Heinrich Klüver, who took exception to Ellis's pronouncement that mescaline "visions" were "indescribable," published *Mescal*, in which he introduced a detailed classification of mescaline-induced imagery by "hallucinatory constants." Klüver methodically cataloged the visual forms he believed constituted the mescal experience's primary aspect into form constants such as spirals, cobweb shapes, lattice or chessboard designs, tunnels, and cones.

KNAUER AND MALONEY, upon injecting 0.2 gm. of the sulfate of mescaline into the subcutaneous tissue of the forearm, obtained four hours after the injection the following report from one of their subjects: "Immediately before my eyes are a vast number of rings, apparently made of extremely fine steel wire, all constantly rotating in the direction of the hands of a clock; these circles are concentrically arranged, the innermost being infinitely small, almost point like, the outermost being about a meter and a half in diameter. The spaces between the wires seem brighter than the wires themselves. Now the wires shine like dim silver in parts. Now a beautiful light violet tint has developed in them. As I watch, the center seems to recede into the depth of the room, leaving the periphery stationary, till the whole assumes the form of a deep funnel of wire rings. The light, which was irregularly distributed among the circles, has receded with the center into the apex of the funnel. The center is gradually returning, and, passing the position when all the rings are in the same vertical plane, continues to advance, till a cone forms with its apex toward me." In the following the subject describes "beautiful crimsons, purples, violets, blues and greens" quickly succeeding one another. The background of this "gorgeous color panorama was first like faintly illuminated ground glass; it is now a silvery tint, and is deepening into a yellow like pure gold. . . . On pressing upon my eyes, the whole picture seemed to materialize." The wires became "more solid, more real and quite distinct from the background." "The wires are now flattening into bands or ribbons, with a suggestion of transverse striation, and colored a gorgeous ultramarine blue, which passes in places into an intense sea green. These bands move rhythmically, in a wavy upward direction, suggesting a slow endless procession of small mosaics, ascending the wall in single files. The whole picture has suddenly receded, the center much more than the sides, and now in a moment, high above me, is a dome of the most beautiful mosaics, a vision of all that is most gorgeous and harmonious in color. The prevailing tint is blue, but the multitude of shades, each of such wonderful individuality, make me feel that hitherto I have been totally ignorant of what the word color really means. The color is intensely beautiful, rich, deep, deep, deep, wonderfully deep blue. It is like the blue of the mosque of Omar in Jerusalem. . . . The dome has absolutely no discernible pattern. But circles are now developing upon it, the circles are becoming sharp and elongated . . . now they are rhomboids; now oblongs; and now all sorts of curious angles are forming and mathematical figures are chasing one another wildly across the roof. The colors are changing rapidly—from blue green to black, to brown—passing successively through an infinite variety of transitional shades . . ." Six hours after the injection the subject sees "a beautiful palace, filled with rare tapestries, pictures, and Louis Quinze furniture . . ." In the rooms ladies appear "without motion . . . as a series of portraits. . . ." Twenty hours after the injection there are outlines "suggesting crocodiles, lizards and other reptiles . . . they arouse absolutely no sensation of fear." There are "visions of human intestines, of sections of abdomens, and sections of the pregnant uterus. . . ."

As a second example of mescal visions we quote from the report of Weir Mitchell who, "at 12 noon of a busy morning," took 1½ drachm of an extract "of which each drachm represented one mescal button." One hour hereafter, little over a drachm was taken and at about four o'clock half an ounce of this extract in three doses. Soon Mitchell found himself "deliciously at languid ease." At 5:40 he noticed a number of star points and fragments of stained glass with closed eyes. He went into a dark room: "The display which for an enchanted two hours followed was such as I find it hopeless to describe in language which shall convey to others the beauty and splendor of what I saw." "Stars . . . delicate floating films of color . . . then an abrupt rush of countless points of white light swept across the field of view, as if the unseen millions of the Milky Way were to flow a sparkling river before the eye . . . zigzag lines of very bright colors . . . the wonderful loveliness of swelling clouds of more vivid colors gone before I could name them. . . ." Then, for the first time, "definite objects associated with colors" appeared. "A white spear of grey stone grew up to huge height, and became a tall, richly finished Gothic tower of very elaborate and definite design, with many rather worn statues standing in the doorways or on stone brackets. As I gazed every projecting angle, cornice, and even the face of the stones at their joinings were by degrees covered or hung with clusters of what seemed to be huge precious stones, but uncut, some being more like masses of transparent fruit. These were green, purple, red, and orange; never clear yellow and never blue. All seemed to possess an interior light, and to give the faintest idea of the perfectly satisfying intensity and purity of these gorgeous color-fruits is quite beyond my power. All the colors I have ever beheld are dull as compared to these. As I looked, and it lasted long, the tower became of a fine mouse hue, and everywhere the vast pendant masses of emerald green, ruby reds, and orange began to drip a slow rain of colors. . . . After an endless display of less beautiful marvels I saw that which deeply impressed me. An edge of a huge cliff seemed to project over a gulf of unseen depth. My viewless enchanter set on the brink a huge bird claw of stone. Above, from the stem or leg, hung a fragment of some stuff. This began to unroll and float out to a distance which seemed to me to represent Time as well as immensity of Space. Here were miles of rippled purples, half transparent, and of ineffable beauty. Now and then soft golden clouds floated from these folds, or a great shimmer went over the whole of the rolling purples, and things, like green birds, fell from it, fluttering down into the gulf below. Next, I saw clusters of stones hanging in masses from the claw toes, as it seemed to me miles of them, down far below into the underworld of the black gulf. This was the most distinct of my visions." In his last vision, Mitchell saw the beach of Newport with its rolling waves as "liquid splendours huge and threatening, of wonderfully pure green, or red or deep purple, once only deep orange, and with no trace of foam. These water hills of color broke on the beach with myriads of lights of the same tint as the wave." Again, the author considers it totally impossible to find words to describe these colors. "They still linger visibly in my memory, and left the feeling that I had seen among them colors unknown to my experience."

William James received a supply of mescal buttons from Mitchell. He tried the drug and reports on the results in a letter to Henry James: "I took one bud three days ago, was violently sick for 24 hours, and had no other symptom whatever except that and the Katzenjammer the following day. I will take the visions on trust!" Even Mitchell writes,"These shows are expensive. . . . The experience, however, was worth one such headache and indigestion, but was not worth a second."

We refer now to our personal observation to demonstrate some other aspects of mescal visions. 23 gm. of the powdered buttons were taken in doses of 13 and 10 gm. Half an hour after taking the second dose vomiting occurred. Soon hereafter phenomena of the following kind could be observed with closed eyes: "Clouds from left to right through optical field. Tail of a pheasant (in center of field) turns into bright yellow star; star into sparks. Moving scintillating screw; 'hundreds' of screws. A sequence of rapidly changing objects in agreeable colors. A rotating wheel (diameter about 1 cm.) in the center of a silvery ground. Suddenly in the wheel a picture of God as represented in old Christian paintings.–Intention to see a homogeneous dark field of vision: red and green shoes appear. Most phenomena much nearer than reading distance.–The upper part of the body of a man, with a pale face but red cheeks, rising slowly from below. The face is unknown to me.–While I am thinking of a friend (visual memory-image) the head of an Indian appears.–Beads in different colors. Colors always changing: red to violet, green to bright gray, etc. Colors so bright that I doubt that the eyes are closed.–Yellow mass like salt-water taffy pierced by two teeth (about 6 cm. in length).–Silvery water pouring downward, suddenly flowing upward.–Landscape as on Japanese pictures: a picture rather than a real landscape.– Sparks having the appearance of exploding shells turn into strange flowers which remind me of poppies in California.– (Eyes open): streaks of green and violet on the wall. Then a drawing of a head changing into a mushroom (both of natural size). Then a skeleton (natural size) in lateral view turned about 30° to the left. Head and legs are lacking. Try to convince myself that there are only shadows on the wall, but still see the skeleton (as in X-ray).–(Eyes closed). Soft deep darkness with moving wheels and stars in extremely pleasant colors.–Nuns in silver dresses (about 3 cm. height) quickly disappearing.–Collection of bluish ink-bottles with labels.–Red, brownish and violet threads running together in center.–Autumn leaves turning into mescal buttons.–Different forms emitting intense greenish light.–Forms in different colors; contours often dark.–Strange animal (length perhaps 10 cm.) rapidly turns into arabesques.–Gold rain falling vertically. On stationary background rotating jewels revolving around a center. Then, with a certain jerk, absence of all motion.–Regular and irregular forms in iridescent colors reminding me of radiolaria, sea urchins and shells, etc., in symmetrical or asymmetrical arrangement.–Shells illuminated from within radiating in different colors, moving towards the right, turned about 45° towards the right and somewhat towards me. A little piece in every shell is broken out.–Slow majestic movements along differently shaped curves simultaneously with 'mad' movements.–Feeling there is 'motion *per se*.'–Man in greenish velvet (height about 7–8 cm.) jumping into deep chasm.–Strange animal turns into a piece of wood in horizontal position."

from **Miserable Miracle**

H e n r i   M i c h a u x

"And men with caffeined thought will change the world," wrote the French poet and painter Henri Michaux. Some time in the late 1940s or early 1950s, after having read with interest the growing abundance of doctors' reports on mescaline experiments—as well as visionary poesy by Rimbaud and Artaud—Michaux decided to conduct his own experiments for art's sake.

He painted and wrote extensively while under the influence. Fellow poet–drug advocate Allen Ginsberg has paid homage to Michaux on numerous occasions as a man who well understood the "honorific use of drugs." One of the several books he published on his mescaline-induced hallucinogenic experiences, *Miserable Miracle* (1956) was published in translation by City Lights Books in 1963 on the insistence of Michaux-advocate Anaïs Nin. Here is his foreword to that volume.

THIS BOOK IS AN EXPLORATION. By means of words, signs, drawings. Mescaline, the subject explored.

From the thirty two autograph pages reproduced out of the hundred and fifty written while the inner perturbation was at its height, those who can read handwriting will learn more than from any description.

As for the drawings, begun immediately after the third experiment, they were done with a vibratory motion that continues in you for days and days and, though automatic and blind, reproduces exactly the visions to which you have been subjected, passes through them again.

It being impossible to reproduce the entire manuscript, which directly and simultaneously translated the subject, the rhythms, the forms, the chaos, as well as the inner defenses and their devastation, we found ourselves in difficulties, confronted by a typographical wall. Everything had to be rewritten. The original text, more tangible than legible, drawn rather than written, would not, in any case, suffice.

Flung onto and across the paper, hastily and in jerks, the interrupted sentences, with syllables, flying off, frayed, petering out, kept diving, falling, dying. Their tattered remnants would revive, bolt, and burst again. The letters ended in smoke or disappeared in zigzags. The next ones, similarly interrupted, continued their uneasy recitation, birds in the midst of the drama, their wings cut in flight by invisible scissors.

Sometimes words would be fused together on the spot. For example, "Martyrissibly" would recur to me time and time again, speaking volumes. I couldn't get rid of it. Another repeated untiringly, "Krakatoa!" "Krakatoa!" or sometimes a quite ordinary word like "crystal" would return twenty times in succession, giving me a great harangue all by itself, out of another world, and I could never have augmented it in the least or supplemented it with some other word. Alone, like a castaway on an island, it was everything to me, and the restless ocean out of which it had just come and of which it irresistibly reminded me, for I too was shipwrecked and alone and holding out against disaster.

In the huge light-churn, with lights splashing over me, drunk, I was swept headlong without ever turning back

How to describe it! It would require a picturesque style which I do not possess, made up of surprises, of nonsense, of sudden flasher, of bounds and rebounds, an unstable style, tobogganing and prankish.

In this book, the margins, filled with what are epitomes rather than titles, suggest very inadequately the *overlappings* which are an ever-present phenomenon of mescaline. Without them it would be like talking about something else. I have not used any other "artifices." It would have required too many. The insurmountable difficulties come (1) from the incredible rapidity of the apparition, transformation, and appearance of the visions; (2) from the multiplicity, the pullulation of each vision; (3) from the fan-like and umbellate developments through autonomous, independent, simultaneous progressions (on seven screens as it were); (4) from their unemotional character; (5) from their inept, and even more, from their mechanical appearance: gusts of images, gusts of "yes's" or of "no's," gusts of stereotype movements.

I was not neutral either, for which I do not apologize. Mescaline and I were more often at odds with each other than together. I was shaken, broken, but I refused to be taken in by it.

Tawdry, its spectacle. Moreover it was enough to uncover one's eyes not to see any more of the stupid phantasmagoria. Inharmonious mescaline, an alkaloid derived from the Peyotl which contains six, was really like a robot. It knew only how to do certain things.

Yet I had come prepared to admire. I was confident. But that day my cells were brayed, buffeted, sabotaged, sent into convulsions. I felt them being caressed, being subjected to constant wrenchings. Mescaline wanted my full consent. To enjoy a drug one must enjoy being a subject. To me it was too much like being on "fatigue duty."

It was with *my* terrible buffetings that *It* put on its show. I was the fireworks that despises the pyrotechnist, even when it can be proved that it is itself the pyrotechnist. I was being shoved about, I was being crumpled. In a daze, I stared at this Brownian movement—disturbance of perception.

I was distraught and tired of being distraught, with my eye at this microscope. What was there supernatural about all this? You scarcely got away from the human state at all. You felt more as if you were caught and held prisoner in some workshop of the brain.

Should I speak of pleasure? It was unpleasant.

Once the agony of the first hour is over (effect of the encounter with the poison), an agony so great that you wonder if you are not going to faint (as some people do, though rarely) you can let yourself be carried along by a certain current which may seem like happiness. Is that what I thought? I am not sure of the contrary. Yet, in my journal, during all those incredible hours, I find these words written more than fifty times, clumsily, and with difficultly: *Intolerable, Unbearable.*

Such is the price of this paradise (!)

(Translated by Louise Varèse)

from **"An Opium Eater in America"**

William Blair

Written on the request of the author's physician, this account describes a period of opium use by a young English immigrant. It was subsequently printed in New York in the July 1842 issue of *The Knickerbocker*. Blair, who had first taken opium at the age of fourteen, found copious time to study philosophy, languages, and literature. Within the range of drug-experience literature, his autobiography is significant as one of the first that was consciously modeled after Thomas De Quincey's *Confessions of an English Opium Eater* (1821).

I HAD DURING THOSE FIFTEEN MONTHS thought and read much on the subject of revealed religion, and had devoted a considerable portion of my time to an examination of the evidences advanced by the advocates of Christianity, which resulted in a reluctant conviction of their utter weakness and inability. No sooner was I aware that so complete a change of opinion had taken place, than I wrote to my patron stating the fact, and explaining the process by which I had arrived at such a conclusion. The reply I received was a peremptory order to return to my mother's house immediately; and on arriving there, the first time I had entered it for some years, I was met by the information that I had nothing more to expect from the countenance of those who had supplied me with the means of prosecuting my studies to "so bad a purpose." I was so irritated by what I considered the unjustifiable harshness of this decision, that at the moment I wrote a haughty and angry letter to one of the parties, which of course widened the breach, and made the separation between us eternal.

What was I now to do? I was unfit for any business, both by habit, inclination, and constitution. My health was ruined, and hopeless poverty stared me in the face; when a distinguished solicitor in my native town, who by the way has since become celebrated in the political world, offered to receive me as a clerk. I at once accepted the offer; but knowing that in my *then* condition it was impossible for me to perform the duties required of me, I decided on *taking opium!* The strange confessions of De Quincey had long been a favorite with me. The first part had in fact been given me both as a model in English composition, and also as an exercise to be rendered into

Patavinian Latin. The latter part, the "Miseries of Opium," I had most unaccountably always neglected to read. Again and again,when my increasing debility had threatened to bring my studies to an abrupt conclusion, I had meditated this experiment, but an undefinable and shadowy fear had as often stayed my hand. But now that I knew that unless I could by artificial stimuli obtain a sudden increase of strength I must *starve* I no longer hesitated. I was desperate. I believed that something horrible would result from it, though my imagination, the most vivid, could not conjure up visions of horror half so terrific as the fearful reality. I knew that for every hour of comparative ease and comfort its treacherous alliance might confer upon me *now*, I must endure days of bodily suffering; but I did not, could not, conceive the mental hell into whose fierce corroding fires I was about to plunge!

All that occurred during the first day is imperishably engraved upon my memory. It was about a week previous to the day appointed for my début in my new character as an attorney's clerk; and when I arose, I was depressed in mind, and a racking pain, to which I had lately been subject, was maddening me. I could scarcely manage to crawl into the breakfast-room. I had previously procured a drachm of opium, and I took two grains with my coffee. It did not produce any change in my feelings. I took two more–still without effect; and by six o'clock in the evening I had taken ten grains. While I was sitting at tea, I felt a strange sensation, totally unlike any thing I had ever felt before; a gradual *creeping thrill*, which in a few minutes occupied every part of my body, lulling to sleep the before-mentioned racking pain, producing a pleasing glow from head to foot, and inducing a sensation of dreamy exhilaration (if the phrase be intelligible to others as it is to me), similar in nature but not in degree to the drowsiness caused by wine, though not inclining me to sleep; in fact so far from it, that I longed to engage in some active exercise; to sing, dance, or leap. I then resolved to go to the theatre–the last place I should the day before have dreamed of visiting; for the sight of cheerfulness in others made me doubly gloomy.

I went; and so vividly did I feel my vitality–for in this state of delicious exhilaration even mere excitement seemed absolute elysium–that I could not resist the temptation to break out in the strangest vagaries, until my companions thought me deranged. As I ran up the stairs I rushed after and flung back every one who was above me. I escaped numberless beatings solely through the interference of my friends. After I had been seated a few minutes, the nature of the excitement was changed, and a "waking sleep" succeeded. The actors on the stage vanished; the stage itself lost its reality; and before my entranced sight magnificent halls stretched out in endless succession, with gallery above gallery, while the roof was blazing with gems, like stars whose rays alone illumined the whole building, which was thronged with strange, gigantic figures, like the wild possessors of a lost globe, such as Lord Byron has described in "Cain;" as beheld by the Fratricide, when guided by Lucifer he wandered among the shadowy existences of those worlds which had been destroyed to make way for our pigmy earth. I will not attempt farther to describe the magnificent vision which a little pill of "brown gum" had conjured up from the realm of ideal being. No words that I can command would do justice to its Titanian splendor and immensity.

At midnight I was roused from my dreamy abstraction; and on my return home the blood in my veins seemed to "run lightning," and I knocked down (for I had the strength of a giant at that moment) the first watchman I met: of course there was "a row," and for some minutes a battle-royal raged in New Street, the principal thoroughfare of the town, between my party and the "Charleys;" who, although greatly superior in numbers, were sadly "milled;" for we were all somewhat scientific bruisers, that sublime art or science having been cultivated with great assiduity at the public school, through which I had as was customary fought my way. I reached home at two in the morning with a pair of "Oxford spectacles" which confined me to the house for a week. I slept disturbedly, haunted by terrific dreams and oppressed by the Night-mare and her nine-fold, and awoke with a dreadful headache; stiff in every joint, and with deadly sickness of the stomach, which lasted for two or three days; my throat contracted and parched, my tongue furred, my eyes bloodshot, and the whole surface of my body burning hot. I did not have recourse to opium again for three days; for the strength it had excited did not till then fail me. When partially recovered from the nausea the first dose had caused, my spirits were good, though not exuberant; but I could eat nothing, and was annoyed by an insatiable thirst. I went to the office, and for six months performed the services required of me without lassitude or depression of spirits; though never again did I experience the same delicious sensations as on that memorable night, which is an "oasis in the desert" of my subsequent existence; life I cannot call it, for the *vivida vis animi et corporis* was extinct.

In the seventh month my misery commenced. Burning heat, attended with constant thirst, then began to torment me from morning till night: my skin became scurfy; the skin of my feet and hands peeled off; my tongue was always furred; a feeling of con-traction in the bowels was continual; my eyes were strained and discolored, and I had unceasing head-ache. But internal and external heat was the pervading feeling and ap-pearance. My digestion became still weaker, and my incessant costiveness was painful in the extreme. The reader must not however imagine that all these symptoms appeared suddenly and at once; they came on gradually, though with frightful rapidity, until I be-came a *morborum moles,* as a Romanic physician whose lucubrations I met with and pe-rused with great amusement some years since in a little country ale-house (God knows how it got there) poetically expresses it. I could not sleep for hours after I had lain down, and consequently was unable to rise in time to attend the office in the morning, though as yet no visions of horror haunted my slumbers. Mr. P., my employer, bore with this for some months; but at length his patience was wearied; and I was informed that I must attend at nine in the morning. I could not; for even if I rose at seven, after two or three hours' unhealthy and fitful sleep, I was unable to walk or exert myself in any way for at least two hours. I was at this time taking laudanum, and had no appetite for any thing but coffee and acid fruits. I could and did drink great quantities of ale, though it would not, as nothing would, quench my thirst.

Matters continued in this state for fifteen months, during which time the only comfortable hours I spent were in the evening, when freed from the duties of the office, I sat down to study, which it is rather singular I was able to do with as strong zest and as unwearied application as ever; as will appear, when I mention that in those fifteen months I read through in the evenings the whole of Cicero, Tacitus, the Corpus Poetarum (Latinorum), Boëthius, Scriptores Historiae Augustinae, Homer, Corpus Graecarum Tragediarum, a great part of Plato, and a large mass of philological works. In fact, in the evening I generally felt comparatively well, not being troubled with many of the above mentioned symptoms. These evenings were the very happiest of my life. I had ample means for the purchase of books, for I lived very cheap on bread, ale, and coffee; and I had access to a library containing all the Latin classics–Valpy's edition in one hundred and fifty volumes, octavo, a magnificent publication–and about fifteen thousand other books. Toward the end of the year 1829 I established at my own expense and edited myself a magazine (there was not one in a town as large and as populous as New York!) by which I lost a considerable sum; though the pleasure I derived from my monthly labors amply compensated me. In December of that year my previous sufferings became light in comparison with those which now seized upon me, never completely to leave me again.

One night, after taking about fifty grains of opium, I sat down in my arm-chair to read the confession of a Russian who had murdered his brother because he was the chosen of her whom both loved. It was recorded by a French priest who visited him in his last moments, and was powerfully and eloquently written. I dozed while reading it; and immediately I was present in the prison-cell of the Fratricide; I saw his ghastly and death-dewed features, his despairing yet defying look, the gloomy and impenetrable dungeon; the dying lamp, which seemed but to render "darkness visible;" and the horror-struck yet pitying expression of the priest's countenance; *but there I lost my identity.* Though I was the recipient of these impressions, yet I was not myself separately and distinctively existent and sentient; but my entity was confounded with that of not only the two figures before me, but of the inanimate objects surrounding them. This state of compound existence I can no farther describe. While in this state I composed the "Fratricide's Death," or rather it composed *itself* and forced itself upon my memory without any activity or volition on my part.

And here again another phenomenon presented itself. The images reflected, if the expression be allowable, in the verses rose bodily and with perfect distinctness before me, simultaneously with their verbal representatives; and when I roused myself (I had not been *sleeping* but was only *abstracted*) all remained clear and distinct in my memory. From that night for six months darkness always brought the most horrible fancies and opticular and auricular or acoustical delusions of a frightful nature, so vivid and real, that instead of a blessing, sleep became a curse; and the hours of darkness became hours which seemed days of misery. For many consecutive nights I dared not undress myself nor "put out the light," lest the moment I lay down some *monstrum horrendum, informe, ingens* should blast my sight with his hellish aspect! I had a double sense of sight and sound; one real, the other visionary; both equally strong and apparently real; so that while I distinctly heard imaginary footsteps ascending the stairs, the door opening, and my curtains drawn, I at the same time as plainly heard any actual sound in or outside the house, and could not remark the slightest difference between them, and while I *saw* an imaginary assassin standing by my bed bending over me with a lamp in one hand and a dagger in the other, I could see any real tangible object which the degree of light that might be then in the room made visible. Though these visionary fears and imaginary objects had presented themselves to me every night for months, yet I never could convince myself of their non-existence; and every fresh appearance caused suffering of as intense and as deadly horror as on the first night! And so great was the confusion of the real with the unreal, that I nearly became a convert to Bishop Berkeley's non-reality doctrines. My health was also rapidly becoming worse; and before I had taken my opium in the morning, I had become unable to move hand or foot, and of course could not rise from my bed until I had received strength from the "damnable dirt." I could not attend the office at all in the morning, and was forced to throw up my articles, and as the only chance left me of gaining a livelihood, turn to writing for magazines for support. I left B. and proceeded to London, where I engaged with Charles Knight to supply the chapters on the use of elephants in the wars of the ancients for the "History of Elephants," then preparing for publication in the series of the Library of Entertaining Knowledge. For this purpose I obtained permission to use the Library of the British Museum for six months, and again devoted myself with renewed ardor to my favorite studies.

But "what a falling off was there!" My memory was impaired; and in reading I was conscious of a confusion of mind which prevented my clearly comprehending the full meaning of what I read. Some organ appeared to be defective. My judgment too was weakened, and I was frequently guilty of the most absurd actions, which at the time I considered wise and prudent. The strong common sense which I had at one time boasted of, deserted me. I lived in a dreamy, imaginative state, which completely disqualified me for managing my own affairs.

from **Boxcar Bertha**

Boxcar Bertha Thompson

There is some controversy whether Boxcar Bertha was in fact a fictional character created by Ben L. Reitman, a well-known hobo physician and radical during Depression-era America. It is possible a woman named Bertha Thompson existed, and that Boxcar Bertha—whose story is told by Reitman in an "as-told-to autobiography" originally published in 1937—was a composite of several women hoboes Reitman had met in his travels. However, the current King of the Hoboes, "Steam Train" Maury Graham, who was a boy during the 1930s, claims to have heard tell of her near-legendary exploits riding the rails. Following is an excerpt from Bertha's story, centering on her first experiences as a young, free-thinking hobo.

ANNA AND JAKE AND OTHER HABITUAL USERS smoked the pipe in recumbent position, lying either on the bed or on a mattress on the floor. Before this stage of the procedure they were careful to stuff all keyholes, and to paste adhesive tape over the cracks around the door and to hang wet sheets over the doors and windows.

The actual smoking process was very complicated, and very quick, only about ten seconds to smoke a pill. Anna, whom I watched many times, placed the stem against her lips and inhaled quickly. She took six or eight short deep breaths, and, then, as her lungs filled, one final, prolonged draw to get all of the smoke possible from the pill into her lungs.

For the habitual smoker the desire is to produce a state of self-satisfaction that he must have. Really he smokes not so much for pleasure as to avoid pain and mental anguish which he suffers if free from opium. Anna was a habitual smoker and had a hunger only opium could satisfy. She put it this way:

"I smoke my habit off before going to bed and I smoke my habit off when I wake up in the morning."

To smoke her habit off meant to take enough opium to protect her from pain and anxiety.

With the pleasure smoker who takes the pipe only occasionally, the reaction is quite different. I watched a number of women just learning to smoke. After the first pill they began to experience buoyancy and a sense of well-being. They got talkative. These emotions increased until the fourth pill, and then they became drowsy and quickly fell asleep. Even after eight hours' sleep they retained some of the same buoyant feeling. As far as I could learn, neither the habitual nor the pleasure smoker had any fantastic dreams or illusions of grandeur, nor did they become bold or courageous.

The sex life of a pipe smoker is lessened. Desire is suspended and capacities are extremely weakened. Anna admitted to me that what sex she had meant little to her or to any of them on the regular habit. On the other hand, the pleasure smoker has his desires greatly stimulated by the pipe, although it retards considerably the culmination of the sex act.

Lucille and Jimmie used "white stuff," heroin and morphine, which are the alkaloids of opium. "White stuff" comes in small tablets, cubes, or in powder. It is sold in New York for twenty dollars an ounce, and was shipped out to our group by mail in ten ounce lots. They never kept more than an ounce in their possession at one time. They kept the balance in a safety deposit box in a Chicago bank, and when they were out of town they arranged for a friend to send it to them. Lucille and Jimmie always carried a small heroin "plant," or supply, sewed in their clothing, to be ready in case of emergency, such as an arrest. Heroin was more easily used than morphine, as it could be inhaled.

Lucille told me that her "junk" habit cost her at least thirty-five dollars a month. If anything interfered with their source of supply in New York, they had to pay thirty-five dollars an ounce instead of twenty from a different dealer in Chicago.

I did not know then, but I do now, that very few women hoboes use drugs in any form. The number I have known is not even one percent. In the first place, women of the road are invariably broke, and junk costs money. The same is true of the women who spend much of their time in shelter homes. The only sisters of the road who indulge in it are those whose hoboing is secondary to their racket. Crooks or prostitutes who occasionally hobo their way about sometimes go in for dope. In the south this is much more common than in the north. The specialty there is marijuana cigarettes.

Marijuana is called among the users, "muggles." It is really a form of hasheesh, slightly changed when grown on American soil. It came to this country first from Mexico. New Orleans and all the southern cities are full of it. In New Orleans it is grown commonly in the back yards of the Old Town. It is available also in every northern city. In south Chicago there is a whole field growing wild which is harvested by Mexicans and various small wholesale dealers.

Marijuana is popular because it is prepared without trouble and because it gives tremendous effect at very low cost. The leaves and blossoms are gathered, dried, and rolled into cigarettes slightly thinner than the ordinary package cigarettes, and twisted together on the ends so that none of the substance may be spilled. In almost every city they may be had as low as twenty-five cents each. In New Orleans they are two for a quarter. One cigarette, if smoked by those who know the way, will give a thorough "muggles jag" to at least three persons for an entire night.

Otto was the only one of the grifters I was with who had ever used marijuana. He stopped, he said, because he didn't intend to get into the dope habit. Just twice while I was with him did he make a buy, once in Philadelphia, where he just walked into a poolroom and secured one cigarette at the cigar counter, and the other time on a party down on Dumaine Street in New Orleans.

We had driven down to New Orleans from Savannah on one of the road trips and the gang had put in three days grifting [shoplifting], making good hauls. Otto had had a narrow escape, being pinched the last day and having to pay two hundred dollars to a fix to get him out. It was summer and terribly hot. The night was stifling as we walked down in the little streets of the French quarter. Suddenly he declared he wanted "a weed" and after asking a few questions of some of the loafers around Tony Vaccaro's saloon, we made a purchase of a half dozen cigarettes in a little charcoal store on Saint Ann Street. Otto didn't even wait to get back to the hotel. He lit one right there and walked out with it. After a few short drags he handed it to me.

"Try it, kid," he said, already cheering up, "it will kill the blues. Now don't waste it. Draw the smoke inward in short drags and hold it in your lungs for a minute and then let it out very slowly. There . . . there's enough for a beginning. Did it put on the rose-colored glasses?"

I didn't get much effect at first. The cigarette was sweetish in flavor. The flat dead smell almost nauseated me. But after the second drag I began to feel very happy and light-hearted. Otto promptly snubbed out the cigarette carefully in the palm of his hand and put it in his pocket.

"Here's once we save butts, kid," he told me jovially, "that's good to the last shred. Here, smoke a regular cigarette now. That will keep the effect of the other longer."

As we went on down toward the old French market, all the objects in the street suddenly became very vivid. Colors were stronger. Objects and people larger. The lights shone more brightly, and the edges of their flares diffused into reds and greens. We found ourselves very gay and joking. Everything Otto said seemed exceedingly important. People were amusing to us.

(as told to Ben L. Reitman)

from **Opium: Diary of a Cure**

Jean Cocteau

Versatile artist, cautious mystic, and avant-celebrity, as a young man Cocteau took up the use of opium, to which he became addicted. He considered *Diary of a Cure* (1930), his dramatic account of his use, addictions, and cure, to be one of his most important works. Witty and profound, it is extraordinarily insightful and passionate and serves as a testament to the durabilty —and the irresponsibility —of the creative artist. His memorable descriptions of opium use record the fervent imagination of a man struggling with the irony of the presence of the possibility of achieving vision through chemical means while existing in a bodily form that cannot sustain it.

I BECAME ADDICTED TO OPIUM A SECOND TIME under the following circumstances.

To begin with, I could not have been thoroughly cured the first time. Many courageous drug addicts do not know the pitfalls of being cured, they are content merely to give up and emerge ravaged by a useless ordeal, their cells weakened and further prevented from regaining their vitality through alcohol and sport.

Incredible phenomena are attached to the cure; medicine is powerless against them, beyond making the padded cell look like a hotel-room and demanding of the doctor or nurse patience, attendance and sensitivity. I shall explain later that these phenomena should be not those of an organism in a state of decomposition but on the contrary the uncommunicated symptoms of a baby at the breast and of vegetables in spring.

A tree must suffer from the rising of its sap and not feel the falling of its leaves.

"Le Sacre Du Printemps" orchestrates a cure with a scrupulous precision of which Stravinsky is not even aware.

I therefore became an opium addict again because the doctors who cure–one should really say, quite simply, who purge–do not seek to cure the troubles which first cause the addiction; I had found again my unbalanced state of mind; and I preferred an artificial equilibrium to no equilibrium at all. This moral disguise is more misleading than a disordered appearance: it is human, almost feminine, to have recourse to it.

I became addicted with caution and under medical supervision. There *are* doctors capable of pity. I never exceeded ten pipes. I smoked them at the rate of three in the morning (at nine o'clock) four in the afternoon (at five o'clock), three in the evening (at eleven o'clock). I believed that, in this way, I was reducing the chances of addiction. With opium I suckled new cells, which were restored to the world after five months of abstinence, and I suckled them with countless unknown alkaloids, whereas a morphine addict, whose habits frighten me, fills his veins with a single known poison and surrenders himself far less to the unknown.

I am writing these lines after twelve days and twelve nights without sleep. I leave to the drawings the task of expressing the tortures inflicted by medical impotence on those who drive out a remedy which is in process of becoming a despot.

Opium leads the organism towards death in euphoric mood. The tortures arise from the process of returning to life against one's wish. A whole spring-time excites the veins to madness, bringing with it ice and fiery lava.

I recommend the patient who has been deprived for eight days to bury his head in his arm, to glue his ear to that arm, and wait. Catastrophe, riots, factories blowing up, armies in flight, flood–the ear can detect a whole apocalypse in the starry night of the human body.

A person undergoing a cure experiences brief periods of sleep, and awakenings which remove the taste for sleep. The organism seems to emerge from hibernation, that strange economy of tortoises, marmots and crocodiles. Our blindness, our obstinacy in judging everything according to our own rhythm of existence, used to lead us to mistake the slowness of plant life for an absurd serenity. Nothing illustrates better the drama of a cure than those speeded-up films which expose the grimaces, gestures and contortions of the vegetable kingdom. The same progress in the world of sound will no doubt enable us to hear the cries of plants.

Do not expect me to be a traitor. Of course opium remains unique and the euphoria it induces superior to that of health. I owe it my perfect hours. It is a pity that instead of perfecting curative techniques, medicine does not try to render opium harmless.

But here we come back to the problem of progress. Is suffering a regulation or a lyrical interlude?

It seems to me that on an earth so old, so wrinkled, so painted, where so many compromises and laughable conventions are rife, opium (if its harmful effects could be eliminated) would soften people's manners and would cause more good than the fever of activity causes harm.

My nurse says to me "You are the first patient whom I have seen writing on the eighth day."

I fully realize that I am planting a spoon in the soft tapioca of my young cells, that I am delaying matters, but I am burning myself up and will always do so. In two weeks, despite these notes, I shall no longer believe in what I am experiencing now. One must leave behind a trace of this journey which memory forgets. One must, when this is impossible, write or draw without responding to the romantic solicitations of pain, without enjoying suffering like music, tieing a pen to one's foot if need be, helping the doctors who can learn nothing from laziness.

During an attack of neuritis one night, I asked B.: "You, who do not practise and are up to your eyes in work at the Salpêtriere and are preparing your thesis, why do you attend me at my home day and night? I know doctors. You like me very much but you like medicine more." He replied that he had at last found a patient who talked, that he learnt more from me, because I was capable of describing my symptoms, than at the Salpetriere where the question: "Where does it hurt?" invariably brought the same reply: "Don't know, doctor."

The reawakening of one's senses (the first clear symptom of recovery) is accompanied by sneezes, yawns, sniffling and tears. Another sign: the poultry in the hen house opposite exasperated me and so did those pigeons which trot up and down the tin roof, their hands behind their backs. On the seventh day the crow of the cock pleased me. I am writing these notes between six and seven in the morning. With opium nothing exists before eleven o'clock.

Clinics receive few opium addicts. It is rare for an opium addict to stop smoking. The nurses only know the counterfeit smokers, the elegant smokers, those who combine opium, alcohol, drugs, the setting (opium and alcohol are mortal enemies), or those who pass from the pipe to the syringe and from morphine to heroin. Of all drugs "the drug" is the most subtle. The lungs absorb its smoke instantaneously. The effect of a pipe is immediate. I am speaking of the real smokers. The amateurs feel nothing, they wait for dreams and risk being seasick, because the effectiveness of opium is the result of a pact. If we fall under its spell, we shall never be able to give it up.

To moralize to an opium addict is like saying to Tristan: "Kill Yseult. You will feel much better afterwards."

Opium cannot bear impatient addicts, bunglers. It moves away, leaving them morphine, heroin, suicide and death.

If you hear someone say: "X . . . has killed himself smoking opium," you should know that it is impossible, and that this death conceals something else.

Certain organisms are born to become a prey to drugs. They demand a corrective, without which they can have no contact with the outside world. They float. They vegetate in the half-light. The world remains unreal, until some substance has given it body.

It does happen that these unfortunates can live without ever finding the slightest remedy. It does happen, too, that the remedy they find kills them.

It is a matter of luck when opium steadies them and provides these souls of cork with a diver's suit. For the harm done by opium will be less than that caused by other substances and less than the infirmity which they try to heal.

I remain convinced, despite my failures, that opium can be good and that it is entirely up to us to make it well-disposed. We must know how to handle it. Nothing is worse than clumsiness on our part. A strict regime (laxatives, exercise, perspiration, rest-periods, care of the liver, keeping hours which do not encroach on one's night sleep) would permit the use of a remedy jeopardize by half-wits.

Let no one say to me: "Habit forces the smoker to increase the dose." One of the riddles of opium is that the smoker never has to increase his dose.

The drama of opium, as I see it, is none other than the drama of comfort and the lack of comfort. Comfort kills. Lack of comfort creates. I am speaking of the lack of both material and spiritual comfort.

To take opium without yielding to the absolute comfort which it offers is to escape, within the domain of the spirit, from the stupid worries of life which have nothing to do with the lack of comfort in the domain of the senses.

If a hermit lives in a state of ecstasy, his lack of comfort becomes the height of comfort. He must relinquish it.

There is in man a sort of fixative, that is to say, a sort of absurd feeling stronger than reason which allows him to think that the children who play are a race of dwarfs, instead of being a bunch of "get out of there and leave room for me."

Living is a horizontal fall.

Without this fixative any life perfectly and continually conscious of its speed would become intolerable. It enables the condemned man to sleep.

I lack this fixative. It is, I suppose, a diseased gland. Medicine takes this infirmity for an excess of conscience, for an intellectual advantage.

Everything convinces me of the functioning, in others, of this absurd fixative, as indispensable as habit, which conceals from us each day the horror of having to get up, shave, dress and eat. Even if it were only the photograph album, one of the most comical ways of turning a helter-skelter into a succession of solemn monuments.

Opium gave me this fixative. Without opium, plans, marriages and journeys appear to me just as foolish as if someone falling out of a window were to hope to make friends with the occupants of the room before which he passes.

If the universe were not moved by a very simple mechanism, it would break down. The whole of this movement, which seems to us a complicated timepiece, must resemble an alarm clock. Thus the need to procreate is doled out to us by the gross, blindly. A mistake does not cost nature much, given the odds in her favor. A mistake which becomes refined, a vice, is nothing more than one of nature's luxuries.

We are no longer, alas, a race of farmers and shepherds. The fact that we need another system of therapy to defend our over-worked nervous system cannot be questioned. For that reason it is imperative to discover some means of rendering harmless those beneficial substances which the body eliminates so unsatisfactorily, or of shielding the nerve cells.

Tell this obvious truth to a doctor and he will shrug his shoulders. He talks of literature, Utopia, and the obsessions of the drug addict.

Nevertheless, I contend that one day we shall use those soothing substances without danger, that we shall avoid habit-making, that we shall laugh at the bugaboo of the drug and that opium, once tamed, will assuage the evil of towns where trees die on their feet.

The mortal boredom of the smoker who is cured!

(Translated by Margaret Crosland and Sinclair Road)

from "The Hashish Club"

Théophile Gautier

A high-profile literary personality in mid-nineteenth-century Parisian bohemian circles, Théophile Gautier, poet, novelist, and critic, counted among his decadent achievements the cofoundation of the infamous Assassin's Club, c. 1845. After French conquests of Arabic lands in the nineteenth century, hashish—a staple of the Near and Far East—found its way to Europe, inevitably becoming the exotic passion of many a would-be romantic. Artists had found a new means to exasperate their bourgeois neighbors. Gautier remained something of a regular visitor to the club, and shortly before his death in 1872 he wrote a vivid account of it, from which two passages are here excerpted.

Fantasia

Then I looked toward the ceiling and saw a multitude of heads without bodies, like cherubim. Their expressions were so comical, their features so jovial, so radiantly happy that I was powerless before their spell. Their eyes squinted, their smiles broadened; their noses wrinkled; these were faces to brighten the darkest humor. Swarms of merry faces swirled round and round creating a giddy, dizzying effect.

Little by little the drawing room filled with extraordinary figures, figures found only in etchings by Callot and in aquatints by Goya: a potpourri of shabby finery and rags, of animal and human shapes. On another occasion I might have been uneasy in such company, but there was nothing threatening in these monsters. Mischief, not malice, glinted in their eyes. It was good humor and good humor alone that bared these crooked teeth and pointed fangs.

Like King of Carnival, I occupied the center of a bright circle, into which each figure stepped by turn, with exaggerated ceremony, to murmur witty remarks in my ear. Although I cannot recall a single one, these remarks seemed enormously funny to me at the time and roused me to wild mirth.

With each new apparition, Homeric, Olympian, boundless, deafening laughter, echoing beyond all time and space, broke forth around me like peals of thunder. Voices, now yelping, now rumbling cavernously, cried "No, it's too funny, stop! My God, what fun I'm having! . . . It's getting worse all the time! . . . Stop! I can't take any more! . . . Ha! Ha! Ha! What a farce! What a good pun! Stop! I'm choking to death, I can't breathe! Don't look at me like that! . . . Help me up, my sides are splitting!" But despite these half-jesting, half-pleading protestations, the fearful hilarity mounted steadily, the uproar grew louder, the floors and walls of the house rose and shook like a human diaphragm racked with frenzied, irresistible, pitiless laughter.

Soon, instead of accosting me one by one, these grotesque phantoms beset me en masse, flapping long Pierrot sleeves, tripping in the tattered skirts of wizards' robes, squashing cardboard noses in ridiculous collisions, shaking clouds of powder from their wigs, singing, off-key, silly songs with impossible rhymes. Every type invented by the raillery of folklore and art was there, magnified tenfold, hundredfold in power. It was a strange concourse: a Neapolitan Pulcinella rubbed its black muzzle against the floured mask of a French Paillasse, who shrieked in fright; the Doctor from Bologna flicked snuff in the eyes of Father Cassandro; Tartaglia rode piggyback on a clown, Gilles kicked Don Spavento in the bottom; Karagheuze, armed with his obscene staff, fought duels with an Oscan buffoon. Farther off raged a confused struggle of figments from foolish daydreams, hybrid creatures, formless mixtures of man, beast and tool, monks with wheels for feet and cauldrons for bellies, warriors clad in dishes wielding wooden swords in birdlike claws, statesmen turned by cranks, like roasting spits, kings waist deep in turrets shaped like pepperpots, alchemists with heads like bellows and limbs like retorts, strumpets formed of odd-shaped gourds—anything that might be drawn by the feverish pencil of a cynic, when drink prompts his hand. "It swarmed, it climbed, it ran, it leapt, it groaned, it whistled"—as Goethe says in his *Walpurgisnacht.*

To escape the crush of baroque figures, I took refuge in a dark corner, from which I could observe them giving themselves over to wild dancing, such as the Renaissance had never seen in the days of Chicard, nor the Opera during the reign of Musard, King of the Disheveled Quadrille. In each entrechat and balance, these dancers wrote, a thousand times better than Moliere, Rabelais, Swift or Voltaire have, such profoundly philosophical comedies, such broad and scathing satires, that I was forced to clutch my sides in my retreat.

Still wiping his eyes, Daucus-Carota executed unbelievable pirouettes and caprioles, especially for a man whose legs were mandrake root, and kept repeating over and over in a mockingly piteous voice: "Today you must die of laughter."

You who have admired the sublime stupidity of Oudry, the raucous foolishness of Alcide Tousez, the audacious idiocy of Arnal, the simian muggery of Ravel, you who think you know what a comic mask should be, had you been present at this Gustave's ball inspired by hashish, you too would agree that the funniest players in our little theaters are fit only to be carved on hearses or on tombstones.

What weirdly convulsed faces! What winking sarcastic eyes behind those avian membranes! What facetiously dodecahedral noses! What bellies stuffed with Pantagruelian mockery! Across this teeming harmless nightmare flashed sudden resemblances, irresistible in their effect, caricatures to make Daumier and Garnavari envious, fantasies to make the marvelous artists of China, the Phidiases of the Poussah and the Booby, swoon with satisfaction.

Still, not all the visions were misshapen or ludicrous. There was charm too within this carnival of form. Near the fireplace a small face with peachy cheeks bobbed back and forth in its frame of yellow hair, baring thirty-two tiny teeth, the size of grains of rice, in an endless fit of laughter, emitting high, tremulous, silvery, prolonged notes embroidered with trills and graces, that pierced my eardrums and drove me to folly with the intensity of their nervous energy.

The uproarious mirth was at its height; one could hear only convulsive sighs and inarticulate chuckling. The laughter lost pitch and turned to a growl, spasm succeeded pleasure; the constant refrain of Daucus-Carota was about to come true. Several Hashishin had already collapsed on the floor with that soft weight of drunkenness that renders falls harmless. Exclamations such as "My God, I'm so happy! What bliss! I'm floating in ecstasy! I am in paradise! I'm diving into an abyss of delight!" shot back and forth, garbling, drowning one another out. Hoarse cries sprang from agonized chests; arms stretched out toward fleeting visions; heads and heels beat tattoos against the floor. It was high time to fling a drop of cold water on this burning steam, or else the kettle would have burst. This human vessel, which has such small capacity for pleasure and such great capacity for sorrow, could not have withstood a greater pressure of happiness.

One of the members of the club who had not taken part in our voluptuous intoxication so that he might supervise our fantasies and restrain those who might imagine that they had sprouted wings from exiting through the windows, got up, opened the piano, and sat down to play. A magnificent chord sounded, silencing all clamor, and shifted the course of our intoxication.

Treadmill

I rose with great difficulty and headed toward the door of the drawing room. My progress was painfully slow, for an unknown force made me take one step backward for every three steps forward. In my reckoning it took me ten years to reach the door. Daucus-Carota trailed along behind me, sneering and mumbling in false commiseration: "If he goes on at this rate, he'll be an old man by the time he gets there."

Despite these taunts, I reached the adjoining room. Its dimensions had changed beyond recognition; it stretched on and on without end. A light that glimmered at the far side of the room seemed as remote as a fixed star. Discouragement overwhelmed me and I was on the point of stopping when the small voice, nearly brushing me with its lips, said, "Don't lose heart. You are expected at eleven."

I called desperately on inner resources of strength; only by enormous exertions of my will could I manage to dislodge my feet from the floor; at every step I had to uproot them like trees. The mandrake-legged monster escorted me, mocking my struggles and chanting in a sing-song voice: "The marble is winning, the marble is winning!"

Indeed I could feel my feet turning into stone, felt marble enveloping me up to my hips like the Daphne in the Tuilleries; I was statue halfway up my body, like the enchanted princes of the *Thousand and One Nights*. My stone heels crashed frightfully against the floor: I was quite capable of playing the Commander in *Don Juan*.

I had gained, however, the landing of the stairs, and I attempted to descend them. They were dimly lighted and in my delirious brain they assumed gigantic, cyclopean proportions. Their farther reaches, plunged in shadow, seemed to plumb the twin abysses of heaven and hell. Looking up, I descried in vast perspective the superposition of innumerable flights, ramp upon ramp, as if to scale the heights of the Tower of Lylacq; looking down, I foresaw a precipice of steps, a maelstrom of spirals and giddying convolutions. 'These stairs must pierce the world from one end to the other," I said, continuing my mechanical pace. "I shall reach bottom the day after Doomsday." The figures in the paintings looked down on me with pity in their eyes, several squirmed in anguish, like mutes longing to give important counsel at a critical moment. It seemed that they would warn me of some pitfall that I must avoid, but the dreary forces of inertia dragged me onward; the steps were soft and sagged beneath my weight, like the mysterious ladders of Masonic initiations. Sticky, flaccid stones squelched like toads' bellies; new landings, new flights presented themselves continually to my resigned step, those that I had passed reappeared before me. This weary round lasted for one thousand years, as far as I could tell. Finally I reached the entrance hall, where another, no less fearful persecution awaited me.

The chimera with the candle in its claws that I had noticed when I entered, barred my way with clearly hostile intentions; her greenish eyes seethed with irony, her sly mouth grinned maliciously; she moved toward me trailing her bronze caparison in the dust, but this was not a gesture of submission; fierce twitches swept over her leonine hindparts; Daucus-Carota goaded her on like a dog that one sets on attack: "Bite him! Bite him! Marble flesh for a brazen mouth, what a feast!"

Without giving way to my fear of this awful beast, I pressed on. A gust of cold air struck my face and the night sky, swept free of clouds, appeared suddenly before me. A thick seeding of stars dusted the veins of this great block of lapis lazuli with gold. I was in the courtyard.

To convey the effect of that somber architecture upon my spirits I should need the point with which Piranesi graved the black varnish of his miraculous copper plates: the courtyard had grown to the size of the Champs de Mars, and with the space of a few hours had fringed itself with giant buildings that cut the skyline in a filigree of spires, domes, towers, gables and pyramids, worthy of Rome or Babylon.

My astonishment was profound; I had never dreamed that the Ile Saint-Louis harbored such magnificent monuments, which would, in any case, occupy twenty times its real area and I could not imagine without grave apprehension the awesome power of those magicians that could raise such structures within a single night.

"You are the plaything of hollow illusions: this courtyard is quite small," murmured the voice. "It is twenty-seven paces long and twenty-five paces wide."

"Yes, yes," muttered the forked abortion, "paces in seven-league boots. You will never arrive by eleven o'clock. You started out fifteen hundred years ago. Your hair has turned half gray. Go back upstairs, that is the wisest thing to do."

When I refused to comply with his instruction, the loathsome monster caught me in the meshes of his roots and grappling, dragged me back, despite my efforts to free myself, forced me up the stairs that had occasioned so much torment, and set me once again, to my dismay, in the drawing room that I had fled under such hardship.

At this point the intoxication completely overpowered me; I went stark mad. Daucus-Carota somersaulted to the ceiling, shrieking: "You fool, I gave you back your head, but I scooped the brains out first!"

Raising my hand to the crown of my head, I discovered a gaping hole. A rush of sorrow swept over me and I lost consciousness.

(Translated by John Githens)

from **Journey to the Orient**

Gérard de Nerval

A friend and literary peer of Gautier, the poet Nerval remained a member in good standing with the Hashish-eaters Club, although he apparently long resisted the exotic pleasures to which the club was devoted. As a young boy, Nerval had been schooled in Arabic and Persian languages, and later in life he spent two years in the Middle East. Drawing on these experiences, he wrote a romantic and visionary travelogue, *Voyage en Orient* (1851). Primarily a work of fiction, it presents a nonetheless truthful portrait of a remarkable foreign land. In the following excerpt a disguised ruler of the kingdom of Egypt has wandered into a tavern where some of his subjects are smoking hashish.

O N THE RIGHT BANK OF THE NILE, some distance from the port of Fostat and the ruins of Old Cairo, not far from Mount Mokatam that overlooks the new city, there was, about the year 1000 of the Christian era, which is the fourth century of the Hegira, a small village inhabited in large part by people of the Sabian sect.[1]

There is a delightful view from the last houses along the river: with its waves the Nile seems to caress the island of Roddah, to hold it aloft, as a slave would carry a basket of flowers. On the other bank is Giza, where just after sunset the gigantic triangular shapes of the pyramids pierce through the violet haze at their base. The tops of the doom palms, the sycamores, and the pharaoh figs stand out black against this light background. Herds of water buffalo, which the Sphinx seems to guard from afar as she lies in the plain like a watchdog, move toward their watering place in a long file and the lights from the fishing boats poke golden stars through the dense dark along the river bank.

In the Sabian village, at the place from which one can best see this view, was a white-walled *okel,* or tavern, surrounded by carob trees, whose terrace had its foot in the water, and where every night the boatmen going up or down the Nile could see the night lamps flickering in their pools of oil.

A curious observer on a boat in the middle of the river, looking through the arcades of the *okel,* would have easily discerned the travelers and patrons inside, seated on palmwood cages in front of little tables, or on divans covered with matting, and most assuredly he would have been astonished at their strange appearance. Their extravagant gestures, succeeded by stupid immobility, the insensate laughter, the occasional inarticulate cries, by these he would have guessed that this was one of those houses where the infidels, defying the prohibition, came to intoxicate themselves with wine, *bouza* (beer), or hashish.

One evening a ship, steered with that certainty which comes from a thorough knowledge of the place, put in at the foot of the staircase whose bottom steps were in the water, and from it jumped a young man of worthy appearance, who seemed to be a fisherman, and who, climbing the steps with a firm and rapid tread, sat down in a corner of the room at a place that seemed to be his own. No one paid any attention to his arrival: He was evidently a patron.

At that same moment, from the opposite, landward door there entered a man dressed in a black woolen tunic, with uncustomarily long hair which he wore under a *takieh,* or white cap.

His sudden appearance caused some surprise. He sat down in a corner in the shadows, and soon, the general hilarity taking over, no one looked at him any longer. Though his clothes were shabby the newcomer had no mark on his face of the uneasy humility of misery. His firmly drawn features had the severe lines of a lion's. His eyes, of a blue as somber as sapphire, had an indefinable power; they frightened and charmed at the same time.

Yusuf, the young man who came by boat, immediately felt in his heart a secret sympathy for this unknown person, whose unusual presence he had noticed. Not yet having joined in the revelry, he approached the divan where the stranger sat cross-legged.

"Brother," said Yusuf, "you seem tired; no doubt you come from far away. Would you like some refreshments?"

"Indeed," replied the stranger, "my journey was long. I came into the *okel* to rest a bit; but what can I drink here, where only forbidden things are consumed?"

"You Moslems dare to take nothing but pure water, but we of the Sabian sect may, without breaking our law, quench the thirst with the blood of the vine or the pale brew made from barley."

"And yet I see no fermented drink before you."

"Oh, I renounced that coarse sort of intoxication long ago," said Yusuf, signaling to a slave, who placed on the table two little glasses worked with silver filigree, and a box filled with a greenish paste, in which was stuck an ivory spatula. "This box contains the paradise your prophet promised his believers, and if you were not so scrupulous I would place you within an hour in the houris' arms, without making you pass over the bridge of al-Sirat," he continued, laughing.

"But this paste is hashish, unless I'm mistaken," replied the stranger, pushing away the glass in which Yusuf had put a dose of the fantastic mixture. "And hashish is forbidden."

"Everything pleasant is forbidden," said Yusuf, swallowing the first spoonful.

The stranger looked at him steadily with his dark blue eyes, and the skin of his forehead contracted so violently that his hair followed its undulations; one moment he seemed about to jump on the carefree young man and tear him to pieces, but he calmed himself, his features became smooth once again, and suddenly changing his mind he put out his hand, took up the glass, and slowly began to sample the green paste.

After several minutes the effects of the hashish began to be felt by Yusuf and the stranger: a sweet languor spread over their bodies and a vague smile came to their lips. Though they had spent scarcely half an hour seated side by side, it seemed they had known one another for a thousand years. Then the drug began to act more strongly on them, and they began to laugh, became excited, and talked with great volubility, especially the stranger, a strict observer of the prohibition, who had never tasted hashish and who felt its effects very strongly. He seemed gripped by extraordinary exaltation; swarms of new, unheard-of, inconceivable thoughts crossed his soul in fiery whirlwinds; his eyes glittered as if lit from within by the reflection of an unknown world; then his superhuman dignity righted itself, the vision darkened, and he let himself drift through the beatific fields of *kif*.

"Well, comrade," said Yusuf, seizing on this pause in the unknown man's intoxication, "what do you think of these fine pistachio preserves? Do you still curse good people like these, peaceably assembled in a low room, who want only to be happy in their own way?

"Hashish makes man like God," replied the stranger in a slow, deep voice.

"Exactly," said Yusuf with enthusiasm. "Water drinkers can only know the coarse and material aspect of things. Hashish, in clouding the eyes of the body, enlightens those of the soul; the mind, once separated from the body, its weighty keeper, flies away like a prisoner whose jailer has fallen asleep with the key in the cell. It wanders happy and free in space and light, talking familiarly with the genii it meets, who astound with their sudden and delightful disclosures. It crosses in one easy bound through regions of indescribable happiness, all in the space of one minute that seems eternal, so quickly the sensations follow each other. I myself have a dream that reappears again and again, always the same yet always slightly different: I am returning to my boat, reeling with the splendor of my visions, and close my eyes against the constant flow of jacinths, carbuncles, emeralds, and rubies that form the background for the wondrous fantasies of hashish; as if in the very heart of the infinite I see a heavenly figure, more beautiful than all the poets' creations, who smiles at me with a piercing sweetness, then descends from heaven to me alone. Is it an angel, a fairy? I do not know. She sits by my side in the boat, the coarse wood of which instantly changes to mother-of-pearl, floating on a silver river, pushed along by perfumed breezes."

"A fortunate and peculiar vision," the stranger murmured, shaking his head.

"That is not all of it," Yusuf continued. "One night, when I had taken a weaker dose, and I had come out of my intoxication, just as the boat was passing the tip of the island of Roddah, a woman very like the one in my dreams looked at me with eyes that, though they were human, had nonetheless the brilliance of heaven; her veil, half opened, revealed in the moonlight a vest covered with precious stones. My hand reached out and touched hers; her soft skin, as smooth and fresh as a petal, and her rings, as the carvings on them grazed my skin, entirely convinced me of her reality."

"Near Roddah?" asked the stranger meditatively.

"I was not dreaming," pursued Yusuf, not noticing his improvised confidant's remark. "The hashish only brought forward a memory that had fled deep into my soul, for this divine face was known to me. Where indeed had I seen her before? In what world did we meet? What earlier life had thrown us together? There are questions I could not answer, but this strange meeting, this bizarre adventure, did not surprise me at all: it seemed entirely natural that this woman, who met my ideal so completely, should be there in my boat in the middle of the Nile, as if she had jumped out of one of those large flowers that bloom on the water's surface. Without asking for any explanation I threw myself at her feet, and as to the apparition of my dream I poured out to her all the most burning and sublime words of my exalted love. Words of immense meaning came to me, expressions that enclosed all the universe in thoughts, mysterious sentences that vibrated with the echo of vanished worlds. My soul was projected into past and future; I was convinced I had felt the love I expressed throughout all eternity.

"Even as I spoke I saw her large eyes become bright, throwing out their rays; her transparent hands extended toward me, breaking up into beams of light. I felt caught in a net of flames, and despite myself and the dream of the night before I fell backward. When I roused myself from the invincible delightful torpor that bound my body I was on the riverbank opposite Giza, leaning against a palm tree, and my slave was sleeping peacefully beside the boat, which he had pulled up onto the sand. A rosy glow fringed the horizon: It was almost dawn."

"This is a love that in no way resembles earthly love," said the stranger, not objecting in the slightest to the improbabilities of Yusuf's story, for hashish makes one credulous of all marvels.

"I have never told my incredible tale to anyone, so why have I confided in you, whom I have never seen? It's hard to explain. Some mysterious attraction draws me toward you. When you entered this room a voice cried in the depth of my soul, 'Here he is, finally.' Your arrival has calmed a secret disquiet that gives me no rest. You are he whom I have waited for without knowing it. My thoughts bound forward to meet you, and I have had to tell you all the mysteries of my heart."

"What you feel," replied the stranger, "I also feel, and I shall tell you what I have never dared admit even to myself. You have an impossible passion, I have a monstrous one; you love a phantom, I love–you will tremble–my sister! Yet a stranger thing is that I feel no remorse at this: in vain I condemn myself; I am absolved by a mysterious power that I feel in myself. My love has no earthly impurities. It is not lust that pushes me toward my sister, though she equals in beauty the phantom of my dreams; it is an indescribable attraction, an affection deep as the sea, wide as the sky, such as a god might feel. The idea of my sister marrying a man is disgusting, horrible, sacrilegious: in her spirit there is something divine that I can see through the veil of flesh. Despite the name they give it on earth, she is the bride of my immortal soul, the virgin destined for me from the earliest days of creation. Now and again I feel I can recapture across the darkness of the ages the reasons for our secret union. Things that happened before the arrival of men upon earth come to my memory, and I see myself under the golden boughs of Eden, sitting beside her, being attended by obedient spirits. If I were to marry any other woman I would debase and dissipate the soul of the world that beats in me. By the concentration of our divine blood I want to found an immortal race, a definitive god, more powerful than all those who have come until now under various names and aspects."

While Yusuf and the stranger were exchanging these extended confidences, the patrons of the *okel,* stirred by the hashish, were engaged in amazing contortions, inane laughter, ecstatic swoons, and convulsive dances, but bit by bit the hemp's strength wore off, calm returned, and they lay down on the divans in the prostrate condition that usually follows this kind of excess.

A man of patriarchal bearing, whose beard flowed over his trailing robes, came into the *okel* and went to the middle of the room.

"Brothers, arise!" he said in a resounding voice. "I have just consulted the heavens; the hour is propitious to sacrifice a white cock before the Sphinx in honor of Hermes and Agathodaemon."

The Sabians got to their feet and seemed ready to follow their priest, but the stranger, hearing this proposal, colored deeply, his blue eyes turned black, terrifying lines furrowed his brow, and he uttered a low growl that made everyone start in fear, as if a real lion had fallen into their midst.

"Ungodly blasphemers! Vile beasts! Idol worshipers!" he roared in a voice of resounding thunder.

This angry explosion produced amazement in the crowd. The unknown man had such an air of authority and raised the folds of his cloak so menacingly that no one dared answer his insults.

The old man went up to him and said, "What evil do you see, brother, in sacrificing a cock, according to the ritual, to the good spirits Hermes and Agathodaemon?"

The stranger ground his teeth at the very mention of the names.

"If you do not share the Sabians' beliefs, why have you come here? Are you a follower of Jesus, or Mohammed?"

"Mohammed and Jesus are impostors!" cried the man with immense, blasphemous power.

'Then you must be of the Parsi religion. You venerate fire—"

"They are all fantasies, mockeries, lies!" said the man in the black cloak, with redoubled indignation.

"Then whom do you worship?"

"He asks me whom I worship! I worship no one, because I am God myself! The one, the true, the only God, before me the others are only shadows!

Hearing this claim, inconceivable, unheard of, and insane, the Sabians threw themselves on the blasphemer, and would have injured him badly, but Yusuf, shielding him with his body, led him out backward onto the terrace beside the Nile, even though he protested loudly, yelling like a madman. Then, pushing it off from the bank with a vigorous kick, Yusuf maneuvered the boat into the middle of the river. Soon the current caught them up. "Where shall I take you?" Yusuf said to his friend.

"Down there, on Roddah, where you see the lights burning," replied the stranger, who had calmed down in the night air.

With a few pulls on the oars they reached the island's beach, and the man in the black cloak, before leaping onto the bank, said to his protector, offering him an ancient ring that he removed from his finger, "Wheresoever you find me again, you have only to show me this ring, and I will do for you whatever you wish." Then he walked away, disappearing through the trees that border the river. To make up for lost time Yusuf, who wanted to attend the sacrifice, began to move the boat quickly through the Nile's waters with redoubled energy.

Footnote:

[1] The Sabians are mentioned in the Koran and were a semi-Christian sect, at first tolerated in Islam because they were thought to have a written revelation. Hence they were usually not treated as cruelly as infidels.

(Translated by Andrew C. Kimmens)

A Modern Opium Eater

Anonymous

This account of a journalist's opium addiction, published in the June 1914 edition of *American Magazine*, begins as the sob story of an imprisoned man and concludes as a caveat to all potential opium users foolish enough to allow themselves be enslaved by such an "insidious" drug. The ready availability of opiates from American apothecaries through the turn of the century produced not only numerous addicts but many reformers (in many instances ex-addicts), who passionately cited cases of ruined lifes in support of their calls for stricter legal controls. "Writing cures" such as the following were intended to provide the ex-user a cathartic assuagement of guilt and to address the public's cry for temperance. This essay remains a vivid testimonial on the psychology of pain —as well as the maddening pleasure—of a life of addiction.

FIVE YEARS AGO I WAS EDITOR and manager of a metropolitan daily newspaper. To-day I am a convict serving my second penitentiary sentence–a "two-time loser" in the language of the underworld, my world now. Between these extremes is a single cause–opium.

For five years I have been a smoker of opium. For five years there has not been a day, scarcely an hour, during which my mind and body have not been under the influence of the most subtle and insidious of drugs. And now, after weeks of agony in a prison where an honest warden has made it impossible to secure the drug, I am myself again, a normal-minded man, able to look back critically and im-partially over the ruinous past. If I can set down here fairly and simply the story of those years, I shall have done some-thing, I think, that may save many an unfortunate whose feet have turned toward the road I traveled.

Few people in the United States realize the extent to which opium and kindred drugs are being used to-day in this country. You, my reader, may have read of the Federal Government's strict prohibitive law against the importation of smoking opium, and concurred idly and without interest. But do you know that the United States Revenue Service has a roster of over three thousand known users of opium in San Francisco alone? Countless other thousands are unregistered. Every other great city in the country has similar rosters, and numbers its "fiends" by thousands and tens of thousands. Hundreds of cans of the contraband drug are sold daily in New York, Chicago, Denver, New Orleans, Salt Lake, and Portland. The United States army posts have been in-vaded, and thousands of the wearers of our country's uniform are users of opium, morphine, and cocaine.

The severest penalties have not seemed even to check the habit.

Starting at the Presidio in San Francisco with transports returning from the Orient, the drug habit has spread among the enlisted men in the army by leaps and bounds. The reason is easily found. Not one man in a hundred, once he has tested the peace, the mindease, the soothed nerves and the surcease from all sorrows, disappointments, and responsibilities that come from a *first* use of opium, ever again has the will-power to deny himself that delightful nepenthe. Opium is like the salary loan shark–a friend to-day, smoothing difficulty and trouble with a free and easy hand. Tomorrow it becomes a master, exacting a toll a hundredfold more terrible than the ills it eased.

My first experience with opium was accidental. As a San Francisco reporter I had specialized in Chinatown and Chinese subjects. Not a licensed guide in the city knew the real Oriental quarter as I knew it. I had taken scores of friends to opium dens on slumming parties, but had never touched a pipe nor been tempted to do so. When I became a newspaper executive and finally attained the chief position of responsibility on the —— I naturally spent less time in Chinatown, but I still kept in touch with my news sources, sources that scored many a good "beat" for my paper.

At the time of which I write I was overworked. I was the one experienced newspaper man in an office of "cubs." Every line of copy in our eight-and ten-page sheet passed through my hands. I wrote the more important headlines, planned the "make-up," and in addition directed the efforts of the business office force. In short, I was doing the work of three or four men and the strain was beginning to tell on me. When my day's work was done I was always utterly exhausted. I slept brokenly and sat down to my daily task absolutely unrefreshed. I was approaching a nervous breakdown and knew it, but conditions on my sheet were such that I could see no immediate relief.

One evening I attended an important dramatic opening that I did not care to intrust to any of my inexperienced cubs. From the theater I started for the club where I passed a few hours occasionally. On the street I met a fellow newspaper man, a dramatic critic, who, like myself, has since passed into oblivion.

"Take me for a stroll through Chinatown," he asked. "There are some things I want to see first-hand, and you're the one man I know who can get behind their doors."

We went. During our trip my friend suggested a visit to a "hopjoint." I led the way to one little known to ordinary slummers. The mummified Chinese in charge was an old acquaintance of mine and welcomed us warmly. He was smoking opium when we entered and the unventilated cell in which he lived was heavy with the fumes of the drug. I took one deep breath of the pungent, sweetish, smoke-laden air. My friend squatted on the bunk chatting with the Chinese. Again and again I inhaled the smoke fresh from the pipe, taking it in thirstily to the very bottom of my lungs. To my amazement, my weariness, my nervousness, my brain-fag slipped from me like a discarded garment.

"Say, Lee," I demanded, when I realized the delightful exhilaration that was stealing over me, "cook me up a couple of yen poks" [pills]. "I'm going to smoke a few."

Willingly he toasted the brownish syrupy drug over his dim lamp, rolled the pill into shape, deftly attached it to the bowl and then handed me the pipe and guided it over the flame while I drew into my lungs my first pill of opium.

In sixty seconds I was another man. My barren brain, in which I had been conning over an introduction to the criticism I must write before I slept, leaped to its task. The ideas, the phrases, the right words, which, until then, had eluded my fagged mentality, came trooping forth faster than I could have written them had I been at my desk. My worries and responsibilities fell from me. I remember even to-day that as I smoked my third or fourth pill the solution of a problem that had been a bugbear for days came into my mind like an inspiration.

I smoked six pills before we left. As my friend and I separated he looked at me curiously.

"I've often wondered how you do the work you do and hold up," he said. "Now I know. I'm going to try that myself the next time I'm stuck for my Sunday page story. My brain is virile and as clear as crystal and I didn't take a pill–just breathed the air. I've surprised your secret, old man. Good night."

I didn't tell him he had seen me smoke my first pill.

A half hour later I wrote a column of dramatic criticism that was quoted on the bill-boards and I reeled it off as fast as my fingers could hit the typewriter keys. I was never at a loss for a word. The story in its entirety seemed to lie ready in my brain. My task finished, I went to bed without my customary drink, and dropped asleep as peacefully as a child. For the first time in weeks I slept soundly and awoke refreshed and clear-minded with a zest for the day's labor.

That was the beginning. After that I visited Lee, first at intervals of several days, then, by degrees, more frequently, until finally I became a daily user of opium. I shall never forget one conversation with the old Chinese den-keeper on the occasion of my third or fourth smoke. He looked up with his bland smile of welcome as I came in. It was evident that the man *expected* me. This nettled me. Nothing could have convinced me then that the drug could ever become a necessity to me.

"Well, Lee," I said throwing myself on the bunk, "chef me up a few extra big ones to-night. I'll take more to-night, for this will be about my last smoke. I'm going to quit."

In silence he adjusted my favorite bowl to the pipe. In silence he deftly toasted the pill, completed the operation and twirled the ivory mouthpiece around to me. Greedily I drew the fragrant smoke into my lungs. He noticed my eagerness. Indeed, I could not even pretend to conceal it. He watched me inhale the smoke until my lungs puffed out like a pigeon's breast, then exhale it slowly, in little puffs, regretting each. At last he spoke.

"You no quit," he said softly. "Every man alleetime say he quit. Every man alleesame you. Smoke one time, smoke two time, smoke tlee time, then smoke alleetime. Chineman, white man, chokquay" [negro] "alleesame. No can quit. Bimeby you die you quit. Bimeby maybe you bloke,—no more money, no more fliend bollow money, no can stealem money, maybe you quit one, two days. Bimeby maybe you go jail, no got fliend bling you hop, no got money givem policeman catchem hop, you quit. You got money, no go jail, you no quit. I heap sabe. Bimeby you see."

I laughed at his warning. Had I but known it, the wisdom of ages, the experience of untold thousands of wrecked lives were summed up in the halting words I allowed to pass me unheeded.

When I became a regular smoker I bought a "layout"–pipe, bowls, lamp, tray, yen hocks, everything–and indulged my habit in the "joint" of a white smoker where I was a favored patron and could lie at ease, privately, without fear of discovery.

By this time the cost of opium had become a very appreciable and permanent expense. From a few pills at first I increased my allowance day by day until it took thirty or forty "fun" (a Chinese measure; there are 76 fun in an ounce) to give me the mental relief I craved. The physical craving–the body's demand for it–can be satisfied with approximately the same amount each day. The mental craving–the mind's demand–increases daily. What satisfies tonight is too little to-morrow, and so on. To feel even normal I now needed three or four times the half-dozen pills which at first had given me such exquisite pleasure. To get the exhilaration, the soothed nerves, the contentment I craved, I, like each of the millions before me, had to use more and more each day.

Thirty-six fun of opium at retail costs, at an average, three dollars. A fifty-cent tip to my "cook" and a quarter for the privilege of the room in which I smoked made my habit cost me about four dollars a day, which made a ghastly hole in even the good salary I earned. I began to buy my opium by the can, paying from $25 to $30 for tins averaging 460 fun. The elimination of the retailer's profit helped temporarily, but the ever-increasing demands of my habit soon overcame the saving.

I had been a user of opium about eight months when I first began to realize a mental change in myself–a new moral viewpoint, so to speak. I handled a story of the arrest of a criminal with real regret, while the news of a clever crime with the perpetrators safely at liberty was a personal gratification. The realization of this change came about peculiarly.

A big story broke one day. A prominent official had robbed the city of a large sum. The man had disappeared. Detectives and a hundred reporters hunted the town over for him. His home, his friends, his relatives, and every outward bound train were watched without result. I handled the story, personally, from the desk. As I rewrote an introduction to the mystery, I kept revolving in my mind the problem of the absconder's disappearance. Where had he hidden himself? The problem was complicated by the belief that a woman with whom he was infatuated was with him.

I was still pondering over the mystery as I lay smoking that evening. I had reached the stage now in which I rushed from my work to the layout and lay beside it smoking and dreaming until far into the night. That night, my habit appeased, I lay seemingly half asleep, but with an alert mind working automatically without effort of will. "Suppose

I were in S—'s place," I argued. "What would I do? Try to get away by rail? Nonsense. I would know that every outlet in the city was guarded and, besides, with pictures scattered broadcast over the country, an appearance in any other city would be an invitation to arrest. Hide in a local hotel? With prying bell-boys, clerks, and chambermaids?–never. My own and relatives' homes of course were impossible. Where, then, would I go?"

The answer came to me like a flash. I roused my lethargic body with a sudden start. *I knew where that criminal would hide.* Given its full quota of opium, my brain furnished the solution. If his flight had been planned in advance he would have his companion rent an inconspicuous, detached, furnished cottage where they could live alone and at ease while the hue and cry wore itself out. Then, when the hunt slumbered, a disguise, an automobile to an obscure port and a steamer to Honduras.

But the missing man had been forced to leave without preparation, owing to the unexpected appearance of expert accountants. What then? The alternative lay ready. One of the French roadhouses, a small one preferably, kept without attendants by some man and his wife of the type whose lips are sealed effectively with gold. Of course! How simple!

At seven o'clock next morning I started in a motor car with a list of six roadhouses I had selected. My experiences during the hunt are not relevant here. It suffices to say that at the fifth house I located my man. By means of a trick note I brought him down to me, white-faced and shaking. We had been acquaintances for years.

"What are you going to do?" he stammered, "turn me over to the police?"

"I don't wear a star," I replied angrily. Opium hates the law. "I haven't a drop of 'copper' blood in me. You're perfectly safe. But I want a signed confession covering this entire business. It can't harm you, for they've got the goods on you anyway if you're caught. I'll hold up the story till our late edition. Meanwhile, it's your move."

His face lighted with relief.

"I'll do it," he cried. "Have a drink."

A half hour later I was glancing over a signed document that meant a "beat" that was worth while.

As I rose to go he waved me back and ordered another drink.

"You've been 'right' with me," he said, "and I feel I can trust you. I'm a bit puzzled about the safest sort of a 'get-away,' from here. What would you do in my predicament?"

I replied without a second's hesitation.

"In your place," I said, "I would 'phone to some public garage for a machine to be here at noon. About eleven o'clock you and your friend stroll off through the woods in the rear. It's less than a mile to Pierre's. Maybe you know him?" He nodded. "Well, he would forget his own mother's name for a century note. When the machine gets here you'll be gone. Have the proprietor here send the chauffeur down to San M—, telling him to wait at the railway depot there for you until eight o'clock to-night. Leave plenty of money to pay him in advance. Tell the boss here to tell the exact truth to the police when they come: that you went away before the car came and ordered it sent down empty to the San M— railway station. The detectives will have the chauffeur in custody before night, but there isn't a man who wears a star who will believe the truth. When he says he didn't see you at all and has been traveling around with an empty machine, they'll laugh at him. Meanwhile lie close at Pierre's. They'll never look for you within a mile of here in identically the same kind of a house. It's too simple for their complex intellects."

As I talked, looks of startled wonder flashed from his heavy, puffed eyes.

"Man!" he cried. "Are you a mind reader? First you locate me here, then you tell me word for word the exact idea I had in mind."

"I'll tell you more," I said laughingly. "You'd be hidden in a little furnished house somewhere instead of here, if the experts hadn't come on you so unexpectedly."

He leaped to his feet.

"You're uncanny," he cried. "I did intend that. Thank heaven, you're not one of those police hounds. Are you an opium smoker?"

"Are you?" I retorted, ignoring his question.

"Yes," he said, and we smiled together.

This brings me to the crux of the incident, the reason for its telling. It is proof of the most important point I wish to make, which is that an equal number of brain convolutions *plus* an adequate amount of opium will *invariably produce precisely the same impulses and ideas.* Take two men of similar intellects and propound a problem, preferably in criminality. If both men are users of opium their minds will arrive at exactly the same result by exactly the same mental processes. I have tested it scores of times and the results were the same nineteen times out of twenty.

In this lies the proof of the terrible power of opium over the mind of its slave. It controls his every thought and impulses as absolutely as the brain controls the muscles. And opium-made plans, plots, inspirations–call them what you will–are devious, tricky, shrewd because of their abnormality. No one but another smoker will ever come within leagues of guessing what a "fiend" will do under any given set of conditions. A normal brain and an opium brain have nothing in common.

There is but one exception to this rule. An opium smoker suffering for the drug and lacking the money to buy what alone can still the frightful agony in nerve and limb is as simple as a coot. He will try anything that promises money. The more foolhardy the stunt, the more it appeals to him.

Returning for a paragraph to the absconder, he made his escape exactly as we had planned. A year later he returned from the Orient, deserted by his companion and broken physically and financially. He surrendered himself and went to prison. Another niche in Oblivion for a slave of opium. I remembered, as I read of his fate, the similarity in our ideas on that foggy morning out at the little French roadhouse. But now I was too close behind him on the road to the penitentiary to worry myself with the future as long as I had opium and plenty of it.

This fugitive's confession was the last dividend granted me by the drug by which I was now enslaved. Thereafter, and always, it wrested from me bit by bit everything that a man holds dear and sacred, giving nothing in return but the temporary power to forget. The paper on which I worked was absorbed by another and I passed out of the newspaper business forever. I was rather glad at the time. I had just that many more hours a day to lie musing by my layout.

What were my thoughts during these hours? I have never read anything, not even De Quincey's "Opium-Eater," that gives a truthful and lucid impression of what "opium dreams" really are. The ordinary conception of them is miles from the truth. There is no riot of wonderful and strange colors dancing before the eyes. There are no visions of Orientalized beauty, no loving women, sweetly-perfumed, no luxurious air castles filled with jewels, gold and sensuous luxury. Instead, the brain works automatically on the important projects of everyday life. It plans and plots, rejects and reconstructs–always trickily and by devious means–and, finally, evolves a clean-cut idea. The intervening difficulties are lessened, the ultimate rewards accentuated.

All this is absolutely without effort. You lie quiescent, your whole being apparently deep in lethargy, your eyes half-closed and unseeing. You are perfectly content, at peace with the world and yourself. Meanwhile the brain, working of its own volition, independently of you, exactly as if it were a distinct personality, raps out with Gatling-gun rapidity various solutions of the problems it has set itself. It works always, however, in devious channels. If there is a direct road between two points, it mistrusts and rejects it, taking the crooked path.

Time ceases to exist. Night after night I have lain down after the theater to smoke. Finally rousing myself to leave, believing it midnight or a little later, I would look at my watch. Five o'clock! Impossible! Not until I raised the curtain to a gray dawn could I believe. Night after night this happened. I smoked for five years and was surprised anew each time when the day seemed to come hours before its time.

And now I was ripe for the final stage of the opium habit– criminality. I had sunk step by step morally until there remained no semblance of the character that once had won me trust and respect. After I abandoned newspaper work I dabbled in many semi-legitimate businesses. I occupied myself with prize-fight promotion, gambling clubs and stock tricks, all verging on swindles, but permeated with the subtleness of the drug that created them.

At last there came a day, inevitable in the history of all drug fiends, when I found myself without the money to buy the opium my body and brain demanded. My credit was gone. I was a derelict with but a single purpose, to relieve with opium the anguish of a thousand tortured nerves.

I stepped into a store, wrote a bad check, passed it and took a taxicab to the joint. The latter is characteristic of the habit. Provided enough money remains for the smoke immediately in prospect nothing else matters. There is no future in the Land of Opium.

Having smoked and being once again mentally alert I realized keenly my danger of arrest. My mind, acute as ever, warned me that check-passing could lead ultimately to but one fate–a striped suit. I resolved never again to take such chances. It was not that scruples troubled me. My opium-sated brain simply refused to countenance such idiocy.

Three days later, again needing money to satisfy my habit, I drew another worthless check and entered a prominent book store. Almost at the threshold I met a detective whom I knew well. We chatted for a moment. Then, deliberately, I entered that store, ordered a complete edition of valuable books sent to a fictitious address, and in return for my check received $37.50 in change. In twenty minutes I was in the joint, breathing in the smoke that was more to me than liberty. Under the stimulus of the drug my brain kept ringing its warning. It is difficult to explain this mental duality. Given its opium, my mind was like a guardian, a mentor, pointing out reprovingly the folly of that same mind, committed while in want of opium.

I hid myself in an obscure hotel and was safe while my money lasted and I had my drug. That gone I walked brazenly down the main street of the city intending to pass another check. I was arrested by the detective I had chatted with before the store, convicted, and sentenced to a year in the penitentiary.

I do not intend to exploit here the horrors, the ignominy of that year. What it means to "do time" is subject enough for an article such as this. It is sufficient to say that I was able to secure opium while a convict. Meanwhile I lived in an environment and under conditions, both moral and physical, that *create criminals* instead of correcting them. I was discharged, uncured of the drug habit, and returned to society a hundredfold more dangerous a menace than before.

By this time I had many friends among professional thieves. From the very first I had been "right," which, translated, means that my loyalty to the underworld was established, that I was held to be above the suspicion of being a "stool-pigeon," no matter what the cost or reward. When I left prison I was received with open arms and was offered "work" of various kinds on a number of different criminal "mobs."

Once, moved by some fleeting impulse, I applied for work to a paper on which I once had made a reputation. My rebuff sent me flying back to my layout and thiefdom, never to return. I "joined out" with a mob and we prospered financially. Given plenty of opium, I was a good money getter. I took the minimum of risk and made the maximum of money. I lived on opium. Physically, I was a wreck. Mentally, I was as scheming a criminal as ever wore stripes. Months passed. Untroubled by conscience, ignored responsibilities and broken faith, I went on downward–living to smoke, smoking to live.

Then the inevitable happened once again. A heavy gambling loss took our reserve fund. The arrest of one of the mob for a triviality was the excuse for police extortion that took the remainder of our "bank roll." Our money gone, we were warned to stay off the streets, and had not the means to travel. One night the opium ran out. I secured a can on credit. That was soon gone.

I endured twelve hours without the drug; then, with a companion, went down-town, induced a man wearing several thousand dollars worth of diamonds to accompany me to a room in a prominent down-town hotel, and at midday without a mask and with my photograph in the police gallery of "known criminals," I deliberately put a revolver to his head and told him to put up his hands. He did so. I took his diamonds and money, bound and gagged him, and then blithely walked out of the place, passing hundreds of men, including two detectives.

The brazen effrontery of the crime staggered even the police.

Stopping only to lay in a supply of opium, we boarded a car and in half an hour were in the little furnished house I had rented, with the "long-stem" (pipe) passing round and round the circle. I smoked heavily and dozed. When I awoke it was night. Our circle was still unbroken, the pipe still passed from lip to lip. But now, opium once again having made me as near normal as was possible, I sensed danger, imminent, immediately impending. It was not alone the knowledge of guilt, it was something more definite, something intuitive. In the underworld there is a species of foresight termed "hop-head hunches." They are regarded with superstitious awe the country over. Knowing that something threatened, I scattered the boys out, sending all but one down-town. We two remained. We had slept while the others smoked, and now needed more opium, and, needing it, no danger could drive us from the layout until we were satisfied. We intended to leave the moment we finished smoking, but before we had inhaled a dozen pills a heavy knock, peremptory, insistent, sounded on the door.

We both knew its significance. Snapping off the lights, I peered out into the night. Everywhere were armed detectives. The entire house was surrounded. We were trapped. Their gleaming gun barrels proved they expected a battle, and had I *needed* opium just then instead of being newly saturated with it, they would have had it. It is upon such chances that life and death and murder turn in lives such as mine. Being near enough to normality to realize the absolute futility of resistance, I turned to my pal.

"It's the pinch, old boy," I said.

In that moment, facing arrest that could only result in a long term in the penitentiary, there was but one thought, one anxiety in my mind. Would the "plant" of opium I carried on my person for emergencies such as this escape detection, I wondered. Beyond that I was unconcerned. That thought is as eloquent as a volume in explanation of a drug user's mind.

I threw open the door and admitted the officers, who covered evident nervousness with a show of brusqueness. The stolen gems were not found, for during the afternoon, having smoked, my opium self had warned me to hide them safely. The usual police methods–"third degree" some call it–were tried, but without result. Each of us was told that the other had confessed and each was offered leniency at the expense of his comrade. That neither of us weakened proves that there lies even in humanity's dregs the remnants of decency. There is really loyalty and honor (according to a strangely twisted code) among some thieves. Incidentally, the diamonds were not found until returned by us voluntarily.

Trial and conviction followed after the usual delays, and to-night I write this in a penitentiary cell. No one who has never lost the freedom of the "outside"–that perpetual elusive dream of every convict–can realize what "doing time" means. But even the horror of prison life, the monotonous, hopeless sameness of each hour, each day, each month, each year, is not too great a price for what it has given me. For I am freed from opium's shackles.

In this institution the drug traffic that makes many like places mere colleges for crime has been absolutely stamped out. Being unable to get opium or morphine, and being given intelligent and humane medical treatment during the agonizing weeks during which the body and mind are breaking away from a habit almost as deep-rooted as life itself, men here are cured of the opium habit. I do not know what more can be said in laudation of any penitentiary.

I was asked a few days ago to describe the sensations of the opium "habit," the word with us meaning the anguish that follows the need of the drug. It is a difficult task, for it is like no other suffering. In the first stage come restlessness, irritability, eyes that stream tears, and the mental incompetency I have tried to make plain heretofore. This quickly passes into the most exquisite physical torture. Thousand pound weights drag each separate joint apart by infinitesimal degrees. Every jangling nerve throbs and twitches the muscles with a pain that would make a toothache seem perfect ease. Every pore in the body drips a clammy perspiration. The bodily functions are entirely disorganized. Abdominal cramps follow nausea. An irresistible force seems to be slowly dragging each muscle and nerve apart.

Meanwhile the brain fights for the drug as life fights death. A million impossible schemes for getting opium suggest themselves as some inner force seems to be expanding within the skull until every bone is strained to the breaking point. A weight like a gigantic hand seems to be squeezing the naked brain as you would squeeze a sponge. Hundreds of drug fiends have committed suicide in jails where they were confined without adequate medical attention. Three tried it in one week recently in a single jail in the West, and hundreds more will follow in their footsteps if they can secure a weapon. This merits attention.

The final stage of the "habit" is insanity. The fiend becomes a raving maniac if unrelieved, but here the physician forestalls this by ever so slight a margin and with a hypodermic injection of morphine send the unfortunate off to sleep. The next day it is the same torture over again until the needle again saves tottering reason. But each time the injection is lighter and finally the torture, too, lessens, imperceptibly at first, until the system begins to try to readjust itself to the new conditions. The mind, however, remains rebellious to the very last, crying out for the drug even after the body has begun to mend.

I do not believe that any man with an opium or morphine habit of years' standing can deny himself the drug if it is within reach.

I do not believe that any man, no matter what his previous character may have been, can use opium continuously and not have the *impulse* to be crooked. He may not be crooked, he may lack the nerve or the necessity to steal, but the impulse will be there, and if it ever becomes a question of theft or a "habit" he will thieve. I do not say this because of my own experience. It is the history of every opium smoker I have ever known.

That I have been freed from the servitude of the past years seems almost too unreal to be possible, and yet I confidently believe that this is true. For nearly a year I have not touched opium in any of its forms and all physical need for it disappeared long ago. But what about the mental craving? If I were free now to use it or not, would I do so? I believe I would not. I believe I am free from opium forever for this reason: I fear it too intensely. My mind now is free from the taint of the drug. My will is not undermined and controlled by it. Being normal mentally, I am able to realize fully what it has cost me. And so I believe that I could keep a bottle of morphine in my cell and never be tempted to touch it. But if I were to take just one dose–that fatal first pill–I believe I would slip rapidly and irretrievably into my former condition of absolute thralldom. I repeat that I fear opium and its power too deeply ever to test myself with that first pill.

I am the fourth man I have ever known who has escaped–if I have escaped. Each of the four was saved exactly as I have been, in an institution like this where honesty of purpose is placed above the easy money that can be made by letting the drug traffic go on behind prison walls. It would surprise most readers to know how many penitentiaries are managed without such qualms.

And now one final word. If ever you are invited to try a pill of opium or to still a pain with morphine, or, most important of all, to give your children any medicine, patent or otherwise, that contains opium, morphine, laudanum, heroin or any of their kindred alkaloids, remember the old Chinese lying beside his opium layout and mumbling his warning.

"You no quit . . . You smoke one time, then smoke two time, then smoke tlee time, then smoke allee time . . . You no quit. I heap sabe. Bimeby you see."

That, reader, will be as bitterly true for you as it had been for me if you ever try that fatal first pill.

Drugs That Shape
Men's Minds

Aldous Huxley

Perhaps in part owing to a lifelong problem with his eyesight, Aldous Huxley was drawn to the visions of mysticism in all its variations. Well before 1953, when Huxley first experimented with psychoactive substances, he'd extensively explored those aspects of many religions that might serve as a means to expand ordinary consciousness. In the last decade of his life, now a revered litterateur and thinker, Huxley devoted much of his time to introducing a wide audience to the spiritual possibilities attainable through the use of psychedelics. With passionate idealism he advocated mass access to mind-altering substances. The following essay was originally published in *The Saturday Evening Post* in 1958.

IN THE COURSE OF HISTORY many more people have died for their drink and their dope than have died for their religion or their country. The craving for ethyl alcohol and the opiates has been stronger, in these millions, than the love of God, of home, of children; even of life. Their cry was not for liberty or death; it was for death preceded by enslavement. There is a paradox here, and a mystery. Why should such multitudes of men and women be so ready to sacrifice themselves for a cause so utterly hopeless and in ways so painful and so profoundly humiliating?

To this riddle there is, of course, no simple or single answer. Human beings are immensely complicated creatures, living simultaneously in a half dozen different worlds. Each individual is unique and, in a number of respects, unlike all the other members of the species. None of our motives is unmixed, none of our actions can be traced back to a single source and, in any group we care to study, behavior patterns that are observably similar may be the result of many constellations of dissimilar causes.

Thus, there are some alcoholics who seem to have been biochemically predestined to alcoholism. (Among rats, as Prof. Roger Williams, of the University of Texas, has shown, some are born drunkards; some are born teetotalers and will never touch the stuff.) Other alcoholics have been foredoomed not by some inherited defect in their biochemical make-up, but by their neurotic reactions to distressing events in their childhood or adolescence. Again, others embark upon their course of slow suicide as a result of mere imitation and good fellowship because they have made such an "excellent adjustment to their group"–a process which, if the group happens to be criminal, idiotic or merely ignorant, can bring only disaster to the well-adjusted individual. Nor must we forget that large class of addicts who have taken to drugs or drink in order to escape from physical pain. Aspirin, let us remember, is a very recent invention. Until late in the Victorian era, "poppy and mandragora," along with henbane and ethyl alcohol, were the only pain relievers available to civilized man. Toothache, arthritis and neuralgia could, and frequently did, drive men and women to become opium addicts.

De Quincey, for example, first resorted to opium[1] in order to relieve "excruciating rheumatic pains of the head." He swallowed his poppy and, an hour later, "What a resurrection from the lowest depths of the inner spirit! What an apocalypse!" And it was not merely that he felt no more pain. "This negative effect was swallowed up in the immensity of those positive effects which had opened up before me, in the abyss of divine enjoyment thus suddenly revealed. . . . Here was the secret of happiness, about which the philosophers had disputed for so many ages, at once discovered."

"Resurrection, apocalypse, divine enjoyment, happiness. . . ." De Quincey's words lead us to the very heart of our paradoxical mystery. The problem of drug addiction and excessive drinking is not merely a matter of chemistry and psychopathology, of relief from pain and conformity with a bad society. It is also a problem in metaphysics–a problem, one might almost say, in theology. In *The Varieties of Religious Experience* (1902), William James has touched on these metaphysical aspects of addiction:

> The sway of alcohol over mankind is unquestionably due to its power to stimulate the mystical faculties in human nature, usually crushed to earth by the cold facts and dry criticisms of the sober hour. Sobriety diminishes, discriminates and says no. Drunkenness expands, unites and says yes. It is in fact the great exciter of the Yes function in man. It brings its votary from the chill periphery of things into the radiant core. It makes him for the moment one with truth. Not through mere perversity do men run after it. To the poor and unlettered it stands in the place of symphony concerts and literature and it is part of the deeper mystery and tragedy of life that whiffs and gleams of something that we immediately recognize as excellent should be vouchsafed to so many of us only through the fleeting earlier phases of what, in its totality, is so degrading a poison. The drunken consciousness is one bit of the mystic consciousness, and our total opinion of it must find its place in our opinion of that larger whole.

William James was not the first to detect a likeness between drunkenness and the mystical and pre-mystical states. On that day of Pentecost there were people who explained the strange behavior of the disciples by saying, "These men are full of new wine."

Peter soon undeceived them: "These are not drunken, as ye suppose, seeing it is but the third hour of the day. But this is that which was spoken by the prophet Joel. And it shall come to pass in the last days, saith God, I will pour out of my Spirit upon all flesh."

And it is not only by "the dry critics of the sober hour" that the state of God-intoxication has been likened to drunkenness. In their efforts to express the inexpressible, the great mystics themselves have done the same. Thus, St. Theresa of Avila tells us that she "regards the centre of our soul as a cellar, into which God admits us as and when it pleases Him, so as to intoxicate us with the delicious wine of His Grace."

Every fully developed religion exists simultaneously on several different levels. It exists as a set of abstract concepts about the world and its governance. It exists as a set of rites and sacraments, as a traditional method for manipulating the symbols, by means of which beliefs about the cosmic order are expressed. It exists as the feelings of love, fear and devotion evoked by this manipulation of symbols.

And finally it exists as a special kind of feeling or intuition–a sense of the oneness of all things in their divine principle, a realization (to use the language of Hindu theology) that "thou art That," a mystical experience of what seems self-evidently to be union with God.

The ordinary waking consciousness is a very useful and, on most occasions, an indispensable state of mind; but it is by no means the only form of consciousness, nor in all circumstances the best. Insofar as he transcends his ordinary self and his ordinary mode of awareness, the mystic is able to enlarge his vision, to look more deeply into the unfathomable miracle of existence.

The mystical experience is doubly valuable; it is valuable because it gives the experiencer a better understanding of himself and the world and because it may help him to lead a less self-centered and more creative life.

In hell, a great religious poet has written, the punishment of the lost is to be "their sweating selves, but worse." On earth we are not worse than we are, we are merely our sweating selves, period.

Alas, that is quite bad enough. We love ourselves to the point of idolatry; but we also intensely dislike ourselves–we find ourselves unutterably boring. Correlated with this distaste for the idolatrously worshipped self, there is in all of us a desire, sometimes latent, sometimes conscious and passionately expressed, to escape from the prison of our individuality, an urge to self-transcendence. It is to this urge that we owe mystical theology, spiritual exercises and yoga–to this, too, that we owe alcoholism and drug addiction.

Modern pharmacology has given us a host of new synthetics, but in the field of the naturally occurring mind changers it has made no radical discoveries. All the botanical sedatives, stimulants, vision revealers, happiness promoters and cosmic-consciousness arousers were found out thousands of years ago, before the dawn of history.

In many societies at many levels of civilization attempts have been made to fuse drug intoxication with God-intoxication. In ancient Greece, for example, ethyl alcohol had its place in the established religion. Dionysus, or Bacchus, as he was often called, was a true divinity. His worshipers addressed him as *Lusios*, "Liberator," or as *Theoinos*, "Godwine." The latter name telescopes fermented grape juice and the supernatural into a single pentecostal experience. "Born a god," writes Euripides, "Bacchus is poured out as a libation to the gods, and through him men receive good." Unfortunately they also receive harm. The blissful experience of self-transcendence which alcohol makes possible has to be paid for, and the price is exorbitantly high.

Complete prohibition of all chemical mind changers can be decreed, but cannot be enforced, and tends to create more evils than it cures. Even more unsatisfactory has been the policy of complete toleration and unrestricted availability. In England, during the first years of the eighteenth century, cheap untaxed gin—"drunk for a penny, dead drunk for two-pence"—threatened society with complete demoralization. A century later, opium, in the form of laudanum, was reconciling the victims of the Industrial Revolution to their lot—but at an appalling cost in terms of addiction, illness and early death. Today most civilized societies follow a course between the two extremes of total prohibition and total toleration. Certain mind-changing drugs, such as alcohol, are permitted and made available to the public on payment of a very high tax, which tends to restrict their consumption. Other mind changers are unobtainable except under doctors' orders—or illegally from a dope pusher. In this way the problem is kept within manageable bounds. It is most certainly not solved. In their ceaseless search for self-transcendence, millions of would-be mystics become addicts, commit scores of thousands of crimes and are involved in hundreds of thousands of avoidable accidents.

Do we have to go on in this dismal way indefinitely? Up until a few years ago, the answer to such a question would have been a rueful "Yes, we do." Today, thanks to recent developments in biochemistry and pharmacology, we are offered a workable alternative. We see that it may soon be possible for us to do something better in the way of chemical self-transcendence than what we have been doing so ineptly for the last seventy or eighty centuries.

Is it possible for a powerful drug to be completely harmless? Perhaps not. But the physiological cost can certainly be reduced to the point where it becomes negligible. There are powerful mind changers which do their work without damaging the taker's psychophysical organism and without inciting him to behave like a criminal or a lunatic. Biochemistry and pharmacology are just getting into their stride. Within a few years there will probably be dozens of powerful but—physiologically and socially speaking—very inexpensive mind changers on the market.

In view of what we already have in the way of powerful but nearly harmless drugs; in view, above all, of what unquestionably we are very soon going to have—we ought to start immediately to give some serious thought to the problem of the new mind changers. How ought they to be used? How can they be abused? Will human beings be better and happier for their discovery? Or worse and more miserable?

The matter requires to be examined from many points of view. It is simultaneously a question for biochemists and physicians, for psychologists and social anthropologists, for legislators and law-enforcement officers. And finally it is an ethical question and a religious question. Sooner or later—and the sooner, the better—the various specialists concerned will have to meet, discuss and then decide, in the light of the best available evidence and the most imaginative kind of foresight, what should be done. Meanwhile let us take a preliminary look at this many-faceted problem.

Last year American physicians wrote 48,000,000 prescriptions for tranquillizing drugs, many of which have been refilled, probably more than once. The tranquillizers are the best known of the new, nearly harmless mind changers. They can be used by most people, not indeed with complete impunity, but at a reasonably low physiological cost. Their enormous popularity bears witness to the fact that a great many people dislike both their environment and "their sweating selves." Under tranquillizers the degree of their self-transcendence is not very great; but it is enough to make all the difference, in many cases, between misery and contentment.

In theory, tranquillizers should be given only to persons suffering from rather severe forms of neurosis or psychosis. In practice, unfortunately, many physicians have been carried away by the current pharmacological fashion and are prescribing tranquillizers to all and sundry. The history of medical fashions, it may be remarked, is at least as grotesque as the history of fashions in women's hats–at least as grotesque and, since human lives are at stake, considerably more tragic. In the present case, millions of patients who had no real need of the tranquillizers have been given the pills by their doctors and have learned to resort to them in every predicament, however triflingly uncomfortable. This is very bad medicine and, from the pill taker's point of view, dubious morality and poor sense.

There are circumstances in which even the healthy are justified in resorting to the chemical control of negative emotions. If you really can't keep your temper, let a tranquillizer keep it for you. But for healthy people to resort to a chemical mind changer every time they feel annoyed or anxious or tense is neither sensible nor right. Too much tension and anxiety can reduce a man's efficiency–but so can too little. There are many occasions when it is entirely proper for us to feel concerned, when an excess of placidity might reduce our chances of dealing effectively with a ticklish situation. On these occasions, tension mitigated and directed from within by the psychological methods of self-control is preferable from every point of view to complacency imposed from without by the methods of chemical control.

And now let us consider the case–not, alas, a hypothetical case–of two societies competing with each other. In Society A, tranquillizers are available by prescription and at a rather stiff price–which means, in practice, that their use is confined to that rich and influential minority which provides the society with its leadership. This minority of leading citizens consumes several billions of the complacency-producing pills every year. In Society B, on the other hand, the tranquillizers are not so freely available, and the members of the influential minority do not resort, on the slightest provocation, to the chemical control of what may be necessary and productive tension. Which of these two competing societies is likely to win the race? A society whose leaders make an excessive use of soothing syrups is in danger of falling behind a society whose leaders are not over-tranquillized.

Now let us consider another kind of drug–still undiscovered, but probably just around the corner–a drug capable of making people feel happy in situations where they would normally feel miserable. Such a drug would be a blessing, but a blessing fraught with grave political dangers. By making harmless chemical euphoria freely available, a dictator could reconcile an entire population to a state of affairs to which self-respecting human beings ought not to be reconciled. Despots have always found it necessary to supplement force by political or religious propaganda. In this sense the pen is mightier than the sword. But mightier than either the pen or the sword is the pill. In mental hospitals it has been found that chemical restraint is far more effective than strait jackets or psychiatry. The dictatorships of tomorrow will deprive men of their freedom, but will give them in exchange a happiness none the less real, as a subjective experience, for being chemically induced. The pursuit of happiness is one of the traditional rights of man; unfortunately, the achievement of happiness may turn out to be incompatible with another of man's rights–namely, liberty.

It is quite possible, however, that pharmacology will restore with one hand what it takes away with the other. Chemically induced euphoria could easily become a threat to individual liberty; but chemically induced vigor and chemically heightened intelligence could easily be liberty's strongest bulwark. Most of us function at about 15 per cent of capacity. How can we step up our lamentably low efficiency?

Two methods are available–the educational and the biochemical. We can take adults and children as they are and give them a much better training than we are giving them now. Or, by appropriate biochemical methods, we can transform them into superior individuals. If these superior individuals are given a superior education, the results will be revolutionary. They will be startling even if we continue to subject them to the rather poor educational methods at present in vogue.

Will it in fact be possible to produce superior individuals by biochemical means? The Russians certainly believe it. They are now halfway through a Five Year Plan to produce "pharmacological substances that normalize higher nervous activity and heighten human capacity for work." Precursors of these future mind improvers are already being experimented with. It has been found, for example, that when given in massive doses some of the vitamins–nicotinic acid and ascorbic acid are examples–sometimes produce a certain heightening of psychic energy. A combination of two enzymes–ethylene disulphonate and adenosine triphosphate, which, when injected together, improve carbohydrate metabolism in nervous tissue–may also turn out to be effective.

Meanwhile good results are being claimed for various new synthetic, nearly harmless stimulants. There is iproniazid, which, according to some authorities, "appears to increase the total amount of psychic energy." Unfortunately, iproniazid in large doses has side effects which in some cases may be extremely serious! Another psychic energizer is an amino alcohol which is thought to increase the body's production of acetylcholine, a substance of prime importance in the functioning of the nervous system. In view of what has already been achieved, it seems quite possible that, within a few years, we may be able to lift ourselves up by our own biochemical bootstraps.

In the meantime let us all fervently wish the Russians every success in their current pharmacological venture. The discovery of a drug capable of increasing the average individual's psychic energy, and its wide distribution throughout the U.S.S.R., would probably mean the end of Russia's present form of government. Generalized intelligence and mental alertness are the most powerful enemies of dictatorship and at the same time the basic conditions of effective democracy. Even in the democratic West we could do with a bit of psychic energizing. Between them, education and pharmacology may do something to offset the effects of that deterioration of our biological material to which geneticists have frequently called attention.

From these political and ethical considerations let us now pass to the strictly religious problems that will be posed by some of the new mind changers. We can foresee the nature of these future problems by studying the effects of a natural mind changer, which has been used for centuries past in religious worship; I refer to the peyote cactus of Northern Mexico and the Southwestern United States. Peyote contains mescalin–which can now be produced synthetically–and mescalin, in William James' phrase, "stimulates the mystical faculties in human nature" far more powerfully and in a far more enlightening way than alcohol and, what is more, it does so at a physiological and social cost that is negligibly low. Peyote produces self-transcendence in two ways–it introduces the taker into the Other World of visionary experience, and it gives him a sense of solidarity with his fellow worshippers, with human beings at large and with the divine nature of things.

The effects of peyote can be duplicated by synthetic mescalin and by LSD (lysergic acid diethylamide), a derivative of ergot. Effective in incredibly small doses, LSD is now being used experimentally by psychotherapists in Europe, in South America, in Canada and the United States. It lowers the barrier between conscious and subconscious and permits the patient to look more deeply and understandingly into the recesses of his own mind. The deepening of self-knowledge takes place against a background of visionary and even mystical experience.

When administered in the right kind of psychological environment, these chemical mind changers make possible a genuine religious experience. Thus a person who takes LSD or mescalin may suddenly understand–not only intellectually but organically, experientially– the meaning of such tremendous religious affirmations as "God is love," or "Though He slay me, yet I will trust in Him."

It goes without saying that this kind of temporary self-transcendence is no guarantee of permanent enlightenment or a lasting improvement of conduct. It is a "gratuitous grace," which is neither necessary nor sufficient for salvation, but which, if properly used, can be enormously helpful to those who have received it. And this is true of all such experiences, whether occurring spontaneously, or as the result of swallowing the right kind of chemical mind changer, or after undertaking a course of "spiritual exercises" or bodily mortification.

Those who are offended by the idea that the swallowing of a pill may contribute to a genuinely religious experience should remember that all the standard mortifications–fasting, voluntary sleeplessness and self-torture–inflicted upon themselves by the ascetics of every religion for the purpose of acquiring merit, are also, like the mindchanging drugs, powerful devices for altering the chemistry of the body in general and the nervous system in particular. Or consider the procedures generally known as spiritual exercises. The breathing techniques taught by the yogi of India result in prolonged suspensions of respiration. These in turn result in an increased concentration of carbon dioxide in the blood; and the psychological consequence of this is a change in the quality of consciousness. Again, meditations involving long, intense concentration upon a single idea or image may also result–for neurological reasons which I do not profess to understand–in a slowing down of respiration and even in prolonged suspensions of breathing.

Many ascetics and mystics have practiced their chemistry-changing mortifications and spiritual exercises while living, for longer or shorter periods, as hermits. Now, the life of a hermit, such as Saint Anthony, is a life in which there are very few external stimuli. But as Hebb, John Lilly and other experimental psychologists have recently shown in the laboratory, a person in a limited environment, which provides very few external stimuli, soon undergoes a change in the quality of his consciousness and may transcend his normal self to the point of hearing voices or seeing visions, often extremely unpleasant, like so many of Saint Anthony's visions, but sometimes beatific.

That men and women can, by physical and chemical means, transcend themselves in a genuinely spiritual way is something which, to the squeamish idealist, seems rather shocking. But, after all, the drug or the physical exercise is not the cause of the spiritual experience; it is only its occasion.

Writing of William James' experiments with nitrous oxide, Bergson has summed up the whole matter in a few lucid sentences. "The psychic disposition was there, potentially, only waiting a signal to express itself in action. It might have been evoked spiritually by an effort made on his own spiritual level. But it could just as well be brought about materially, by an inhibition of what inhibited it, by the removing of an obstacle; and this effect was the wholly negative one produced by the drug."[2] Where, for any reason, physical or moral, the psychological dispositions are unsatisfactory, the removal of obstacles by a drug or by ascetic practices will result in a negative rather than a positive spiritual experience. Such an infernal experience is extremely distressing, but may also be extremely salutary. There are plenty of people to whom a few hours in hell–the hell that they themselves have done so much to create–could do a world of good.

Physiologically costless, or nearly costless, stimulators of the mystical faculties are now making their appearance, and many kinds of them will soon be on the market. We can be quite sure that, as and when they become available, they will be extensively used. The urge to self-transcendence is so strong and so general that it cannot be otherwise. In the past, very few people have had spontaneous experiences of a pre-mystical or fully mystical nature; still fewer have been willing to undergo the psychophysical disciplines which prepare an insulated individual for this kind of self-transcendence. The powerful but nearly costless mind changers of the future will change all this completely. Instead of being rare, pre-mystical and mystical experiences will become common. What was once the spiritual privilege of the few will be made available to the many. For the ministers of the world's organized religions, this will raise a number of unprecedented problems. For most people, religion has always been a matter of traditional symbols and of their own emotional, intellectual and ethical response to those symbols. To men and women who have had direct experience of self-transcendence into the mind's Other World of vision and union with the nature of things, a religion of mere symbols is not likely to be very satisfying. The perusal of a page from even the most beautifully written cookbook is no substitute for the eating of dinner. We are exhorted to "*taste* and see that the Lord is good."

In one way or another, the world's ecclesiastical authorities will have to come to terms with the new mind changers. They may come to terms with them negatively, by refusing to have anything to do with them. In that case, a psychological phenomenon, potentially of great spiritual value, will manifest itself outside the pale of organized religion. On the other hand, they may choose to come to terms with the mind changers in some positive way—exactly how, I am not prepared to guess.

My own belief is that, though they may start by being something of an embarrassment, these new mind changers will tend in the long run to deepen the spiritual life of the communities in which they are available. That famous "revival of religion," about which so many people have been talking for so long, will not come about as the result of evangelistic mass meetings or the television appearances of photogenic clergymen. It will come about as the result of biochemical discoveries that will make it possible for large numbers of men and women to achieve a radical self-transcendence and a deeper understanding of the nature of things. And this revival of religion will be at the same time a revolution. From being an activity mainly concerned with symbols, religion will be transformed into an activity concerned mainly with experience and intuition—an everyday mysticism underlying and giving significance to everyday rationality, everyday tasks and duties, everyday human relationships.

Footnotes:
[1] De Quincey's *Confessions of an English Opium-Eater* (London, 1822) was the first drug confessional and case history in literature.
[2] *Two Sources of Religion and Morality* (1935).

from **Straight with the Medicine:**

Narratives of Washoe

Followers of the Tipi Way

The members of the Washoe Tribe of western Nevada and on the eastern slopes of the Sierra in California who are followers of the Native American Church refer to their religion as the Tipi Way. Officially established in 1918, the church, whose sacrament is peyote, did not come to these regions until several decades later. The serious-ness with which its followers regard the sacramental herb is a testament to a conviction—simple, strong, and poetic—that sustains an otherwise troubled people.

For followers of the Tipi Way, every one is shaman, and salvation comes through the natural elements of the God-given world.

THIS HERB HERE . . . THIS PEYOTE . . . this little green thing grows in the desert. There ain't no water where It grows, but It's got plenty water in It. When you eat It you ain't thirsty. It fills you up. You ain't hungry.

The whole world is in there. When I am looking at this fine little Peyote here my mind is praying. I can't think of nothing bad. All is good. It shows you everything there is to see . . . all the people in the world . . . all the different animals . . . all the places. It shows you all that's in the sky. . . everything under this earth here.

With this little Herb you can hear all the Indians in the world singing. You hear their songs and they can hear you. It makes your eyes like x-ray so you can see what's inside things. You can see inside a person and see if he is in good health or he got some sickness in there. It makes your mind like a telegram. You can send your thoughts far away to some other person and that person can send messages to you. It works like electricity. That's why when someone has this Medicine working inside them or when there's a Meeting going on somewhere people can feel It. They know It even if they is twenty miles away. They can hear the songs and feel the people's thoughts.

The Creator put this Herb on Earth for all the people. But Indians is the only ones left know how to use It. Jesus tried to tell the white people how to use It. They forgot, I guess. They eat some kind of bread and drink wine in their church. Maybe they figured that's what He meant. But He meant this Herb . . . this Medicine. He was just a man like anybody, but the Creator showed Him the way. . . showed Him where He put the Peyote on the earth for the good of the people. That's why we got Jesus as one of the main Ones in this Indian Tipi Church. We say we have the Peyote, the Creator and Jesus. That's how we believe.

Some white people try to make laws against this Herb. They go against their own life. They don't understand It, so they don't want nobody to have It. But they can't stop It. It grows where the Creator put It. It grows in them Gardens in Texas, in Arizona and all over Mexico. There is millions of Them. Each one of Them little green Herbs is singing His own songs the Creator give Him. Any Indian Member in good standing can hear Them all singing if he go on a run down there to get the Medicine. It is the music the Creator put on this earth to make the mind of humans good and clear. It is for happiness and good health.

The old Indians didn't have no books like the Bible. They didn't have no writing or no books like the white people to read and write what they believe. Indians just think and tell what they believe. But Peyote is like a Bible to us here. Peyote is our Bible. When I'm with this Herb sometimes It is like a book . . . like turning pages in a book. I want to know something, and I can turn to here, and here, and there. I want to know something else, so I say, 'What is the meaning of that?' And then it is there . . . everything is in there. It is like that with the Peyote. So I think white people got one kind of book and we got another kind.

When you see this little Herb you see our Church and our Bible. If we keep on the Road It shows us we will have good life. Everything we got to depend on is right here in this Medicine the Creator give us.

(as told to Warren L. d'Azevedo)

Report about the Effects of Peyote on Stanislaw Ignacy Witkiewicz

S . I .   W i t k i e w i c z

The Polish avant-gardist Stanislaw Witkiewicz (1885–1939) applied his eccentric brilliance to a remarkably wide variety of the arts—painting, photography, literature, cultural criticism, and theatre. The following transcript, "reported" on June 20, 1928, and originally published in *Narcotics* (1933) in an expurgated version, is an account of Witkacy's (his nom de plume) first experiment with peyote. It was composed during the experiment first by Witkacy's wife—referred to by her nickname, Nina—and then by the artist himself, while still under the influence of the mind-altering substance. Writing while intoxicated frequently results in an indulgent rambling that is decipherable only to the user and whose meaning is lost once the experience is over. Witcacy was able, for the most part, to objectify his experience and write insightfully in a functional way that engages the curious reader's patient (third) eye.

A T 5:40 W. TOOK 2 GROUND-UP PILLS of pan-peyote. After a few minutes he began to feel lightness and cold throughout his body and became afraid of being sick to his stomach. 6 o'clock–yawning and chills, pulse 88. 6:15 feels wonderful, nerves completely soothed. W. takes another dose (2 pills) and eats 2 eggs with tomatoes and drinks a small cup of coffee with just a drop of milk. 6:25 feels a little bit abnormal, like after a small dose of cocaine, pulse 80. The tired feeling after three portrait sittings disappeared totally. W. walks around the room with a steady step and closed the blinds on the windows tightly. 6:40 pulse 72–feels slight, agreeable stupor and light-headedness. The inactivity bothers him, he's bored and would like to smoke a cigarette. 6:50 W. takes a third dose–stares with tremendous interest at an airplane in flight–then lowers the blinds again and lies down on the bed. Pupils normal, pulse 84. Strange feeling, waits for visions without any results, finally out of boredom smoked a cigarette but didn't finish it. 7:20 got up, took the last pill and lay down again. Starts to feel apathetic and disheartened. After lying down for half an hour, W. got up and felt sick, pulse a little weak, pupils somewhat enlarged, voice changed. Asked for coffee and stays lying down, as soon as he tries to get up, feels sick. 8:30 sees swirls of filaments, bright against a dark background. Next there start to appear animal phantoms, sea monsters, little faces, a man with a beard, but he still does not consider this to be visions, only the kind of heightened images that occur before falling asleep. Someone in a black velvet hat leans from an Italian balcony and speaks to the crowd. Definitely feels a heightening of the imagination, but still nothing extraordinary. Feels better, but when he gets up has dizzy spells and feels "odd," in an unpleasant way, at the same time a strange feeling in his muscles. 9 o'clock begins to see rainbow colors, but still does not consider this to be visions. 9:30–various sculpture in sharp relief, tiny faces, feels "weird," but good. Sees rainbow stripes, but incomplete–the following colors predominate: dirty-red and lemon-yellow. Desire to forget reality. Huge building, the bricks turn into gargoyle faces, like on the cathedral of Nôtre-Dame in Paris. Monsters similar to plesiosauruses made out of luminous filaments. The trees turned into ostriches. A corpse's brain, abscesses, sheaves of sparks bursting out of them. On the whole unpleasant apparitions. On the ceiling, against a red background horned beasts. A gigantic abdomen with a wound–the insides turn into coral at the bottom of the sea. A battle among sea monsters. Dr. Sokolowski turns into a cephalopod. Spatial "distortion." Cross-section of the earth. Fantastic luxuriousness of plant life. 10 o'clock languor continues. Stupor. Battle among senseless things. A series of chambers which change into an underground circus, some strange beasts appear, interesting class of people in the boxes, the boxes turn into (?). Impressions of two visible layers–the images are only black and white, and the rainbow colors are as it were separately. Land and sea monsters and frightful human mugs predominate in the visions. Snakes and giraffes, a sheep with a flamingo's nose, cobras crawled out of this sheep, a double-crested grebe with a seal's tail–bursting jaws, volcanoes change into fish. African vision. 11 o'clock terrific appetite, but at the same time total laziness so that eating a few tomatoes took over half an hour. With the monsters in the background a yellow pilot's cap appeared, then a uniform, then the face of Col. Beaurain in a yellow light. Out of the wild, chaotic coils a splendid beach came to the fore, across it along by the sea a Negro boy rides a bicycle and changes into a man with a small beard, and the toys which the Negro boy was apparently carrying turned into Mexican sculpture which, while looking at W., climbed up ladders. A series of female sex organs, out of which spill out guts and live worms as well as a green embryo turning somersaults.

W. himself writes the continuation.

Kogda perestanu kushat' pomidory (Russian: when I finish eating the tomatoes). A song. 20 before twelve midnight. *Polosatiye* (Russian: striped) monsters at the side. The bottom of the ocean. A shark. Bubbles of gas. Sea anemone. A battle of sea-monsters to the left. Anonymous jaws. Previously about 10:30, hairy machines. Abstract creations, machinishly alive, ramrods, cylinders, grasshoppers and their battles. (Marvelous) Anteaters twisting backwards; spiny anteaters. Rodent covered with bristles of that kind etc. Col. Beaurain in a cap at 11 lighted in yellow. Zawadzka, deformed, giving someone a flirtatious wink. 12:10 A.M. Pulse 72. Time swollen. Metallic and precious stones. *Living* Indian sculpture (started with a gold miniature of Beelzebub). Hellish transformations of stylized mugs and animals (mixed up together) ending with a brood of snakes on a Grand Scale. Coils of snakes turning into monsters. Nina sleeping nearby changes into a mask *from staring at her*, moves her eyes in a horrible fashion (*en realité* goes on sleeping without moving). A second time–the same thing–monstrous moving masks.

Narcotics create styles in sculpture and architecture. An elbow with a coat-of-arms. An arm turned into snakes (yellow and blue), conquered by discolorating monsters with crab-eyes. Green snake-worlds against a brown background. Worlds. Grüenwald's Isenheim (Altar) and something like Lucas Cranach. Monsters of this sort mixed up with corpses in a state of decay. The Negro, who rotted in my eyes, evaporated halfway in the form of a shaft of sparks. Often it all is seen crosswise. A cross-section of earth in the tropics. Machines–turbines–the Center of the World and their brakes made out of fur. Monstrous speed. I had the impression that hours (days?) had elapsed–but it was a quarter of an hour. What can you do to enjoy yourself in such a short time? I drew just to "go through the motions," although the lines were something special. But it was a waste of time compared to what there was to be seen. (12:30).

Snakes too "good to be true." Stylization and colors. Pearly tanks of the Assyrian kings. (I often interrupt the visions in order to write them down). So many things vanish in this whirl. The portrait of old Kossak (hanging in my room) came to life and started to move.

I return to *that other* world. Such a large number of reptiles (colored) are *monstrous*. Higher (metaphysical) acrobatics by chameleons. (How is it that they too do not perish doing those somersaults?)

Again only a quarter of an hour has elapsed. *La plante qui émerveille les yeux.* Brain-strain-storms. The vodka was tasteless. Hunger pains. Total contempt for cigarettes. Mobile china made out of reptiles. Piggish monsters came out of Beaurain's eye. A pile of pigs came spilling out. A stage. Artificial monsters. Pigsnouts in green four-cornered caps (those worn by eighteenth-century Polish patriots).

12:55–I am going to try not to write, and to enter more into the spirit of things. I put out the lights as an experiment. I cannot stand not writing it down: cross-section of reptile machine (of course this is hardly a fraction of what I'm seeing).

Desisterization of doublesharks on water dolthives.

1:02–I put out the light again.

1:15–2nd series of drawings. I roar with laughter.

1:17–I lie down. (No–I pace back and forth and eat sweets).

1:25–(Drawing with the Mokrzysies) Check what the M's were doing at this time. I shut my eyes for a second–I see an animal behind broken lids. Transformations of animals into people in a continuous fashion *á la fourchette*.

1:28–I put out the light and decide not to write things down. I cannot stop writing. Centuries have elapsed, but by the clock it is 7 minutes after 1:30. It began with the Bolsheviks (Trotsky) and their transformations. Supergenitals in crayfish-red colors, sexual intercourse *in natura* and next the *incarnation of sexual pleasures* in various little monsters rubbing up against one another and fighting among themselves, in crayfish-red color. Sometimes cobalt eyes flickered on top of filaments. It ended in reptiles.

1:40–pulse 68. Alien hands are writing. I close my eyes by the lighted lamp. Primeval matter with snakes. It started with a scene from *Macbeth* from the side and from below. A gigantic sister of mercy intersected with frightful genitals seen from underneath. I feel a bit like smoking. I stare at the childhood portrait of Nina. Nina smiles and moves her eyes, but *does not want* to look at me. I have had enough reptiles. Seals in a sea *thick* as grease. Whole series of brown-green sculpture representing peyote scenes. (Executed in a highly artistic way.) A monastery by the moonlight undermined by snakes and a monstrous female organ in a cliff, upon which a violet spark has descended. The monastery crashed down on me into the sea. (Grabinski.)

1:52–Seems that the visions are growing weaker.

2:05–Centuries have elapsed. Entire mountains, worlds and droves of visions. Too many reptiles. Finally a cave made out of pigs–out of a gigantic moving pig, composed of little piggish tiles.

The Chinese knew peyote. All Chinese dragons and all of India come from that source. The artists are the initiated. *Eine allgemeine Peyote-theorie.* Panpeyoteism.

Peyote

The two branches of art

China, India, Persia   *America-Mexico, Africa-Egypt*

Our navel of decline. Perhaps peyote will resurrect art.

Music and a phonograph from down below spoil the seriousness of the visions. Should I smoke? At times there were red and blue dancing paper figures.

2:11–One vodka and a few tomatoes. Notes. I close my eyes by the lamp. A vision of Gucio Z. *snaked* (by snakes) yellow and black. And then realistically sleeping on his right stomach-side. Headache. Glass visions–criminal ones. Supertramps. The start of a fantastic theatre. Alcor–the double star–2 stars (160 years a revolution) turned very fast.

2:30–A madman's brain with gurgling eyes in the clutches of a hellish snake-cephalopod.

After vodka sad and gloomy visions. A yellow eye pudent amid soot. *Superhuman* edifices with columns turned into mountain-genitals (big as Giewont) made of shiny pink stones.

2:35–Violet sperm-jet straight in the face, from a hydrant of mountain-genitals (down below there are superedifices).

2:45–I eat Graham bread and butter. Glancing through the curtained windows at unsightly apartment buildings. Reminding me of a certain horrendous view of the Poldeks' apartment building on View Street. Will there be visions? The Poldeks sleep *separately* under one quilt. Poldek on his back and Wanda on her right side, curled up (towards the window). Visions (renewed) of tiny little faces. The thought that Kotarbinski could make better use of this world and my reptiles than Rafal Malczewski or I.

2:53—Superasses keep on constantly coming down like waterfalls.

2:58—Procession of elephants and a pearly camel (in a mask) magnificently proportioned (tremendous realism). Eyes peeping at and embracing female organs.

3:00—A little guy of the Micinski type tearing off to the moon and his adventures after landing by parachute in a state of addlepatedness. Elves on a see-saw (Comic number). The Queen of Sheba's horny genitals in an astral museum.

3:05—I said "enough visions" and put out the light. Next cane cadavero-erotic visions (*Macabre* number). A skull (which had dropped down) floating across an abdomen—so hideous that I turned the light out as quickly as I could. Erotic rain of skirtish flowers (crocuses). Smiling man with a beard (Valois) enclosed in gigantic ox-snouts.

3:10—Hades according to my personal conception. Skeleton in a circular desert and specters *á la Goya*. Goya must have known Peyote.

3:30—Tiring visions. A battle of centaurs turned into a battle of fantastic genitals. Conversion, but not to any religion, rather in the realm of life. Renouncing drugs. Soulfulness. The crab of iniquity crawled out of the wound in a skull. The partridge-ification of a goshawk. The marvelously wise, goshawkly-human eyes grew dull and stupid, became duplicated and flew away in bird heads beyond the round horizon.

3:45—A Pharaoh similar to me. Processions. Totemistic rites (somewhat goshawkly-reptilian). On shields—then floating away in the form of animal spirits. Reptiles in sexual entanglements. Minettes of iguanas.

3:50—Snakes in desert springs. (Realistic number.) Again a vision (repetition with variation) of a madman's brain ulcerated to the point of gangrene (*a propos* no more drinking) and a bird-amphibian face pecking a monster's brain (and holding it in its clutches) lifted up its head in my direction and looked at me lasciviously. Sexual abyss with a blond wooly hippopotamus. Eyes in the midst of it.

3:58—Bristling concepts and from out of these concepts, instead of the truth (it stood with its back artificially turned to me), there came forth a strange animal, and then an ordinary wild pig.

4:05—The birth of a diamond goldfinch. A rainbow-colored basset hound spurted into fireworks of black and pink butterflies on bent pink sticks. Egyptian and Assyrian processions. A female slave behind a column and from out of this there then came forth an unfinished palace tale, drowned in greasy genitals.

4:10—In these visions I saw all my inner wretchedness.

4:15—Transformation of a skeleton into an ethereal body (diamond-like).

4:20—Third series of drawings. I want to smoke.

4:27—Drawings (2) finished (?).

About 3 o'clock a variety of processions in different styles, for example: rococo, present-day and antiquity. (Mélange of styles as though at the races–seen from below.)

4:30–Crotch from Zakroczym. I cannot be completely saved, since I cannot renounce sex.

Nina's portrait won't look anymore, because I have lost my secret power over things. In the dark depths of the coils of my brain the remnants of visions are lying in wait (I have deserved these–the Indians are right, Peyote punishes the guilty).

4:40–Slight headache. Fatigue from visions. Desire for sleep without visions. Pulse 72. Ordinary reality more and more often seems normal, and not horrendous as heretofore. Curving of space slowly vanishes. (Einstein put into practice).

4:43–Vision of fat old women hanging by ropes in the mountains (Hala Gasiennicowa). (Vision of unintelligible symbolism.) The Strazyskis in their living room on a sofa turned into a bed. He by the window with his feet towards the window, she on her right side with her head towards the library. Now she woke up, 4:49, he's asleep.

4:55–Realistic eye of Pilsudski–it comes gently out from its eye-socket and springs (already ethereal) straight at me through space. It hits some point in the Ukraine and from there swarms of geometricalized, striped black worms pour out onto the entire world.

5:00–The mysterious tale of a lady from the Eastern Provinces (a blonde), a gendarme, a Russian Orthodox priest, an old man in a nobleman's uniform. English Fieldmarshals–one a cuirassier of the guard, the other in a pointed hat–pulling a wagon with a Hindu statue through the rain (punishment). All these reptiles are monsters bred in me by alcohol and cocaine. There was so little of that, and so many reptiles.

5:04–Hideous monster with whiskers, cat-like, crawling out of a fatty female organ–being born.

5:08–Grim fleet with faces under the rudders. I have had *enough visions.*

5:11–Rotting foot, the shoe disintegrates. Pink worms, similar to phalluses, crawl out, change into erect lingams. (Foot and shoe gangrene)

5:18–Ideal young lady slowly changed an ambling, bubble-shaped horror.

5:20–I think I am the incarnation of the King of the Tatra Mountain Snakes. (Tatra vision.) The Small Meadow in winter, and it ended as a *monstrous* reptile on Przyslop Mietusi.

5:25–I put out the light. Zygmunt Unrug (a heretic), seen in profile, drawn into a vortex of snakes. A shield with a coat of arms grew into a snake and collapses. Alongside, visions of another shield with a lion, his legs astride. Visit to the Sokolowskis in Brwinów. Slinking monsters; chocolate-colored with black and gold.

5:33–Deformation of Nina asleep with her eyes open. Before that, transformation of the pitcher in the corner. I put out the light. Brighter and brighter in the room due to the daylight. Immediately thereafter vision of nicotine–small yellow eye in a corpse's skull. Next of alcohol–a marvelous hummingbird snake crawls out; and Coco–a woman's eye, white as a pigeon's and from underneath a small woman's hand which grows into white snake reins, prodding and squeezing my neck. White feminine fluffy down and a beautiful eye, a blue one. An empty blister on the leg, protruding into infinity.

5:47–Vision of a deluxe reptile (dinosaur), *pour les princes*. Rather humorous number as an encore. Sunny knight under glass (after a geographic vision with the sun on the mountains from both *sides*). Caricatures of male characters in costumes. An affair of honor involving French officers and wild combinations with a young Russian. Frenchmen and Bedouins on Percherons fill in a well with monsters. General Porzeczko's ulcerated tits.

6:15–Hydrocychnytine. Stinkotine. Music, a lower art, gave birth to itself–but only Peyote could have given birth to such a cunning thing as painting or sculpture, and then it went on its own–just like that.

6:17–I take valerian. Desire to smoke. Mundane quarter-asses barked at by flying dragons (on a cone). Hideous reptile, *bleu acier*, at the bottom of shallow water, flat as a ray without a head, alongside but at the top . . . a snake peeped out from this. Disappearing towers and a gigantic mourner lights the sun of truth–a little metal figure with a bare backside. I, as a little boy on a catafalque, turn into a wild pig.

6:30–Drank up the rest of the valerian. I have decidedly had *enough* visions. The total ugliness of naturalism compared to the riches of these forms. Sins against Mother. And here Peyote gave me a vision, although I thought that it would not dare. How my wrongs and sins are destroying my Mother's health.

6:38–Parade of contemporary masks with duplications and caricatures *in the eyes,* constrictions, contractions, and repulsions. Realistic character of a harum-scarum (scared his harem).

6:50–The Strazyskis start to wake up. Vision of the transformations of a marvelous woman, then sexual tentacular getting hooked. How much evil there is in me. And I consider myself good. Frightful visions of Mother. Nina on her wedding trip with an unknown gentleman, in a hammock on the Riviera.

7:15–Dozing without *real* visions. Normal sleeping dreams. Franz Joseph and Franek Orkan–one and the same. Marvelously indecent woman gives birth to a monster. Hideous sexual intercourse with a horde of reptiles.

8:15–Morning activities. Fear of the light. However, state still highly abnormal. Pupils somewhat narrower than at the maximum. Fading visions of rainbow-colored whirls of filaments.

9:00–Visions still, but weaker and not so awful. Many visions. *Reptiles.*

9:20–Multiform flat green snake in a shallow pond.

10:00–Remnants of visions.

10:15 to 12:00–Sleep. Then relatively normal state. Slight stupor and spatial disorientation. Weak enlargement of the pupils.

(Translated by Daniel Gerould and Jadwiga Kosicka)

Permissions

Pages 239 and 240 constitute an extension of the copyright page.

EXCERPT FROM *The Underworld of the East* by James Lee © 1936 James S. Lee; excerpt from "The Poem of Hashish" by Charles Baudelaire, translated by Andrew C. Kimmens © 1977 Andrew Kimmens, reprinted by permission of William Morrow and Co., Inc.; "General Security: The Liquidation of Opium" by Antonin Artaud, translated by L. Dejardin © 1965 City Lights Books, reprinted by permission of City Lights Books; excerpt from *Drugs and the Mind* by Robert S. de Ropp © 1957 Robert S. de Ropp; "A Brief Oral History of Benzedrine Use in the U.S." by Herbert Huncke © 1990 Herbert E. Huncke; "A Fundamental Experiment" by René Daumal, translated by Roger Shattuck, translation © 1959, 1987 Roger Shattuck, reprinted by permission of Roger Shattuck; excerpt from *Lame Deer: Seeker of Visions* by John (Fire) Lame Deer with Richard Erdoes © 1972 John (Fire) Lame Deer and Richard Erdoes, reprinted by permission of Simon & Schuster, Inc.; "Seeking the Magic Mushroom" by R. Gordon Wasson © 1957 R. Gordon Wasson; excerpt from *LSD: My Problem Child* by Albert Hofmann, translated by Jonathan Ott © 1983 Albert Hofmann, reprinted by permission of Jeremy Tarcher, Inc.; excerpt from *The Hasheesh Eater* by Fitz Hugh Ludlow © 1857 Fitz Hugh Ludlow; excerpt from *Movers and Shakers* by Mabel Dodge Luhan © 1935, 1963 Mabel Dodge Luhan, reprinted by permission of Curtis Brown, Ltd.; excerpt from *Really the Blues* by Mezz Mezzrow © 1946 Milton Mezzrow and Bernard Wolfe, reprinted by permission of Carol Publishing Group, Citadel Underground; excerpt from *An Essay on Hasheesh* by Victor Robinson © 1925 Victor Robinson; excerpt from *The Diary of Anaïs Nin, 1947–1955* by Anaïs Nin © 1955 Anaïs Nin, reprinted

MORAVAGINE
Blaise Cendrars

"Blaise Cendrars [is] the Indiana Jones of French literature. . . . " —*Voice Literary Supplement*

"The only parallels that come to mind are with Celine and Beckett." —*New Boston Review*

"Rip-roaring fiction and imaginative adventuring on all planes of experience." —*Times Literary Supplement*

"A deeply moving book. . . . "—*Factsheet Five*

"How can I convince the skeptic that I was ravished by Cendrars's *Moravagine?* How does one know immediately that a thing is after one's own heart?" —Henry Miller

Perhaps the most brilliant of all this legendary French writer's more than twenty works, *Moravagine* is the semiautobiographical account of a doctor who rescues Moravagine from his solitary confinement in a remote Swiss mental asylum. Embarking on a series of adventures extravagant, unpredictable, and monumental as a biblical epic, they wander the world over—inciting Russia to revolution, terrorizing the streets of Berlin, crossing the Atlantic to America and the Amazons, where they narrowly escape a group of cannibalistic Jivaro, and finally returning to the narrator's home, Paris, at the outbreak of World War I.

Translated from the French by Alan Brown
5 1/4" x 8 1/4", 250 pages • $9.95 pb • ISBN: 0-922233-04-7

VENUS IN FURS
and Selected Letters
Leopold von Sacher-Masoch

"*Venus in Furs* is the quintessential Sacher-Masoch novel . . . a deviant classic." —*New York Press*

". . . Sacher-Masoch's correspondence with Emilie Mataja [offers] and intriguing parallel to the novel's exploration of dark obsessions." —*Blitz*

"A deeply felt, intelligent and powerful morality play of our time, marvelously written." —*Small Press*

Illuminating his darkest obsessions in *Venus in Furs*, Leopold von Sacher-Masoch created Severin and Wanda—a "suprasensual" man who craves abuse and domination, and a cruel, icy Venus brought to life. The novel and the accompanying remarkable series of letters (translated and published here in English for the first time) between Sacher-Masoch and Emilie Mataja, a nineteen-year-old aspiring writer, provide unique insight into the compulsive imagination of the man from whose name the term "masochism" is derived.

5 1/4" x 8 1/4", 224 pages • $9.95 pb • ISBN: 0-922233-01-2

PANORAMA OF HELL
Hideshi Hino

"One of the most shockingly bizarre graphic novels ever seen in this country." —*Toxic Horror*

"Maniacal, perverse . . . it's a gorefest to make the most outrageous slasher films look tame." —*New York Press*

"A brain-scraping, gut-breaking revelation from postnuclear Japan." —*Metro*

"With . . . *Panorama of Hell* . . . Americans have a real chance to attempt to understand the depth of nuclear horror . . ." *LA Weekly*

"A striking and relentless masterwork." —*Samhain* (UK)

Through the confessions of a fiendish Hell painter born in the aftermath of the bombing of Hiroshima, Hideshi Hino tells a nightmarish story in this extraordinary graphic novel. With black humor, stunning vision, and unflinching imagery, *Panorama of Hell* takes the reader on an unforgettable journey of reeling hallucination and maddening reality. Amid a desolate postnuclear landscape, the reclusive artist feverishly works to depict on canvas a hell greater than that he has already endured on earth. *Panorama of Hell* is the first horror *manga* to be translated into English. Hideshi Hino is the author of *Shocking Theatre,* a thirteen-volume series of graphic novels, of which *Panorama of Hell* is his personal favorite.

Translated from the Japanese by Screaming Mad George, Charles Schneider, and Yoko Umezawa

6" x 9", 200 pages • $9.95 pb • ISBN: 0-922233-00-4

ORDERING INFORMATION

BLAST BOOKS is distributed to the bookstores, wholesalers, and libraries exclusively by Publishers Group West, 4065 Hollis Street, Emeryville, CA 94608. Call (800) 365-3453, or in California call collect (415) 658-3453.

INDIVIDUALS
Send your order to Blast Books, P.O. Box 51, Cooper Station, New York, NY 10276. Add $2.00 postage and handling for the first book and 50¢ for each book thereafter.